# People and Computers XVI - Memorable Yet Invisible

W0043871

Springer-Verlag London Ltd.

Xristine Faulkner, Janet Finlay
and Françoise Détienne (Eds)

# People and Computers XVI
# - Memorable Yet Invisible

## Proceedings of HCI 2002

Springer

Xristine Faulkner, BA PGCE, PGDip, MSc
South Bank University, London, UK

Janet Finlay, BA, Ms, Dphil
Leeds Metropolitan University, Leeds, UK

Françoise Détienne
INRIA, The French National Institute for Research in Computer Science Control, France

British Library Cataloguing in Publication Data
HCI 2002 (Conference : 2002)
  People and computers XVI : memorable yet invisible :
  proceedings of HCI 2002
  1.Human-computer interaction - Congresses
  I.Title II.Faulkner, Xristine III.Finlay, Janet
  IV.Detienne, Francoise
  004'.019
  ISBN 978-1-85233-659-2

Library of Congress Cataloging-in-Publication Data
A catalog record for this book is available from the Library of Congress.

Apart from any fair dealing for the purposes of research or private study, or criticism or review, as permitted under the Copyright, Designs and Patents Act 1988, this publication may only be reproduced, stored or transmitted, in any form or by any means, with the prior permission in writing of the publishers, or in the case of reprographic reproduction in accordance with the terms of licences issued by the Copyright Licensing Agency. Enquiries concerning reproduction outside those terms should be sent to the publishers.

ISBN 978-1-85233-659-2      ISBN 978-1-4471-0105-5 (eBook)
DOI 10.1007/978-1-4471-0105-5
http://www.springer.co.uk

© Springer-Verlag London 2002
Originally published by Springer-Verlag London Limited in 2002
Softcover reprint of the hardcover 1st edition 2002

The use of registered names, trademarks etc. in this publication does not imply, even in the absence of a specific statement, that such names are exempt from the relevant laws and regulations and therefore free for general use.

The publisher makes no representation, express or implied, with regard to the accuracy of the information contained in this book and cannot accept any legal responsibility or liability for any errors or omissions that may be made.

Whilst we have made considerable efforts to contact all holders of copyright material contained within this book, we have failed to locate some of them. Should holders wish to contact the Publisher, we will be happy to come to some arrangement.

Typeset: by *Winder.*
Printed and bound at the Athenæum Press Ltd., Gateshead, Tyne and Wear
34/3830-543210  Printed on acid-free paper  SPIN 10880486

# Contents

# *Preface: Memorable yet Invisible*

The sixteenth annual British HCI Conference chose as its theme 'Memorable yet Invisible'. The theme aimed to explore how we can address the issue of seamless interaction with systems, yet making interaction a positively memorable experience rather than a negative one. As usual, the HCI community responded enthusiastically to the challenge of the conference theme. In putting together the conference programme we were spoilt for choice and we are sure that our final programme will be memorable. We selected 23 papers out of 60 papers submitted. The quality of submissions was very high indeed as can be seen from this volume.

In putting together the programme this year we followed a two stage review process. The first stage consisted of between 3 and 5 reviewers who had identified themselves as experts in the area addressed by the allotted papers. These reviews, together with the paper were then passed to a member of the programme committee, for a second stage review in which the first stage reviews were summarised and the papers given an overall score. The meta reviews and first stage reviews were checked for discrepancies by the programme chairs then ranked for consideration by the committee. Twenty three papers were finally chosen to be included in the programme and are offered here in the proceedings.

The conference theme is in evidence in some of the paper categories and several authors addressed the ideas of the memorable and the invisible computer; while others looked at novel ways of solving the problems associated with humans interacting with computer systems. We note the number of submissions from abroad with great pleasure. Although this is the conference of the British HCI Group it undoubtedly is international in its catchment, with contributions from Finland and America, from Canada to Australia to Japan.

The papers in this collection are arranged according to the categories we organised for the conference itself. This is to aid delegates if they wish to read papers prior to the presentations but also to give those of you who could not be with us at HCI 2002 some of the spirit of the conference.

When putting together a conference and the associated proceedings, many people deserve our thanks. However, we would like to draw attention to the first stage reviewers without whom the integrity of the conference could not be maintained. Reviewing is an invisible task and sometimes a thankless one. It is to them and to our authors that the greatest thanks is due and without whom 'Memorable yet Invisible' would not take on the meaning it has for us. Our second thanks go to the committee members who helped assemble the fare before you. We would also like to make a very special mention of Russel Winder and his team for work on production. Finally, thanks are due to Tom Lancaster and Simon Hall who helped with all of the tiresome administration and produced endless spreadsheets to aid our task.

All that remains is for us to commend the selected papers to you and for you to enjoy them.

*Fintan Culwin*
*Xristine Faulkner*
*Janet Finlay*
*Françoise Détienne*

*May 2002*

# The Committee

| | |
|---|---|
| Conference Chair | Fintan Culwin *South Bank University* |
| Full Papers | Françoise Détienne *INRIA — The French National Institute for Research in Computer Science and Control* |
| | Xristine Faulkner *South Bank University* |
| | Janet Finlay *Leeds Metropolitan University* |
| Doctoral Consortium | Sally Fincher *University of Kent at Canterbury* |
| Interactive Experiences | John Rosbottom *University of Portsmouth* |
| Panels | Richard Butterworth *Middlesex University* |
| Posters | Pete Chalk *University of North London* |
| | Jenny Le Peuple *London Guildhall University* |
| Short Papers | Helen Sharp *The Open University* |
| Tutorials | Eamonn O'Neill *University of Bath* |
| Workshops | Steve Draper *University of Glasgow* |
| Publicity | Tom McEwan *Napier University* |
| | Lachlan M MacKinnon *Heriot-Watt University* |
| Sponsorship | Alistair Kilgour *Real Axis Consulting* |
| Treasurer | Bob Steele *Sheffield Hallam University* |
| HCI Liaison | Chris Roast *Sheffield Hallam University* |
| Past Conference Chair | Gilbert Cockton *Sunderland University* |
| Past London Chair | Bob Spence *Imperial College London* |
| Registration | Sylvia Alexander *LTSN Information & Computer Sciences* |
| Student Volunteers | Simon Hall *South Bank University* |
| Web Site | Thomas Lancaster *South Bank University* |
| EUPA liaison | Nigel Bevan *Serco Usability Services* |
| | Martin Maguire *Loughborough University* |

# The Reviewers

| | |
|---|---|
| R. Arangarasan | *University of Wisconsin-Madison, USA* |
| S. Balbo | *Modem Media, USA* |
| T. Barlow | *SAS Institute Inc., USA* |
| G. Baxter | *University of York, UK* |
| S. Björk | *PLAY, Interactive Institute, Sweden* |
| A. Blandford | *UCL, UK* |
| R. Boardman | *Imperial College, UK* |
| S. Bødker | *University of Aarhus, Denmark* |
| N. Bonnardel | *University of Provence, France* |
| N. Braun | *Computer Graphics Center, Darmstadt, Germany* |
| S. Brewster | *University of Glasgow, UK* |
| S. Cairncross | *Napier University, UK* |
| M. Colbert | *Kingston University, UK* |
| M. Crerar | *Napier University, Edinburgh, UK* |
| E. P. Curran | *University of Ulster, Ireland* |
| M. Czerwinski | *Microsoft Research, USA* |
| A. Dey | *Intel Research, USA* |
| E. Dubois | *University of Glasgow, UK* |
| L. Dunckley | *Thames Valley University, UK* |
| M. Eibl | *GESIS, Germany* |
| D. England | *Liverpool John Moores University, UK* |
| S. Errore | *IBM Rome, Tivoli Lab, Italy* |
| S. Fenley | *King's College, London, UK* |
| F. Ferlazzo | *La Sapienza, University of Rome, Italy* |
| B. Fields | *Middlesex University, UK* |
| P. Forcheri | *Istituto Matematica Applicata-Consiglio Nazionale Ricerche, Italy* |
| G. Ghinea | *Brunel University, UK* |
| S. Grant | *Information Strategists, UK* |
| T. Gross | *Fraunhofer Gesellschaft, Germany* |
| L. Hammerton | *University of Sussex, UK* |
| J. Hoffmann | *Darmstadt University of Technology, Germany* |
| S. Holmlid | *LinLab, Ericsson Radio Systems, Sweden* |
| K. Hone | *Nokia Mobile Phones, University of Tampere, Finland* |
| K. Hornbæk | *University of Copenhagen, Denmark* |
| S. Howard | *University of Melbourne, Australia* |
| E. T. Hvannberg | *University of Iceland, Iceland* |
| P. Jefferies | *De Montfort University, UK* |
| H. Johnson | *University of Bath, UK* |
| T. Jokela | *University of Oulu, Finland* |
| M. Jones | *University of Waikato, New Zealand* |
| C. Karin | *Limburg University Center, Belgium* |
| E. Kemp | *Massey University, New Zealand* |
| P. Ketola | *Nokia Mobile Phones, University of Tampere, Finland* |
| B. Khazaei | *Sheffield-Hallam University, UK* |
| A. Kilgour | *Heriot-Watt University, UK* |

| M. Kirby | *University of Huddersfield, UK* |
| D. C. Lane | *Leeds Metropolitan University, UK* |
| J. Lee | *IBM, USA* |
| S. MacFarlane | *University of Central Lancs, UK* |
| T. Mandl | *Universität Hildesheim, Germany* |
| P. Markopoulos | *Technical University Eindhoven, Netherlands* |
| M. Masoodian | *The University of Waikato, New Zealand* |
| P. McAndrew | *Open University, UK* |
| R. McCrindle | *The University of Reading, UK* |
| M. Mlchior | *Symbian, USA* |
| D. Morse | *The Open University, UK* |
| M. Muller | *IBM Research, USA* |
| R. Navarro-Prieto | *Motorola Labs, USA* |
| A. Palmer | *University of Waterloo, Ontario, Canada* |
| D. Petrelli | *University of Sheffield, UK* |
| M. Pohl | *University of Technology, Vienna, Austria* |
| I. B. Rebelo | *Federal University of Santa Catarina, Brazil* |
| N. Reeves | *University of Gloucestershire, UK* |
| D. Rigas | *University of Bradford, UK* |
| M. Riordan | *Dun Laoghaire Institute of Art, Design and Technology, Ireland* |
| A. Sebok | *OECD Halden Reactor Project, Norway* |
| B. Shackel | *HUSAT Research Institute, Loughborough University, UK* |
| A. Sloane | *University of Wolverhampton, UK* |
| J. Stage | *Aalborg University, Denmark* |
| M. A. Sujan | *University of Karlsruhe, Germany* |
| D. Tabary | *LAMIH, France* |
| M. Treglown | *University of Nottingham, UK* |
| P. Turner | *Napier University, UK* |
| S. Turner | *Napier University, UK* |
| C. C. Venters | *Manchester Visualisation Centre, UK* |
| J. Whatley | *University of Salford, UK* |
| P. Wild | *University of Bath, UK* |
| S. Wilson | *University College London, UK* |
| B. Wise | *General Electric Corporate R&D, USA* |
| M. A. Wise | *General Electric Corporate* |
| J. O. Wobbrock | *Carnegie Mellon University, USA* |
| W. Wong | *University of Otago, New Zealand* |
| A. Woodcock | *Coventry University, UK* |
| M. Zajicek | *Oxford Brookes University, UK* |

# Keynotes

# Fun, Communication and Dependability: Extending the Concept of Usability

## Andrew F Monk

*Department of Psychology, University of York,*
*York YO1 5DD, UK.*
Email: *a.monk@psych.york.ac.uk*

**Designing information and technology products for the home has drawn attention to the narrowness of traditional conceptions of usability. Design methods and guidelines were developed in work contexts and so are mainly concerned with ease-of-learning, low level ease-of-use and task fit. These are all issues in the home but there are other important components of usability. How do we make the product enjoyable to use? How do we design for effective human-human communication? How doe we make these systems dependable? The paper illustrates these issues through two design problems, the Virtual Pub and Mavis' smart home. Drawing on the history of HCI, suggestions are made about how these new conceptions of usability could be further developed for design for the home, and more widely.**

**Keywords:** usability, methodologies, guidelines, fun, enjoyment, effective communication, dependability.

## 1 Technology in the Home: A Stimulus for Change

The technology we use in our homes is becoming increasingly sophisticated. Entertainment systems such as multi-channel interactive TV require complex interfaces. Future visions of ubiquitous computing in the home involve networked appliances linked to sensors and effectors that react automatically to our behaviour. The manufacturers and vendors of this technology are aware that human factors are crucial in determining uptake. We are paid to use the technology provided at work. If it breaks down regularly or is tedious to use we will put up with it. Attitudes to technology we have bought ourselves are somewhat different. We need it to be reliable, attractive and enjoyable to use.

This paper will argue that conventional approaches to usability are too narrowly focused to properly inform the design of technology for the home. It will suggest some issues that need to be addressed in order to broaden the concept of usability. These are: enjoyment (fun), effective communication and dependability. Designing for the home has highlighted these issues but they are also important in work and educational contexts. In this sense designing for the home context is a stimulus for a more wide ranging change in the way we conceptualise usability.

## 2  Usability as Ease-of-learning, Low Level Ease-of-use and Task Fit

What do I mean by conventional approaches to usability? To design a product to support someone's work in the office one needs to achieve usability through ease-of-learning, low level ease-of-use and task fit. HCI research has been very successful in this area and there is considerable agreement on how to do this. For the first two ease-of-learning and low level ease-of-use one may rely on standards and guidelines. ISO 9241[1] specifies how and when menus, forms and other dialogue styles should be used. International standards have to be agreed by numerous committees and have the weight of law behind them. However, the less formal style guides have probably been more influential. These prescribe how the interface should work for a particular operating system. The knowledge they contain has been incorporated into the tools that are used to create software. Thus, a designer using a software development tool such as Visual Basic will find it very hard to disobey the Windows Microsoft Windows style guide (Microsoft, 1995) even if they have never read it. This prevents the designer from developing idiosyncratic interfaces that do not behave in the way users expect. At the very least, by enforcing a degree of consistency, style guides ensure ease-of-learning. When a user learns to do something in one context, that knowledge will transfer positively to new contexts. This is important as even small inconsistencies can result in negative transfer. It is a common experience to upgrade software only to find it extremely difficult to suppress ingrained habits learned with the old system. In fact, the Windows style guide and those that came before it draw on the results of years of painstaking empirical and analytic work from the HCI research community and they do guarantee low level ease-of-use. In this way I have argued (Monk, 2000) that Visual Basic is a theory of HCI. Software tools encapsulate style guides, and style guides encapsulate the research.

When designing a product for use in the office then, ease-of-learning and low level ease-of-use are achieved by specifying the product of design, that is how the interface should appear and behave. Task fit is achieved by specifying the process of design, how the designer should behave. Here again there is considerable agreement and an international standard, ISO 13407. There are also text books, for example Dix et al. (1998), and proprietary methodologies such as Contextual Inquiry (Holtzblatt & Jones, 1993) and Monk's Lightweight Techniques (Monk, 1998). There are certain common elements to all these processes and these are illustrated in Table 1.

---

[1] See http://www.iso.ch for details.

**Understanding the work context**
*Methods*: focus groups, interviews, observation
*Representations*: the rich picture

**Understanding the work**
*Methods*: focus groups, interviews, observation
*Representations*: Hierarchical Task Analysis (HTA), scenarios

**Testing a top level design against your understanding of the work**
*Methods*: Scenario walkthrough, Cognitive Walk Through
*Representations*: Story boards, dialogue modelling

**User testing of more detailed prototypes**
*Methods*: Usability Labs., Cooperative Evaluation
*Representations*: Paper prototypes, simulations

**Table 1:** Common processes in user centred design.

---

The user-centred design process starts by obtaining an understanding of the context for the work. In broad terms, how does the work get done? Who are the stakeholders in this system and what are their concerns? The methods used to elicit this information, interviews and observation, are unremarkable, though they require a great deal of skill to carry out well. What the various proprietary methodologies prescribe are representations, ways of recording and thinking about the information obtained through interviews and observation. The Rich Picture (Checkland & Scholes, 1990; Monk, 1998) is one such representation. It consists of a cartoon style depiction of the key stakeholders, their concerns and how the work passes between them. It is common to give each stakeholder a 'thought bubble' expressing his or her main concerns about the work. Writing down the findings in this way focuses the analysis and allows the analyst to reason about the completeness of her understanding. It can also be taken back to the analyst's informants to check the understanding obtained. The rich picture, like all the other representations listed in Table 1, is also a valuable tool for communicating with designers.

Table 1 also lists some of the representations that have been proposed for recording and reasoning about the work done by a particular operator. A high level design can be tested against this understanding. Finally, a detailed prototype of the interface can be built and refined by user testing.

So, what parts of this conventional view of usability can be used to design for the home? The standards and style guides used to achieve ease-of-learning and low level ease-of-use for software for the office will be of some use. Unfortunately, most are for graphical interfaces operated with a mouse and a keyboard. In the home controls and displays tend to be smaller. We have to return to basic principles of interaction design and develop style guides and software tools that reinforce those guidelines for the new forms of interaction needed in the home.

The design methodologies, and associated representations, specified to achieve task fit will also be applicable at some level. There are tasks to be done in the home. Setting the video recorder or doing the laundry are work and are amenable to these methods. But, where is the task in actually watching the TV or talking on the telephone?

In the domestic environment user concerns go well beyond task fit. To take another example, various products have been devised for the elderly that make allowances for fading eyesight and poor manual dexterity. Many of these apparently useful products have failed simply because they are ugly and stigmatising. We need to go back to basics, to identify new usability concepts, parallel to ease-of-learning, ease-of-use and task fit, but with a broader reach. In the sections that follow I will speculate about some such concepts under the headings: enjoyment, effective communication, and dependability. Note, the words 'fun' and 'enjoyment' are used interchangeably in this paper. 'Fun' makes for an arresting title but 'enjoyment' may be more useful in a taxonomy of usability as it implies a less specific user experience.

## 3   Enjoyment

To make this discussion more concrete, consider the following design problem. Broadband Internet makes group conversations using voice an alternative to telephone conferencing that may be sufficiently inexpensive to be used for leisure purposes. In addition, graphical support for this leisure experience could be provided over the Internet in the form of pictures and text. How would you design an inexpensive terminal, let us call it 'the virtual pub', to make it possible for geographically distributed friends to get together without anyone having to travel?

Conventional concepts of usability can be applied to the problem of connecting the friends up and then operating the other features one might want to include. But what are these features, and what are they there to achieve? One requirement is clearly that the conversations should be enjoyable or fun and so the terminal should include features that facilitate fun conversations. This is equivalent to identifying ease-of-learning as a requirement for office products. On its own it is not worth a lot. We need to understand the concept of enjoyment further before we can guide design. Let us examine the history of HCI to see how that might be done.

Several years of empirical and analytic work were required to identify the properties of a user interface necessary for ease-of learning. Different forms of consistency were identified, for example, and these in turn lead to the formation of the guidelines that eventually gave rise to the style guides used today. The empirical work needed to gain this understanding followed the psychological paradigm of experimentation. Different user interfaces were constructed and compared by having users work with them. Measures pertaining to particular criteria to do with ease-of-learning, e.g. learning time, were devised to make these comparisons. The analytic work similarly drew on ethnographic studies or simply the common experience of reader and author with different systems to find examples that could identify features of an interface that lead to good or bad ease-of-learning.

Can we follow this process with the high level concept of 'enjoyment'. The key is to break enjoyment down into components that are sufficiently specific that we can agree when they are there or not, and if possible, how to measure them. There is some existing work from outside of HCI that can be drawn on here. In the psychological tradition, Csikszentmihalyi and colleagues, see for example Csikszentmihalyi & Rathunde (1993), have examined the conditions necessary for a 'flow' experience. They interviewed people like rock climbers who spent large amounts of their time on difficult activities that have no apparent external motivation. An important common theme in the experiences of all these people was 'flow'. The activity takes them over shutting out all other concerns. In sport this experience has been described as being 'in the zone'. The conditions necessary to get a flow experience were:

1. an activity with clear goals and good feedback as to whether these goals are being achieved, and

2. a close match between the difficulty of the task and the ability of the user.

Computer games have these characteristics, scores provide goals and feedback. Difficulty is matched to ability through the levels within the game.

More mundanely, we have all had the experience of getting so involved in a task that we shut out everything else and it becomes an end in itself. This is rather different from the peak experience described by Csikszentmihalyi's informants and may be better described as 'high engagement' rather than flow. Csikszentmihalyi & Rathunde (1993) developed a short list of questions that can be used repeatedly to assess minute-to-minute changes in flow, rather as the NASA TLX[2] measures minute-to-minute changes in workload. Csikszentmihalyi & Rathunde's scale can also be used to measure engagement.

Flow and engagement are concepts that apply to the individual. Our design problem, the Virtual Pub, is about enjoyment in the form of engagement *as a group*. A sociological view of high engagement as fun is provided by Goffman (1961) through his concept of a focused gathering:

> "For the participants, this involves: a single and cognitive focus of attention; a mutual and preferential openness to verbal communication; a heightened mutual relevance of acts; an eye-to-eye ecological huddle that maximises each participant's opportunity to perceive the other participants' monitoring of him." (Goffman, 1961, p.18).

The transcript in Table 2 is from a yet unpublished transcript by Darren Reed that we think exhibits these characteristics. It comes from a telephone conference between a facilitator and three older women. The 'Friendship Links' telephone conference is one of a series organised by Hackney Borough Council for the benefit of isolated old people. For a large part of the recording the conversation is stilted, as Laura (the facilitator) goes around them one at a time trying to find some common interest. At the point where this extract starts she succeeds in generating smooth participation for the first time with a topic of favourite authors. Note how they are all jumping in with spontaneous contributions. Square parentheses indicate overlapping speech, and '=' at the end of one turn and the start of another indicates that the two

---

[2] See http://iac.dtic.mil/hsiac/products/tlx/tlx.html for details.

```
Laura: oh yes [ and which is what is your favourite author
Ida:          [ ye
Ida:     (0.2) (sniff) well i like er daniel steele=
Laura: =oh yes yes
Ida:     or catherine cookson=
Laura: =oh YEs yes dorothea and I [ like catherine cookson
Dorothea:                          [ °yeah° ((cough))
Renie:                            [ thats mar favourit
Ida:                             [ () I like=
Laura: =an you as well renie=
Renie: =yeah=
Ida:     = yes I like er ACHullee there as lot of (.) good books i like really,
Laura: mm
Renie: the trouble is with er books once you've picked them up you dont want to put
Renie: them down [ do you
Ida:              [ NO:: No
Laura:           [ no::
Laura:           [ its ()
Ida:              [ they are good yeah                     .
```

**Table 2:** Extract from a transcript demonstrating a focused gathering.

utterances were 'latched', i.e. one immediately followed the other with almost no pause between them. The amount of overlap and latching in this extract is much higher than elsewhere in the transcript. At last they are engaged in a common experience.

To summarise this far, a high level of engagement as an individual or as a group would seem to be an important component of enjoyment and an important ingredient in many recreational activities. We can also identify some ways of measuring or detecting it, through rating scales or in conversations, that can be used in field studies and experiments. Using these measures, new features for the Virtual Pub could be evaluated by examining their ability to produce recreational experiences that exhibit a high level of engagement from the whole group. Analytic studies can proceed by making arguments about features that may induce or prevent high engagement. To take one example, a way of inducing engagement as a group would be for each participant to bring a 'gift'. This would take the form of a picture that would be displayed on all the Virtual Pub terminals. Participants would download their gifts to a Web site prior to the session and the software would cycle through the gifts so that each participant would get a turn at being the centre of attention for the group. There are existing photo sharing Web sites that already do something like this.

One can think of other elements of enjoyment. Aesthetic attraction would seem to be important, also narrative completeness. Again, there are existing bodies of research that can be adapted to our purpose. Who knows, in the process of broadening the concept of usability HCI researchers may identify completely new components of fun and enjoyment.

## 4 Effective Communication

Despite the implications of the phrase 'human–computer interaction', a large part of the research within the discipline of HCI is concerned with electronic products that support human-human interaction. Enjoyment is a very new issue for HCI. Effective communication is an old one. Communication is studied under various headings, notably, 'computer supported cooperative work', 'electronically mediated communication' and 'computer mediated communication'. Hundreds of papers and books have been written on these topics. It is thus surprising that there has not been the same effort to encapsulate the results of this research in guidelines and design methodologies. The technological infrastructures for electronic communication depends on widespread agreement to adopt standard ways of doing things and international standards abound in this area. However, I am not aware of any international standards that prescribe user-centred guidelines on how text-based or voice communication should work, in the way that ISO 9241 prescribes how menus should work. Neither am I aware of an international standard prescribing a user centred methodology for the design of communication technology. There is also little in the way of agreed representations for reasoning about the problem.

Consider again the Virtual Pub. What features should we include to facilitate effective communication? To answer this question it is necessary to consider the nature of spoken conversation as a collaborative activity. Grice (1957) gives the following example. A couple are lying in bed. Anne says to Bill "What time is it?" Bill says "The milkman has just come". This reply only has meaning if Anne can assume that Bill is seeking to answer her question and knows that Anne knows when the milkman usually delivers the milk. As can be seen from Table 2, spoken language is poorly formed and disjointed in comparison to the sloppiest written language, and yet it is incredibly efficient. Clark (1996) explains how this efficiency arises through the collaborative obligations between the speaker and the hearer. For each utterance, the speaker and hearer are collaborating at a number of levels. At the most basic level, the listener is listening and the speaker is speaking. At a higher level, the speaker is designing what she says using her knowledge of the listener, and the listener is trying to understand given his knowledge of her knowledge. The listener has an obligation to signal whether he has understood and the speaker has an obligation to monitor these signals and repair potential 'trouble' when she spots it.

The efficiency of spoken conversation is achieved, within the collaborative framework described above, using certain conversational devices described by Conversation Analysts, see for example Hutchby & Wooffitt (1998). This very influential branch of sociology is also the basis of Clark's account. I shall concentrate on just three conversational devices that I will dub, 'interpersonal awareness', 'fluent turn allocation' and 'deixis'.

First consider the concept of interpersonal awareness (Short et al., 1976). A group of friends socialising in the same room are able to see each other, the environment they are in, and what they are doing in that environment. If one person slipped out to the toilet and another was taking a call on his mobile phone everyone would know. In the Virtual Pub this kind of awareness may be much harder to achieve. Another kind of awareness that may be absent in mediated communication is gaze awareness. Experiments at York (Monk & Gale, 2002) have shown that we can accurately judge what someone is looking at in the immediate environment and that this knowledge can be used to make language more efficient. Again, unless the virtual pub gives you a view of all the participants *and* their surrounding environment, this will not be possible.

In one-to-one telephone conversations we have learned tricks to provide awareness. For example, if someone has a very long turn at talking, the other is obliged to make encouraging noises at the other end to prove they are still there. With a group conversation this may be harder to do. General awareness of who is attending in the Virtual Pub could be supported by low quality video with a wide angle view, for example, though this would not support full gaze awareness or eye contact.

Second, fluent turn allocation is similarly something that is hard when you cannot see the other person, and is even harder in a group. Conversation is structured as turns and Conversation Analysts have devoted a great deal of work to describing how a group conversation moves smoothly from one speaker to the next. When turn allocation is hard conversations become less fluent. The average turn size goes up and this impedes the rapid feedback necessary in the collaborative endeavour described above.

One important signal used in turn allocation is gaze and eye contact. An interesting potential solution to the problem of turn allocation has been provided by Vertegaal (1999). His GAZE system monitors the gaze of a participant using a camera and computer vision techniques. Instead of sending a video signal, which could be very expensive in a group conversation, one of a small number of alternative gaze positions is determined and used to control the graphical display of each participant. The display shows where each of the others is looking by using a few stored photos. So if Anne is looking at your photo on her display and Ben is looking at Anne's photo on his, your display will contain a photo of Anne looking straight ahead (at you) and Ben looking to the left (assuming Anne's photo is left of Ben's).

Third deixis simply means pointing with language. Whenever we say 'that one' we are using deixis. Take the example of a meeting around a whiteboard. During the meeting various lists and diagrams will be put on the whiteboard. Later in the conversation these can provide a very powerful and efficient way of expressing oneself. Just by pointing, verbally or physically, to some item on the whiteboard one can reference a whole raft of previous talk that would take a long time to specify any other way. Something similar is happening during recreational conversations when we pass around a letter or a postcard, or a pack of holiday snaps.

The importance of deixis suggests features such as virtual photograph albums. The idea of a graphical 'gift', described in the discussion of enjoyment above, could also serve this purpose. Such a device would provide a commonly experienced object or field of reference so that deictic references to 'that' 'there' could be directed toward a common spatial context.

It is possible then to identify elements necessary for effective communication that one would want to support in the Virtual Pub. The examples given here are interpersonal awareness, fluent turn allocation and deixis. These are all specific enough and sufficiently well understood that we can make a priori arguments about the kinds of features which would facilitate them. It is also possible to identify them in a conversation and they can be used as criteria in experiments or field studies comparing alternative systems. The next step would seem to be some intensive analytic and empirical work to devise guidelines and methodologies for designers.

## 5 Dependability

Dependability has been a concern of Computer Scientists for many years, see for example Sommerville (2000). In the office we are used to software that 'crashes' on a regular basis. However, if you are building software to control a power station, or the control surfaces of an aircraft, you need to be able to prove that the software is very unlikely to fail or even to behave in an inappropriate manner. At York we are part of a large interdisciplinary project exploring how this work on 'dependable systems' can be applied to socio-technical systems in general and the home in particular[3]. To explain why this is important I need to develop another design problem.

One of the big opportunities provided by so-called 'smart technologies' for the home is the possibility of enabling older and disabled people to remain independent and live in their own homes when they would otherwise have to move to some sort of institution. Imagine you are planning to install some technology in the home of an elderly woman, let us call her Mavis. She has severe arthritis and it has been decided to install motorised windows and doors with push button controls. These are linked through a wireless network and so we can also provide central locking. When she goes out, she can shut all open windows and lock both doors with one button press. She suffers from low blood pressure and could easily faint so we also install a personal fall monitor. This wearable device communicates with a call centre from which appropriate actions are initiated and carers informed. She also has some cognitive problems so we monitor her activity to check she is not leaving the house at unusual times. This monitoring is also mediated via a call centre. This clearly needs to be a dependable system, if it goes wrong it can be a threat to life, but safety is not the only concern. Three components of dependability will be considered here: safety, privacy and integrity.

With a network of interconnected devices, designing for safety is not straightforward as the failure or unexpected behaviour of one component can affect the whole system. With a socio-technical system the components include technology and humans, that is Mavis, the call centre, the carers and so on. Dependable systems detect errors before they lead to catastrophic failures. Humans are good at detecting and repairing failures. If, for example, the central locking system fails and Mavis is locked out, she should be able to contact the call centre and get emergency help. However, it is not enough to assume that because there is human supervision of the system all will be well. A case must be made for each possible error and the failures that could result. Technology designers often have a poor understanding of how people function in a socio-technical system and need help in doing this safety analysis.

---

[3]See the DIRC Web site http://www.dirc.org.uk.

Privacy is an important issue in the home. Mavis may be willing to give away some privacy in order to maintain her independence on the basis that the privacy she would lose should she have to move to an institution would be much greater. However, she needs to understand the precise nature of the transaction she is making. For example, people are very resistant to having cameras in their homes. This may be quite unreasonable if the camera is simply acting as a sophisticated movement detector. Of course, if the video images are transmitted outside of the home, their fears may be justified. Mavis needs to understand, and agree to who has access to the monitoring data collected and what these people know about her from it. She is then in a position to make an informed decision about whether the privacy given away is worth the independence gained.

Integrity is defined as security from external threats. If your door locks are controlled by a wireless link there is the possibility that a burglar with a scanner could obtain entry to your home. Could a person with malicious intent monitor the data being sent to the call centre to determine when Mavis is out of the house? In the early days of remote central locking for cars, thieves managed to steal cars in this way. More sophisticated encryption techniques were devised and the problem is now solved. The purpose of dependability analysis is to identify threats to the integrity of a system before they occur rather than after the event as in the above example.

Dependability of human–computer systems is a relatively new area for HCI — but see the work of Harrison and colleagues, for example, Pocock et al. (2001). By breaking it down into component issues we can start to see how progress can be made. Dependability is an area where analysis is more important than empirical work. We cannot build alternative systems and see which kills the least people! The application of smart home technology to support older and disabled people is new, even though the technology itself may be old. There is much work to be done before we understand the problem well enough to specify methodologies or guidelines.

## 6  Conclusion

The two design problems considered here, the Virtual Pub and Mavis' smart home, illustrate how restricted the view of usability as ease-of-learning, ease-of-use and task fit is. The additional concepts suggested here are summarised in Table 3 along with some of the components of these concepts discussed. These all need further development and some may not stand the test of time. In this connection the history of the development of current conceptions of usability may be useful. This sees guidelines, representations and methodologies as the ultimate goals of usability engineering. It suggests empirical and analytic processes for achieving those goals.

At the beginning of this paper it was suggested that the home can act as a stimulus to change our ideas about usability, that our conception of usability must be broadened in other design contexts as well. Fun is not restricted to the home. Educational software needs to engender a high level of personal engagement for example. All the components of effective communication: interpersonal awareness, fluent turn allocation and deixis, apply in the workplace just as well as the home. Dependability has always been an issue in safety critical work contexts and integrity and privacy are rapidly becoming major issues in office technology. It is not

Conventional conceptions of usability
    Ease-of-learning
    Low level ease-of-use
    Task fit
Enjoyment
    High engagement (as an individual or as a group)
    Aesthetic attraction
    Narrative completeness
Effective communication
    Interpersonal awareness
    Fluent turn allocation
    Deixis
Dependability
    Safety
    Privacy
    Integrity / security

**Table 3:** Components of usability identified in this paper.

overstating the case to say that a broader view of usability is crucial if HCI is to continue to successfully represent the needs of the user.

## Acknowledgements

I would like to thank all the members of the York Usability Research group, Jan Blom, Mark Blythe, Gordon Baxter, David Grayson, Darren Reed, Hokyoung Ryu, and Peter Wright who have contributed to this article through their original ideas and comments on drafts. Further information about the work of the group is available at www.yorkusabilityresearch.org. The author is supported by EPRC through Grant No. GR/M86446, and the DIRC project, also by PACCIT (award L328253006).

## References

Checkland, P. B. & Scholes, J. (1990), *Soft Systems Methodology in Action*, John Wiley & Sons.

Clark, H. H. (1996), *Using Language*, Cambridge University Press.

Csikszentmihalyi, M. & Rathunde, K. (1993), The Measurement of Flow in Everyday Life: Towards a Theory of Emergent Motivation, *in* J. E. Jacobs (ed.), *Proceedings of the 40th Nebraska Symposium on Motivation*, University of Nebraska Press, pp.57–97.

Dix, A., Finlay, J., Abowd, G. & Beale, R. (1998), *Human–Computer Interaction*, second edition, Prentice–Hall Europe.

Goffman, E. (1961), Fun in Games, *in* E. Goffman (ed.), *Encounters: Two Studies in the Sociology of Interaction*, Bob Merril, pp.15–31.

Grice, H. P. (1957), "Meaning", *Philosophical Review* **66**, 377–88.

Holtzblatt, K. & Jones, S. (1993), Contextual Inquiry: A Participatory Technique for System Design, *in* D. Schuler & A. Namioka (eds.), *Participatory Design: Principles and Practices*, Lawrence Erlbaum Associates, pp.177–210.

Hutchby, I. & Wooffitt, R. (1998), *Conversation Analysis. Principles Practices and Applications*, Polity Press.

Microsoft (1995), *The Windows Interface Guidelines for Software Design*, Microsoft Press.

Monk, A. F. (1998), Lightweight Techniques to Encourage Innovative User Interface Design, *in* L. Wood (ed.), *User Interface Design: Bridging the Gap between User Requirements and Design*, CRC Press, pp.109–29.

Monk, A. F. (2000), User-centred Design: The Home Use Challenge, *in* A. Sloane & F. van Rijn (eds.), *Home Informatics and Telematics: Information Technology and Society*, Kluwer, pp.181–90.

Monk, A. F. & Gale, C. (2002), "A Look is Worth a Thousand Words: Full Gaze Awareness in Video-mediated Conversation", *Discourse Processes* **33**(3), 257–78.

Pocock, S., Harrison, M., Wright, P. & Johnson, P. (2001), THEA: A Technique for Human Error Assessment Early in Design, *in* M. Hirose (ed.), *Human–Computer Interaction — INTERACT '99: Proceedings of the Eighth IFIP Conference on Human–Computer Interaction*, Vol. 1, IOS Press, pp.247–54.

Short, J., Williams, E. & Christie, B. (1976), *The Social Psychology of Telecommunications*, John Wiley & Sons.

Sommerville, I. (2000), *Software Engineering*, sixth edition, Addison–Wesley.

Vertegaal, R. (1999), The GAZE Groupware System: Mediating Joint Attention in Multiparty Communication and Collaboration, *in* M. G. Williams, M. W. Altom, K. Ehrlich & W. Newman (eds.), *Proceedings of the CHI99 Conference on Human Factors in Computing Systems: The CHI is the Limit*, ACM Press, pp.294–301.

# Anthropomorphism

# Invisible but Audible: Enhancing Information Awareness through Anthropomorphic Speech

## Nuno M Ribeiro[†] & Ian D Benest[‡]

[†] *CEREM, Universidade Fernando Pessoa, P4249–004 Porto, Portugal.*
Tel: *+351 22 507 1306*
Email: *nribeiro@ufp.pt*
URL: *www.cerem.ufp.pt/~nribeiro*

[‡] *Department of Computer Science, University of York, York YO10 5DD, UK.*
Tel: *+44 1 904 43 2736*
Email: *ian.benest@cs.york.ac.uk*
URL: *www.cs.york.ac.uk/~idb*

Information awareness is the process by which people obtain knowledge about the status of personal information that is important to them. This is usually provided graphically. When the information would otherwise be hidden from view, it must be brought to the front automatically or manually making users stop what they are doing and interact with the system. This design strategy ignores the human costs of interrupting the user. A solution is to use speech output to make the delivery invisible, but the incorporation of speech invokes anthropomorphic feelings whose cues must be carefully controlled if the system is to be regarded as humanised. This paper describes an empirical study designed to investigate how the content contextually cues the significance of visually hidden information, and how the delivery, including attentive interruptions, linguistic variation and politeness, impacts on the social acceptability of a speaking system. The results indicated that heuristic-oriented people felt a degree of rapport with the speech-based system, and that it enabled them to appreciate the content of hidden information more strongly than those who were analytic

in nature. **Overall, the system was unexpectedly well accepted, leading to
the abstraction of design guidelines for those speech-based systems that
exploit invisibility to enhance information awareness.**

**Keywords:** information awareness, anthropomorphic interfaces, speech
output, interruptions, linguistic variation, politeness, notifications,
reminders.

# 1  Introduction

## 1.1  *Problems with Visible Interfaces*

Current graphical interfaces for personal information management (PIM) are based
on principles, mostly arising from the desktop metaphor, that "limit the computer–
human interface" (Gentner & Nielsen, 1996) in a number of ways. First, *finding
hidden information*, such as information nested in a hierarchy or hidden behind
opened windows, requires cognitive effort that can adversely distract attention from
the user's main activity. Second, when people need to be notified of new or updated
information, current interface approaches rely on playing a sound or blinking an icon
to grab the user's attention. However, these techniques give insufficient information
about the interruption and require the user to investigate further. Third, where
systems display a notification window, it obscures any information already being
displayed (Raskin, 2000) due to screen display space limitations (Shneiderman,
1993). Additionally, existing approaches that alert the user do not include an
evaluation of its importance before it interrupts. Thus, users often suffer a loss
in concentration through needless graphical notifications. Finally, applications
that interrupt make use of their own icons or notification windows. This *lack of
integration for alerts* requires the user to have to remember and recognise the source
of the information (Sawhney & Schmandt, 2000). So the information should be
conveyed in an active and unobtrusive way with due regard to the user's degree of
interruptibility and commitment to a task. The interface should be able to sense the
context in which the user is working and act appropriately. Here, *notifications* are
viewed as alerts to the imminence or occurrence of new events while *reminders* are
viewed as alerts to *past* events of which the user needs to be reminded.

## 1.2  *Exploiting Speech Output*

Research is required to determine the kinds of information processing for which
spoken output is a benefit and is in fact preferred (Cohen & Oviatt, 1995). In this
paper, it is argued that the limitations of current techniques used for information
awareness may be reduced by the adoption of speech output in such a way that it
complements, rather than replaces, the graphical user-interface.

Using speech output for notifying and reminding the user should make
interruptions less disruptive since the user's attention can be obtained without
interfering with the visual "locus of attention" (Raskin, 2000). Moreover, speech
output potentially allows for the provision of more meaningful alerts: it can be
used both to alert the user as to the occurrence of an event and to provide sufficient
semantics about that event. Furthermore, speech output provides an integrating

mechanism for disparate sources to deliver alerts in a timely manner. Of course, in an open-plan environment, the aural channel promotes information leakage unless an ear-piece is employed. The ability to broadcast to a wider audience also needs to be minimised so that it is no more irritating than when someone is speaking on the telephone in the same environment.

## 1.3   Anthropomorphic Delivery

Research has found that people react socially to computers (Reeves & Nass, 1996), but the reception of speech invokes even stronger social responses (Nass et al., 1994). When speech is used, the system must *reinforce its social acceptability* by complying with human expectations regarding social interaction; the system must reflect the same social norms that people employ in conversation. This paper suggests that to reinforce the social acceptability of a speaking system, the design must take into account at least three critical anthropomorphic aspects: attentive spoken interruptions, linguistic variation and politeness.

Interruptions are inevitable in a computer-based system that notifies and reminds; so the system must know: the information priority and urgency, what to say to grab the person's attention, and how to interrupt the audio channel. Furthermore, interruptions are raised by the occurrence of events, and these are inevitably repetitive. For visual interfaces, it is extremely important to maintain consistency in the presentation of information, but for speech output the repetition of the same utterance over and over again will irritate and distract the person. So, while the semantic consistency must be maintained, the message must be conveyed with variation. The types of linguistic variation people usually employ in a conversation, which have no impact on the meaning they intend to convey, include small variations of intonation and prosody, variation in the words used to construct sentences, and variation in word position.

Being interrupted is sufficiently annoying *per se*, even though it may be urgent, very relevant to the person, and conveyed in a non-repetitive way. The strategy usually employed by people who are interrupting is to be polite in order to attenuate the adverse effects of the interruption. Thus, the design must use typical polite expressions, particularly when getting the person's attention.

## 1.4   Contextual Content

The fundamental concepts that should drive the design of the alerting messages are those that relate to the psychological principles that underlie the processes people use in personal information management.

Psychological evidence indicates that *recognition is superior to recall* (Houston, 1986) and thus, a system that attempts to enhance information awareness should support the weaker recall function. This suggests that speech should support the initial recall-directed function, leaving the recognition function (the presentation of the full details) for the most suitable graphical presentation.

Humans also have a *poor memory for details* (Houston, 1986); people interpret information in the *context* in which it appears, rather than storing that information in memory exactly as it was acquired. This fact prompts the need to provide recallable and recognisable characteristics in order to improve information recall, and these are provided by contextual elements, or *cues*, that characterise the situation in which an event occurs (Barreau, 1995). These cues include such elements as the subject matter, the addresses of the information or the intended use for the information. For the purpose of this work, the contextual cues are called *forward cues*; the reason is that they provide sufficient information to allow the person to appreciate what will be found ahead. It is suggested that the following context elements should be adopted in speech-based alerts: Kind, Time, Quantity, People, Nature, Description and Place (Ribeiro, 2002).

## 2   Experimental Environment

A speaking assistant for information awareness was developed to provide an experimental environment for testing users' perceptions and reactions to anthropomorphised spoken notifications and reminders. It also established the extent to which exploiting speech as part of a complementary invisible mechanism to the existing graphical presentation of information, offers advantages over purely graphical-based approaches for information awareness. The system was designed so that it supports the user's continued awareness of dynamic personal information which is hidden from view, by extracting selected contextual information for the *cues* required by the human cognitive system, and conveying those cues as part of spoken notifications and reminders in the email, diary and printing domains. The system was designed to follow typical conversational norms, including attentive interruptions, linguistic variation and politeness.

The experimental environment architecture is illustrated in Figure 1. There are three main types of software agent: the *specialised* agents (the email, printer and diary agents), which are personal information monitoring agents, the *service* agents (the user monitor agent), which provide environmental information required by the specialised agents, and an *interface* agent (the speaking agent). In addition, there is a defined inter-agent communication protocol. It was implemented on a MS Windows NT platform running the Microsoft Agent extensions (see http://www.microsoft.com/msagent), and the Lernout & Hauspie TruVoice text-to-speech (TTS) engine.

## 3   Method

The following research questions were considered:

- How *useful* would people find it if they were interrupted using spoken language at the interface to convey information that is hidden from view?

- Would polite, linguistically varied and attentive interrupting speech, reinforce the *social acceptability* of the interface?

- How *humanised* would such a system appear to be?

A quasi-natural experiment was designed to simulate a situation in which users searched for specific information in order to answer a set of questions and write a report on the information found. In parallel, the users had to perform

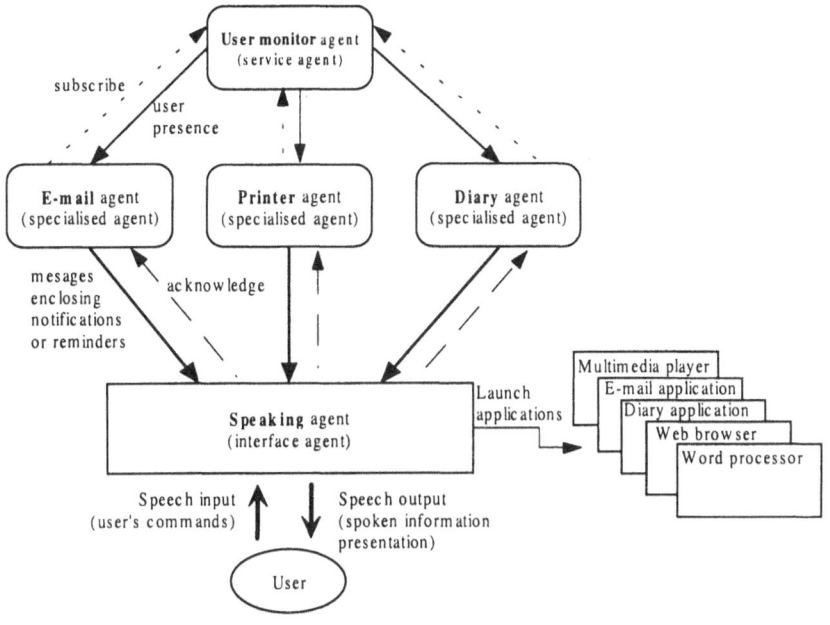

**Figure 1:** Experimental environment architecture.

other common activities such as printing, managing email and performing to-do's previously entered in their diary. There was no control group; the system itself was not being evaluated against any other system. The experimental situation was not intended to reveal the true motivation of the study. The overall objectives of the experiment were as follows:

- To assess the perceived *adequacy* of the *anthropomorphic characteristics* in relation to the overall goal of providing a humanised work environment; and to identify any *differences* in these perceptions according to users' inherent psychological preferences for acquiring and processing information.

- To assess the perceived *usefulness* and the *degree of humanisation* of the system; identifying any *differences* in perceptions when compared with ones emanating from previous experience with the MS Office Assistant.

## 3.1 Experimental Design and Procedure

Participants were told that this experiment was being conducted to investigate how easy it is for people to use an interactive system to find information in an environment where there is some interruption. The experimental sequence is given in Figure 2.

Participants were told to use the World Wide Web to find answers to forty-eight questions. It was stressed that knowing the answer to a question would not be sufficient, and that they should find evidence to support the answer and paste it

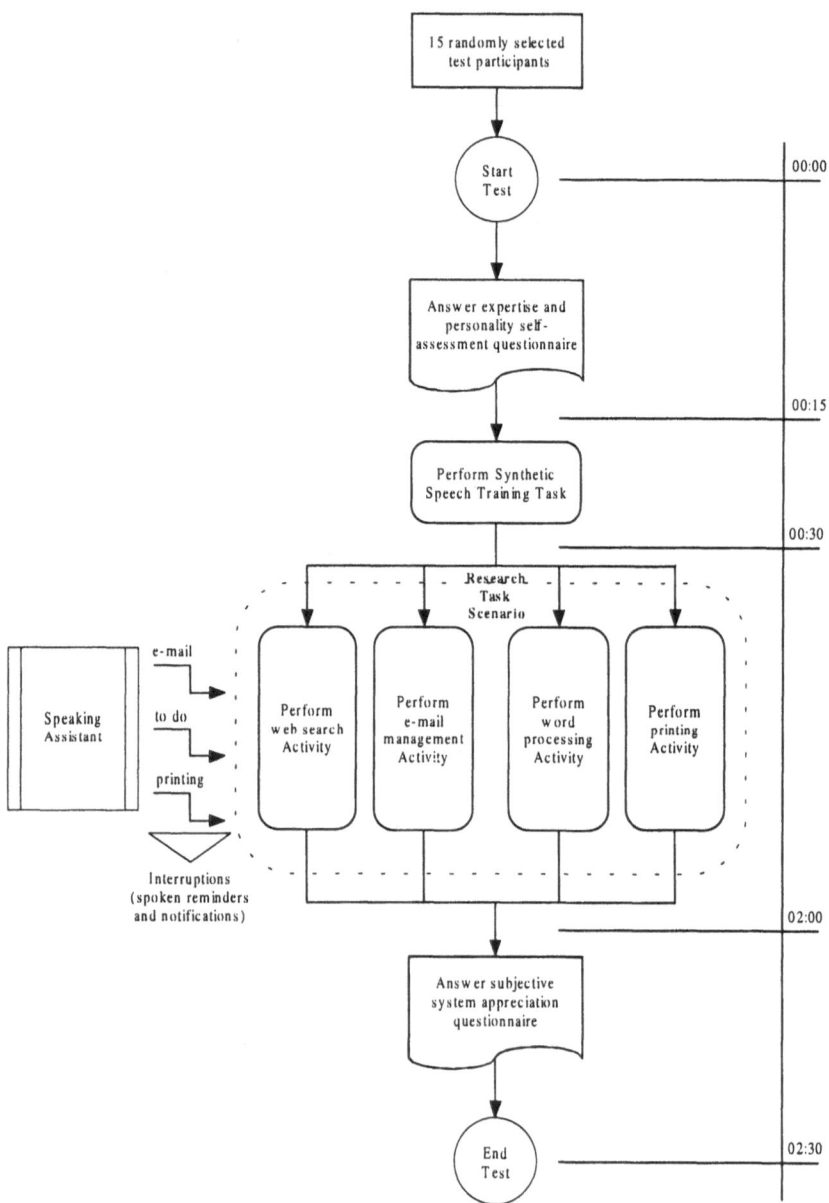

**Figure 2:** Experiment design and procedure.

into a word-processor document along with its Uniform Resource Locator (URL). Once participants had finished each group of questions they were told to print off their word processor document. Additionally, they used an email client to read, reply and print selected email messages. 15 self-selected participants performed the experiment. Each had to complete an expertise and personality self-assessment questionnaire. A 15minute training session with the particular speech synthesiser was given at the start, though all were actually familiar with speech synthesis. Each person took two and a half hours to complete the exercise. Each interrupting event was precisely timed. At the end of the session, participants completed a subjective appreciation questionnaire designed to measure their opinions and attitudes concerning the assistance offered by the system's prototype.

## 3.2 Measures

To collect data, two questionnaires were used. The first questionnaire was completed before participants started the task. The second questionnaire was completed after the task was finished. The design of these questionnaires took into account guidelines and advice presented in the literature (Alreck & Settle, 1994; Bouchard, 1976; Saunders et al., 2000).

The independent variables (IV), collected through the first questionnaire describe the participants: gender, age range, level of operating system proficiency, degree of familiarity with speech synthesis, and the participant's personality type as given by the self-test (Tieger & Tieger, 1995) that determines the Myers–Briggs Type Indicator (MBTI). The MBTI categorises people according to their dominant psychological preferences in each of four pairs of personality traits; it relies on the person's honesty. It is completed remote from any specific situation so it is not an accurate predictor of action in any situation. As the experimental environment poses little threat, it was thought unlikely that any of the participants would deviate from their indicated personality trait during the experiment.

The dependent variables (DV) were the measures taken in the second questionnaire. In this study, only subjective measures consisting of users' opinions, feelings or attitudes about the system characteristics were taken. These measures were obtained by having participants rate their perception about specific system characteristics on 5-point and 7-point scales.

For assessing the *adequacy of the anthropomorphic characteristics* in relation to the overall goal of providing a humanised work environment, users were asked to rate the suitability of given adjectives to describe certain system features on 7-point numeric scales ("1" = "Not at all", "7" = "Very much so"). Each adjective corresponds to one dependent variable, as shown in Table 1.

In order to assess the perceived *overall quality of the system's assistance*, participants were asked to use 5-point Likert scales (Alreck & Settle, 1994) to rate their level of agreement with given statements about the system ("1" = "Strongly Disagree", "2" = "Disagree", "3" = "Neither Disagree nor Agree", "4" = "Agree", "5" = "Strongly Agree"). Each statement corresponded to one dependent variable, as shown in Table 2.

In order to assess the perceived usefulness and humanisation of the speaking assistant, participants were asked to use a 7-point semantic differential scale (Osgood

| Anthropomorphic characteristics | Dependent Variables (adjectives) |
|---|---|
| Interruptions | Appropriate |
| | Useful |
| | Disruptive |
| Music interruptions | Natural |
| | Interfering |
| Attention-getters | Useful |
| | Annoying |
| | Natural |
| Spoken message semantics | Easy to recognise words |
| | Easy to understand meaning |
| | Helpful |
| | Appropriate |
| Politeness | Degree |
| | Appropriate |
| | Irritating |
| Linguistic variation | Irritating |

**Table 1:** Dependent variables for assessing anthropomorphic characteristics.

| Characteristics | Dependent variables (statements) |
|---|---|
| Task assistance | The speaking assistant made the task easier to perform |
| | The system was assisting me. |

**Table 2:** Dependent variables for assessing the speech-based assistance quality.

| Dimensions | Dependent variables (semantic differential) | |
|---|---|---|
| | 1 | 7 |
| Assistant pleasantness | Unpleasant | Pleasant |
| Assistant helpfulness | Unhelpful | Helpful |
| Assistant convenience | Inconvenient | Convenient |
| Assistant reliability | Unreliable | Reliable |
| Assistant comfort | Uncomfortable | Comfortable |
| Assistant efficiency | Inefficient | Efficient |
| Assistant satisfaction | Unsatisfying | Satisfying |
| Assistant unobtrusiveness | Unobtrusive | Intrusive |
| Assistant likeability | Horrible | Lovely |

**Table 3:** Dependent variables for assessing usefulness and humanisation.

| | Mean | Median | Mode | Std Deviation |
|---|---|---|---|---|
| Interruptions: appropriateness | 5.67 | 6 | 6 | 1.05 |
| Interruptions: usefulness | 5.87 | 6 | 6 | 0.92 |

**Table 4:** Average ratings for interruptions.

| | Mean | Median | Mode | Std Deviation |
|---|---|---|---|---|
| Interruptions: not disruptive (recoded) | 5.00 | 5 | 6 | 1.65 |

**Table 5:** Average ratings for interruptions' non-disruptiveness.

et al., 1967) and rate their overall feelings about the system for nine different dimensions. Each pair corresponded to one dependent variable (Table 3).

## 3.3 Participants Profile

The 15 participants were selected by being the first ones to respond to a message broadcast throughout the Department. They consisted of nine undergraduate students, five postgraduate students and one staff member. Four were females and eleven were males; their ages ranged between 18 and 45 years old. Participants were provided with a small financial reward. Time prohibited a larger and more diverse sample. All participants had adequate domain knowledge of the task suggested, and they judged themselves as medium or high proficiency users of the MS Windows NT operating system. All had either heard speech synthesis a few times or many times before the experiment. Their psychological characteristics were fairly distributed with no strong correlations between the participants' characteristics.

## 3.4 Experimental Results and Discussion

### 3.4.1 Adequacy of Anthropomorphic Behaviours

The first set of results relates to the user's perceptions of appropriateness and usefulness of the interruptions produced by the speaking assistant. The users' mean ratings are presented in Table 4: users moderately agreed that the interruptions generated by the system were perceived as both appropriate and useful.

To investigate the quality of the interruptions an index of *relevance* was created by aggregating both items (Cronbach alpha = 0.87). (As a correlation coefficient, Cronbach's alpha (Norušis, 1994) provides a measure of confidence as to how reasonable it is to aggregate the items.) The mean rating was 5.76 out of 7, with a standard deviation of 0.92, indicating that on average users thought the interruptions were relevant. No significant differences were found. Three users observed that the system only delivered relevant (necessary) information, and four liked being interrupted with spoken notifications, which they classified as timely.

The second result (in Table 5) relates to the perceived disruptiveness caused by spoken interruptions. This was recoded during analysis in order to obtain an index of non-disruptiveness. It indicates that on average users slightly agree that the interruptions did not disrupt them, while the majority agreed that interruptions

|                                                                      | Mean | Median | Mode | Std Deviation |
|----------------------------------------------------------------------|------|--------|------|---------------|
| Music interruption: naturalness                                      | 6.20 | 6      | 6    | 0.68          |
| Music interruption: music did not interfere with spoken message (recoded) | 6.07 | 6      | 7    | 1.33          |

**Table 6:** Average ratings for music interruption.

|                                              | Mean | Median | Mode | Std Deviation |
|----------------------------------------------|------|--------|------|---------------|
| Attention-getters: usefulness                | 4.87 | 6      | 6    | 1.68          |
| Attention-getters: not annoying (recoded)    | 5.00 | 5      | 6    | 1.56          |
| Attention-getters: naturalness               | 4.93 | 5      | 5    | 1.16          |

**Table 7:** Average ratings for spoken attention-getters.

were not disruptive. If the result had indicated a perception of disruptiveness then the suitability of speech as an alternative to graphical based interruptions would be questionable. This suggests that speech has a role to play as a complementary invisible mechanism for delivering information with minimal disruption.

This finding is also supported by five positive opinions about the unobtrusive nature of spoken alerts. The comment here was that the messages did not demand immediate action. So, the verification of the items of information mentioned in the message could be postponed until the user's current task was finished, or until the user's attention could be diverted from the current task. Thus, users were able to decide when to deal with the interruption without any other overt action.

The third set of results concerns the way the system deals with the audio channel when it is already in use for other audio presentations. The main concern was to maximise the naturalness of the interruption while minimising the interference between the spoken message and an existing audio presentation. In order to test the suitability of a fading approach, music was continuously playing in the background (at a suitable volume that was kept constant during the experiment). User's average ratings can be found in Table 6. As noted, these are very positive results regarding the fading technique for the audio channel modulation, with users definitely agreeing on the naturalness of the modulation and on the low level of interference. To investigate further the *quality* of the modulation, both variables were aggregated (Cronbach alpha = 0.61) during analysis. Consistently, the mean rating obtained was 6.1 out of a possible 7, with a standard deviation of 0.89. No significant differences were found across the users' personality characteristics under analysis.

However, the experiment was limited in that it only tested interruptions of music. Thus, further research is needed to investigate the appropriateness of this technique to interrupt other multimedia presentations, such as video clips.

The fourth set of results relates to the investigation of the quality of speech-based attention-getting. In order to obtain users' perceptions along these dimensions, participants were asked to consider the way the system obtained their attention, by

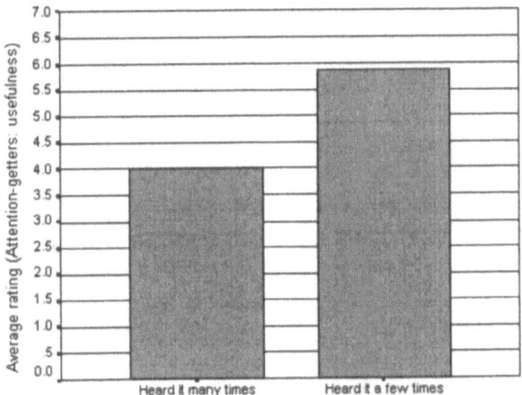

**Figure 3:** Average ratings for attention-getters' usefulness by familiarity with TTS.

saying for example "Excuse me". Table 7 illustrates users' average ratings. These results indicate that users slightly agree on the usefulness, naturalness and non-annoying nature of the expressions used to grab their attention. However, there is a considerable variation in the results. This may be indicating that additional research is needed in order to achieve more humanised ways of getting a user's attention. The index of the *quality* of attention-getting (aggregation of all three variables — Cronbach alpha = 0.72) confirms this: the mean rating obtained was 4.93 out of a possible 7, with a standard deviation of 1.18.

In order to clarify these results three users mentioned that the attention-getters promoted reliable interruptions by preventing them from missing important information, and another user mentioned that attention-getting was pleasant because it prevented the occurrence of sudden interruptions, which could lead to them missing part of the delivered information. However, one user commented on the annoyance caused by the low level of linguistic variation in the short utterances that the system used to grab their attention. Another three users were annoyed because there was not enough intonation in the speech-based attention-getters. So varying the intonation with which these expressions are spoken, might alter the way they sound, and thus solve both problems.

One interesting difference between user groups was found. As Figure 3 illustrates, users who were less familiar with text-to-speech (TTS) synthesis tended to find attention-getters more useful (M = 5.86) than those with greater familiarity (M = 4.00), t(13) = −2.497, p = 0.027. It may be the case that the spoken attention-getters are really performing a useful function for the first group of users by drawing their attention before the actual message is spoken and momentarily helping them to focus their attention and improve their understanding of the synthesised speech. For the second group, this result indicates a neutral opinion.

|                                                  | Mean | Median | Mode | Std Deviation |
|--------------------------------------------------|------|--------|------|---------------|
| Semantics: words easy to recognise               | 5.60 | 6      | 6    | 1.45          |
| Semantics: meaning easy to understand            | 6.00 | 6      | 7    | 1.07          |
| Semantics: messages helpful to understand event  | 5.93 | 6      | 6    | 0.80          |
| Semantics: messages detail appropriateness       | 5.40 | 6      | 6    | 1.64          |

**Table 8:** Average ratings for spoken message semantics.

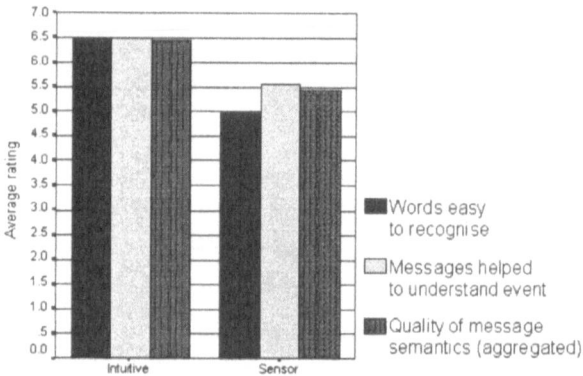

Personality Traits (MBTI): Intuitive(N) / Sensor(S)

**Figure 4:** Average ratings for message semantics by N/S.

The next set of results covers the investigation as to whether there was an adequate level of semantics in the spoken alerts so that they enhanced the user's awareness of information that was hidden from view. The average ratings are given in Table 8. Participants found the message contents to be understandable, making them well aware of events that they promoted. These were positive indicators for the *forward* cues. To validate this conclusion, an index of *semantic quality* was derived by the aggregation of three variables: "words easy to recognise", "meaning easy to recognise" and "messages helped to understand the event" (Cronbach alpha = 0.63). The mean rating was 5.84 (out of 7), with a standard deviation of 0.86.

However, some variation in opinions was apparent and significant differences were found in average ratings. Figure 4 illustrates the differences along the Intuition/Sensing personality dimension (N/S): Intuitive participants rated significantly higher (M = 6.50) the facility in recognising words when compared with Sensor participants (M = 5.00), t(13) = 2.213, p = 0.045. Intuitives also rated significantly higher the help provided by the spoken messages (M = 6.50) when compared with Sensor participants (M = 5.56), t(13) = 2.701, p = 0.018. Intuitives tend to be more heuristic in their approach to information gathering, whereas Sensors tend to be more analytic information gatherers.

|  | Mean | Median | Mode | Std Deviation |
|---|---|---|---|---|
| Level of politeness | 6.07 | 6 | 6 | 0.70 |
| Appropriateness of polite messages | 5.20 | 6 | 6 | 1.37 |
| Polite messages do not irritate (recoded) | 4.60 | 4 | 7 | 1.92 |

**Table 9:** Average ratings for the perception of system politeness.

These differences can be regarded as positive indicators. Given that messages work as surrogates to the actual event-triggered information (by providing an overview of what happened), people will acquire that information without having to interrupt their current activity. This corresponds to the way people with an Intuition preference like to take in information: they prefer to see the 'big picture', focusing on the meaning behind facts. Sensors prefer to focus on the practical details of facts to find out about events. Since the main objective of spoken alerts is to provide sufficient cues to promote the awareness of information, these results seem to support this objective. Moreover, six users mentioned that the notifications of email messages, which include information about the subject and the sender of new messages, helped them decide whether to look at, or to ignore, newly arrived messages. Furthermore, ten participants mentioned the usefulness of notifications about the printer queue as helping them carry on with their work until they were sure their documents were printed.

The next set of results clarifies what level of politeness is appropriate for a system to appear to be a humanised work companion. Here, the main thrust was to reveal whether politeness in general is perceived to be an aspect of spoken interaction that reinforces the social acceptability of the computer (by reducing its rudeness). In order to collect the users' opinions about the appropriateness of politeness, the system prototype provided simple polite utterances whenever the user's attention was to be obtained. Participants were first asked to indicate whether they noticed the system politeness; all of them did. Then, they were asked to rate their opinion of the polite messages (Table 9).

On average, participants agreed that the messages were polite and they slightly agreed that the polite messages were appropriate. However, the result is not so positive as far as the irritation caused by the polite attention-getters: some participants felt quite irritated, while others did not feel irritated at all. Users mentioned as particularly annoying the way in which the system kept repeating *"Excuse me"*. They also felt annoyed with naïve attention-grabbing utterances such as *"If you're not too busy"*. These comments clearly indicate that careful choices must be made regarding the polite expressions, but it also indicates that the system should not be overly polite all the time. In fact, although people like politeness, the typical human behaviour is not to be overly polite all the time. Sometimes, a neutral, or more serious tone is the appropriate human response to a situation.

The next result illustrates the importance of minimising user irritation by adopting linguistic variation. Participants were invited to indicate whether they had noticed this system behaviour. Only eleven participants answered positively. These

|                                           | Mean | Median | Mode | Std Deviation |
|-------------------------------------------|------|--------|------|---------------|
| Varied messages do not irritate (recoded) | 6.09 | 6      | 7    | 1.04          |

**Table 10:** Average ratings for non-irritating varied spoken messages.

|                                                      | Mean | Median | Mode | Std Deviation |
|------------------------------------------------------|------|--------|------|---------------|
| The speaking assistant made the task easier to perform | 4.07 | 4      | 4    | 0.80          |
| The system was assisting me                          | 4.13 | 4      | 4    | 0.83          |

**Table 11:** Average ratings for system assistance (on a 1 to 5 scale).

people were asked to indicate their feelings about the linguistic variation. Table 10 gives the average ratings (N = 11). It can be seen that participants did not feel irritated at all with linguistic variation (this variable was recoded). This is a positive result since the system was designed precisely to reduce irritation by varying otherwise repetitive messages. No significant differences were found.

For the four participants who did not notice the linguistic variation even though it was a salient system feature, it suggests that the system exhibited a high degree of naturalness: those features, which go unnoticed, behave in a natural way. Thus, non-repetitive spoken messages do *not* have a negative impact on users.

### 3.4.2 Assessing Speech-based Assistance Quality

The following set of results reveals the degree of assistance the system is perceived to provide in supporting the awareness of information that is hidden from view. Participants were asked to consider the influence of the system in all the activities they had to perform in order to conduct successfully the research task (e.g. they were required to check for particular email messages, and they had to print specific documents). The average ratings can be found in Table 11.

Participants definitely agreed that the system provided valuable assistance for those tasks requiring them to be aware of dynamic information that was hidden from view. The index of this *assistance quality*, obtained through the aggregation of both variables (Cronbach alpha = 0.97), confirms that the system was perceived as providing good-quality assistance for information awareness. The mean rating obtained was 4.10 out of a possible 5, with a standard deviation of 0.80. Significant differences concerning users' ratings of these variables were only found along the Intuition/Sensing dimension, as Figure 5 shows.

Intuitive participants rated significantly higher (M = 4.67) the importance of the system to assist with the experimental task than Sensor participants (M = 3.67), $t(13) = 2.962$, $p = 0.011$. Intuitive users also found that the system assisted them to a greater extent (M = 4.67) than Sensor users (M = 3.78), $t(13) = 2.317$, $p = 0.037$. Consistently, these results reveal that the system supports a heuristic style of information acquisition. Enhancing the awareness of the meaning behind events, the system was seen to aid the process of acquiring visually hidden information.

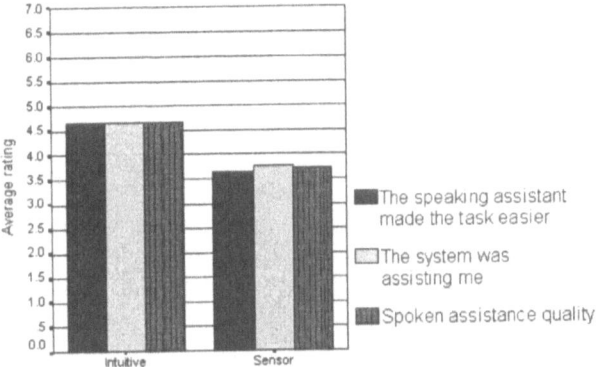

Personality Traits (MBTI): Intuitive(N) / Sensor(S)

**Figure 5:** Average ratings for system assistance by N/S personality traits.

|                                               | Mean | Median | Mode | Std Deviation |
|-----------------------------------------------|------|--------|------|---------------|
| Speaking assistant: pleasantness              | 4.73 | 4      | 4    | 1.10          |
| Speaking assistant: helpfulness               | 5.80 | 6      | 5    | 0.86          |
| Speaking assistant: convenience               | 5.33 | 5      | 5    | 0.90          |
| Speaking assistant: reliability               | 5.60 | 6      | 7    | 1.55          |
| Speaking assistant: comfort                   | 5.47 | 6      | 6    | 1.13          |
| Speaking assistant: efficiency                | 4.87 | 5      | 5    | 1.36          |
| Speaking assistant: satisfaction              | 5.07 | 5      | 6    | 0.88          |
| Speaking assistant: unobtrusiveness (recoded) | 4.73 | 5      | 6    | 1.94          |
| Speaking assistant: likeability               | 5.00 | 5      | 5    | 1.00          |

**Table 12:** Average ratings for perceptions about system's humanisation and usefulness.

### 3.4.3  Assessing Humanisation and Usefulness

This section presents the results found in studying the extent to which the anthropomorphic characteristics implemented in the prototype promote the perception of both a humanised and useful assistant (Table 12).

On average all users' perceptions of the system were positive. These results indicate that users found the spoken assistance particularly helpful and reliable.

In order to analyse the results, two indices were derived through the aggregation of the variables. The index for system *usefulness* was obtained by the aggregation of the helpfulness, convenience and comfort variables (Cronbach alpha = 0.85). The index for *humanisation* was obtained by aggregating the remaining six variables (Cronbach alpha = 0.74). Table 13 shows that the system was considered both useful and humanised.

There were three significant differences found along the Intuition/Sensing dimension. As Figure 6 illustrates, Intuitives tended to find the system more pleasant

|                                               | Mean | Std Deviation |
|-----------------------------------------------|------|---------------|
| Speaking assistant: usefulness (aggregated)   | 5.53 | 0.85          |
| Speaking assistant: humanisation (aggregated) | 5.00 | 0.90          |

**Table 13:** Average ratings for system usefulness and humanisation.

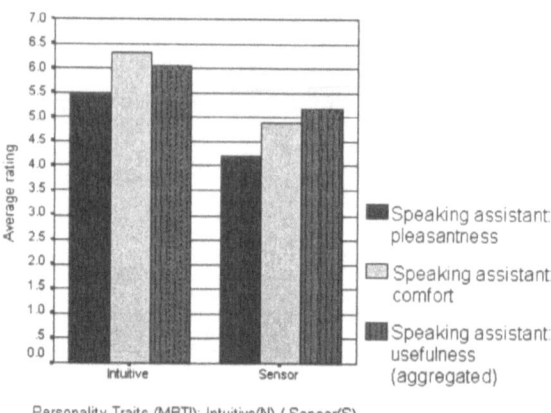

**Figure 6:** Average ratings for system pleasantness, comfort and usefulness by N/S.

(M = 5.50) than Sensors (M = 4.22), t(13) = 2.629, p = 0.021. Similarly, Intuitives also found the system significantly more comfortable (M = 6.33) than Sensors (M = 4.89), t(13) = 3.091, p = 0.009. There was also a difference in terms of the system usefulness (aggregation of helpfulness, convenience and comfort): Intuitives found the system more useful (M = 6.05) than Sensors (M = 5.18), t(13) = 2.181, p = 0.048. These results are consistent with the results found during the analysis of the specific system characteristics: the speaking assistant seems to be effectively supporting a heuristic approach to information acquisition.

Significant differences were also found along the Feeling/Thinking dimension as shown in Figure 7. Feelers found the system more pleasant (M = 5.25) than Thinkers (M = 4.14), t(11.569) = 2.271, p = 0.043. Similarly, Feelers found the system far less intrusive (M = 6.13) than Thinkers (M = 3.14), t(13) = 4.677, p = 0.000. This is the most significant difference found during the study.

It might be that such behaviours as interrupting just to convey relevant information, varying otherwise repetitive messages, and drawing attention in a polite way, make the system appear to base its decision as to when to interrupt, on person-centred values. That is, participants may have perceived the system to be evaluating the impact of its interruptions on their attention, and trying to behave in a way that preserves harmony. This is precisely the kind of behaviour that would be noticed by Feelers, because it is their distinctive mode of making decisions. This may

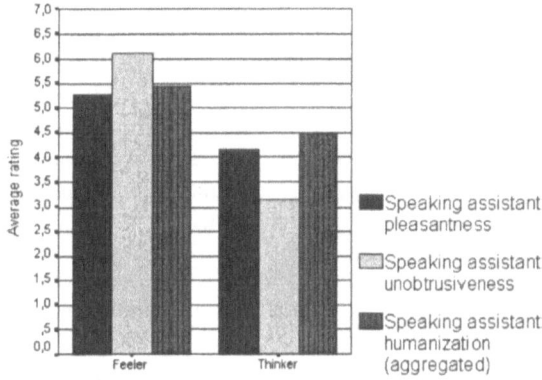

**Figure 7:** Average ratings for pleasantness, unobtrusiveness and humanisation by F/T.

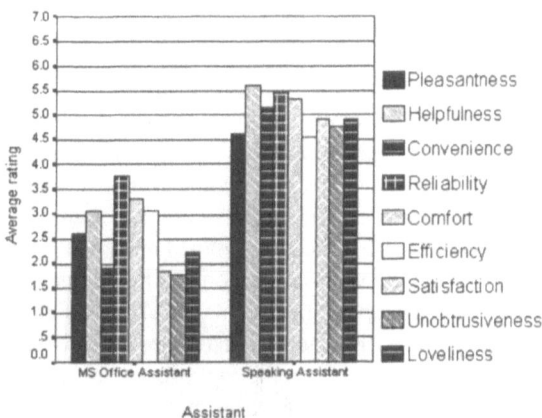

**Figure 8:** Differences in ratings for the MS Office Assistant and the Speaking Assistant.

explain why Feelers found the system less intrusive, more pleasant, and globally more humanised (M = 5.45) than Thinkers (M = 4.47), t(13) = 2.470, p = 0.028.

The last result of this study concerns the comparison of users' perceptions of the Speaking Assistant with those of the MS Office Assistant. Figure 8 illustrates the differences in users' average ratings for the nine dimensions introduced above (N = 13).

It should be noted that this is comparing the participants' reactions to the way each system delivers information. On average, the speech-based (invisible) approach to interrupting (as implemented in the Speaking Assistant prototype) was rated significantly higher than the graphical approach employed by the MS Office

Assistant over all dimensions under analysis. Interestingly, the major differences were found in the ratings of helpfulness and convenience (dimensions related to the system usefulness), and in the ratings of satisfaction and unobtrusiveness (dimensions related to the system's humanisation). All the differences shown in Figure 8 are statistically significant. This may be indicating that speech induced anthropomorphism, used to enhance the awareness of dynamic information that is hidden from view, is a potentially beneficial alternative to an approach that is purely based on the graphical delivery of information.

## 3.5   *Conclusions*

The experiment described in this paper was an initial, but thorough, study of the effects caused by speech induced anthropomorphism, when used at the interface to enhance the awareness of information that is hidden from view. The findings reported here and elsewhere suggest some important implications for the design of speech-based systems for personal information awareness. First, speech appears to be an appropriate and visually unobtrusive means of alerting the user to information that is hidden from view. It can be used in this way to complement the graphical presentation of the information. Second, speech should be used to convey short summaries about event-triggered information, and this may be achieved by including context cues that characterise the events. This facilitates the heuristic acquisition of information in that it enables people to appreciate the meaning of event-triggered information. Third, since using speech invokes an unconscious social response on the user, it should be conveyed following typical social norms such as importance-sensitive and well-structured interruptions, and linguistic variation. Using these anthropomorphic characteristics reinforces the social acceptability of the speech-based system and enhances the perception of a humanised assistant. Fourth, using speech is likely to give the system a personality. The choice of linguistic style may reinforce the social acceptability of the speech-based system, but it also may irritate users if it is not used in a way that is consistent with the personality that is expected. *Spontaneity* seems to be the key aspect that users would welcome in future speech-based systems. This should promote the perception of an interrupting behaviour that arises naturally. With built-in spontaneity, speech should not be the cause of irritation. A longitudinal study is necessary to determine whether over time, speech however mechanically humanised it is, eventually becomes too irritating to be acceptable. Future work might also compare and contrast the interference levels caused by using either speech cues or non-speech cues.

## References

Alreck, P. L. & Settle, R. B. (1994), *The Survey Research Handbook: Guidelines and Strategies for Conducting a Survey*, second edition, McGraw-Hill.

Barreau, D. K. (1995), "Context as a Factor in Personal Information Management Systems", *Journal of the American Society for Information Science* **46**(5), 327–39.

Bouchard, J. (1976), Field Research Methods: Interviewing, Questionnaires, Participant Observation, Systematic Observation, Unobtrusive Measures, *in* M. D. Dunnette (ed.), *Handbook of Organizational Psychology*, Rand McNally, pp.363–413.

Cohen, P. R. & Oviatt, S. L. (1995), The Role of Voice in Human-Machine Communication, *in* D. B. Roe & J. Wilpon (eds.), *Voice Communication Between Humans and Machines*, National Academy of Sciences, pp.34–75.

Gentner, D. & Nielsen, J. (1996), "The Anti-Mac Interface", *Communications of the ACM* **39**(8), 70–82.

Houston, J. R. (1986), *Fundamentals of Learning and Memory*, third edition, Harcourt Brace.

Nass, C., Steuer, J. & Tauber, E. R. (1994), Computers are Social Actors, *in* B. Adelson, S. Dumais & J. Olson (eds.), *Proceedings of CHI'94: Human Factors in Computing Systems*, ACM Press, pp.72–7.

Norušis, M. J. (1994), *SPSS Professional Statistics 6.1*, SPSS Inc.

Osgood, C. E., Suci, G. J. & Tannenbaum, P. (1967), *The Measurement of Meaning*, University of Illinois Press.

Raskin, J. (2000), *The Humane Interface: New Directions for Designing Interactive Systems*, Addison–Wesley.

Reeves, B. & Nass, C. (1996), *The Media Equation: How People Treat Computers, Television and New Media Like Real People and Places*, Cambridge University Press.

Ribeiro, N. M. (2002), Enhancing Information Awareness Through Speech Induced Anthropomorphism, PhD thesis, Department of Computer Science, University of York.

Saunders, M., Lewis, P. & Thornhill, A. (2000), *Research Methods for Business Students*, Pearson Education.

Sawhney, N. & Schmandt, C. (2000), "Nomadic Radio: Speech and Audio Interaction for Contextual Messaging in Nomadic Environments", *ACM Transactions on Computer–Human Interaction* **7**(3), 353–83.

Shneiderman, B. (1993), *Sparks of Innovation in Human–Computer Interaction*, Ablex.

Tieger, P. & Tieger, B. B. (1995), *Do What You Are: Discover the Perfect Career for you through the Secrets of Personality Type*, Little Brown.

# User Perception of Anthropomorphic Characters with Varying Levels of Interaction

## Guillermo Power, Gary Wills & Wendy Hall

*IAM Group, Department of Electronics and Computer Science, University of Southampton, Southampton SO17 1BJ, UK.*
Email: *{gp98r, gbw, wh}@ecs.soton.ac.uk*

In this paper we report on experiments investigating how levels of anthropomorphism and interaction affect users assumptions when interacting with anthropomorphic interface agents. User trials were undertaken under three different experimental conditions: no interaction, one-way and two-way interaction.

We demonstrate that the simpler experimental conditions replicated those of the more complex conditions, enabling us to create simpler and quicker experiments for future research.

We identify a number of key patterns in the assumptions made by users as they interacted with changing levels of anthropomorphic abstraction of an interface agent.

The users described the more realistic looking characters as being scary; although, these realistic characters are seen as being more intelligent. While the users scored the abstract characters as being more friendly and pleasant, they also described them as being less interesting and boring.

The perceived value of each of the characters varied with the level of interaction. From these results we concluded it is better to have no interaction with the characters rather than only partial interaction. The character favoured by the users was one of moderate abstraction.

**Keywords:** anthropomorphic, abstraction, interaction, perception.

# 1  Introduction

For the last 20 years the dominant form of user interface has been the Graphical
User Interface (GUI) with direct manipulation. As software gets more complicated
and more and more inexperienced users come into contact with computers, enticed
by the World Wide Web and smaller mobile devices, new interface metaphors are
required. The increasing complexity of software has introduced more options to
the user. This seemingly increased control actually decreases control as the number
of options and features available to them overwhelms the users and 'information
overload' can occur (Lachman, 1997). Conversational anthropomorphic interfaces
provide a possible alternative to the direct manipulation metaphor.

The aim of this paper is to investigate users reactions and assumptions when
interacting with anthropomorphic agents. Here we consider how the level of
anthropomorphism exhibited by the character and the level of interaction affects
these assumptions. We compared characters of different levels of anthropomorphic
abstraction, from a very abstract character to a realistic yet not human character.
As more software is released for general use with anthropomorphic interfaces there
seems to be no consensus of what the characters should look like and what look is
more suited for different applications. Some software and research opts for realistic
looking characters (for example, Haptek Inc., see http://www.haptek.com), others
opt for cartoon characters (Microsoft, 1999) others opt for floating heads (Dohi &
Ishizuka, 1997; Takama & Ishizuka, 1998; Koda, 1996; Koda & Maes, 1996a;
Koda & Maes, 1996b).

On anthropomorphic abstraction, Thorisson (1996) argues that realistic
computer animated faces look abnormal and repulsive. Similarly, McCloud (1993)
proposes that cartoon characters are more likely to be accepted by viewers, because,
when viewers see cartoon characters they see a reflection of themselves; i.e. cartoons
are like an empty shell that enables us to not just watch the cartoon, but to 'become
it'. This is something we aim to show in these experiments.

If we are able to ascertain what assumptions and characteristics users attribute
to anthropomorphic agents and how these vary according to the look of the character,
we will be able to produce a strong basis for anthropomorphic character design for
different kinds of applications. Koda (1996; Koda & Maes, 1996a; Koda & Maes,
1996b) has already gone some way in accomplishing some of these goals using a
poker game as a test bed for experiments.

We also examined how the level of interaction between the user and the agent
affects these assumptions. To accomplish this, three sets of experiments with
different levels of interaction between the user and the animated character were
carried out.

# 2  Character Design

The characters we developed use Microsoft Agent (Microsoft, 1999) and Haptek's
Virtual Friend (see http://www.haptek.com). Microsoft Agent services support the
presentation of software agents as interactive personalities within the Microsoft
Windows environment. It allows developers to easily incorporate anthropomorphic
conversational interfaces into software.

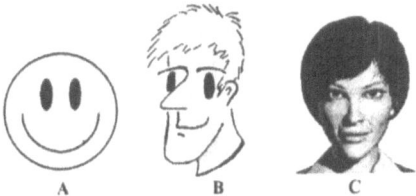

**Figure 1:** Characters used for the two-way interaction experiment.

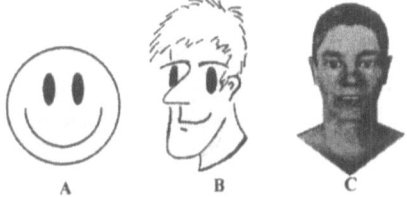

**Figure 2:** Characters used for one-way interaction experiment.

We initially wanted to script a Verbot[1] to create our on-screen character. This, however, proved unsuccessful, as the scripting language it uses is very limited. The only way to enable communication between the Verbot and any other software is by using the command line, as the Verbot has been given the ability to load other programs. This is unfortunate as the Verbot has exceptional lip synchronisation and a wide range of facial expressions. As such we decided to capture the frames from the Verbot software and animate them using the Microsoft Agent software.

For the first two experiments (see Section 3) we had three characters of increasing realism (Figure 1), A being a smiley face, B a cartoon character and C a realistic character.

After negative feedback, from the first two experiments concerning the female character, which was described as being *'scary'* by a number of test subjects, the character was changed to a Haptek's Virtual Friend character called Erin. Erin used the Virtual Friend API, and it is a realistic smoothly animated a 3D character (Figure 2).

As there are no generally accepted guidelines for creating conversational, anthropomorphic interface agents this might be an area worth investigating. Trower (1997) has proposed a set of guidelines for designing effective conversational software agents, which we have considered in the creation of our characters.

## 3  Experimental Design

In this section we describe the three experiments we carried out in chronological order.

---

[1] Verbot is by Virtual Personalities Inc., see http://www.verbot.com.

| Population Information | The two-way interaction experiment was advertised locally at the Department of Electronics and Computer Science at the University of Southampton. |
|---|---|
| Number of Users | 11 |
| Gender Distribution | 8 male and 3 female |
| Age Distribution | Age group 18–30 |

**Table 1:** User profile for the first experiment: Two-way interaction.

- Search for and browse sites on your academic/work interests.
- Search for and browse sites on your hobbies.
- Search for and browse sites on a music group(s) of your choice.
- Search for and browse sites on your favourite sport(s).
- Search for information on a company or product of your choice.
- Search and browse sites on your favourite TV program(s).

**Table 2:** List of tasks for two-way interaction experiment.

## 3.1   First experiment: Two-way Interaction Experiment

In order to observe if some of the features used were not necessary for simpler experiments, we decided to perform the most complex of the experiments first, i.e. the two-way interaction experiment.

For this experiment we implemented software that works as an interface for a Web-based search engine, using code we developed, that accepts Sherlock[2] plug-ins which are used to parse results produced by various search engines.

Two-way communication was allowed between the user and the character in this experiment, see Table 1 for user profile. The ability of this system to target different sources was exploited to give different capabilities to the software. For example, if the user asks the character to find a photograph the software only targets archives that contain pictures. We restricted the software to a few simple functions: 'find Web site', 'find picture' and 'find links'. The 'find Web site' function also targets Google but selects the most relevant Web site. For the find picture function, the software targets the Altavista image index. However, during a pilot experiment we found that it didn't produce very good matches so we deactivated this feature. Having these functions enabled us to instruct users to carry out open-ended tasks (see Table 2).

The natural language parser can handle three types of inputs:

- Commands to find a set of links.

- Commands to find one page.

- Keywords.

---

[2]See http://www.apple.com/sherlock/ for details.

| | Atttribute | Description |
|---|---|---|
| User-friendly Interaction | Friendly | A character for this application should be of favourable disposure and well wishing. Both of which are characteristics, which are encompassed by the word friendly. |
| | Pleasant | Being pleasant is defined as having pleasing manners, demeanour, or aspect; agreeable, cheerful, good-humoured. |
| | Interesting | We wish to provide the user with an interesting character to interact with and look at. This is to maintain user involvement in the interaction. |
| Fulfilling the user's needs and expectations | Intelligence | Is an important trait that has been looked at before (Koda, 1996; Koda & Maes, 1996a; Koda & Maes, 1996b); it has been thought that matching the anthropomorphic character's outward intelligence to its capabilities is crucial if users are not to be frustrated when the software's capabilities do not meet their expectations. |
| | Helpful | We believe that it is vital that an anthropomorphic assistant appear helpful and eager to help. We wanted to see how well the user perceived the software was doing its job as a helper. |

**Table 3:** Attributes to be examined in the experiments.

---

The software parses the first two types of command, extracting search keys and forwards these to Google and waits for the results. A command that cannot be parsed by our software is sent to Netscape Search, which also accepts natural language queries.

To ensure that the user's opinion was not influenced by the tasks they decided to carry out, their actions were restrained by the guidelines given to them.

To ensure that the tests were fair, we decided to give them a set of searches that needed to be done by querying the software. In addition, to ensure that the results were not influenced by the order in which these tasks were undertaken, the order was randomise using a random table (Fowler et al., 1998).

A list of six open-ended tasks was produced, which were divided into three sets of two tasks, (see Table 2). These were printed out and handed to the user as required, when the user finished a set of tasks the next would be given to them and the next character they had to interact with would be started. To further reduce the chances of the experimental procedure affecting the results we randomised the order in which the characters were presented to the users, once again using the random table. In this experiment the characters used had a neutral expression all of the time. That is they did not show any emotion.

The users' opinions were recorded using a questionnaire; this was completed once they had carried out all the tasks as instructed. Here they were asked to rate each character (see Figures 1 & 2) using a seven-point scale for each of the attributes, 1 being the lowest (i.e. un-Helpful) and 7 the highest (i.e. Helpful).

| Population information | The no interaction experiment was advertised across the University of Southampton. |
|---|---|
| Number of Users | 31 |

**Table 4:** User profile for the second experiment: No interaction.

| Population information | In the one-way interaction experiment users were obtained from a lecture on Human Computer Interaction at the Department of Electronics and Computer Science at the University of Southampton. |
|---|---|
| Number of Users | 79 |
| Gender distribution | 77 male and 2 female |
| Age distribution | Between 18–25 |

**Table 5:** User profile for the third experiment: One-way interaction.

In this experiment we asked users to rate a set of attributes. To decide upon these we looked at traits we considered central to the application of a simple anthropomorphic web-searching assistant. We concentrated on two aspects of the interaction that were essential towards forming a fruitful relationship between the user and character and were dictated primarily by its appearance (see Table 3):

- User friendly interaction: We wanted interaction with our character to be an enjoyable experience, so we thought the character should seem to be friendly and pleasant.

- Fulfilling the user's needs and expectations of the software.

The experiment took place in a laboratory and the users were fully instructed on how to communicate with the characters and how to interpret the results.

## 3.2   Second Experiment: No Interaction Experiment

The second experiment consisted of a web-based form where users (see Table 4) were asked to assess the characters just by looking at still pictures i.e. no interaction.

The helpfulness attribute was omitted as it was thought that it wasn't fitting to judge how helpful a person or caricature was from a still picture.

## 3.3   Third Experiment: One-way Interaction Experiment

The third experiment consisted of a lecture presented to undergraduate students (see Table 5) by three different characters (see Figure 2). The main part of the presentation was divided up into three parts. Part one took 12 minutes, part two took 7 minutes and part three took 5minutes. The first part was presented by Character A in Figure 2, part two by Character B and part three by Character C. It was decided that each part should take less time than the previous one to prevent the students from getting bored and irritated with the presentation. The attributes we examined for the characters are shown in Table 3.

Character expressions; for this experiment we had two expressions: neutral and smile. The characters would speak with a neutral expression and smile from time to time. Character C is slightly different from characters A and B, Haptek's character is rendered in 3D and has smoother animation when compared to the other two, it smiles at certain points during the presentation as well.

## 4   Statistical Methods

The results of each test were analysed using the non-parametric Friedman two-way test in order to see if the differences observed in the scores of each character in each test were statistically significant. As required by the Friedman test the scales on the questionnaire were given a weighting. The scale was weighted from one to seven, the total scores were calculated for all the users and then these were normalised from 0 to 1.

Friedman analysis tests the null hypothesis that the $K$ repeated measures or matched groups come from the same population or populations with the same median. The alternative hypothesis is then that at least one pair of conditions or samples has different medians. Therefore, when the value obtained from a Friedman test is significant, it indicates that at least one of the conditions differs from at least one of the other conditions; in order words, in our case at least one of the average scores of one of the characters is statistically significantly different from the average score of one of the others. The test does not tell us which one of the results is different nor how many of the groups are different from one another. In those cases where the value obtained from a Friedman test was significant, we used a multiple comparison between the groups in order to identify which of the sample were different from one another. In this work we used non-parametric statistics since it was not possible to assume that the scores under analysis were drawn from a population distributed in a certain way (distribution-free).

In order to find the degree of confidence for the results for the choice of character (see Section 5.6) we used the chi-square goodness-of-fit method, which is normally utilised to analyse the number of subjects, objects or responses, which fall into various categories.

## 5   Experimental Results and Comments

This section presents the results from all the experiments. The results are presented by comparing the results from each of the three experiments for each of the attributes shown in Table 3.

### 5.1   *Friendliness*

For this characteristic, we clearly observed two distinct patterns in the three experiments:

1. In the one and two-way interaction experiments, we can clearly see that the friendliness rating was proportional to the degree of abstraction of the character, the friendliest being the most abstract character, i.e. Character A, then the cartoon, Character B, and finally the least friendly character being the least abstract character, Character C (see Table 6). In these two experiments

|                     | A    | B    | C    |
|---------------------|------|------|------|
| No Interaction      | 0.94 | 0.71 | 0.57 |
| One-way Interaction | 0.73 | 0.51 | 0.53 |
| Two-way Interaction | 0.73 | 0.73 | 0.48 |

**Table 6:** Shows the normalised scores for Friendliness in all the experimental conditions (no-interaction, one-way interaction and two-way interaction).

---

the differences observed between the average score of each character was statistically significant with a confidence of more that 95%, except for the difference between Character B and C in the non-interactive experiment where the confidence level was only 75%.

2. In the two-way experiment characters A and B were rated equal and both of them were significantly friendlier than Character C (see Table 6). In this experiment the difference between Character C compared to A and B was statistically significant with a confidence level greater than 90%.

It is important to observe that in the two-way-interaction experiment the cartoon and the smiley characters were rated equally, while in the other experiments (no-interaction and one-way-interaction) the degree of friendliness was always proportional to the degree of abstraction of the characters.

In Table 6 we present the score obtained by each character in each of the experiments.

Character A scored higher friendliness levels in the no-interaction experiment, 0.94. The users scored this character less, to 0.73, during the two interactive tests (one-way and two-way interaction).

In the case of character B, the no-interaction experiment results in a score of 0.71, which decreased in the one-way-interaction experiment to a value of 0.51, and then significantly increased by the two-way-interaction experiment to it's highest value of 0.73. This behaviour of the one and two-way interaction test, i.e. reduces and then increases the score, was frequently observed in most of the other characteristics evaluated in this work.

Finally the degree of friendliness of Character C was always inversely proportional to the order of interaction of the test, with a score of 0.57 with no interaction and 0.48 in the case of two-way interaction, showing that the users became more disappointed with the character the more they got to know it.

One factor that remained constant throughout the experiments is that the realistic characters were thought of as being less friendly than the more abstract characters, this is in accordance to McCloud's (1993) and Thorisson's (1996) proposals. We considered that a reason might be that the realistic computer generated characters might be intimidating users. This is supported by the following comments made by the users:

- The following comments were given about the female character used for the first and second experiments (two-way and no interaction):

|                     | A    | B    | C    |
|---------------------|------|------|------|
| No Interaction      | 0.45 | 0.57 | 0.72 |
| One-way Interaction | 0.44 | 0.56 | 0.60 |
| Two-way Interaction | 0.45 | 0.58 | 0.65 |

**Table 7:** Shows the normalised scores for Intelligence in all the experimental conditions (no-interaction, one-way interaction and two-way interaction).

---

- "was scary."

- "scares me."

- "is very scary!"

- "is SCARY!!!!!! She's staring at me. She has a pimple. I think she is laughing at me."

- "C is evil."

- While regarding male character used for the third experiment (one-way interaction); the following comments were given:

  - "is far too scary … "

  - "looks neurotic."

We have considered a few possibilities for why this might be happening, after the first two experiments (two-way and no interaction) we considered that it could either be that particular character that was scaring the users. We decided to choose a different character for the third experiment (one-way interaction), this is when we switched to the Haptek character, which was much better animated and was three-dimensional. However, users still commented they found the realistic character scary. We also considered that users might be expecting realistic looking characters to move in a less cartoon like fashion and more like humans, if this was the case it was something that would be improved by using the better animated character. This idea that users expect more from the more realistic characters can be seen in a comment from one of the users when commenting about Character C (see Figure 2) during the one-way interaction experiment:

- "doesn't behave like a real human, eye movements, you get confused"

However, even though the other two more abstract characters did not "behave like a real human", no comments were made about behaving like humans as the users did not expect them to behave as such.

## 5.2 Intelligence

We also identified that the less abstract a character the more *intelligence* the users will attribute to it, this result was repeated in all three experimental conditions (see Table 7). This replicates Koda's (1996; Koda & Maes, 1996a; Koda & Maes, 1996b) results. It worth considering that apparent intelligence is not necessarily something

|                     | A    | B    | C    |
|---------------------|------|------|------|
| No Interaction      | 0.84 | 0.64 | 0.55 |
| One-way Interaction | 0.63 | 0.51 | 0.49 |
| Two-way Interaction | 0.74 | 0.69 | 0.49 |

**Table 8:** Shows the normalised scores for Pleasantness in all the experimental conditions (no-interaction, one-way interaction and two-way interaction).

---

to aim for when designing a character. If the characters seeming intelligence greatly surpasses it's capabilities then users are likely to be disillusioned when their expectations are not fulfilled.

It was anticipated that users would see the more realistic characters as more intelligent since they seem more human and less like objects, intelligence being a specifically human characteristic it is understandable that users see the more human like characters as more intelligent.

Although, in these experiments it appears that the differences between the average *intelligence* scores of each of the characters was well defined, it was observed from the non-parametric tests carried out during the evaluation of the results that only in the no-interaction experiment is the difference in the scores of any statistical significance with a confidence always greater than 85%.

In the one-way interaction experiment the difference between Character B and C was not statistically significant and the differences between A and B and A and C were significant with a confidence level greater than 95%. On the other hand, on the two-way interaction experiment only the difference between characters A and C was found to be statistically significant with a confidence greater that 90%.

In these tests no significant effects from the degree of interaction were observed on the score obtained by each character, each character having almost the same score in each experiment except Character C in the no-interaction experiment, where it scores it's highest value (see Table 7).

## 5.3  *Pleasantness*

We identified a pattern with the *pleasantness* attribute, which is similar to a pattern observed for friendliness. This is where pleasantness is inversely proportional to the level of abstraction. We observed this pattern in all three experimental conditions (see Table 8).

Although the differences observed in Table 8 appear to be well defined, the non-parametric tests carried out during the evaluation of these results show that in the no-interaction experiment the differences between A and B and A and C were significant with a confidence higher than 95%, but the differences between B and C was not statistically significant. On the other hand in the one-way experiment the differences between A and C and B and C were statistically significant with a confidence level higher than 95%, but the difference between A and B was not significant. In the two-way experiment only the difference between A and C was significant but only with a confidence level of 75%.

|                     | A    | B    | C    |
|---------------------|------|------|------|
| No Interaction      | 0.49 | 0.61 | 0.61 |
| One-way Interaction | 0.45 | 0.52 | 0.50 |
| Two-way Interaction | 0.47 | 0.55 | 0.58 |

**Table 9:** Shows the normalised scores for Interesting in all the experimental conditions (no-interaction, one-way interaction and two-way interaction).

Pleasantness, in the Oxford English Dictionary, is defined as the quality of being pleasant. Pleasant is in turn defined as; having pleasing manners, demeanour, or aspect; agreeable, cheerful, good-humoured. On reflection pleasantness and friendliness are closely related. This association between *friendliness* and *pleasantness* can be clearly seen in Table 6 and Table 8 as they follow similar patterns. Another similarity to the friendliness attribute is that, in the one-way interaction experiment the users gave this attributes its lowest scores. However, the score given by the users increases during the two-way interaction experiment (see Table 8), showing again that it might be better to not have any interaction with the characters if the only interaction possible is merely partial. Once again the overall pattern of the scores is preserved across the difference conditions.

We also considered that less realistic more abstract characters leave more open to the imagination and thus are less likely to be disliked. McCloud (1993) argues that when viewers see cartoon characters they see a reflection of themselves. That cartoons are like an empty shell that enables us to not just watch the cartoon, but to 'become it'.

## 5.4 Interestingness

We have identified that the highly abstract character was classed as being less interesting to look at than the less abstract ones. In all three experimental conditions the abstract character is rated as considerably less interesting than the others (see Table 9).

In this case the different *Interesting* score obtained for each character in each of the experiments were very similar. However, as with other attributes, the users gave the *interesting* attribute its lowest score in the one-way interaction experiment.

The non-parametric tests showed that in the no and one-way interaction experiments the differences observed between the characters A and B and A and C were statistically significant with a confidence level of more than 85%. However, the difference between the characters B and C was not statistically significant. However none of the results obtained in the two-way experiment were found to be statistically significant. For this characteristic it appears that users respond in a similar way independently of the experiment carried out.

## 5.5 Helpfulness

As explained earlier this characteristic was not evaluated as part of the no-interaction condition experiment due to the inconsistency of this attribute with this type of experiment. It appears from the scores obtained in the two remaining experimental

|                     | A    | B    | C    |
|---------------------|------|------|------|
| One-way Interaction | 0.52 | 0.57 | 0.53 |
| Two-way Interaction | 0.55 | 0.57 | 0.53 |

**Table 10:** Shows the normalised scores for Helpfulness in two experimental conditions (one-way interaction and two-way interaction).

|                  | A   | B   | C   |
|------------------|-----|-----|-----|
| Character choice | 27% | 56% | 18% |

**Table 11:** Shows as a percentage the users who choose a character as their favourite in the one-way condition.

conditions that users attributed slightly more helpfulness to the Character B, the cartoon character (see Table 10). However, the non-parametric test for all the experiments where *Helpfulness* was evaluated shows that the difference between the average scores was not statistically significant. It appears that this characteristic is too subjective in order to be analysed by our experiments.

## 5.6    Choice of Character

During the one-way interaction experiment users were asked to choose a favourite character, the overwhelming majority chose Face B, the cartoon character (see Table 11). Analysis carried out for this data shows that the results given in Table 7 are statistically significant with a confidence level of more than 95%.

We also found overall scores for each of the characters (see Table 12) in the one-way interaction experiment by taking into account all the characteristics considered in each experiment. This result is surprisingly similar considering it was clear that most users preferred the cartoon character. We propose the final success of the cartoon character is because it's a middle of the road character that doesn't score too low or too high on any particular attribute. On the other hand both the very abstract character and the realistic characters score very high for some features and very low for others. We put forward the theory that the realistic characters are proving to be too 'scary' as people are expecting them to act like human beings and not cartoons with text to speech voices. The very abstract character although perceived as being friendly and pleasant, is not seen as being very interesting to look at.

We consider that the scariness factor of the realistic characters is something that could be overcome if the user expectations are fulfilled by the character's capabilities. These capabilities include artificial intelligence techniques, realistic animation and human like voices, as this is what the user expects when confronted by a very realistic looking character. We see this as merely a technological barrier that once broken would allow us to create very realistic believable agents (Mateas, 1997; Bates, 1994) which people might not find so awkward to interact with.

This is implied by user comments like:

- "The more realistic the face the more you are expecting a more realistic voice.

|                     | A    | B    | C    |
|---------------------|------|------|------|
| One-way Interaction | 0.55 | 0.54 | 0.53 |

**Table 12:** Shows the normalised total for each character in the one-way interaction condition.

When this doesn't happen you are less likely to listen as attentively to what is being said."

None of the characters (see Figures 1 & 2) were perfect as demonstrated by the user comments:

- "Face A doesn't really look like a face when talking, just lots of random blobs flashing up. Face C is far too scary ... "

- "Didn't like the eyes of A & B ... "

- "Didn't like the mouth movements of face A."

- "Eyes on face B look freaky ... "

- " ... face B would have been more appealing without black eyes."

All the characters could be improved, for instance the mouth movements of Face A and the eye design of Face B and as mentioned before Face C was described as being scary and neurotic.

## 6  Conclusions and Future Work

We have made the following observations during the course of our experiment:

**The realistic faces were seen as less friendly and even scary:** We propose the scary factor is due to the character's behaviour not matching the user's expectations of the human looking face. We put forward that this is a technological barrier that will be overcome with time.

**The more abstract a character the more friendly/pleasant it seems:** It is possible that less realistic more abstract characters leave more open to the imagination and thus are less likely to be disliked. The *friendliness/pleasantness* attributes are inversely proportional to the level of abstraction.

**The more abstract the character the less intelligence users will attribute to it:** It was anticipated that users would see the more realistic characters as more intelligent since they seem more human and less like objects. Intelligence being a specifically human characteristic it is understandable that users see the more human like characters as more intelligent.

**The more abstract the character the less interesting it is to look at:** It is not surprising that users rate the simpler characters as less interesting to look at than more complex ones.

**The users favoured a moderately abstract character:** The cartoon character is the users favourite even though this is not reflected by score higher overall scores than the other two. We propose that its success is because it scores well in all characteristics as opposed to the other characters, which score, very high for some features and very low for others.

Although partial interaction does lower the scores attributed by the users it does not appear to change the overall patterns displayed by these. Therefore when developing future studies the use of partial interaction could prove a useful tool in developing quicker experiments.

We propose in future work to investigate users attitudes while changing the levels of; emotional facial expressions, gaze, hand gestures and head movements.

Ultimately we plan to devise a Wizard of Oz type experiment where the user will be presented with a seemingly intelligent agent to interact with and help them browse the World Wide Web. This is a method where the user interacts with what appears to be a computer system but is in fact mock up where some of the features missing from the software are provided by a concealed human. This type of interface will then be compared to more traditional methods of browsing and searching the World Wide Web. We also plan to carry out a further one-way interaction experiment where we will again compare three characters of different levels of anthropomorphic abstraction. We will be keeping the smiley face and cartoon characters the same and will change the realistic 3D character for a real human animated using Microsoft Agent. We believe this would be a worthy exercise as it using Microsoft Agent to animate all the characters instead of different technologies, which would reduce the number of variables involved.

## Acknowledgements

This work was partly funded by the EPSRC through a PhD studentship. The authors would like to thank Dr Samhaa El Beltagy for helping with programming issues and for providing the natural language parser used for the experiments. The work undertaken by Gary Wills is supported under the Advanced Knowledge Technologies (AKT) Interdisciplinary Research Collaboration (IRC), which is sponsored by the UK Engineering and Physical Sciences Research Council under grant number GR/N15764/01.

## References

Bates, J. (1994), "The Role of Emotion in Belivable Agents", *Communications of the ACM* pp.122–5. Special Issue on Agents.

Dohi, H. & Ishizuka, M. (1997), Visual Software Agent: A Realistic Face-to-Face Style Interface Connected with WWW/Netscape, *in Proceedings of IJCAI-97 Workshop on Intelligent Multimodal Systems*, pp.17–22. Available at http://www.miv.t.u-tokyo.ac.jp/dohi/ijcai97-ims/paper.html.

Fowler, J., Cohen, L. & Jarvis, P. (1998), *Practical Statistics for Field Biology*, John Wiley & Sons.

Koda, T. (1996), Agents with Faces: The Effects of Personification of Agents, Master's thesis, MIT.

Koda, T. & Maes, P. (1996a), Agents with Faces: The Effect of Personification, *in Fifth IEEE International Workshop on Robot and Human Communication (RO-MAN'96)*, IEEE Computer Society Press, pp.189–94.

Koda, T. & Maes, P. (1996b), Agents with Faces: The Effects of Personification of Agents, *in* A. Sasse, R. J. Cunningham & R. Winder (eds.), *People and Computers XI (Proceedings of HCI'96)*, Springer-Verlag, pp.239–45.

Lachman, R. (1997), *Animistic Interface: Experiments in Mapping Character Animation to Computer Interface*, MIT Press.

Mateas, M. (1997), An Oz-Centric Review of Interactive Drama and Belivable Agents, Technical Report CMU-CS-97-156, School of Computer Science, Carnegie Mellon University.

McCloud, S. (1993), *Understanding Comics The Invisible Art*, Harper Perennial.

Microsoft (1999), *Microsoft Agent Software Development Kit*, Microsoft Press.

Takama, Y. Dohi, H. & Ishizuka, M. (1998), A Visual Anthropomorphic Agent with Learning Capability of Cooperative Answering Strategy through Speech Dialog, *in Proceedings of the Asia Pacific Computer Human Interaction (APCHI'98)*, pp.260–5. Available via http://www.miv.t.u-tokyo.ac.jp/e-pub.html.

Thorisson, K. (1996), Communicative Humanoids: A Computational Model of Psychosocial Dialogue Skills, PhD thesis, MIT.

Trower, T. (1997), "Creating Conversational Interfaces for Interactive Software Agents". Tutorial at CHI'97. Available online at http://www.acm.org/sigs/sigchi/chi97/proceedings/tutorial/twt.htm.

# CSCW

# A Tool for Performing and Analysing Experiments on Graphical Communication

## Patrick G T Healey, Nik Swoboda[†] & James King

*Information, Media, and Communication Research Group, Department of Computer Science, Queen Mary, University of London, Mile End Road, London E1 4NS, UK.*
Email: *{ph, jking}@dcs.qmul.ac.uk*

[†] *ATR Media Information Science Laboratories, 2-2 Hikaridai, Seika-cho, Soraku-gun, Kyoto 619-0288, Japan.*
Email: *nswoboda@mis.atr.co.jp*

**Drawing is a basic mode of human communication.** This paper describes a tool, written in Java, that is designed to support the capture and analysis of interactive graphical communication for experimental purposes. It is based around a simple 'virtual' whiteboard that supports remote and co-present graphical interaction between pairs of subjects. Logs of the subjects' drawing activity and the dynamics of the communicative exchange are captured for subsequent statistical analysis. The software supports experimental manipulation of graphical interaction by providing control over update and layout of the whiteboard area. It also supports manipulation of patterns of group interaction through the management of multiple simultaneous shared whiteboard connections. Lastly, a playback tool supports fine-grained analysis of collaborative drawing activity.

**Keywords:** collaboration, communication, drawing in interaction.

## 1   Introduction

Drawing is an integrated part of a variety of ordinary interactions. Familiar examples include the sketch maps, explanatory diagrams, and plans which are produced and adapted during informal conversation. Graphical interaction is also integrated into some specialised interactions such as design conversations between architects and clients (Neilson & Lee, 1994). It can be particularly important when communicative resources are limited. Anecdotally, people who do not share a first language often recruit sketches of situations or objects in order to sustain their interaction. In a clinical context, drawing is considered to be a key mode of interaction for people with aphasia whose linguistic abilities are otherwise restricted (Lyon, 1995; Sacchett et al., 1999).

Technological support for co-present and remote graphical interaction is ubiquitous. Electronic or 'virtual' whiteboards were an important component of early collaboration systems such as Colab (Stefik et al., 1987). They are a standard component of remote conferencing applications and of generic tools, such as the Java Shared Data Toolkit, for creating applications to support collaboration. The potential scope and significance of graphical interaction has also been extended through applications which support new kinds of communicative exchange. For example, Tang & Minneman developed VideoDraw, a system that overlays video of participants' gestures onto the display of a shared whiteboard (Tang & Minneman, 1991). The ClearBoard developed by Ishii and coworkers integrates both gaze and gesture with a drawing based medium to support collaboration in pairs (Ishii & Kobayashi, 1992; Ishii et al., 1995). These technologies provide support for tightly coupled forms of graphical exchange that are not possible with physical media. For example, they allow a number of individuals to work simultaneously on the same area of the same drawing — something that is physically impossible with conventional drawing tools.

The role of drawing in a variety of interactions, and the range of technologies available to support it, indicate the importance of graphical interaction as a mode of communication. Evaluations suggest that virtual whiteboards have a positive impact on the performance of a variety of cooperative tasks (Healey et al., 2000; Traum & Dillenbourg, 1996; Whittaker et al., 1993). Observational work has shown that, in face-to-face design interactions, drawing serves a wide variety of communicative functions (Bly, 1988; Neilson & Lee, 1994; Tang, 1991). Drawing activities may also have a role turn taking and topic management (Bly, 1988; Tang, 1991). However, in contrast to speech and non-verbal signals such as gesture and facial expression, little is known about the communicative organisation of drawing-in-interaction. To date, studies of graphical interaction have relied on direct observation, video analysis, or analysis of photographs and screenshots. See, for example, (Bly, 1988; Bly & Minneman, 1990; Neilson & Lee, 1994; Tang, 1991; Tang & Minneman, 1991; Whittaker et al., 1993). For practical reasons these techniques support only relatively coarse levels of analysis. For example, the identification of classes of graphical object type such as graphs and sketches (Brinck & Gomez, 1992), categories of action such as listing, drawing and gesturing (Tang, 1991) and classification of functions such as mediating interaction, storing information and expressing ideas (Bly, 1988; Tang, 1991).

Video analysis is particularly labour intensive and data collection and coding is time consuming and susceptible to error. This has the result that often only small sample sizes are used restricting the validity and statistical reliability of the analysis. This paper describes a tool for performing and analysing graphical communication

**Figure 1:** Example whiteboard screen (music drawing task).

experiments that exploits the potential whiteboards offer for the direct capture and control of drawing activity. The tool was developed to support our research and the requirements and capabilities of the tool arose out of this. It is designed with three basic aims. Firstly, to provide a more fine-grained and reliable method of capturing drawing activities. Secondly, to support experimental investigation through the selective manipulation of different aspects of graphical interaction. Thirdly, to aid analysis by providing statistics on drawing activity, the dynamics of the interaction, and a customised playback tool.

## 2    The Software Components

The tools have a modular design to allow for modification. They consist of three basic components. Firstly, a simple shared whiteboard that allows pairs of subjects to communicate through drawing. The whiteboard runs across a network allowing users to be either co-present or in different locations. Users draw in freehand by selecting from a palette of colours in the editor bar (see Figure 1). They see all their own and their partner's drawing displayed in the whiteboard window. Secondly, a master program is used to configure, connect and monitor the individual whiteboard processes and to allow multiple pairs of processes to share the same task. These processes run separately on each subjects' computer and record time stamped logs of both users drawing, mouse or pen movements, and button presses. Lastly, data analysis and presentation tools are provided to study the logs of data generated by the subject whiteboard windows. Figure 2 illustrates the relationship between the various components.

### 2.1    The Whiteboard Window

The whiteboard window consists of three areas: the task bar, the editor bar, and the editing space (Figure 1). The task bar displays the buttons or other GUI components

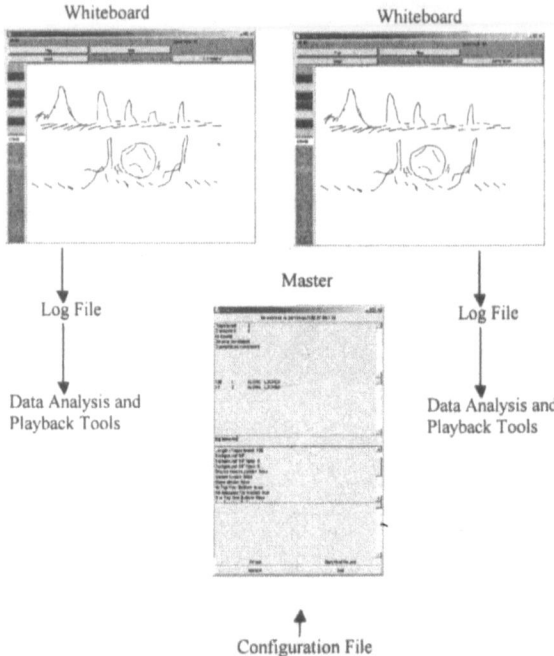

**Figure 2:** System Architecture.

used by subjects in completing the given task. For example, in a music drawing task the task bar includes buttons to control the playback of target and distractor pieces of music and buttons for selection of a piece of music as a response (Healey et al., to appearb; Healey et al., 2001b). In the generic task no buttons are provided in the task bar. The editor bar displays buttons to allow the user to change their current drawing colour or to enter erase mode. It also indicates which colour is currently selected. The software is designed so that the editor bar and task bar are independent. This allows additional functionality in the task bar or the editor bar to be programmed without affecting the other components. The editing space is where the user draws and sees what his or her partner has drawn. The whiteboard outputs logs of drawing and other subject behaviour for later analysis.

### 2.1.1    The Whiteboard Internals

Central to the whiteboard is the concept of a *subject event*. Subject events consist of particular subject interactions with the task bar or the editor. An example of an event is a button press or a point in a line drawn by one of the subjects. Each line has a starting and ending time stamp, a list of points, and a colour. Subject events are sent between the pairs of whiteboards and between the editor and the code that controls the experimental task being performed. Subject events are also written to a log file for subsequent playback and analysis. The logs are stored in ASCII format to allow

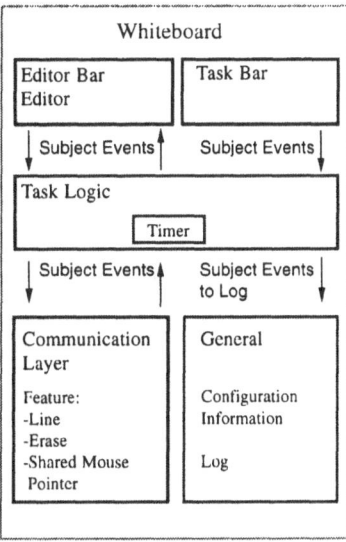

**Figure 3:** Diagram of the whiteboard Internals.

for importing into spreadsheets or other analysis programs. In order to minimise the possible performance problems associated with writing to the log files, subject events are stored in memory and only written to file at the end of each experimental trial. Figure 3 illustrates the whiteboard's internal structure.

### 2.1.2 Data Logging

In the log file, the whiteboard stores enough information to completely re-create the user's view of the screen at any point during the experiment. This logging information includes:

- All the lines drawn and erases as lists of time stamped points.

- Time of each button press or GUI component access in the task bar.

- Time taken to complete the task or trial.

- Task dependent information such as the name of the background image displayed or the music played etc.

- The result of the task, such as response accuracy.

- Experimental configuration parameters, such as the length of the experiment and size of the whiteboard.

As noted above, the subject events generated for both members of a pair are stored on each subject's machine. This redundancy provides useful protection in the case of accidental data loss. Because timing is provided by the local machine clocks network delays can lead to discrepancies in the times recorded for a subject event on each machine. The size of the discrepancy varies with network traffic but can be calculated in any given case (and potentially discounted) from the differences in the timings of events in the two log files. The maximum discrepancy we have noted in experiments run across a single subnet is 30ms.

## 2.2   Master Program

Monitoring and control of the whiteboard processes is provided by the master program. For example, it specifies the length of each trial and the order of subject pairing. The Master begins by reading a configuration file describing the task to perform. This configuration file is a human readable and editable ASCII text file. Once a configuration file is loaded the master displays the current options and checks the pattern of connections between machines. The master program allows the experimenter to start, monitor, and repeat experimental blocks or trials. This program has been used in real experimental settings to control and manage the connections of 14 pairs of subjects all working simultaneously. Though untested, it should also support experiments with larger groups of subjects.

## 3   Manipulating Subject Interactions

This tool is intended to support the experimental investigation of graphical interaction. To this end a significant part of its functionality has been developed to support the manipulation of the level of communicative interaction possible between experimental subjects. Currently this is implemented in two main ways. The first is manipulation of interaction through the selective blocking of drawing on regions on the whiteboard, the second is through manipulation of the topology of the interaction.

## 3.1   Spatial Blocking of Interaction

One salient contrast between speech and drawing as modes of communication is that drawings have a spatial organisation. Studies of graphical interaction have indicated that this is exploited not just semantically, for example to represent the spatial orientation of objects, but also as a resource for coordinating the communicative interaction. For example, there is observational evidence that the spatial organisation of drawing is exploited in topic management (Bly, 1988). Intuitively, activities such as underlining, circling, and arrowing are also important elements of graphical interaction, especially where people modify each other's drawings.

The tool exploits the control that the whiteboard software provides to support experimental manipulations of spatial layout. In the current implementation this consists in adding a dividing line to the centre of the editor area. This can be drawn either horizontally or vertically. This division itself may influence subject's use of the drawing area by fostering a sense of ownership of a particular area of the screen. More substantial interference with spatial layout is provided by a blocking function. This can be used along with the split screen option to prevent one subject from drawing in one half of the screen and prevent their partner from drawing on the other half of the screen.

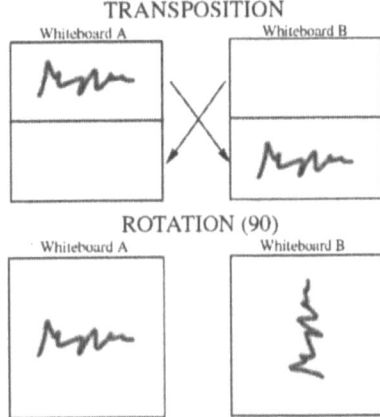

**Figure 4:** Schematic representation of transposition and rotation.

The blocking function can also be applied globally in order to prevent any simultaneous drawing. In this case only one member of a pair is able to make graphical input at a given time. One example of the use of this feature, is in a music matching task. In this task, a *drawer* has a single piece of music that must be described, by drawing, to a *guesser* who is presented with two pieces of music. One of these pieces of music is the same as the drawers while the other is a distractor. The guesser's goal is to select the common piece of music on the basis of the drawing made by the drawer. This pattern can be repeated across trials and the roles of drawer and guesser can optionally be swapped between members of a pair — see, for example, Healey et al. (to appearb; to appeara; 2001b).

## 3.2 Manipulating Topology

The tool also supports two manipulations of the topology of the drawing surface (Figure 4). The first of these, transposition, builds on the division of the screen into regions described above. Where the screen is divided horizontally a person draws in, say, the top half of the whiteboard but this is displayed to their partner in the bottom half of the screen. Similarly, transposition of a screen divided vertically will cause what is drawn on the left to be displayed on the right-hand section of their partner's screen. This manipulation interferes with subjects ability to align their drawings. For example, it prevents them drawing arrows to link elements of each other's drawings. If desired, this option can be used in combination with blocking to interfere with both direct and indirect coordination of drawing activities.

The second manipulation of topology that the tool supports is rotation. Existing whiteboards typically provide the same orientation for all observers, i.e. up on the whiteboard is the same for everyone. For people sharing a piece of paper across a table this is not the case. To simulate this kind of interaction, the whiteboard can rotate a subject's drawing by 0°, 90° or 180° before displaying it on the partner's whiteboard. This can be done to simulate the pair facing each other across a table with a shared drawing space in the middle or the subjects side by side with a shared drawing space between them.

## 4   Additional Features

The tool supports a number of additional features that can be switched on or off, independently of the task, to support experimental studies.

### 4.1   *Background Image*

A background GIF image can be displayed at any position in the editor space. This feature has been used in a map task to assess if the orientation of a map affects the way people communicate directions and perform problem solving tasks involving multiple locations and movement between locations (Umata et al., 2000).

### 4.2   *Time Limit and Breaks*

Tasks can be configured with a time limit after which a decision is forced or the task has deemed to have failed or finished normally. The time remaining before a decision is required can also be displayed on the task bar. It is also possible to configure breaks in the experiment based on the elapsed time of the experiment or the number of repetitions completed.

### 4.3   *Input and Display*

Input devices can be changed to alter the fluency of drawing. The whiteboard tool has been used with mouse and stylus input on Wacom tablet-screens with MACs, with stylus input on Fujitsu stylistic 3400 touch screen portable computers, and with mouse input on PCs running Windows and Linux.

### 4.4   *Shared Mouse Pointers*

Previous studies of collaborative drawing have highlighted the importance of cues to indicate and manage reference and focus of attention (Tang, 1991; Tang & Minneman, 1991; Greenberg et al., 1995). In physical drawing spaces these cues are normally provided by hand gestures and gaze. The simplest way to provide cues to focus of attention on a virtual whiteboard is through shared mouse pointers. The whiteboard tool can be configured to allow a subject to see the current location of their partner's mouse pointer. The partner's mouse pointer is differentiable from the subject's own by colour and shape and is hidden when the partner draws to avoid distraction. With this option activated, it is possible to record all mouse/pen movements not involved in the act of drawing.

### 4.5   *Task Performance Feedback Levels*

In cases where it is possible for the program to calculate aspects of task performance such as accuracy, it is possible to provide feedback to a pair about their performance. For example, in the music drawing task described above the program can determine, on the basis of the selection made, whether the subjects were successful in communicating about a piece of music. This is communicated to them after each trial using a pop-up dialogue.

## 5  The Data Analysis and Presentation Tools

Experimental data is recorded on a trial by trial basis.  Logging of task related performance is always performed at the finest level of granularity possible so that all the information is available for subsequent analysis.

### 5.1  *Statistics*

The comprehensive nature of the data logged by the whiteboard means that a variety of statistics can be generated for each phase of an experiment. Statistics are generated for each person individually and each pair. The individual statistics include:

- The total number of lines drawn, and erases made.

- The total line and erase lengths.

- The total time spend drawing and erasing.

- The total number of different colours used.

- Screen usage (distribution of screen areas in which drawing occurs).

Per pair statistics include:

- Number of colours used by a subject not used by their partner (i.e. differences).

- The amount of drawing in which the pair draw over each others lines.

- The amount of the partners drawing erased by the partner.

- The amount of simultaneous drawing and erasing.

### 5.1.1  *Visual Complexity Measure*

The logged data allows for the recreation of drawings, accurate at the pixel level, from any point during their construction.  A psychophysical measure of visual complexity can be calculated for any given image (Pelli et al., to appear).

### 5.2  *Playback Tool*

In addition to support for the statistical analysis of the logged data, a drawing play-back tool has been developed to support detailed analysis of the content and organisation of the graphical exchange (see Figure 5). The playback tool has buttons at the top which load log files and start, pause, and stop playback. The total time taken to complete the trial is displayed and a box displays the number of milliseconds elapsed since the start of the trial. Below this there is a time-line (see Figure 6), with a calibrated scale divided into of 1, 5 and 10 seconds. Inside the time line two rows of horizontal lines display the distribution of each subject's drawing activities. For example, if a subject draws in blue, a blue line corresponding to the duration of this drawing is presented on the time-line. The time-line also indicates in hollow black lines the points at which erasing occurred. Button presses on the task bar are also shown in the time-line. Because the activities of the two participants are represented in parallel this provides a useful visual representation of the size and

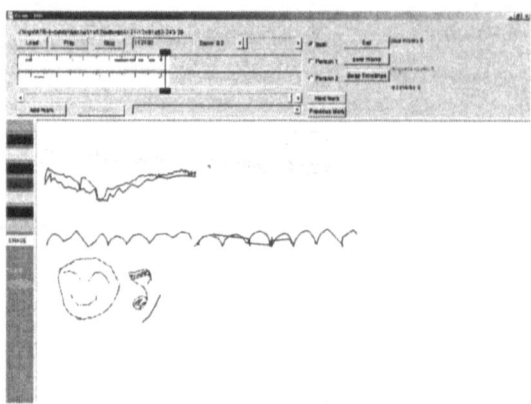

**Figure 5:** Playback and coding tool.

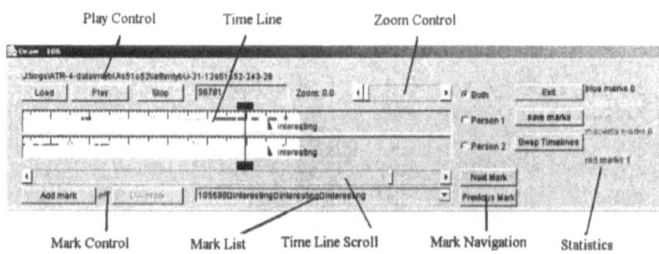

**Figure 6:** Playback controls.

pattern of contributions to the exchange. During replay the drawing is played back to the editor space. In synchrony with this the time-line scrolls past and a horizontal black line indicates the point in the log that is currently displayed. The time-line can also be zoomed to allow for inspection of the interaction at a coarse or fine grain.

This tool can be used simply to play back, in real time, a particular trial or episode of drawing. This can provide an overview of the pattern of interactions that occurred in a particular condition of an experiment, or for a particular experimental item. It is similar to a VCR in that it allows the user to wind, rewind, play, and stop the drawing at any point. The user can also navigate the playback of the log by scrolling the time-line backwards and forwards, entering a target time in milliseconds in the time display or by clicking on a particular point in the time-line. In each case only the drawing up to the selected moment in time is displayed. Radio buttons beside the time-line allow for a switching between display of only one or both participants' drawing.

Event coding is supported through the 'Add Mark' and 'Del Mark' buttons (see Figure 6). This initiates a short dialogue that allows the user to specify the colour and label (if desired) for a mark and whether it should be added to one or both drawer's time-lines. Once marks have been added users can navigate by moving directly to the next/previous mark. This functionality is designed to support content based analysis, such as the points at which words or drawing elements are completed, and interaction analysis such as the completion of turns or repairs.

## 5.3 Picture Capture Tool

The capture tool takes a logged trial and produces a FIG format image file of the state of the editor area at any point in the experiment. The FIG file can be manipulated by a variety of free and public domain tools and can be converted into GIF, JPEG, PDF or postscript. This image generating tool also allows each member of a pairs' drawings to be isolated and displayed in separate pictures, and can also be used to produce a time-line of the drawing activity of the pair.

## 5.4 Further Work

The current implementation could be extended in a number of ways to provide more control over patterns of interaction and update that may prove to be of experimental interest. Some developments currently under consideration are:

- Integration of synchronised audio capture to aid analysis of multi-modal exchanges[1].

- Incremental update by sending drawings by line or group of lines instead of point by point to the partner.

- Control of 'turn-taking' through the use of a send button which only updates the partner's display when the the drawer chooses or, conversely, a poll button that controls receipt of drawings.

- Support for n-way graphical interaction.

## 6 Conclusion

Our purpose in this paper has been threefold. Firstly, to highlight the importance of graphical interaction as a mode of communication. Secondly to outline some methods and techniques of analysis that whiteboard technology makes available. Thirdly to document the whiteboard tool and make it available for use in the research community[2]. Although a number of sophisticated whiteboard tools have been developed — see the examples in Greenberg et al. (1995) — we are not aware of any that provide direct support for experimental investigation and analysis. The present tool has been used successfully to carry out a number of experiments in Japan and the UK — see, for example, Healey et al. (to appearb; to appeara; 2001b; 2001a) and Umata et al. (2000). These experiments have involved a variety of collaborative

---

[1] An effective interim solution is to record the whiteboard interaction on, for example, digital video. This allows the data from the whiteboard to be combined with the analysis of events in other modalities. Although care needs to be taken with time synchronisation.

[2] The tool, developed by the MAGIC consortium and ATR Media Information Sciences Laboratories is available for research use on a GPL licence. The documentation and source code can be found at http://www.dcs.qmul.ac.uk/research/imc/magic.html.

drawing tasks including the joint construction of sketch maps and graphs as well as more abstract tasks such as the music drawing task described above. It has also been used in experiments investigating the influence of maps on direct and indirect reference in dialogue.

Our experience indicates that this is a useful tool for investigating the details of graphical interaction. It supports a level of analysis and reliability which is almost impossible to achieve with existing techniques such as video analysis. It also provides a new degree of experimental control, supporting direct experimental manipulation of the graphical exchange. Two practical advantages of this tool are that it automatically produces statistics on the drawing activities that can be correlated with other measures and it allows multiple pairs of subjects to be run simultaneously. Some important limitations are that it currently only supports dyadic interaction and the development of new experimental tasks requires specific programming effort. Development of the tool continues but we believe it is now at a stage where it has the potential to contribute to research on graphical interaction and multi-modal communication more generally.

## Acknowledgements

This research was generously supported by the UK research councils; ESRC and EPSRC, under the PACCIT programme award 'MAGIC: Mutimodality and Graphics in Interactive Communication' and by ATR Media Information Science Laboratories, Kyoto, Japan through a contract with the Telectommunications Advancement Organisation of Japan entitled "A study of innovational interaction media for the development of a highly networked society". We would also like to thank Yasuhiro Katagiri and Ichiro Umata for their help and support.

## References

Bly, S. (1988), Use of Drawing Surfaces in Different Collaborative Settings, *in* D. G. Tatar (ed.), *Proceedings of CSCW'88: Second Conference on Computer Supported Cooperative Work*, ACM Press, pp.250–6.

Bly, S. & Minneman, S. L. (1990), Commune: A Shared Drawing Surface, *in Proceedings of the Conference on Office Information Systems*, ACM Press, pp.184–92.

Brinck, T. & Gomez, L. (1992), A Collaborative Medium for the Support of Conversational Props, *in* J. Turner & R. Kraut (eds.), *Proceedings of CSCW'92: ACM Conference on Computer Supported Cooperative Work*, ACM Press, pp.171–8.

Greenberg, S., Hayne, S. & Rada, R. (1995), *Groupware for Real-time Drawing: A Designer's Guide*, McGraw-Hill.

Healey, P. G. T., Garrod, S., Fay, N. Lee, J. & Oberlander, J. (to appeara), Interactional context in graphical communication, Poster to be presented at the 24th Annual Conference of the Cognitive Science Society.

Healey, P. G. T., King, J., Peters, C., Umata, I., Katagiri, Y. & Swoboda, N. (2001a), Interactional Constraints on Representational Form., Paper presented at the *ESCOOP2001: The XII Conference of the European Society for Cognitive Psychology* and the XVIII Annual Conference of the British Psychological Society Cognitive Psychology Section, Edinburgh, Scotland.

Healey, P. G. T., McCabe, R. & Katagiri, Y. (2000), A comparison of graphics and speech in a task-oriented dialogue, *in* M. Anderson, P. Cheng & V. Haarslev (eds.), *Theory and Application of Diagrams. Proceedings of the First International Conference, Diagrams 2000*, Vol. 1889 of *Lecture Notes in Artifical Intelligence*, Springer-Verlag, pp.245–56.

Healey, P. G. T., Swoboda, N., Umata, I. & Katagiri, Y. (2001b), Representational form and communicative use, *in* J. D. Moore & K. Stenning (eds.), *Proceedings of the 23rd Annual Conference of the Cognitive Science Society*, pp.411–6.

Healey, P. G. T., Swoboda, N., Umata, I. & Katagiri, Y. (to appearb), Graphical representation in graphical dialogue, To appear in a special issue of the *International Journal of Human Computer Studies* on Interactive Graphical Communication.

Ishii, H. & Kobayashi, M. (1992), Clearboard: A Seamless Medium for Shared Drawing and Conversation with Eye Contact, *in* P. Bauersfeld, J. Bennett & G. Lynch (eds.), *Proceedings of CHI'92: Human Factors in Computing Systems*, ACM Press, pp.525–32.

Ishii, H., Kobayashi, M. & Grudin, J. (1995), Integration of Interpersonal Space and Shared Workspace: ClearBoard Design and Experiments, *in* S. Greenberg, S. Hayne & R. Rada (eds.), *Groupware for Realtime Drawing: A Designer's Guide*, McGraw-Hill.

Lyon, J. G. (1995), "Drawing: Its Value as a Communication Aid for Adults with Aphasia", *Aphasiology* 9(1), 34–50.

Neilson, I. & Lee, J. (1994), "Conversations with Graphics: Implications for the Design of Natural Language/Graphics Interfaces", *International Journal of Human–Computer Studies* 40, 509–41.

Pelli, D. G., Burns, C. W., Farell, B. & Moore, D. C. (to appear), "Identifying Letters", *Vision Research* .

Sacchett, C., Byng, M., Marshall, J. & Pound, C. (1999), "Drawing Together: Evaluation of a Therapy Programme for Severe Aphasia", *International Journal of Language and Communication Disorders* 34(3), 265–89.

Stefik, M., Foster, G., Bobrow, D. G., Kahn, K., Lanning, S. & Suchman, L. (1987), "Beyond the Chalkboard: Computer Support for Collaboration and Problem Solving in Meetings", *Communications of the ACM* 30(1), 33–47.

Tang, J. C. (1991), "Findings from Observational Studies of Collaborative Work", *International Journal of Man–Machine Studies* 34(2), 143–60.

Tang, J. C. & Minneman, S. L. (1991), "VideoDraw: A Video Interafce for Collaborative Drawing", *ACM Transactions on Office Information Systems* 9(2), 170–84.

Traum, D. R. & Dillenbourg, P. (1996), Miscommunication in Multi-modal Collaboration, *in* L. Dybkjaer, N. O. Bernsen & H. Dybkjaer (eds.), *Proceedings of the AAAI'96 Workshop on Detecting, Repairing and Preventing Human–Machine Miscommunication*, pp.37–46.

Umata, I., Shimojima, A. & Katagiri, Y. (2000), Talking Through Graphics: An Empirical Study of the Sequential Integration of Modalities, *in* L. R. Gleitman & A. K. Joshi (eds.), *Proceedings of the 22nd Annual Conference of the Cognitive Science Society*, Lawrence Erlbaum Associates, pp.529–34.

Whittaker, S., Geelhoed, E. & Robinson, E. (1993), "Shared Workspaces: How Do They Work and When Are They Useful?", *International Journal of Man–Machine Studies* **39**(5), 813–42.

# A Comparison of Text Messaging and Email Support for Digital Communities: A Case Study

## Elizabeth Longmate & Chris Baber

*Educational Technology Research Group, Electronic, Electrical and Computing Engineering, University of Birmingham, Edgbaston, Birmingham B15 2TT, UK.*

Tel: *+44 121 414 4308*

Email: *e.longmate@bham.ac.uk*

**The increase in personal and mobile technologies as well as increasing access to organisational media suggests new ways in which community development can be supported. In this paper, we describe the differences between text messaging and email as ways of supporting community activities. A case study of a group of University students is presented. A framework for characterising and comparing communities is described. This is used to analyse the role of the technologies in the development of a sense of community amongst the students. The students completed communication diaries. Differences in the use of the technologies are identified and described. These are explained in terms of a claims analysis in which literature claims are compared with the collected data. The discussion focuses on the social use of technology and the integration of media within the community setting.**

**Keywords:** text messaging, email, digital communities, principal components analysis, framework, diary studies.

## 1 Introduction

This paper aims to understand how text messaging or Short Messaging Service (SMS) and email are used by a group of University classmates. The study examines how these technologies support the development of their community and its activities. Within educational settings the introduction of technology is becoming more commonplace (Light & Light, 1999). The increase in students' personal, mobile technologies as well as the increasing access to organisational media suggests new ways in which community development can be supported within educational settings. Creating community within learning contexts is thought to be beneficial for students and their communities (Haythornthwaite et al., 2000). This study explores the role of two technologies, SMS and email, in supporting community amongst a group of students. SMS is a relatively new technology, especially popular with young people. Mobile phone use and SMS in particular is becoming more expressive and social in character (Ling & Yttri, 1999; Kopomaa, 2000). Email use has been extensively studied within an organisational context (Garton & Wellman, 1995). Studies have also revealed its potential in supporting social relationships (Parks & Floyd, 1996). This paper reports on two studies. The first describes the development of a community framework. This allows the use of the two technologies to be compared in a community context. This framework is then employed within the second study. The second study is a longitudinal investigation into the use of email and SMS by a group of University classmates. The main purpose was to understand how their use of technology contributed to community development. Differences between email and SMS are discussed through a claims analysis this compares the literature's claims with the data collected from the second study. The paper begins with a brief introduction to the two technologies and a review of technology supported community within educational settings.

## 1.1 The Use of Technology to Support Community Development

The introduction of technology to aid the development and support of communities has been reported across a range of settings including University undergraduate courses (Light & Light, 1999). The use of technology within educational settings allows for increased interaction between the students. These interactions are important in developing a sense of community between the students. The emphasis on creating community within learning settings is fuelled by research that reveals a number of positive benefits for individuals and their communities. Strong interpersonal ties increase willingness to share information and resources, increase the flow of information and the availability of support (Haythornthwaite et al., 2000).

The majority of Computer Mediated Communication (CMC) studies have focused on extending academic discussion and thus learning resources. However, the introduction of email lists, for example, does not always increase the academic discussion either between students or between students and lecturers (Light et al., 1997). Students often feel that there is little encouragement to use such systems. Staff, likewise consider reading and posting messages a low priority. Course requirements or incentives increase participation but do not ensure 100% involvement (Bagherian & Thorngate, 2000).

Distance learning courses have provided an opportunity to examine the social rather than the academic outcomes of CMC systems. Students often use CMC systems for practical reasons rather than for academic achievement and such systems have been enthusiastically adopted as a social medium (Johnson & Huff, 2000). A few studies have focused upon the question of community development amongst distance learners. Haythornthwaite et al. (2000) showed that distance students successfully used the prescribed technologies to develop a sense of community. Initial face-to-face sessions were also an important part of the community building process. The authors noted that whilst fellow students were central to the development of the community, certain others provided additional support. The students included lecturers, technical and administrative staff within the wider definition of their community. Other important figures included family members and those people who provided social and emotional support. This support was necessary for the students to complete their work and so feel part of the course. Distance learning students have to use technology in order to interact and complete their course requirements. Co-located students are not compelled to use technology in order to interact with one another. Consequently, technology may have a different part to play in supporting co-located community. This longitudinal study examines the spontaneous use of SMS and email in supporting community development within a group of co-located students.

## 1.2 Characteristics of SMS and Email

**SMS:** allows the exchange of short messages up to 160 characters in length. The cost of sending a text message varies but is approximately 10 pence/16 euro cent. Users enter characters via the mobile phone keypad. Despite the restrictions in length and the awkwardness of input, SMS is used for a range of communication purposes. People use SMS to plan social events, to send short pieces of information and reminders. In addition to these instrumental or task based purposes, SMS is also used for expressive purposes, i.e. to convey social or emotional content (Ling & Yttri, 1999) with an emphasis on entertainment and socialising.

**Email:** allows rapid transmission of digitised text to multiple others across time and space (Garton & Wellman, 1995). Email systems allow messages to be stored, manipulated and processed. Messages can be edited and forwarded to other parties. In addition to the text body of an email, attachments allow other types of data to be sent. Email attachments might include photographs, software programs and video clips.

## 1.3 Factors Affecting Media Use

A number of factors have been proposed to explain media choices and use under different conditions. These include task–media fit, group norms and social network factors.

### 1.3.1 Social Presence and Task–Media Fit

Technology-mediated interactions, especially CMC have often been regarded as inferior to face-to-face interactions. Short et al. (1976) suggested that the inability of CMC to transmit nonverbal cues would have a negative effect on interpersonal communication. Interactions mediated by CMC exhibit less 'social presence' than face-to-face interactions, i.e. the salience of the 'other' in mediated interactions is diminished. Recent reviews, however, have questioned the extent to which the social presence literature is generalisable to all communications media and to all applications, see for example Gunanwardena & Zittle (1997).

Daft & Lengel (1986) have described CMC as a less 'rich' medium. Rich media such as face-to-face communications convey a lot of information through cues and gestures, they also allow immediate feedback and use natural language. As such it is predicted that rich media will be chosen in situations where the sender wishes to reduce equivocality i.e. provide a careful explanation for an unclear situation. Leaner media such as written communication will be chosen in situations where the sender wishes to reduce uncertainty by providing large amounts of detailed information. These task–media fit theories suggest that communication outcomes are determined by the attributes of the technology.

### 1.3.2  Norms and Social Network Factors

The task–media approach has failed to recognise the social context in which communication takes place. Where people are highly motivated to communicate they modify or adapt the 'lean' CMC environment to support their needs (Baym, 1998). The development of group norms and conventions also affects the use of media within a specific context (DeSanctis & Poole, 1994). Within educational settings, for example, email is a prevalent form of communication and lecturers' email addresses are available on their Web pages.

A social network approach allows an understanding of media use that takes into consideration how communicators maintain multiple relations through multiple media, see for example Haythornthwaite & Wellman (1998). A social network consists of actors (individuals or organisations) and the relations and ties that bind them together. The strength of the tie depends on a number of factors. Strong ties are characterised by higher intimacy, closer friendships, expressive and instrumental exchange and more frequent interaction. Weak ties are characterised by weaker acquaintance, fewer and less intimate exchanges (Granovetter, 1973). Social network theorists believe that individual and group behaviour is affected more by the nature of the ties and networks in which actors are involved than by the norms and attributes they possess. Thus grouping individuals as 'students' does not reveal the nature of their interactions and their communication networks (Haythornthwaite et al., 2000).

Media use may also relate to other factors such as cost, accessibility and privacy. The very act of sending or receiving a message regardless of its content may be important. This is referred to as 'meta-content' (Ling & Yttri, 1999). The possible factors affecting media use will be examined during the course of this study.

## 2   Study One: A Framework for Studying Community

To examine the role of the technologies in supporting community development a framework for assessing the community context is now introduced. This framework guides the analysis of the community. Difficulties in defining the term community have increased in recent times with the inclusion of online communities and the increase in technology mediated community activities (Hamman, 1999). Definitions are either too narrow and forfeit the complexity of the term or else try to be all encompassing and hence too vague. Following the approach taken by Whittaker et al. (1997), we define the term community by 'prototypical' attributes. The framework presented in this paper extends the notion of prototypical attributes to cover the digital context of the community. Important attributes can then be grouped and used as a way of characterising the community and guiding the observational study.

## 2.1 Methodology for Principal Components Analysis (PCA)

An initial set of 20 attributes was identified using:

- A review of the theoretical literature surrounding 'community'.

- Case studies of specific communities (Pereira, 1993; Rheingold, 1993; Hamman, 1999; Zaff & Sloan-Devlin, 1998; Carroll & Rosson, 1996).

### 2.1.1 Ratings Procedure

Twenty-five communities, both digital and physical, were reviewed in terms of the attributes. The Web-based communities included SeniorNet a site for the over 50s and a Web-based learning group. The physical communities included a Christian Union group and a community network providing information on local services and events. Physical communities provide a well-researched standard by which to compare and contrast digital communities. A detailed picture of each community was developed. This involved observing and documenting characteristic features and an examination of relevant literature. The community descriptions were then assessed in terms of the attributes. The authors rated the importance of each attribute to the different communities along a scale of 1 to 5 where 1 means 'not important' and 5 means 'very important'. The ratings were based on the literature review and the results of participant observations. Another researcher also rated a sample of the communities along these dimensions. There was 89% agreement between the two sets of ratings. The scores from the ratings were then subjected to a PCA. This identified the important components.

### 2.1.2 Results

A PCA using SPSS with Varimax rotation and Kaiser normalisation was performed. An inspection of the data at the first stage of the procedure resulted in the removal of six of the initial attributes. Attributes with correlations of <0.3 were automatically removed. Other attributes were removed as they were highly correlated with another attribute, for example, face-to-face and same physical location. The final PCA consisted of fourteen attributes (see Table 1). Three factors or components were extracted accounting for 78% of the variance. The components, and their attributes are shown in Table 1.

**Component one — Membership:** This component concerns the relationships and interactions between the members and the way this leads to the functioning of the community.

**Component two — Organisation:** The structure of the community through the provision and distribution of content and expertise.

**Component three — Mediation:** The processes by which the community communicates.

| Component | Attributes |
|-----------|-----------|
| Membership | Personal investment |
| | Identity |
| | Strength of human feeling |
| | Shared history |
| | Multiple relations |
| | Informal communication |
| Organisation | Voluntary membership |
| | Provided content |
| | Ongoing |
| | Homegrown experts |
| | Member control |
| | Member generated content |
| Mediation | Use of digital technology |
| | Face-to-face communication |

**Table 1:** Components and attributes of PCA.

These components provide a framework to guide the study and structure the results. Each component has an associated community process, which will also be discussed during the case study results.

# 3  Study Two: Longitudinal Study of SMS and Email Usage

A group of University students provides an opportunity to study the development of group interactions over time. It allowed the roles of the technology within the group to be investigated. The students' own assessment of the group can also be monitored.

## 3.1  Research Setting

The students were all enrolled on the undergraduate Interactive Systems (IS) course at the University. The students were aged 18 to 21. The course was full time and was delivered through traditional lectures, tutorials and laboratory sessions within the department. Students were automatically assigned an email account upon registration. There is, however no formal requirement to make use of this facility. Email facilities within the department were free. Students also had email access at home. Stage 1 of the study took place 6 weeks into the course before any group work had taken place. Stage 2 took place towards the end of the second semester, week 22. By this time the students had performed a group work project and a set of examinations.

### 3.1.1  Method

Text messaging and email diaries were distributed to a class of 22 students. Completion of the diaries was voluntary. Some students were unable to take part in the study because they were not SMS or email users. To be included in the study participants must have completed both diaries to the required standard. This involved completing a minimum of five entries per diary. A number of diaries were returned which did not meet the criteria, and contained too few entries. Diaries that did not meet these criteria were rejected. Seven participants met the criteria representing a 30% response rate. Six men and one woman took part and completed Stages 1 and 2. Our strict inclusion criteria meant a reduction in the number of potential respondents. As such it was not possible to gather data from the non-respondents and in turn the results of this study cannot be generalised to the rest of the class. Nevertheless the study provides a set of interesting results.

During each stage all the participants kept communication diaries for ten days. Participants kept an email diary and a text-messaging diary. A diary entry was completed for every message that was sent or received. Other information collected included: the name of the message partner, the location when the message was sent or received, the content of the message and whether or not the message was related to any other communication. Demographic information was collected and following the diary phase participants completed a social network questionnaire. This captured additional data regarding the communication partners such as the length of time known, the type of relationship and the location relative to the diarist. Participants also indicated the other ways in which they communicated with the partners e.g. by landline telephone and face-to-face. Participants also completed an identity questionnaire. This assessed their feelings of affiliation towards the course, the department and the University. Finally, following the completion of Stage 2 four of the participants took part in a group interview. This covered attitudes towards email and SMS and the issue of community. The interview helped establish the members of the wider community including lecturers, family and friends.

## 4   Results

The analysis of the diary and questionnaire data is divided into three main areas. The first is the analysis of the group's community status. The next examines how the two technologies were used, noting any changes that occurred over the year. Finally the data are examined against the community framework developed in study one. This allows an assessment of how the two technologies supported the development of the community.

Tables 2 & 3 present a summary of the results. Table 2 indicates the message characteristics of the two technologies over the year. Table 3 includes the characteristics of the communication partners. Table 4 shows how the messages were distributed between different kinds of partner, e.g. classmates, friends and lecturers. The tables suggest that differences exist between the uses and the functions of the two technologies and between the two stages of the study. These results suggest interesting differences concerning the community's support and development.

### 4.1   Is This a Community?

Given the nature of the group and their shared context it would seem plausible to assume the students are acting as a community. They have a common interest in that they are engaged in the same course and attend the same lectures and tutorials. A shared interest or location, however, does not guarantee the development of a sense of community. To assess the presence of community an identity questionnaire was

| | Total messages | Sent/ Rec. | | Immediate/ future use | | Related/ unrelated message | | Instrumental/ expressive or both | | Location when message sent/ received | |
|---|---|---|---|---|---|---|---|---|---|---|---|
| SMS (T1) | 95 | Sent | 45 | Immediate | 71 | Related | 54 | Instrumental | 45 | Home | 54 |
| | | Rec | 50 | Future | 24 | Unrelated | 41 | Expressive | 25 | Travelling | 13 |
| | | | | | | | | Both | 25 | University | 23 |
| | | | | | | | | | | Café | 5 |
| Email (T1) | 36 | Sent | 7 | Immediate | 20 | Related | 16 | Instrumental | 18 | Home | 16 |
| | | Rec | 29 | Future | 16 | Unrelated | 20 | Expressive | 12 | University | 20 |
| | | | | | | | | Both | 6 | | |
| SMS (T2) | 106 | Sent | 57 | Immediate | 86 | Related | 60 | Instrumental | 74 | Home | 63 |
| | | Rec | 49 | Future | 20 | Unrelated | 46 | Expressive | 24 | Travelling | 10 |
| | | | | | | | | Both | 8 | University | 19 |
| | | | | | | | | | | Café | 14 |
| Email (T2) | 39 | Sent | 10 | Immediate | 31 | Related | 18 | Instrumental | 21 | Home | 27 |
| | | Rec | 29 | Future | 8 | Unrelated | 21 | Expressive | 13 | University | 12 |
| | | | | | | | | Both | 5 | | |

**Table 2:** Email and SMS message characteristics.

| | Total number of partners | Location of partner | | Close relationship | | Length of relationship | | Partner relationship | |
|---|---|---|---|---|---|---|---|---|---|
| SMS (T1) | 36 | Other town | 8 | Very close | 3 | <3months | 2 | Classmate | 4 |
| | | Same town | 19 | Quite close | 9 | 3months–1year | 15 | Friend | 25 |
| | | Same building | 9 | Close | 18 | 1–3years | 9 | Family | 1 |
| | | | | Not close | 6 | >3years | 10 | Team mate | 2 |
| | | | | | | | | Neighbour | 4 |
| Email (T1) | 12 | Other town | 3 | Very close | 1 | <3months | 5 | Classmate | 1 |
| | | Same town | 4 | Close | 3 | 3months–1year | 2 | Friend | 3 |
| | | Same building | 5 | Not close | 8 | 1–3years | 2 | Family | 1 |
| | | | | | | >3years | 3 | Lecturer | 6 |
| | | | | | | | | Organisation | 1 |
| SMS (T2) | 43 | Other town | 8 | Very close | 17 | <3months | 1 | Classmate | 9 |
| | | Same town | 26 | Quite close | 3 | 3months–1year | 19 | Friend | 22 |
| | | Same building | 9 | Close | 19 | 1–3years | 8 | Family | 4 |
| | | | | Not Close | 4 | >3years | 15 | Team mate | 3 |
| | | | | | | | | Neighbour | 5 |
| Email (T2) | 25 | Other town | 11 | Very close | 7 | <3months | 2 | Classmate | 2 |
| | | Same town | 14 | Quite close | 1 | 3months–1year | 13 | Friend | 10 |
| | | | | Close | 4 | 1–3years | 5 | Family | 3 |
| | | | | Not close | 13 | >3years | 5 | Lecturer | 7 |
| | | | | | | | | Organisation | 3 |

**Table 3:** Email and SMS partner characteristics.

| | Total number of messages | Number of messages exchanged between different partners | | | |
|---|---|---|---|---|---|
| SMS (T1) | 95 | Classmates | 18 | Team mates | 2 |
| | | Friends | 56 | Neighbours | 15 |
| | | Family | 4 | | |
| Email (T1) | 36 | Classmates | 3 | Family | 7 |
| | | Lecturer | 14 | Organisations | 3 |
| | | Friends | 9 | | |
| SMS (T2) | 106 | Classmates | 35 | Team mates | 4 |
| | | Friends | 47 | Neighbours | 16 |
| | | Family | 4 | | |
| Email (T2) | 39 | Classmates | 2 | Family | 2 |
| | | Lecturer | 12 | Organisations | 4 |
| | | Friends | 18 | | |

**Table 4:** Distribution of Email and SMS messages between different partner types.

given to the diarists at Stage 1 and again at Stage 2. The questionnaire was based upon Chin et al.'s (1999) Perceived Cohesion scale and had a Cronbach's alpha of 0.85. The identity questionnaire examined feelings of identification with various groups within the University. At Stage 1 of the study the questionnaire revealed high levels of affiliation with the different groups. Most diarists considered themselves members of the student population and members of the IS community. There was a slight overall change in identity scores between the first and second questionnaires. When the groups were examined in more detail there was a clearer pattern of change. Diarists showed a decrease in belonging to the student population category but increased feelings of membership and belonging within the IS community. The group interview supported this view. One diarist argued that it was difficult not to feel like a member. He suggested that the location of the department (away from the main campus) and the small size of the class were important factors. Given that a sense of belonging and community exists between the members of the IS course, the remaining questions concerning the use of SMS and email become more valid and interesting.

## 4.2   The Use of SMS and Email

There are a number of differences in the way email and SMS were used. Usage patterns also changed over the course of the year.

### 4.2.1   Message Characteristics

The volume of messages differed between the media. Table 2 indicates that diarists sent and received approximately two and half times as many text messages as emails over the two stages of the study. There was also a large difference between the sent and the received messages. Approximately equal numbers of SMS messages were sent and received. However the email diaries reveal that over three quarters of the entries were received messages. Students received far more emails then they sent. The difference may be due to the students' multiple group memberships. Many received emails are general course related announcements and do not require a reply.

### 4.2.2   Message Location

Across Stages 1 and 2 over half the SMS messages were sent or received at home (Stage 1: 54/95 and Stage 2: 63/106). Nearly a quarter were sent at the University and the rest were sent when travelling, or at cafés or bars. Emails were sent and received either at the University department or at home.

### 4.2.3   Immediacy of Messages

SMS is used in an immediate manner. Over three quarters of the messages were for immediate use rather than future reference (71/95 and 86/106). Email messages are more evenly distributed between immediate and future use. Mobile phones are typically 'on' and are therefore accessible. This means that sending and receiving SMS messages requires less effort than sending or receiving email messages, which usually have to be accessed specifically. SMS allows immediate contact and can be used as a way of checking a partner's availability. SMS seems to demand a response and recipients do not want to feel as if they are 'missing out' on new information or gossip (Ling & Yttri, 1999). SMS is a highly interactive medium. Over half are related to a previous communication. These include previous SMS messages, face-to-face conversations and landline phone conversations. Email messages are more likely to be single messages and over half are unrelated to another communication.

### 4.2.4   Partner Characteristics

SMS was used to support the communication between a greater number of partners than email. In Stage 1 the average number of SMS partners was 5 (range of 3 to 7). The average number of email partners was 3 (range of 3 to 4). This pattern was repeated in Stage 2. Considering the location of the message partner, over half of SMS partners lived in the same town as the diarist (19/36 and 46/43). Email appears to support longer distance relationships than SMS. More email partners lived in a different town to the diarist compared with SMS. Table 3 indicates that the majority of SMS partners are classified as friends. Other exchanges were between classmates, neighbours and family members. Far fewer emails were exchanged between friends and more were exchanged between the diarists and the lecturing staff. Email is used for less intimate relationships (Kanfer, 1999). Over half of email relationships were described as 'not close' (8/12 and 13/25). Only a tenth of SMS relationships were described similarly.

## 4.3   Changes in the Use of the Technology Over the Course of the Year

The use of SMS and email has changed over the course of the year. The use of both technologies has increased slightly over the study period. More interestingly the specific use of the two technologies has altered over the course of the year. The number of communication partners has increased between Stages 1 and 2. This is the case for both email and SMS.

### 4.3.1 Distribution of Messages Between Different Partner Types

Table 3 shows that the number of SMS partners described as classmates doubled between Stages 1 and 2. Table 4 indicates that the actual number of messages exchanged between the diarists and classmates also doubled from 18/95 to 35/106. Classmate exchanges represent one third of all the messages sent during Stage 2 compared with less than one fifth at Stage 1. Email exchanges between classmates remained more constant across the two stages.

### 4.3.2 Instrumental and Expressive Content

The content of SMS messages has changed over the course of the study. Between Stages 1 and 2 the number of SMS messages containing expressive content such as greetings, jokes, friendly insults and advice has stayed the same but messages containing instrumental content such as reminders and plans increased from approximately half to three quarters of all messages (44/95 to 74/106). SMS messages often contained both types of content. Instrumental messages include those exchanged between classmates concerning the planning and organisation of social as well as work related events. There was no change in the overall level of instrumental and expressive content in the emails but information content specifically increased. Between the first and second stages of the study a number of group projects took place. The instrumental increase in SMS may reflect the increased use of the medium as a way of keeping in touch and coordinating group work. In addition SMS was used more to contact people in the same building in Stage 2 compared with Stage 1.

> "(Using SMS is) more about organisation, meet here at this time and we'll do some work." (Male interviewee)

## 4.4 Email and SMS in Supporting the Community

The community analysis framework used to examine the role of email and SMS in supporting community development, identified changes in the community's character and processes. These changes are related to changes in the groups' activities and their use of the technology during the year.

### 4.4.1 Membership

**Identity and shared history:** The identity questionnaire revealed a strong sense of affiliation with the IS community. Identity processes and mechanisms are described in more detail in the 'process' section below. Developing a shared history is important for the growth of social identity. Taking part in group projects and inhabiting a shared location both contribute to the development of a shared history.

**Personal investment:** There are plenty of opportunities for members to make a personal investment in the community. The size of the community ensures that people remain visible within the community and can be credited with their knowledge and input.

**Human feeling:** There is a sense of shared human feeling within the group. Rheingold (1993) argues that a sense of shared human feeling is a necessary condition for the development and maintenance of a group's sense of community. Members help each other out with project work and alert one another to problems or changes with lectures or allocated marks. The community consisted of a number of different relationships. The diarists communicated with friends, classmates and support staff. They also communicated with family members, neighbours and team mates.

**Multiplex relations:** Relations within the community are multiplex (Haythornthwaite & Wellman, 1998). Although a partner might primarily be classified as a classmate they may also be considered a friend. Some of these relationships have developed over the course of the study. This is reflected in the increased number of relationships existing for 3 months to one year. Relations with classmates have become closer and the number of classmates who were also thought of as friends increased. The number of additional media used with classmates has also increased. The number of media increases as a function of relationship length. This is the case for SMS and email-supported relationships. This gradual strengthening of relations is also apparent with neighbours. Lecturer relations, however, did not develop in terms of closeness or media usage.

**Informal communication:** Whilst the group is essentially a task-based group, students engage in a lot of informal communication. This includes jokes, friendly insults and greetings messages. Email messages tended to be more formal and often included several pieces of formal identification within signatures, e.g. *Yours, Matthew Rice (j111) Registration number 318888*. This contrasts with the more informal tone of SMS arrangements:

> Have u been captured by the squirrels r u coming in today? Meet u
> @ clock tower?

**Process — Identity:** The diaries reveal how social and individual identities were established and maintained through the use of technology. As forms of asynchronous communication, SMS and email communication allow users to compose their 'face' in Goffmanian terms. SMS allows very personalised dialogue including abbreviations and signatures, for example, *inabit*. The email diaries reveal different forms of 'self' presentation. The larger capacity of email allows more information to be included in the presentation of personal identity. Email and SMS also help to maintain a sense of group identity. Group emails sent to students from a member of staff reinforce a sense of group membership. Both email and SMS maintain the sense of group identity during periods without face-to-face contact. SMS exchanges often contain shared group references and meanings.

> Who was our lecturer for 1H1?

SMS is also used to keep fellow students informed about lectures. Referring to common experiences associated with the course is another way group identity is supported. One diarist, for example, asked a classmate how many pages he had completed in his essay. SMS also supports the extended IS community, i.e. friends and flatmates within student accommodation who provide support for IS class members.

> How did the exam go? The whole of floor 9 wishes you luck

### 4.4.2   Organisation

**Voluntary and ongoing membership:** This is a voluntary community.   The students have a common interest which has brought them together to study at University.   Unlike work groups based around discrete tasks, the life expectancy of this community is a lot longer.   Students can expect to be in each other's company for at least three years.

**Provided and member generated content:** The   community   contains   provided content and member-generated content.   Provided content via staff includes face-to-face and email communication.   In addition to oral information staff send group emails reminding students to attend progress meetings with their tutors. Email is also used to answer student queries regarding class marks.

**Homegrown experts:** The community contains a number of provided experts. These include the lecturers and the support staff.   The community members themselves also act as experts.   Within project groups, students are quick to exploit members' differing interests and expertise.   The group interview revealed the division of tasks upon the basis of expertise.   Some students, for example, were particularly skilled in programming through hobbies, previous courses or extra curricular paid work. These students acted as programming experts and answered other members' queries. Despite the similar age of the IS classmates, diverse backgrounds and interests ensures that there is a large pool of diverse community expertise.

**Member control:** There is limited member control within the community. Students had been automatically assigned to group project teams. They did, however, retain some control over their projects. Classmates made decisions regarding their roles within the group and how to manage the work.   Importantly they also made decisions as to how to communicate with each other.

> "The first thing we did was to swap phone numbers."   (Male interviewee)

**Process — Interactivity:** An interactive email or SMS discussion like a good dialogue should generate many replies to topics. It indicates that members are engaged in the discussion (Bagherian & Thorngate, 2000). In this study over half of SMS messages were related to a previous communication (54/95 and 60/106). Nearly half of the emails were also related to another communication. The majority of SMS messages related to another text message but SMS interactivity spans media.   Discussions started in one medium, e.g. face-to-face or mobile phone, are often continued via text messages.   Emails are usually related to a text message or a mobile phone call rather than to another email. Over the course of the study the percentage of emails relating to face-to-face communication increased. Interactive messages show a coherent engaged discussion is taking place. People are not just sending random anonymous messages via email or SMS. The SMS diaries revealed approximately equal numbers of single messages and messages with replies. However over three quarters of the email messages are single messages suggesting that email is a less interactive medium or is at least less immediately interactive.

### 4.4.3  Mediation

The community contains both face-to-face and technology mediated communications. There are frequent face-to-face discussions amongst friends and within group projects. The community uses a variety of media. These include SMS, email, mobile and landline calls as well as face-to-face communications. Diarists use a wider variety of media with friends, whereas diarists tended to limit communications with staff to email.

**Process — Integration:** The social network questionnaires revealed that SMS relationships are supported by multiple media. All of the relationships documented in the SMS diaries were supported by at least one other form of communication and a third were supported by four other media, face-to-face, mobile calls, landline calls and email. The email diaries reveal that about a third of relationships were email only. SMS and to some extent email are used as just one part of the communications between partners. The media are used to support face-to-face communications and to support each other.

> "You can always speak to someone then send them a text message to remind them." (Male interviewee)

### 4.4.4  Summary

SMS and email have been used to consolidate relationships within the community. SMS has been used to strengthen existing relationships and email to maintain weaker ties. The community is founded on a series of work-based relations. SMS is used to build upon this foundation and extend the community through the inclusion of social interactions. The study provides evidence that the group of IS students have started to form a community. Diarists feel more like members of the community at the end of the year compared to the beginning. In addition to face-to-face interactions, the use of email and SMS has supported this process of community development. Email has also supported the relationships between the students and the lecturers. Lecturers and staff make up the extended IS community. They provide support and fulfil roles essential for the community. Email and SMS supported relationships within the wider community. The students' wider community includes friends, neighbours and family members. These people provide support for the IS students to complete their work and participate in the community.

## 5  Discussion

The results of the second study suggest that SMS and email are used in different ways and for different purposes. Following the group interview the data were examined

| Literature Claim | Interview Evidence | Diaries *Support/Refute* |
|---|---|---|
| Individuals will prefer email in order to exchange information to reduce uncertainty. | "Email is just more useful, you can put more stuff into it." | *Support*: Over 50% of emails were >10 lines. Emails included attachments and details of dates, times and phone numbers. *Refute*: SMS messages also contained plans and information. |
| SMS displays more Social Presence than email. | "SMS messages tend to be quite personalised." "Email is quite impersonal so you can write to somebody you haven't heard from for ages without feeling awkward." | *Support*: Goodnight messages, jokes or 'general chatting'. Messages contained personal signatures. *Refute*: Email messages to friends and family also contained expressive content |
| Email use is determined by group norms and conventions | "Yeah we contact staff via departmental email." | *Support*: In Stage 1, 50% of emails were exchanged between diarists and members of staff. Communication with staff is via email or face-to-face only |
| Email supports less close relationships | "Email is impersonal its not embarrassing to contact people you don't know." | *Support*: 57% of email messages were exchanged between 'not close' partners compared to 13% of SMS partners. |
| SMS is used because it is a mobile communications medium | "I am pretty much anywhere (when I send and receive SMS), cos I generally have my phone with me." | *Support*: 18% of messages were sent or received at University, 9% whilst travelling. *Refute*: 58% of messages were sent or received at home |
| SMS use relates to an historical relationship | "Cos you know that if you've got their number that you are pretty alright sending them a text message." | *Support*: 80% of SMS partners were friends and 100% of SMS partners also communicated face-to-face. |
| Group and individual behaviour is affected by the kinds of ties and networks people are involved in. | "I wouldn't text message him cos I don't know him that well." | *Support*: Number of communication media increased as a function of closeness. Close ties exchange both expressive and instrumental messages. |

**Table 5:** Claims analysis for SMS and email.

along with the diaries in order to explore the series of literature claims discussed in Section 1.3. A comparison of the literature claims with the data collected from the diaries and the group interview is shown in Table 5. The important themes from this claims analysis are discussed below.

## 5.1   Social Presence

Technology does not appear to remove the social presence or salience of the other in these mediated interactions. Both SMS and email emphasised the *realness* of the other person and SMS in particular was perceived as being a social medium (Gunanwardena & Zittle, 1997). The interview revealed that SMS was thought to be a useful way of flirting, saying goodnight or even asking someone if they wanted a cup of tea. Receiving an SMS message reaffirms group membership (Ling & Yttri, 1999).

## 5.2   Task–Media Fit

Diarists were keen to point out that they thought using email or SMS was a task-based decision. Email was used if a lot of information needed to be conveyed. Although SMS messages do contain instrumental content they also contain expressive content and meta-content. Text messaging is often more about contact then content. Making contact and remaining available is a key feature of SMS use. The mobile nature of SMS over email was repeatedly emphasised and several people saw the development of mobile email as a potential threat to SMS. The issue of mobility is really one of accessibility. It is about being able to contact people and being contactable wherever people are.

I'm lost! need directions to your house.

## 5.3   Privacy and Cost

Privacy is an important factor in remaining accessible. It is an important issue for teenagers or those living in a shared house. Using mobile phones and SMS guarantees contact with the intended recipient. This bypasses anyone else in the house that might be acting as 'gatekeeper' to the landline telephone (Lacohee & Anderson, 2001). Cost does not appear to be a decisive factor when comparing SMS and email. More SMS messages were sent then emails despite the fact that email access is free at the University. Reasons for not using email included problems with accessibility and restrictions over access to other, non-University email accounts.

## 5.4   Group Norms

Although diarists often made reference to the specific attributes of the technologies, the data from the diaries reveal the importance of the relations and the ties within the network as well as group norms. Students adhere to the group norms surrounding email and use it to seek information from the lecturers and the staff. There is little student-student communication via email. Email is the most prevalent medium within the University organisation. Staff used email to send out announcements to the whole course in addition to formal messages to specific students.

## 5.5   Social Network Ties

There is a network of strong ties supported by SMS. Communication partners have close relationships and communicate expressive and instrumental relations. SMS partners are usually friends, family, neighbours or classmates. Diarists did not use SMS to communicate with the staff. The diaries show that in comparison with SMS email supports weak ties or non-close relations. Under some circumstances email can also support close relations. Emails sent and received at the diarists' homes were often exchanged between friends and family particularly over long distances. Previous work has noted that in work oriented relations media use is often affected by the nature of the tasks. In social relations, the nature of the relationship is the most important factor in determining media usage (Haythornthwaite & Wellman,

1998). The results of this study, however, suggest that the nature of the relationship appears to be influential even across work-oriented relations. In work-based relations between staff and students email is used regardless of the nature of the task. In these circumstances a diarist would still send an email even if the message contained little detailed information and the sender needed the recipient to respond quickly. Despite the benefits of SMS expressed during the interview, diarists were unsure as to the use of the medium with lecturers and staff. Use was still dependent on the relationship with the recipient.

## 5.6 Relationship History

The length or history of the relationship with the recipient was also an important factor in media use. There seems to be a protocol to be followed in using SMS. Relationships supported by SMS have their origins in face-to-face meetings (Ling & Yttri, 1999). Mobile phone numbers are then exchanged and this then 'allows' text messages to be exchanged. The exchange of mobile phone numbers indicates a certain level of trust within a relationship (Licoppe & Heurtin, 2001). Receiving a text message from a complete stranger can be unnerving and may not be an appropriate method of making first contact. Email is a more formal and impersonal medium. Lecturers' email addresses unlike mobile phone numbers are often in the public domain via Web pages. Email allows contact to be established without a prior history of exchange.

## 6 Conclusion

This detailed case study has provided interesting insights into how a group of students have used SMS and email to support their developing community. The increase in affiliation with the IS community over the year has been mirrored by an increase in the strength of relationships amongst classmates. Closer relations are characterised by the use of multiple media. Although email maintained weak ties it was infrequently checked and used compared to SMS and it was rarely used between students. Technology has a role to play even within co-located settings. Interactions via the two technologies support the community even when its members are away from the shared location. The technologies are also used to support relations within the extended community of lecturers, family and friends.

As this study shows, media use is not simply an issue of task–media fit. The group interview and the diary data together paint a more complex picture of relationship factors and specific group norms. It has highlighted the integration of multiple media within a digital community and has noted relationship history as an issue concerning SMS use. This case study has provided support for the social approach to the study of technology use. Relationship factors influenced media use across a wider range of interactions than previously found. The results also add credence to the use of personal mobile technologies as providing support for task-based interactions. The study highlights the importance of multiple data sources as a way of understanding the complex pattern of factors affecting technology use.

## Acknowledgements

We wish to thank the students of the Interactive Systems course. This work is sponsored by NCR.

## References

Bagherian, F. & Thorngate, W. (2000), "Horses to Water: Student Use of Course Newsgroups", http://www.firstmonday.dk/issues/issue5_8/thorngate/index.html. first monday: Peer-reviewed Journal on the Internet.

Baym, N. K. (1998), The Emergence of Online Community, *in* S. G. Jones (ed.), *Cybersociety 2.0 Revisiting Computer Mediated Communication and Community*, Sage Publications, pp.35–68.

Carroll, J. M. & Rosson, M. B. (1996), "Developing the Blacksburg Electronic Village", *Communications of the ACM* **39**(12), 69–74.

Chin, W. W., Salis, W. D., Pearson, A. W. & Stollak, M. J. (1999), "Perceived Cohesion in Small Groups: Adapting and Testing the Perceived Cohesion Scale in a Small Group Setting", *Small Group Research* **30**(6), 751–66.

Daft, R. L. & Lengel, R. H. (1986), "Organizational Information Requirements: Media Richness and Structural Design", *Management Science* **32**(5), 554–71.

DeSanctis, G. & Poole, M. S. (1994), "Capturing the Complexity in Advanced Technology Use: Adaptive Structuration Theory", *Organization Science* **5**(2), 121–47.

Garton, L. & Wellman, B. (1995), Social Impacts of Electronic Mail in Organisations: A Review of the Research Literature, *in* B. R. Burleson (ed.), *Communication Yearbook*, Vol. 18, Sage Publications, pp.434–53.

Granovetter, M. (1973), "The Strength of Weak Ties", *American Journal of Sociology* **78**(6), 1360–80.

Gunanwardena, C. N. & Zittle, F. J. (1997), "Social Presence as a Predictor of Satisfaction within a Computer Mediated Conferencing Environment", *American Journal of Distance Education* **11**(3), 8–26.

Hamman, R. B. (1999), "Computer Networks Linking Network Communities: A Study of the Effects of Computer Network Use Upon Pre-existing Communities", http://www.socio.demon.co.uk/mphil/short.html. Also available at CyberSociology Magazine, http://www.cybersoc.com.

Haythornthwaite, C. & Wellman, B. (1998), "Work, Friendship and Media Use for Information Exchange in a Networked Organisation", *Journal of the American Society for Information Science* **49**(12), 1101–14.

Haythornthwaite, C., Kazmer, M. M., Robins, J. & Shoemaker, S. (2000), "Community Development Among Distance Learners: Temporal and Technological Dimensions", *Journal of Computer-mediated Communication* **6**(1). available at http://www.ascusc.org/jcmc/vol6/issue1/haythornthwaite.html.

Johnson, M. M. & Huff, M. T. (2000), "Student's Use of Computer Mediated Communication in a Distance Education Course", *Research on Social Work Practice* 10(4), 519–32.

Kanfer, A. (1999), "It's a Thin World: The Association Between Email Use and Patterns of Communication and Relationships", http://archive.ncsa.uiuc.edu/edu/trg/info_society.html.

Kopomaa, T. (2000), *The City in Your Pocket: Birth of the Mobile Information Society*, Gaudeamus.

Lacohee, H. & Anderson, B. (2001), "Interacting with the Telephone", *International Journal of Human–Computer Studies* 54(5), 665–99.

Licoppe, C. & Heurtin, J. P. (2001), "Managing One's Availability to Telephone Communication Through Mobile Phones: A French Case Study of the Development Dynamics of Mobile Phone Use", *Personal and Ubiquitous Computing* 5(2), 99–108.

Light, P. & Light, V. (1999), Analysing Asynchronous Learning Interactions. Computer Mediated Communication in a Conventional Setting, *in* K. Littleton & P. Light (eds.), *Learning with Computers: Analysing Productive Interaction*, Routledge, pp.162–78.

Light, P., Colbourn, C. & Light, V. (1997), "Computer Mediated Tutorial Support for Conventional University Courses", *Journal of Computer-assisted Learning* 13(4), 228–35.

Ling, R. & Yttri, B. (1999), Nobody Sits at Home and Waits for the Telephone to Ring: Micro and Hyper-coordination Through the Use of the Mobile Telephone, Technical Report 30/1999, Telenor. http://www.telenor.no/fou/prosjekter/Fremtidens_Brukere/Rich/Nobody sits at home and waits.doc.

Parks, M. & Floyd, K. (1996), "Making Friends in Cyberspace", *Journal of Communication* 46(1), 80–97.

Pereira, C. (1993), Anthology: The Breadth of Community, *in* J. Bornat, C. Pereira, D. Pilgram & F. Williams (eds.), *Community Care: A Reader*, MacMillan, pp.5–32.

Rheingold, H. (1993), *The Virtual Community: Homesteading on the Electronic Frontier*, Addison–Wesley.

Short, J., Williams, E. & Christie, B. (1976), *The Social Psychology of Telecommunications*, John Wiley & Sons.

Whittaker, S., Issacs, E. & O'Day, V. (1997), "Widening the Net: Workshop Report on the Theory and Practice of Physical and Network Communities", *ACM SIGCHI Bulletin* 29(3), 27–30.

Zaff, J. & Sloan-Devlin, A. (1998), "Sense of Community in Housing for the Elderly", *Journal of Community Psychology* 26(4), 381–98.

# An Affordance-based Framework for CVE Evaluation

## Phil Turner & Susan Turner

*HCI Research Group, School of Computing, Napier University, Edinburgh EH9 5DT, UK.*

Email: *{p.turner, s.turner}@napier.ac.uk*

**We argue that a conceptual framework is required to support the practical evaluation of collaborative virtual environments. We propose such a framework based on an extended, three level concept of affordance. The application of the framework is illustrated by way of a case study. We conclude with some reflection on the framework's effectiveness and identify areas where further tools or conceptual work may be required.**

**Keywords:** affordance, collaborative virtual environments, evaluation.

## 1  Introduction

This paper considers the practical and theoretical problems of evaluating collaborative virtual environments (CVE). We were faced with these problems during the Summer of 2001 and while we were able to identify quite a large number of candidate evaluation instruments, the absence of a theoretical framework hindered their organisation and selection. Therefore we found it necessary to develop a framework to support this process. This paper reports the theoretical underpinnings of this framework and how we used it in practice.

So why were we faced with problems given the apparent availability of evaluation tools? Firstly, CVEs are distinguished from other virtual reality applications in that they have a strong collaborative component (*sic*) and as Grudin (1988; 1991), among others has observed, the evaluation of collaborative applications itself is fraught with difficulty, let alone collaboration which is mediated virtually. Tools for the evaluation of collaborative systems have been developed, among others Twidale et al. (1994) and Ramage (1999), but none of them have been specifically tailored or proven with virtual environments. Now consider the concluding words of a recent paper considering the evaluation of virtual reality-based system:

"The paper has ... moved from the specific problems of assessing particular desktop VR interfaces to the general issues of evaluating desktop VR within complex organisations. It is discouraging that we are faced by so many problems and so few solutions."
(Johnson, 1999, p.10)

Although proven instruments do exist for the evaluation of virtual environments, for example Kaur et al. (1999), Kalawsky (1999) and COVEN Consortium (1998), they struck us as too disjoint and insufficiently contextually grounded given that we wanted a holistic evaluation of our CVE-based application. Indeed we were committed by an optimistic project plan to an evaluation which spanned the following dimensions, namely:

1. a low-level usability dimension;

2. a collaborative work dimension; and

3. 'a fit for purpose' dimension.

(We recognise here that that some definitions of usability encompass 'fitness for purpose'. By 'low-level usability' we mean such issues as users being able to find functions, perceive the effect of their actions and use a range of input devices.) So the challenge was to find a means of bring together basic, low-level usability, collaboration and the remarkably slippery 'fit for purpose' aspect. For CVEs as other applications, the basic usability dimension comprises the many of the usual issues of user interaction *with* the UI. However, users must also work *through* the UI to employ these functions to work collaboratively with others in the environment. To these, the virtual nature of the environment adds issues of fidelity, presence and engagement. Finally, for real world organisational users there is the matter of fitness for purpose and consequently confidence in such novel technology. Of course, these dimensions are not orthogonal. A poor choice of input device, for example, may detract from a sense of presence and in turn influence perceptions of fitness-for-purpose.

This paper now moves to a discussion of the conceptual framework we developed and subsequently adopted as a means of organising the evaluation of a CVE-based training application. We describe the context and application of this work by means of a case study in Section 3 and conclude with a discussion of the potential implications of this work.

## 2   An Affordance-based Evaluation Framework for CVEs

As we have said, there is at present no integrative conceptual framework which could be used to organise the selection and application of the diverse evaluation techniques needed to evaluate a CVE. This section develops such a framework. This involves a major reworking and extension of the concept of affordance to include embodiment and cultural-historical thought.

### 2.1   Origins

Rather than thinking of this as a reworking, it is perhaps better described as a restoration. Most people, we would suggest, come across the concept of affordance in any of the many standard textbooks of HCI, or directly from the work of Gibson (1986) or more recently from interesting work by Gaver (1991; 1992). In contrast, we suspect that fewer people are aware of the philosophical and psychological origins in the work of Heidegger and the early Gestaltists Koffka and Lewin. Gibson introduces the roots of the concept by noting that the meaning or value of a thing is perceived as quickly as we recognise its colour. He goes on to quote examples from the 'Principles of Gestalt Psychology' (Koffka, 1935) " ... water says 'Drink me'; thunder says 'Fear me'". He continues that these experiences, " ... are vivid and essential features of the experience itself" (Gibson, 1986, p.138). Similarly, Lewin used the term *Aufforderungscharakter* — invitation character — to describe the property of objects to invite directly perceivable behaviour. Koffka then extended the concept to apply to cultural artefacts such as a postbox which invites the behaviour 'posting of letters'. It was at this point that Gibson disagrees and diverges to his narrower formulation of affordance. However if we unpack the words of the Gestaltist we find resonances with phenomenology and cultural-historical thought.

Phenomenology as proposed by Heidegger is profoundly non-dualistic — rejecting the classic mind-body divide. His philosophy of 'being-in-the-world' — the use of hyphens emphasising that there is no space between the world and ourselves — is remarkably close to the thinking of the Gestaltists. Indeed he pursued his approach to hermeneutics by trying to understand how the world reveals itself to us by way of our interaction with it.

Space prevents a fuller treatment of this theme, so we shall now quickly move on to the cultural-historical thread. Wartofsky famously treats perception as an historical process having been culturally acquired and one which continues to expand with additional individual or group experience (another point of agreement with Heidegger). He has argued that human behaviour transforms the natural world and, "This environment is the world made by *praxis* — nature transformed into artefact ... embodying human intentions and needs in an objective way" and it is this world that we perceive and act upon directly. It is this underlying philosophy which we build upon in the framework developed in this paper.

## 2.2 The Concept of Affordance in Use

The concept of affordance is broadly used in the HCI literature as an heuristic or ad hoc design principle. Silveira et al. (2001), for example, treat affordances as a design solution for designers on behalf of users and in doing so make explicit the mapping between requirements and affordance. Thus a user breakdown in using an application or interactive system is characterised by a user failing to identify (perceive) a particular affordance provided by the designer. Our reasoning is that if we can extend the concept of affordance beyond the low-level, physical or biological properties of an object (e.g. a given object affords grasping / pushing) to include issues such as 'affords embodiment' (thus embracing such embodied behaviours such as collaboration and communication) and 'affords the behaviour for which it was designed' (encompassing 'fit for purpose') then we would simultaneous have a framework for the design and evaluation of CVEs. But is there a precedent for this?

Looking beyond HCI, the use of the term affordance in anthropology is not unusual, for example Cole (1996), Wenger (1998) and Holland et al. (2001).

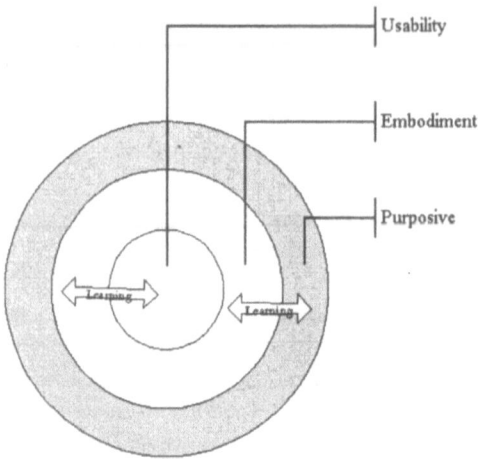

**Figure 1:** A three layer model of affordance.

However what is surprising is the range of affordance identified and cited, which go well beyond Gibson's limited conceptualisation. Cole (1996), for example, recognises the range of affordance offered by a variety of mediating artefacts. These range from the life stories of recovering alcoholics in AA meetings (the stories are said to mediate rehabilitation), patients' charts in a hospital setting (which afford the presentation of a patient's medical history), poker chips (which affords gambling) and 'sexy' clothes (which among other things, affords gender stereotyping). He goes on to note that mediating artefacts embody their own 'developmental histories' which is a reflection of their use. In a similar vein Holland and her colleagues add to this with a discussion of how the men of the Naudada use of the pronoun *ta* (you) to address their wives. This pronoun is the least respectful of all forms of address and is usually reserved for children, dogs and other 'inferiors' and is therefore used as a means of social control. Clearly anthropologists and cultural psychologists find the use of term affordance a useful concept (perhaps merely as short-hand) it does not seem unreasonable to extend the notion to accommodate the raft of issues which is *embodiment* following Robertson's (1997) and Dourish's (2001) recent discussions. Finally, it is the Soviet cultural-historical philosopher Evald Ilyenkov to whom we must turn to provide a theoretical basis for the treatment of the purposive aspects of artefacts which embodies history, use and development (Ilyenkov, 1977). Ilyenkov's thesis on significances is discussed in Section 2.5. Figure 1 summarises this three-layered model of the different flavours of affordance.

The innermost layer might embody the basic usability or ergonomics of the range of controls mediating interaction *with* the device; the second relates to the support for user tasks undertaken *though* the information artefact and the final layer reflects fitness for underlying purpose and the cultural-historical factors arising from the device in use by a community. We have added arrows labelled *learning* to the diagram to illustrate that the boundaries between the layers are dynamic depending on the relative familiarity (*inter alia*) of the artefact in question.

We now describe this model in more detail, illustrating its application to the CVE context.

## 2.3 Low-level Usability

We begin by reminding the reader of the standard description of affordance, with two short quotations from Gibson. The first from 1977, which perhaps encapsulates what is generally understood of affordance:

> "The affordance of the environment is what it offers animals, what it provides or furnishes, for good or ill." (Gibson, 1977)

i.e. affordances are in the environment and are exploited by animals. The second is from 1986:

> "An affordance cuts across the dichotomy of subjective–objective and helps us to understand its inadequacy. It is equally a fact of the environment and a fact of behaviour. It is both physical and psychical, yet neither. An affordance points both ways, to the environment and to the observer." (Gibson, 1986, p.129)

So affordances are neither and both in the world and in the mind of the observer.

These definitions are not without problems as Norman (1988) recognised and who went on to replace the original formulation with a definition which is at one remove, namely that of *perceived affordance*: a user being said to perceive the intended behaviour of an interface widget such as a button or dial. (Many of these observations echo the early work of the ergonomist Hywel Murrell (1965) in the 1950's and 1960's. Murrell notes for example that 'up' means 'more' and 'down' means 'less', rotating a knob clockwise affords the perception of increasing the volume or the amount, likewise an anticlockwise direction signifies a lessening or reduction.) So we either have a disposition to perceive the behaviour of controls in a particular way, or we are picking up their affordances. The design and appearance of these widgets are intended to convey fairly simple behaviours such as sliding, pressing and rotating. Hence adoption of the concept of affordance as a design heuristic. For the purposes of our framework, we consider them to relate to aspects such as the low-level properties of buttons on virtual devices such as telephones, the mouse for moving through the environment, sliders for controlling volume and so forth.

## 2.4 Affordances Supporting User Tasks

We now turn to larger units of human behaviour (beyond, say, merely pressing a button), entailed in accomplishing the user's purpose, thus we are now interested in the tasks and subtasks. In the CVE case, the affordances in question are very largely concerned with co-working in the virtual environment, and are intimately bound up with embodiment. An example might be the task of co-ordinating a team to search a virtual ship for casualties with associated subtasks of finding and communicating with others or reporting progress to a senior officer.

While it can be considered that all our interaction with the world is embodied, see for example the extensive discussion by Dourish (2001), affordances for embodied action are peculiarly central to effective interaction with people and objects in a technologically mediated environment. In the real world, embodied action recognises the constraints of our physical bodies and the limitation of our senses: thus we cannot see each other if we are not co-present; we cannot speak to each other remotely without some form of technological mediation. Equally, embodiment allows us to use a wealth of non-verbal mechanisms and to make assumptions about the perceptual resources and scope for action of other embodied beings. In virtual environments, despite having a body (or avatar) the experience of action is indirectly mediated through keyboard, mouse or joystick, often requiring conscious attention, for example to the speed of mouse movement required to move up stairs without floating to the ceiling. Coordinated action with others is also constrained: fields of vision are usually more limited than in the real world, as are the resources available to determine, say, the referent of another's gesture.

These phenomena have prompted a stream of research into the nature of embodied interaction and its consequences for the design of affordances in media and virtual spaces. Gaver's (1992) extension of Gibson's notion of affordances to media spaces, for example, highlights the role of active perception in technology-mediated interaction. The insight stimulated the development of devices that mimic real world embodiment such as the Virtual Window system, which allowed exploration of a remote scene through moving the head (Gaver et al., 1995). Robertson's (1997) ethnographically-informed study of a distributed design team provides ample evidence of how communication is embodied in the physical world. She identifies a number of what must be regarded as generic, embodied actions, for example, *highlighting some aspect of an object, pointing at something, emitting signs and monitoring of signs, moving in and out of shared space.* In common with Gaver, Robertson notes that our perception is seldom static. Technical systems must support movement, specifically to afford changing perspective, to get a better view to get an object or to move the position of an object. Clearly, while Robertson saw their implications as merely requirements on technology to support cooperative work they can also be seen as affordances. These affordances are realised by actions such as pressing or pushing yet are an order more complex.

A final consideration at this level is the affordances relating to the fidelity of the virtual world to its physical counterpart, presence (by which we mean the sense of being in the virtual world) and engagement (by which we mean the sense of being 'wrapped up' in any action that may be occurring) have a close but somewhat complex association with embodiment. Well-designed embodiment may indeed lead to enhanced perceptions of fidelity, presence and engagement, but action which is particularly engaging, for example in a game, may enable users to overlook breakdowns in embodied action.

## 2.5    *Cultural Affordance?*

We now introduce the concept of cultural affordance which has been developed and broadly based on Ilyenkov's monograph, 'The Problem of the Ideal'[1]. In essence

---

[1] The original paper by Ilyenkov was published in 1979 in Russian but is now free available from the excellent Marxist site which may be found at www.marxists.org — note the plural form. However it is

Ilyenkov addresses the problem of attribution of non-material properties to physical objects. He presents an argument wherein he demonstrates that human purposive activity endows artefacts with values and meaning. (The latter being described as being examples of *ideal* properties, that is, belonging to a class of phenomena which are neither mental nor physical.) He further describes *ideal* properties as *significances* (or to use our term *cultural affordance*). A cultural affordance (CA) is a feature or set of features which arises from the making, using or modifying of the artefact and in doing so endowing it with the values of culture from which it arises. Unlike simple affordance or those which arise from embodiment, CAs can only be recognised (in an extreme sense) by a member of the culture which created it. CAs are exploited with the artefact is in use and will change if the artefact is put to a different use. In Bayonne there is a museum housing a range of Basque farming implements most of which were unfathomable to the authors, neither of whom is Basque nor a farmer. However a number of them could be exploited as decorations, door stops or potentially lethal weapons by changing the context of their use. Similarly, Ilyenkov invites us to consider the differences between a lump of wood and a (wooden) table. The table comes into being by way of purposive human activity, i.e. intending to make a table, working and turning the wood, polishing the surface — processes which embody the ideal properties of that activity. Thus we are able to distinguish between these two objects by virtue of the cultural affordances endowed in the wood by the craftsman. We can further differentiate among tables by way of their cultural affordances — hand-crafted / mass-produced; ornamental / utilitarian; recycled pine / made from wood the from Brazilian rain forest. However, the table to be useful must also embody basic level affordances such as able to support the weight of crockery and so forth, and the affordances arising from embodiment, that is, be of a size which allows people to sit at it.

It is important not to over emphasise the importance of 'human activity endowing natural objects with ideal properties'. Ilyenkov's focus was really on the relationship between humans and nature, and on how it is that humans can come to be capable of knowing the world, and how the world comes to be capable of being known. In Ilyenkov's theory, activity is not just the source of the knowable world, but of the way we inhabit it. The thesis is that it is this constant interchange between activity and an objectified nature that is the root of self-consciousness. What also needs to be accepted, for Ilyenkov's theory to hold, is that while the forms of social life arise from collective action, they are presented to individuals as pre-existing, objective, phenomena. Human development is the process of mastering our objectified (historically developed) world.

So what are the consequences of this cultural-historical analysis of the collective creation and use of artefacts? Immediately we must recognise that this points us to a highly contextual (specifically) use-focused evaluation. In this instance issues include:

- The CVE must show that it can deliver safety-critical training in the maritime and offshore domains to senior professionals.

---

strongly recommended that Bakhurst's (1991) treatment and interpretation of Ilyenkov is consulted first.

- The validation of training by a recognised training and standards body as being of a suitable standard.

- The acceptability of the CVE to the trainers, trainees and employers who will have to use it.

In turn this requires pedagogic evaluation; validation against existing industry standards and user involvement in the determination of acceptability. The use of these instruments is described in the next section. So, having described our proposed framework and its theoretical roots we now turn to how it was applied in the Discover project, which we now introduce.

## 3   The Application of the Framework

Having established the three layer model of affordances, we can now demonstrate how we used it in practice as an evaluation framework. This section shows how it was applied in the Discover project, which we now introduce.

### 3.1   *Introduction to Discover*

The importance of safety–critical training in the maritime and offshore domains is recognised by all stakeholders in these industries, but is almost prohibitively expensive. Current methods require trainees to be co-located at a specialist training site, often equipped with costly physical simulators. The Discover project aimed to provide a CVE based series of team training simulations which would dramatically reduce the need for senior mariners and oil rig workers to have to attend courses at specialist centres. While the system would be made available at such institutions, it could also be used over the Internet from offshore or on board ships. The consortium comprised four marine and offshore training organisations based in the UK, Norway, Denmark and Germany; virtual reality technology specialists, training standards bodies; and a number of interested employers and a UK University.

The CVE itself was designed to run on standard, high-end, networked desktop PCs, the only special purpose equipment being high specification soundcards and audio headsets.  The environment represented the interior of a ship (maritime version) or an offshore platform (offshore version). Users were present as avatars in the environment. Trainee avatars had abilities designed to mimic real action and interaction as closely as possible, and had access to small number of interactive objects such as fire-extinguishers, alarm panels and indeed bodies. Communication again imitated the real world, being mediated through voice when in the same room, or telephone, walkie-talkie or PA when avatars were not co-present. Tutors were not embodied as avatars, but had the ability to teleport to any part of the environment, to see the location of trainees on a map or through a bird's eye view, to track particular trainees and to modify the environment in limited ways, for example by setting fires or locking doors. It should be stressed that the environment was intended to support the training of emergency management and team coordination skills, rather than lower level skills such as using fire extinguishers.

Figure 2 shows the sequence of user trials in Discover, and where the main inputs to each level of the evaluation took place. As can be seen, while each phase

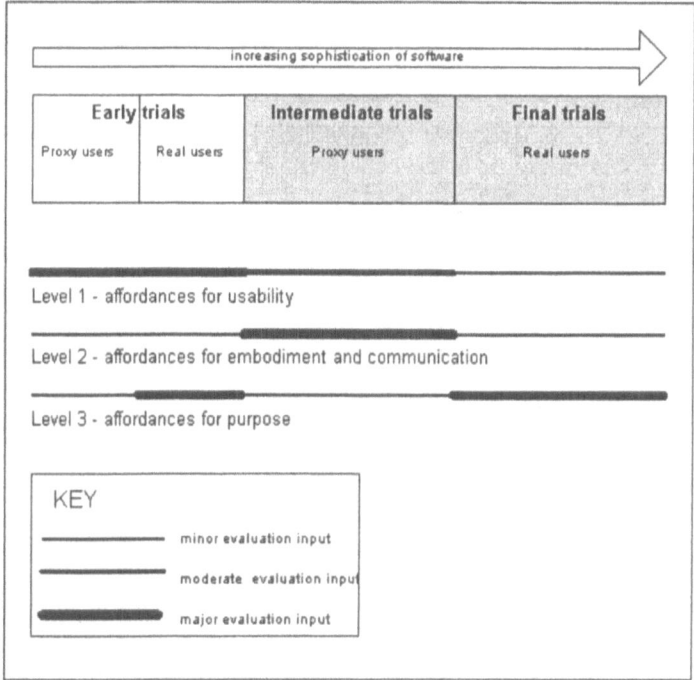

**Figure 2:** Phases of Discover user trials and their focus.

of the trials had a main focus, material pertaining to each of the levels was collected throughout the process. The framework was used to plan the content of the trials and to select appropriate techniques. The following section reprises the generic affordances pertinent to each level, gives specific examples of these for Discover and describes work undertaken. Note that our theme here is the framework and its instantiation, so the evaluation results themselves are not reported.

### 3.2 Evaluating Basic Usability

Affordances to be evaluated at this level are those concerned with the ergonomics and usability of the means provided to interact with the CVE. These include the now standard range of GUI controls, as well input and output devices. Aspects to be considered are their perceptibility, ease of operation, provision of feedback and in general the list of low-level usability heuristics to be found in any textbook.

Here we were concerned, *inter alia*, with affordances of such features as the push-buttons provided to activate virtual communication devices such as the phone and walkie-talkie and the use of the mouse click as a means of opening doors, setting off fire extinguishers and generally activating objects. The design of these had been a subject of much debate as to whether, for realism, a phone should have the usual set of buttons reproduced virtually, or if users would find a dialogue box more convenient. We also needed to evaluate the physical affordances of the mouse for moving through the environment (employers were keen that the system should run on a standard workshop and peripherals), and of the headsets used for verbal communication.

The overall emphasis in the choice and construction of techniques was to obtain basic usability data with minimal consumption of analyst and user resources. These affordances were primarily investigated through user trials, starting from the earliest versions of the software. Subjects for these early trials were in the main 'proxies' who represented the eventual user population as closely as possible in terms of relevant background skills and experience. This allowed us to conserve the scarce resource of 'real' users for both more polished versions of the software and fitness for purpose issues. Subjects undertook realistic single user and collaborative tasks matched to the functionality of the software version under review, monitored by observers.

With later trials the main evaluation focus shifted to the evaluation of embodiment and fitness for purpose issues but usability continued to receive some attention. Post-trial questionnaires were compiled and administered, adapting usability items from standard usability instruments and VRUSE (Kalawsky, 1999), and guided by the insights of Kaur et al. (1999). Although the custom built questionnaire did not now have the strong validation of its parents, the questions could be tailored to the particular context of the Discover CVE while keeping the overall instrument to a manageable length. Observers augmented the self-report data. The trials were supplemented by usability inspections structured by standard heuristics. In the event, most usability problems were identified by a initial, quick expert check of the interface, but the other techniques adopted were able to provide substantive data to back up these observations.

### 3.3   *Evaluating Embodiment and Collaboration*

Here the focus of evaluation is how effectively are actors embodied *in* the environment and how effectively they can collaborate *through* the environment. In addition, we are concerned with evaluating the related issues of perceptions of fidelity, presence and engagement.

Trainees in the Discover environment needed to be able to find each other, to communicate by appropriate means with fellow trainees and tutors, to monitor what others were doing and to interact with various items in the environment, for example to pick up a body (an avatar) overcome by smoke. Tutors had to be able to gather sufficient information from monitoring activity in the CVE to provide guidance and post-training feedback, to communicate with trainees and to modify interactive objects in the CVE such as the location of fires. It had also been stressed by all stakeholders from training and employer organisations that the CVE must be extremely realistic and imbue a strong sense of presence if it was to be considered fit for its purpose of providing training. This was for two reasons. Firstly, existing physical ship simulators are extremely close to their sea-going equivalents, so much so that officers undergoing simulator training can be dismissed should they run the simulator aground. Secondly, one of the key elements in emergency management training is engagement in the emergency scenario, and consequently the experience of a suitable degree of stress.

Here the choice of techniques was constrained by the limited range of ready-made tools for evaluating aspects of collaboration in virtual environments, and again by the availability of subjects. Aspects of communication and coordination (primarily being able to see, hear and address other users) were evaluated in parallel with the ergonomic elements in the very early trials described above. Once the software was reasonably stable and more co-working features had been added, more complex trials were carried out. As before, mainly proxy subjects were used to identify the most immediate issues concerning affordances for embodiment and communication. They undertook exercises structured to include:

- The type of collaborative tasks undertaken in a realistic training situation.

- The underlying collaborative actions identified by the COVEN hierarchical task analysis (COVEN Consortium, 1998).

Short post-use questionnaires were administered using items derived from the task analysis. For users adopting the role of tutor, an additional set of tasks and questionnaire items was derived from Laurillard's (1993) model of teaching and learning. At this point we did not seek to address the efficacy of any teaching or learning, but rather the affordances of the environment for such pedagogic actions as setting/modifying task goals, monitoring trainees and giving feedback. Again, observers monitored the progress, or occasionally lack of progress, of the scenario, supported by checklists mirroring the questionnaire content. Finally, issues of fidelity and presence were also covered. Initially this was through a short series of items in the post use questionnaire and observers' checklist, again adapted from VRUSE.

The final version of the software was evaluated with experienced tutors from one of the training organisations involved in the project. (Evaluation techniques had been planned for trials with 'real' trainees, but in the event personnel could not be made available. This work continues outside the scope of the project at one of the training organisations.) Tutors undertook a realistic training scenario, authored by one of the training organisations. They took turns to play tutor and trainee roles. This time the NASA ITQ questionnaire (a measure of immersive tendencies, Witmer & Singer (1998) was administered before the trial started, followed up by a questionnaire instrument incorporating the collaborative and pedagogic aspects as before, coupled with the NASA PQ — the counterpart to the ITQ which aims to measure presence. These trials were videotaped for further analysis of evaluation data.

## 3.4 Evaluating Cultural Affordances

In the generic case, these affordances relate to the creation and use of an artefact within a community.

The central purpose of the CVE was to support the teaching and learning of emergency management skills for offshore and maritime contexts (pedagogy). Related to this, it was essential that stakeholders should have confidence in the software as affording a means for such training, and trust that the skills learnt in the environment would be effective in real emergencies. (These qualities were strongly dependent on the affordances for realism and presence.)

Clearly, the evaluation of affordance for fitness for purpose can only be undertaken with the participation individuals from the community concerned. In one of the trials of early versions of the software, we had access to several maritime officers (including the captain of a well-known passenger ship) who completed custom-designed questionnaire items about their confidence in the future use of the system as well as taking part in debriefing sessions.

More substantive evaluation for perceived fitness for purpose focused firstly on data from the tutor sessions already discussed above. Here data was collected through custom-designed questionnaire items, post-trial discussions and analysis of verbalisations and behaviour from the video record. As for pedagogic effectiveness, trials are planned with trainees in an employer organisation that will incorporate realistic training scenarios with inbuilt checkpoints for the display of specific management behaviours at appropriate times.   This will be complemented by observations based on the measures of team effectiveness derived by the TADMUS project (Cannon-Bowers & Salas, 1998) in their research into training for decision making under stress, and on the deeper aspects of pedagogy in the Laurillard model. Finally, Discover must receive the seal of approval from industry validating bodies.

However, it will be impractical to run rigorous comparative trials of Discover against conventional training (because of the restricted availability of trainees and the related difficulty of ensuring matched groups). Still less will it be possible to 'prove' the effectiveness of Discover training in genuine emergencies. It remains the case, that at the current state of knowledge, the verification of the transfer of VR-based training into the real world is very much an active issue for research — Caird (1996) explores these issues in some detail. Nor indeed are there methods of assessing the transfer of traditional safety–critical training in these domains.

## 4   Discussion

On a theoretical level, we have presented a radically expanded concept of affordance. Turning to the practice of evaluation, we have shown how it is possible to move from the theory of affordance to the evaluation of a particular instance of collaborative systems, the collaborative virtual environment. The three level model has allowed us to consider the diverse aspects of CVEs and available evaluation techniques in a theoretically structured framework which encompasses basic usability, collaboration and embodiment in the environment, and underlying fitness for purpose.   The application of this has been illustrated in a case study.

### *4.1   The Validity and Scope of the Three Layer Model of Affordance*

As discussed further below, the model has provided an effective means of separating different types of issue in a complex evaluation context. There is also some informal evidence that users found it very natural to partition their feedback in such a manner. By way of illustration of such comments, here are three extracts from discussion among (non-native English speaking) tutors who had just participated in a CVE trial.

"It would be much better to use a joystick as the same as they use in a helicopter. The same as a boy [has] at home. Then it is much easier to move around. It would be more similar to what you are doing moving forward, backward, left, right ... "

"The main problem is knowing which direction and to know what is the front and what is the back of the person ... where you are in fact."

"If they had the alarm plans and the plans of the corridors and all this it would be very good communication training."

## 4.2 The Usefulness of the Framework

In the Discover example, the case study allowed us to consider systematically, level by level, what aspects should be evaluated, where applicable techniques existed and where techniques required modification or development. Focusing on the different levels also allowed us to plan efficient utilisation of the resources available at different stages of the development and evaluation process. For example, by concentrating on Level 1 issues (basic usability) and Level 2 (embodiment and collaboration) when only early versions of the software and 'proxy' users were available, we were able to obtain timely but useful data for developers. In the collation and communication of the evaluation results, we were able to separate concerns, thus preventing, for example, significant issues of perceived fitness for purpose being swamped by large numbers of relatively minor problems such as the layout of a dialogue box. As mentioned above, users also appeared to find the partition a natural one, thus allowing meaningful discussion of pedagogic effectiveness whilst acknowledging that ergonomic issues were still outstanding. The separation of issues also engendered a valuable, albeit rather belated, debate among stakeholders as to the exact intentions for the system rather than a concentration on matters as signage in the virtual ship which had been much in evidence in earlier work. In short, we would commend the approach to others working in similar evaluation contexts.

## 4.3 Further Work

There are two clear areas for further work. Firstly, we suspect that the model and its practical application as an evaluation framework have potential for collaborative applications in general as well as for other instance of CVEs, and this obviously requires further exploration and validation. Secondly, in the specific case of CVEs while techniques exist for addressing most affordances at the level of basic usability and embodiment, covering all these matters with current tools would require unacceptably prolonged inspections, trials and debriefing. What is needed here is a validated, but economical technique to cover basic usability, specialist VR aspects of interaction and issues pertaining to embodiment and collaboration. The scope of work in Discover was able only to make an early, un-validated attempt at this. As for cultural affordances, evaluation techniques are necessarily bound to context-of-use. We would argue that at least where issues of trust and confidence are involved, such domain-specific techniques can only be developed with the participation of the community concerned.

## Acknowledgements

We gratefully acknowledge the contributions of our colleagues on the DISCOVER project in providing the sites and subjects for the fieldwork herein described and in developing the DISCOVER software. The project is financially supported by the EU ESPRIT programme.

## References

Bakhurst, D. (1991), *Consciousness and Revolution in Soviet Philosophy*, Cambridge University Press.

Caird, J. K. (1996), "Persistent Issues in the Application of Virtual Environment Systems to Training", *Human Interaction with Complex Systems* **3**, 124–32.

Cannon-Bowers, J. A. & Salas, E. (1998), *Decision Making Under Stress*, American Psychological Association.

Cole, M. (1996), *Cultural Psychology: Once and Future Discipline?*, Harvard University Press.

COVEN Consortium (1998), Deliverable 3.5 Usage Evaluation of the Online Applications, Technical Report, UCL / University of Nottingham.

Dourish, P. (2001), *Where the Action Is*, MIT Press.

Gaver, W. W. (1991), Technological Affordances, *in* S. P. Robertson, G. M. Olson & J. S. Olson (eds.), *Proceedings of CHI'91: Human Factors in Computing Systems (Reaching through Technology)*, ACM Press, pp.79–84.

Gaver, W. W. (1992), The Affordances of Media Space for Collaboration, *in* J. Turner & R. Kraut (eds.), *Proceedings of CSCW'92: ACM Conference on Computer Supported Cooperative Work*, ACM Press, pp.17–24.

Gaver, W. W., Smets, G. & Overbeeke, K. (1995), A Virtual Window on Mediaspace, *in* I. Katz, R. Mack, L. Marks, M. B. Rosson & J. Nielsen (eds.), *Proceedings of CHI'95: Human Factors in Computing Systems,* ACM Press, pp.257–64.

Gibson, J. J. (1977), The Theory of Affordances, *in* R. Shaw & J. Bransford (eds.), *Perceiving, Acting and Knowing: Towards an Ecological Psychology*, Lawrence Erlbaum Associates distributed by John Wiley & Sons, pp.67–82.

Gibson, J. J. (1986), *The Ecological Approach To Visual Perception*, Lawrence Erlbaum Associates. Originally published in 1979 by Houghton Mifflin.

Grudin, J. (1988), Why CSCW Applications Fail. Problems in the Design and Evaluation of Organizational Interfaces, *in* D. G. Tatar (ed.), *Proceedings of CSCW'88: Second Conference on Computer Supported Cooperative Work*, ACM Press, pp.85–93.

Grudin, J. (1991), "Obstacles to User Involvement in Software Product Development, with Implications for CSCW", *International Journal of Man–Machine Studies* **34**(3), 435–52.

Holland, D., Lachicotte Jr., W. S., Skinner, D. & Cain, C. (2001), *Identity and Agency in Cultural Worlds*, Harvard University Press.

Ilyenkov, E. V. (1977), *Dialectical Logic: Essays on its History and Theory*, Progress Publishers.

Johnson, C. (1999), Evaluating the Contribution of Desktop VR for Safety-Critical Applications, *in* M. Felici, K. Kanoun & A. Pasquini (eds.), *Proceedings of Computer Safety, Reliability and Security, 18th International Conference SAFECOMP'99*, Vol. 1698 of *Lecture Notes in Computer Science*, Springer-Verlag, pp.67–78.

Kalawsky, R. S. (1999), "VRUSE: A Computerised Diagnostic Tool for Usability Evaluation of Virtual/Synthetic Environment Systems", *Applied Ergonomics* **30**(1), 11–25.

Kaur, K., Maiden, N. & Sutcliffe, A. (1999), "Interacting with Virtual Environments: An Evaluation of a Model of Interaction", *Interacting with Computers* **11**(4), 403–26. Special Issue on VR.

Koffka, K. (1935), Principles of Gestalt Psychology, Harcourt Brace.

Laurillard, D. (1993), *Rethinking University Teaching: A Framework for the Effective Use of Educational Technology*, Routledge.

Murrell, K. F. H. (1965), *Ergonomics: Man in his Working Environment*, Chapman & Hall.

Norman, D. A. (1988), *The Psychology of Everyday Things*, Basic Books.

Ramage, M. (1999), A Stakeholder Approach to CSCW Evaluation, PhD thesis, University of Durham.

Robertson, T. (1997), Cooperative Work and Lived Cognitions: A Taxonomy of Embodied Actions, *in* J. Hughes, W. Prinz, T. Rodden & K. Schmidt (eds.), *Proceedings of ECSCW'97, the 5th European Conference on Computer-Supported Cooperative Work*, Kluwer, pp.205–20.

Silveira, M. S., Barbosa, S. D. & Sieckenius de Souza, C. (2001), Augmenting the Affordances of Online Help Content, *in* A. Blandford, J. Vanderdonckt & P. Gray (eds.), *People and Computers XV: Interaction without Frontiers (Proceedings of IHM-HCI'2001)*, Springer-Verlag, pp.279–96.

Twidale, M. B., Randall, D. & Bentley, R. (1994), Situated Evaluation for Cooperative Systems, *in* R. Furuta & C. Neuwirth (eds.), *Proceedings of CSCW'94: ACM Conference on Computer Supported Cooperative Work*, ACM Press, pp.441–52.

Wenger, E. (1998), *Communities of Practice: Learning, Meaning and Identity*, Cambridge University Press.

Witmer, B. G. & Singer, M. J. (1998), "Measuring Presence in Virtual Environments: A Presence Questionnaire", *Presence* **7**(3), 225–40.

# Extending Low-cost Remote Evaluation with Synchronous Communication

## Lynne Dunckley, Lucia Rapanotti[†] & Jon G Hall[‡]

*Department of Computing, Thames Valley University, Wellington Street, Slough SL1 1YG, UK.*

Tel: *+44 1753 69 7739*

Email: *lynne.dunckley@tvu.ac.uk*

[†] *Department of Computing, The Open University, Walton Hall, Milton Keynes MK7 6AA, UK.*

Tel: *+44 1908 654125*

Email: *l.rapanotti@open.ac.uk*

URL: *http://mcs.open.ac.uk/lr38/*

[‡] *Department of Computing, The Open University, Walton Hall, Milton Keynes MK7 6AA, UK.*

Tel: *+44 1908 652679*

Email: *j.g.hall@open.ac.uk*

URL: *http://mcs.open.ac.uk/jgh23/*

**Write-along Low Cost Remote (LCR) evaluation is a highly efficient method for remotely evaluating usability problems with prototype interfaces. A previous study noted that this efficiency comes at the cost of a loss of the conversational nature of the evaluation. In this paper, we assess this loss through a comparison with an extended LCR, which uses real-time conferencing tools to introduce synchronous communication. An experimental investigation was carried out on an interactive prototype interface with known usability problems. In this way the effectiveness of the new method using real-time conferencing tools could be assessed and recommendations for best practice set out.**

**Keywords:** remote usability evaluation, real-time conferencing tools, real world context.

# 1   Introduction

Information systems are being developed to support increasingly complex tasks. Many of these systems are distributed, involving geographically remote users. The growth of network and, particularly, Web technology means that users are communicating with central systems using a wide range of machines and operating systems.

Evaluating and testing such systems is difficult: the network itself and the remote work setting are important parts of the system and produce usage patterns difficult to reproduce in a laboratory. At the same time, bringing developers and users together in remote locations can be impractical, and often prohibitively expensive. These problems are particularly acute where the software is developed for an international market, typically involving usability evaluations in different countries.

In order to take such factors into account, remote usability evaluations have been proposed in the literature. In general, two approaches to remote usability data collection methods have been used. The subjective approach can range from reports from users, user-identified 'critical incidents' to questionnaires, interviews and ethnographic techniques. The objective approach involves automatically collecting data about the application and its users (for example counts, sequence, timing of actions) including audio and video recording; automatic software monitoring; and psychological event monitoring (Hilbert & Redmiles, 1998). Problems with the objective approach include the resource intensive nature of interpreting feedback to extract key issues and that the context, which is vital in interpreting the meaning of the users' actions, is missing from the data (Hammontree et al., 1994; Hartson et al., 1996). In contrast to this, a key benefit of the subjective approach is the ability to capture aspects of the users' needs, thought processes and subjective experiences. However, problems with the subjective approach do exist, particularly if the intention is to collect usability issues and not merely list software bugs (Hartson et al., 1996).

During 1999 a team working at the Open University, UK, developed the Low Cost Remote evaluation method (LCR method) (Dunckley et al., 2000) for the evaluation of high fidelity prototypes linked to the subsequent redesign process. The LCR method is itself a remote adaptation of an evaluation method proposed by Smith et al. (1999) that incorporated structured sessions between designers and users derived from contextual inquiry. In effect, rather than the verbalisation of their experience with a (semi-) working prototype, a user located remotely will record their experiences through a commentary, prompted by a questionnaire, and written concurrently. The original case study, described by Dunckley et al. (2000), held that LCR suffered from a:

> "...temptation for users to explore and interact before they have completed a written answer."

with a concomitant loss of the conversational nature of the face to face designer-user sessions. This paper investigates whether re-establishing a conversation between user and evaluator leads to a more effective LCR method. The cost of this loss can then be assessed.

The paper is structured as follows. Section 2 describes the prototype evaluated in the study. Section 3 summarises the LCR method, and discusses a number of issues raised by Dunckley et al. (2000) that have motivated the investigation reported in this paper. Section 4 describes the new remote evaluation methods based on the deployment of Internet conferencing tools. Section 5 reports on the findings and Section 6 discusses issues of methodology as well as practicalities. Finally, Section 7 concludes the paper.

## 2 The Case Study

The case study we describe involves the Open University (OU). The OU is the major provider of distance-learning education at university level in the UK and Europe. Increasingly, the OU has moved to the electronic provision of its teaching services to students via the Internet and email systems. A component of the course materials, the continuous assessment system, provides the major vehicle for driving the student's distance learning experience: students complete assessments as they study a course. The scripts are marked by associate lecturers (aka tutors) located remotely both from the student and the university campus. Marked scripts are returned to students for feedback on their progression, via the OU.

The move to electronic provision has been facilitated by the development of software for script marking, namely the eTMA (electronic Tutor Marked Assessment) Marking Tool. The original design of the eTMA Marking Tool was subject to conflicting requirements. In operation, the software should require the minimum of support and technical backup. The usage pattern would be one of fairly long gaps followed by intensive use for short periods. Visibility and affordance of design were therefore crucial issues.

The eTMA Marking Tool prototype consisted of four windows, which worked in conjunction with an MS Word document displaying the student's work. The most complex tasks were associated with the 'Score Allocation' window of the tool, where the user is required to enter the score followed by feedback for each question. In contrast, when marking on paper, this order is not enforced. This design rationale came about because a score is a necessary component of the marking, whereas the comment is optional: the user might forget to add the score if the order were reversed. However, the importance of this action sequence needed to be conveyed to the user. An important issue was the visibility of the comments. With a previous version of this software it had been discovered that extensive comments could disrupt the format and display of the eTMA returned to the student. In this prototype the comments were embedded so that they could be seen when returned to the student but disappeared as far as the user was concerned, although they could be glimpsed as the cursor passed over the score in the Word document.

## 3 The LCR Method

The LCR method attempts to capture the user's response to prototype interfaces in a contextual manner and provides a framework to simulate a remote conversation between the developer and the user. The method was strongly influenced by the ideas of contextual inquiry (Holtzblatt & Jones, 1993). There are a number

**For each task**
> *Ask the user to explain what s/he is attempting*
> **For each sub task**
>> *Ask the user to explain what s/he is attempting*
>> **For each stage in Norman's model of interaction**
>>> *Consider asking a question from the checklist*
>> **Next stage**
> **Next sub task**

**Next task**

**Figure 1:** Eliciting user comments in an LCR session.

| Norman's Stages | Remote Evaluation Questions |
|---|---|
| Form a goal | How does the screen help you select a way of achieving your task? |
| Form an intention | What is the most important information visible when you start to allocate the score and make comments? |
| Specify the action sequence | How does the Score Allocation window make it obvious how to allocate scores and make comments? |
| Execute action | |
| Perceive the resultant system state | How has the Score Allocation window changed in order to show what you have achieved? |
| Interpret the resultant state | How do you know what you have done is correct |
| Evaluate the outcome | How would you recognise any mistakes? What action would you take to correct any mistakes? |

**Figure 2:** LCR evaluation framework: sample questions.

of evaluation methods that are variously known by the terms think-aloud, verbal protocol and cooperative evaluation. Many experts recommend think-aloud for most ordinary face-to-face applications, although Goguen (1996) criticises such methods as 'unnatural'. Co-operative evaluation is a variation of think-aloud in which the user is encouraged to see himself as a collaborator in the evaluation rather than just a subject. This is claimed to be less constrained and the user is encouraged to actively criticise the system by the evaluator, who is not necessarily the designer (Wright & Monk, 1991). We were interested in developing remote evaluation methods that could simulate this situation. The approach is based on integrating contextual enquiry approaches with simulated think-aloud methods with the particular aim of promoting developer-user conversations, which the developer does not dominate. A key part of the method is the establishment of a conversation between the user and the developer supported by a series of questions structured within Norman's seven stages of action (Norman, 1998). The process is as exemplified in Figures 1 & 2, with reference to the eTMA prototype evaluation.

The LCR method applies these concepts to enable users to articulate the way in which they would use a prototype interface to complete their normal tasks. Unless the evaluation focuses on specific tasks and context, users tend to evaluate prototypes in abstract terms referring to their general view of the interface and about whether they like the font, colours, etc. Users may not recall problems with the interface outside the context of actually doing work.

In general, remote evaluation experiments reported in the literature have taken place in organisational settings. There, a single group of remote users were observed in their normal work environment, which could, to some extent, be controlled and where audio and video equipment could be set up (Holtzblatt & Jones, 1993). In contrast the eTMA Marking Tool experiment reported by Dunckley et al. (2000) involved users at widely distributed locations. Their social context was the home, with background family noise. Video recording and video conferencing were not feasible options, as most of the users would not have the equipment. Asynchronous evaluation facilitated the experiment due to the time distribution of the users' work patterns. Consequently, LCR was designed to simulate the think-aloud method by providing an electronic, user-completed journal to capture users' responses during interaction with the prototype. Hence the name 'write-along'.

Additionally, the LCR method consisted of an evaluation package with the following components:

1. Detailed evaluation form.

2. Critical incident report form.

3. Summary form of nine open-ended evaluation questions.

To summarise the conclusions of the LCR study by Dunckley et al. (2000):

1. The remote evaluation was effective in providing information from which the developer team could identify usability problems that lead to design changes.

2. Users were able to articulate their experience of using the interface, regardless of their gender and task complexity.

3. Users needed to get used to the conversational style of the LCR framework; repetition of the style of questions for each task assisted this.

4. Since there is some evidence of a learning effect in terms of the questions being asked, the evaluation design should ensure less complex tasks are encountered at first.

It was also found that although users were able to understand the concepts of critical incidents (Castillo et al., 1998) and report these effectively, few usability problems were identified in this way.

The LCR method itself was highly efficient in terms of the resources needed to extract the usability problems from the users' responses. The one element that was a problem in the write-along LCR method which cannot arise in think-aloud protocols is that users get tempted to explore and interact before they have completed the written answer. An actual observer can prevent this in a way that is difficult to simulate in the LCR remote evaluation. We therefore considered that the LCR method needed further development and tool support by the incorporation of audio prompts or active agent technology to maintain the conversational nature of the evaluation. This paper describes the further work that has been carried out. In particular, it describes an investigation into ways to combine the write-along method with audio prompts and reminders. This was carried out by adapting the LCR method for use with two conferencing systems, Lyceum and NetMeeting, as described in the following section.

## 3.1   Real-time Conferencing Investigation

We have adapted the original LCR package based on a write-along method to include audio prompts designed to keep users to the task scenario and to help any who experience critical incidents. Additionally, the evaluator and user can discuss a critical incident immediately instead of the user reporting them for later analysis (Hartson et al., 1996).

We describe an experiment to assess any increase in effectiveness of extending the LCR with real-time conferencing. The conferencing packages used to extend the LCR were Lyceum and NetMeeting. The additional functionality provided by Lyceum was many-to-many voice and data conferencing. That of NetMeeting was to allow the evaluator to view the user's desktop at the same time as peer-to-peer voice conferencing.

We used the same prototype of the eTMA Marking Tool as in Dunckley et al. (2000), as its usability problems had already been identified by that study, and through subsequent conventional usability evaluations as well as actual implementation.

The set of users was drawn from the same population of associate lecturers as those of Dunckley et al. (2000). This is a large population, so we were able to select users with no previous experience of the electronic assessment tool and check that their user profile was comparable to that of Dunckley et al. (2000). By and large, the users were new to Lyceum and NetMeeting. We used the same question and answer framework (see Figure 2), but the questions were adapted to a briefer style needed for audio communication over the Internet.

We also used the same task scenario, which consisted of four tasks:

1. Selecting courses and scripts to mark.

2. Setting part marks for the standard mark scheme.

3. Marking sample scripts.

4. Storing completed marked scripts.

Users were asked to complete Tasks 1 to 4 online, then explore further completion of the tasks offline, using the LCR write-along method, and complete a questionnaire.

## 3.2   Lyceum Trials

Lyceum is a client-server voice groupware system developed at the OU, designed to support real-time collaborative eLearning (Rapanotti & Hall, 2000). Lyceum users can participate in real-time voice conferencing and share collaborative spaces and tools over the Internet. The Lyceum client is designed to run on mid-range Windows PCs with standard multimedia support.

Among Lyceum's features, the following were particularly relevant to our investigation:

1. Participants meet in 'virtual rooms', where they talk to each other and share collaborative tools. During the experiment, one room was used for plenary discussions, and separate rooms were used for individual evaluation activities.

2. Users have access to a collaborative whiteboard and text editor. The whiteboard was used during plenary discussions, while the text editor contained the tasks description and the user's commentary during the individual evaluations.

3. The Lyceum voice tools allow participants to talk and facilitate the moderation of plenary sessions.

### 3.2.1   The Sessions

The Lyceum sessions were designed to allow a number of users and evaluators to work together. We divided the users into groups, each group made up of 4 or 5 people. Each user group engaged in one training and one evaluation session for a total of just over two hours online. Training and evaluation sessions were structured as follows. Each started with a plenary session for all participants, followed by individual evaluation activities in separate virtual rooms, followed by a plenary discussion to close. Each session was run by two evaluators.

The plenary discussions allowed the users to debate prototype usability issues, and were moderated by an evaluator, who also recorded the users' comments. During the individual evaluation activities, the two evaluators would visit the users' separate rooms in a round-robin fashion. As they worked through their tasks, the users completed write-along documents, which were visible to the evaluators.

During all the sessions, the users were located at home, connected to the Lyceum server via an ISP, while the evaluators worked on campus through a LAN.

## 3.3   NetMeeting Trial

In the development of the original LCR method the use of verbal protocols through telephone links was considered, but discounted as impractical due the disruption it would have caused to the users' work, and that it made communication with the evaluator, who could not see the interface, difficult.

In the experiment, we adopted a face-to-face method described by Wright & Monk (1991) for use with NetMeeting, which we used to guide the user–evaluator interaction. NetMeeting is an audio, video and data conferencing system developed and distributed by Microsoft Inc. NetMeeting supports real-time Internet

| Marking Tool Windows | LCR (13 users) | Lyceum (9 users) | | | NetMeeting (4 users) |
|---|---|---|---|---|---|
| | | Online | Offline | Total | |
| Marking Scheme | 10 (R = 3.5) | 2 (R= 3.5) | 3 (R= 3.6) | 5 | 2 |
| Main Window | 7 (R = 2.9) | 2 (R = 3.0) | 3 (R = 3.0) | 5 | 3 |
| Score Allocation | 17 (R = 3.4) | 9* (R = 3.8) | 4 (R = 3.0) | 13 | 5 |
| Total | 34 (R = 3.2) | 13 (R = 3.5) | 10 (R = 3.5) | 23 | 8 |

**Table 1:** Summary of usability problems identified — * includes four new usability issues, identified through the plenary session discussions, that had not been identified in the previous LCR trial.

conferencing and provides collaborative groupware. Users install the NetMeeting[1] application on their desktop and communicate with each other in peer-to-peer mode1 through the Internet. As with Lyceum, NetMeeting runs on mid-range Windows PCs with standard multimedia support.

In our investigation, the most relevant features of NetMeeting were peer-to-peer voice communication and the ability to share the user's desktop across the Internet.

### 3.3.1   The Sessions

In each NetMeeting session one user and one evaluator would work together to perform a remote usability evaluation synchronously.

In each session, user and evaluator were connected peer-to-peer, which allowed them to converse and share collaborative tools. The user's desktop was shared during the session allowing the evaluator to observe events occurring on the user's PC. The evaluator, taking the role of the designer in the face to face method guided the user through the usability evaluation, by conducting a remote conversation.

Difficulties with users' machine base and ISPs meant that it was not possible to obtain audio of an acceptable quality. (We note that similar problems were reported in previous experiments with low cost conferencing software, including NetMeeting (Shah et al., 1998).) Therefore, the NetMeeting sessions were conducted on a campus LAN with evaluator and user located in separate rooms. We made use of two high specification laptops, appropriately configured and tested for NetMeeting use. This allowed the same laptops to be used in all sessions. However, even in this configuration, the audio quality suffered excessive distortion.

## 4   Findings

Evaluation data were collected during the online sessions by the evaluators, as well as extracted from the user-compiled evaluation commentary and summative questionnaire.

Table 1 presents data extracted from the analysis of the users' comments. It contains the number of separate design issues/usability problems identified in the original LCR evaluation (Dunckley et al., 2000), together with the number identified in, respectively, the Lyceum and NetMeeting trials. Note that results

---

[1] NetMeeting can also be used in client/server mode; we did not consider this mode in our experiment.

|  | LCR | Lyceum | NetMeeting |
|---|---|---|---|
| Number of users | 13 | 9 | 4 |
| Total of usability problems | 34 | 23 | 8 |
| Mean of usability problems | 6.23 | 7.55 | 5.75 |
| Standard deviation | 3.76 | 2.78 | 1.89 |

**Table 2:** Statistical summary.

for Lyceum include both those for users working online and subsequently working offline independently.

R in the table refers to the average rating awarded to the usability problems by an independent HCI specialist. The rating of the usability problems is on a scale:

0 — generally usable

1 — minor usability problem

2 — significant usability problem

3 — serious usability problem

4 — catastrophic usability problem

The experimental method adopted was based on a between-groups randomised design where different users were involved in the different sessions rather than the same users being used for all three sessions. The advantage of a between-groups design is that any learning effect resulting from the user repeating the test with the same interface is controlled. The danger of there being significant variation between the groups was handled by carefully selecting the users who were drawn from the same population of associate lecturers and completed a user profile questionnaire prior to selection. The same issues were identifiable from many comments in all the three studies. Table 2 summarises a detailed analysis of user groups vs. method of evaluation. For example, with the LCR method as described by Dunckley et al. (2000), the 13 remote users identified 34 separate usability problems. However, from the table, there is no significant difference between the three methods in terms of the mean or standard deviations of the number of usability problems identified by the different evaluation methods. In addition the difference in means was tested in each case by using a $t$ test. In both cases the differences were not significant and the null hypothesis accepted: Lyceum compared with the LCR gave a value for $t$ of 0.38, and for NetMeeting compared with the LCR results, a $t$ value of 0.53 was obtained. Both results are well below the critical values. Further analysis using ANOVA (one way) gives $F_{(2,23)}$ as 0.60, which is not significant, supporting the hypothesis that in terms of number of usability problems identified there is no significant difference between the three methods.

Although for the LCR- and Lyceum-based methods there was no significant difference in the number of usability problems identified, there was some difference in the nature of the usability problems. The Lyceum plenary sessions identified four usability problems not identified by the previous evaluation: although three had

| *Question*: How does the Score Allocation window make it obvious how to allocate scores and make comments? | |
| --- | --- |
| *User 1*: I am not sure it does. Zero in box[*sic* ] made me experiment with putting score in and I discovered that if you clicked on arrow that this helped you position score in script. | *User A*: Each question or part of question is shown down the left-hand side of the score allocation. I hope this is the score allocation as it has only the name of the student for a title. The numbers are slightly confusing, as the question number and the question part are the same size. |
| *User 2*: There is a question tab at the top of the list of numbers for that question. The window shows a list of marks against a list of text fields. It seemed obvious to insert marks in the text fields and against each of the marks listed. To add a comment the arrow is raised and the text box is displayed whenever you scroll over it. | *User B*: The question numbers are listed. |
| *User 3*: Well, no I'm not sure. Your marking tool is confused. Blast. I pressed Yes for 'I am sure' and now it has put the mark in a silly place in the script. | *User C*: Not really at first. Problem: cursor was at 'start of text' but I could not move it because I could not move the score allocation window: each time I tried the error/warning window about the cursor position came up and became the active window preventing me from dragging the score allocation window away from the ... |

**Table 3:** Samples of users' write-along responses during LCR (to the left) and Lyceum (to the right) sessions.

subsequently been identified by users after implementation, one was a new usability issue not previously identified. As can be seen from Table 1, the severity ratings in the Lyceum trials are the same or slightly higher than those in the LCR trials, which implies that the more severe problems were identified in the Lyceum sessions.

For the LCR- and NetMeeting-based methods, sessions with the 4 users located on campus seemed to identify fewer usability problems. Note that the sessions appeared more stressful due to the tendency for the audio to break up and fewer tasks were completed in the online sessions.

One interesting finding to emerge from the LCR study using the write-along method was that the majority of users' comments read convincingly as though written while looking and exploring the screen. Although the LCR method uses a question and answer framework (see Figure 2), it does so in a style to empower the user by simulating direct conversation with the remote developer on equal terms. Holtzblatt & Jones (1993) describe active engagement as having the sense of a stream of consciousness discussion and this feeling was recognisable in many of the users' responses (see Table 3). This indicated that the users' behaviour was not substantially interfered with by the constraint of writing along in a Word document as they carried out their tasks. In comparison, the comments were terser in the Lyceum sessions. This terseness may be explained as a response to increased time pressure. Table 3

| | *Question*: Were you comfortable communicating with the other users and the evaluators through Lyceum? |
|---|---|
| User 1.2 | Very — once got to recognise voices — at first hard, as had to keep looking at who was talking. Easier 2nd time, as more familiar. |
| User 1.3 | Yes, except that I found at times that the sound reverberated in the ear-piece making it difficult to distinguish what was required. I was comfortable with typing responses. |
| User 1.5 | Very — it appears to be a splendid communications device. |
| User 2.2 | Yes; this seemed more 'human' than simple text conferences; 'hand' seemed a little 'school-like' but its purpose was clear; yes/no flags seemed helpfully basic. |
| User 2.3 | Apart from the connection problems this was OK. |

| | *Question*: Did you feel any anxiety about the way the evaluation was set up? |
|---|---|
| User 1.1 | Not anxiety as such: rather increasing consciousness that I was too unfamiliar with the context of the evaluation to make a very full contribution in the online trial: this was my first experience both with Lyceum and of electronic marking and a marking tool. |
| User 2.1 | Yes. I would have done it differently. We were asked to install the marking tool, but not to run it. It is simple to navigate and I would have felt more at ease in the initial stages of the test if I had been allowed to 'play' with the tool and to examine its components etc. There are no great technical demands with it. |
| User 2.2 | Not sure I'd use the term 'anxiety', I will admit to a little bemusement, and the feeling things other than an electronic marking tool were being assessed. |

**Table 4:** Extracts from users' reflective questionnaires.

gives examples of users' responses to the questions in the two methods — the write-along LCR method (Users 1–3) and the Lyceum-based method (Users A–C).

Users' impressions of the method and tools used in the online evaluations were captured during the plenary discussion and in the post-evaluation questionnaire. Mostly, Lyceum's users found the experience interesting and worthwhile. The voice communication tools were quickly used effectively in the plenary discussion. Users spoke naturally in terms of their own virtual evaluation room and the plenary room. They liked the chance of discussing their ideas online in plenary discussions, and regarded online collaboration a positive part of the process. Some users would have liked the chance to prepare more before the online evaluation. Sample users' views are set out in Table 4.

Users of NetMeeting did not express the same level of satisfaction with their sessions, although most of the problems were due to technical failures. Users reported having problems hearing the evaluator: this made the tasks very demanding. It was noticeable from the transcripts that both participants needed to frequently seek confirmation that what they had said had been received and understood. Users also expressed some anxiety related to the feeling of being constantly under observation.

However, the ability to observe the user's desktop was considered as a real asset by the evaluators, and proved a great advantage when dealing with critical incidents.

Compared to the write-along method, the online sessions stopped the users becoming 'lost' during the evaluation tasks, for instance, by trying to perform a task in the wrong window. In both the Lyceum and NetMeeting sessions, the evaluators were able to correct problems as they arose. On the other hand, when such situations occurred in the write-along investigation of Dunckley et al. (2000), they often resulted in a breakdown of the evaluation. This points to strength of online methods over the write-along.

# 5   Discussion

In this study, we have adapted the LCR method — a text based asynchronous remote evaluation method — for use with real-time audio and other synchronous conferencing tools over the Internet. The aim of the study was to evaluate the feasibility and effectiveness of this adaptation, compared with the original LCR. In the previous section, we have reported some of our findings related to the usability defects captured during the trials, as well as some users' perceptions of the trials. In this section, we reflect on methodological issues as well as discussing some of the practicalities.

## 5.1   On the Methodology

Is it sensible to ask whether our comparison is valid or, because of the experimental conditions and variations between the experiments, we were actually comparing 'apples and pears'.

Most usability evaluations are focused on evaluating differences in the user interfaces. In this case we used the same interface and the experiment was designed to investigate the effectiveness of the different variations in the evaluation methods.

### 5.1.1   User Profile

Each experiment employed different users, but they were samples from the same population of associate lecturers. Every user completed a user profile questionnaire prior to selection.

### 5.1.2   Prototype

The same prototype interface was the subject of each experiment and so each experiment had the same number of extant errors.

### 5.1.3   Method/Treatment

Between the NetMeeting and LCR trials, there were differences in the methods of evaluation. However, these differences were limited to using written questions vs. having an evaluator remotely monitoring and questioning. The main methodological ramification of this difference was that, since the evaluator could see the user's desktop, s/he could help during a critical incident rather than through an asynchronous communication (email exchange) which interrupted the evaluation. The methods of counting/measuring discovered usability problems were the same.

The methods of evaluation of Lyceum and LCR were more dramatically different because the Lyceum experiment involved users interacting as a group.

|  | LCR | Lyceum | NetMeeting |
|---|---|---|---|
| Tool evaluated | Marking tool | Marking tool | Marking tool |
| User training with tool to be evaluated. | None. | None. | None. |
| User training with conferencing tool. | Not required. | Yes. | No. |
| Number of users. | 13 | 9 | 4 |
| Number of usability problems identified. | 34 | 23 | 8 |
| Task description and evaluation questions. | In separate Word document emailed prior to evaluation. | In shared Lyceum text editor available during the session. | In separate Word document, transferred during the session. |
| Documents sharing. | None. | Yes, through Lyceum text editor. | None, but user's Word document visible through desktop sharing. |
| Type of session. | Asynchronous, offline. Individual user. | Synchronous, online. With 4/5 users and two evaluators. Combination of individual and plenary activities. | Synchronous, online. Individual user with peer-to-peer communication with evaluator. |
| Contact with evaluator. | No direct contact. | 2 evaluators per group of 4/5 users. | One-to-one evaluator contact. |
| Audio prompts. | None. | Yes for plenary work; LCR for individual work with occasional audio prompts. | Yes for Task 1, followed by LCR. |
| Group work. | None. | Plenary group discussion. | None. |
| Evaluator's visibility. | Evaluator only sees screenshots after evaluation completed. | Evaluator cannot see desktop, but can see shared task document. | Evaluator sees users desktop at all time. |

**Table 5:** Summary of the experiments.

Again, the methods of counting/measuring the usability problems were the same. The variances between the different experiments are summarised in Table 5.

## 5.2 On the Practicalities

From an operational viewpoint, the following issues were exposed during our investigation.

### 5.2.1 Session Duration

Online evaluation sessions, whether with Lyceum or NetMeeting, can make high demands on the participants in terms of concentration, given that they are required to carry out activities in real-time, with visual and audio input and output occurring at the same time. This effect is compounded by, for example, the often imperfect audio quality, instability of Internet connections and variations in traffic thereon. We found that we had to limit continuous online sessions to one hour in order to contain fatigue.

### 5.2.2   Session Scripts

For each session, evaluators were given designed session scripts. Each script provided a detailed plan of the session, including the set of activities, their sequencing, the tools required, and prompts to help the evaluators moderate the session smoothly. The scripts were very valuable for the evaluators during the sessions, acting as memory aids and helping with time keeping. They also allowed the rehearsal of the sessions and the running of comparable sessions with different groups of users.

### 5.2.3   Beta-testing

We beta-tested all our sessions in-house, before going live. This allowed us to test and finely tune all session designs. Moderating a synchronous online session is a sort of live performance and some general rehearsal is necessary, in particular in the Lyceum's many-to-many scenario. For instance, beta-testing our initial design for the Lyceum evaluation session highlighted the need for familiarising the users with Lyceum prior to the evaluation session, hence the introduction of training sessions. Also, it showed that it was very important to put users into separate virtual rooms. Although each user could work on their own document, even in a plenary room, it soon became evident that users were conscious of their progress vs. that of other users and this caused them anxiety if they felt they were experiencing difficulties other users did not, or were making slower progress.

### 5.2.4   Online and Offline Mix

Compared to the LCR method, the online sessions prevented the users from becoming lost during the evaluation tasks, which sped up the evaluation. On the other hand, working online can be quite slow and tiring. This limits the amount of work that can be carried out during a single session and makes online working unsuitable for usability evaluation of complex software interfaces. Our trials seem to indicate that there is a trade-off to be made: a combination of online and offline work should be adopted; neither solely online nor solely offline sessions appear to be optimal.

### 5.2.5   Technical Support

The amount of technical support required deserves serious consideration. In the current Internet panorama, it is unlikely that any real-time conferencing software could be deployed without technical support, in particular with real-time voice and collaboration. Some technical support will be necessary at least for software installation and proper configuration of the end-users' PCs. More realistically, further support may be required for fine-tuning of the software, to cope with heterogeneous PC settings, and the volatility of today's Internet connections.

### 5.2.6 Recording Facilities

We captured the audio of all sessions for research purposes. Audio capture was accomplished simply by using a high quality tape recorder and microphone connected to one evaluator's speakers. Digital audio and video-capturing software were considered, but could not be run because both Lyceum and NetMeeting require the exclusive use of a PC's sound card. Also, such programs tend to interfere with the conferencing software operation and cause a degradation of their performance. We are aware that this is not a perfect solution, and better methods may be required for larger scale trials, e.g. server-side digital recording.

## 6 Conclusions and Future Work

This paper has reported on an investigation into the development of an effective remote evaluation method applicable to users in their natural working environment. The method uses Internet communication and collaboration technology to facilitate the conversation between remote user and evaluator.

Two online approaches were discussed in the paper, based on adaptations of the write-along method of Dunckley et al. (2000). The investigation found that the write-along method was usefully extended by the addition of voice conferencing, which allowed for better support of the user/evaluator conversation and proved effective when critical incidents occurred.

Among the tools' features, the following were considered of particular value:

1. Many-to-many voice and moderation tools, to support focus group based evaluation.

2. Virtual rooms, to support task-based evaluation.

3. Desktop sharing, to allow the evaluator to deal with critical incidents.

Several issues were not addressed in the trial, and remain open for future investigation. For instance, no attempt was made to evaluate the impact of the quality of network communication over the quality of the evaluation. Although there is an obvious correlation between the two, more data are required to make such an assessment, in particular related to the viability of networked evaluation on a large scale. Importantly, the experiment has not addressed the role of the evaluation method in the context of a software development process and its relation to redesign.

## Acknowledgement

We thank our colleagues at the Open University, in particular the Lyceum development team, for their support, and the LTIC for funding this project.

## References

Castillo, J. C., Hartson, H. R. & Hix, D. (1998), Remote Usability Evaluation: Can Users Report their own Critical Incidents, *in* C.-M. Karat, A. Lund, B. Bederson, E. Bergman, M. Beaudouin-Lafon, N. Bevan, D. Boehm-Davis, A. Boltman, G. Cockton, A. Druin, S. Dumais, N. Frischberg, J. Jacko, J. Koenemann, C. Lewis, S. Pemberton, A. Sears,

K. T. Simsarian, C. Wolf & J. Ziegler (eds.), *Summary Proceedings of CHI'98: Human Factors in Computing Systems (CHI'98 Conference Summary)*, ACM Press, pp.253–4.

Dunckley, L., Taylor, D., Story, M. & Smith, A. (2000), Low Cost Remote Evaluation for Interface Prototyping, *in* S. McDonald, Y. Waern & G. Cockton (eds.), *People and Computers XIV (Proceedings of HCI'2000)*, Springer-Verlag, pp.389–404.

Goguen, J. A. (1996), Formality and Informality in Requirements Engineering, *in* C. Shekaran & J. Siddiqi (eds.), *Proceedings of the Second International Conference on Requirements Engineering (ICRE'96)*, IEEE Computer Society Press, pp.102–8.

Hammontree, M., Weiler, P. & Nayak, N. (1994), "Remote Usability Testing", *Interactions* 1(3), 21–5.

Hartson, R., Castillo, J., Kelso, J., Kamler, J. & Neale, W. (1996), Remote Evaluation: The Network as an Extension of the Usability Laboratory, *in* G. van der Veer & B. Nardi (eds.), *Proceedings of CHI'96: Human Factors in Computing Systems*, ACM Press, pp.228–35.

Hilbert, D. M. & Redmiles, D. F. (1998), An Approach to the Large-scale Collection of Application Usage Data Over the Internet, *in* K. Torii (ed.), *Proceedings of the the 20th International Conference on Software Engineering (ICSE'98)*, IEEE Computer Society Press, pp.136–45.

Holtzblatt, K. & Jones, S. (1993), Contextual Inquiry: A Participatory Technique for System Design, *in* D. Schuler & A. Namioka (eds.), *Participatory Design: Principles and Practices*, Lawrence Erlbaum Associates, pp.177–210.

Norman, D. A. (1998), *The Invisible Computer*, MIT Press.

Rapanotti, L. & Hall, J. G. (2000), Lyceum: The System and its Architecture, *in* E. Riedling & G. Davies (eds.), *Proceedings of ED-ICT2000*, Österreichische Computer Gesellschaft, pp.43–52.

Shah, D., Candy, L. & Edwards, E. (1998), "An Investigation into Supporting Collaboration over the Internet", *Computer Communications* 20(16), 1458–66.

Smith, A., Dunckley, L. & Smith, L. (1999), Importance of Collaborative Design in Computer Interface Design, *in* M. A. Hanson, E. J. Lovesey & S. A. Robertson (eds.), *Proceedings of Contemporary Ergonomics '99*, Taylor & Francis, pp.494–8.

Wright, P. C. & Monk, A. F. (1991), "A Cost-effective Evaluation Method for Use by Designers", *International Journal of Man–Machine Studies* 35(6), 891–912.

# Impedance Matching: When You Need to Know What

## Devina Ramduny & Alan Dix

*Computing Department SECaMS, Lancaster University,*
*Lancaster LA1 4YR, UK.*

Tel: *+44 1524 593490*

Fax: *+44 1524 593608*

Email: *devina@comp.lancs.ac.uk, alan@hcibook.com*

URL: *http://www.hcibook.com/alan/topics/web*

**Feedthrough and awareness of user activities are major issues in CSCW. A key difference between awareness and goal-directed feedthrough lies in the required pace and quality of feedthrough. Getting the right pace of feedthrough is important for usability and to avoid overloading networks. Notification mechanisms should therefore allow dynamic tuning of the pace and volume of update events. This matching of the required and supplied pace of update events we call impedance matching. A separable notification server is often ideally placed to perform impedance matching between end-user clients. These design principles have been applied in an experimental notification server Getting-to-Know.**

**Keywords:** awareness, feedthrough, notification mechanism, separable notification server, event notification, pace, CSCW infrastructure.

## 1 Introduction

Shared interactive networked interfaces present a large number of objects and artefacts through which collaborative users can interact with. Feedthrough (Dix, 1994) — the ability for one participant to sense the effects of another's actions — is essential in such interfaces to promote awareness and facilitate the coordination between users' activities. The faster the rate at which the updates are communicated to the users, the higher is the pace of feedthrough.

In the real world, the feedthrough between participants is mediated by the physical properties of artefacts and space, but in distributed electronic environments, some sort of event or notification needs to propagate through the network so that applications can inform users about remote events.

Our concern in this paper lies in the underlying computational infrastructure that enable systems to support feedthrough, and in particular, in the requirements and design of notification servers. A notification server is a piece of software whose task is to relay the fact that changes in data or other events have occurred. Others have proposed notification servers that are tightly bound to the data they regulate, for example NSTP (Patterson et al., 1996). However, we have previously argued that notification servers should be regarded as separate entities — certainly at a conceptual level and often physically distinct — and this was used as a design driver for our experimental notification server GtK, Getting-to-Know (Ramduny et al., 1998).

As discussed by Dix (1992), different types of task require a different pace of feedthrough. This may be a fraction of a second or hours or days. For example, in Pausch's 'Virtual reality for five dollars a day' he found that rapid feedback of low fidelity wire-frame models was far better than slower photo-realistic rendering (Pausch, 1991). Delivering feedthrough at the wrong pace can be problematic. If it is too slow, users may have to act without up-to-date knowledge of one another's actions. If it is too fast, users may be distracted by irrelevant changes.

Some feedthrough is very goal-directed — information directly used by users in their tasks. However, the collaboration literature constantly emphasises the value of awareness (Dourish & Bellotti, 1992). However, whereas goal-directed activity usually requires detailed and timely feedthrough, awareness is typically longer term and more 'fuzzy'.

For implementation, both the different feedback pace requirements and the difference between goal-directed feedthrough and awareness are largely about quality of service (QoS) (Rada, 1995).

These differences in QoS lead us to conclude that notification servers should be able to modify the rate and quality of notification to match the required feedthrough at the user interface. This facilitates the development of client applications that require rapid detailed feedback for goal-directed activity while supporting lower pace and lower granularity notification for awareness purposes. We call this matching of pace and quality, 'impedance matching' and demonstrate its application in the design of our notification server, GtK.

Due to the limitations on network bandwidth and computer resources, rapid feedthrough for all the shared objects is not always possible in collaborative interfaces. Indeed, even if a maximum rate of feedthrough is provided for each shared object over fast networks, further network congestion will arise. The extra computational load would undoubtedly imply additional delays for all the objects including the ones of higher interests to the users.

Matching the pace and quality of notification to the feedthrough required at the user interface means that we can reduce unnecessary network traffic, thus reducing 'wasted' use and making unintended delays less likely.

In summary, we have three main requirements for notification mechanisms for feedthrough and awareness:

- The notification server should be a separate component.

- It should be possible to control the pace of notification for awareness.

- It should be possible to control the quality/fidelity of the notified information.

In this paper we will focus on the second requirement. The first of these has been discussed in detail in a previous paper (Ramduny et al., 1998) and the last we will leave for future work.

Section 2 shows how notification servers as mediators are ideal for supporting impedance matching by controlling the pace of feedthrough. Section 3 examines how feedthrough demands can be reduced by subsequently reducing the pace and the volume of updates. Section 4 explores the potential triggers for pace impedance by analysing their effect on event propagation. Section 5 introduces the GtK notification server and Section 6 shows how GtK has been augmented to support impedance matching. Finally, Section 7 considers some outstanding issues that arise from impedance matching.

## 2 Where to Control Pace of Feedthrough

As we have already argued, delivering feedthrough that is effective for the user and efficient for the system requires impedance matching to control the pace of feedthrough. However, the best place where this should occur is not obvious. In this section, we will justify our choice of placing impedance matching within the notification server.

### 2.1 Interaction Without Notification Server

For the purpose of this argument, we will assume that each user is interacting through a single client device. For any change, update or user action we can consider the client of the user who initiated the action, the active client, and the clients of the rest of the users who receive feedthrough, the passive clients.

In the absence of the notification server, the active client is responsible for propagating changes to the shared objects to the passive clients. This can either happen through a broadcast mode (Figure 1a) or through a point-to-point interaction between the clients (Figure 1b).

In the first case (Figure 1a), all passive clients receive the same notification events. This means that events have to be delivered at the rate of the fastest client, and any per-user impedance matching has to happen at the passive-client end.

Consider the example of a shared drawing package. All the users may not be actively involved in manipulating the shapes and their sizes on the screen at the same time. So, when changes to the shared cursor are broadcast, the active client must broadcast each pixel movement to everyone, for the sake of the few users who are currently interacting with the particular object.

Although the passive clients can ignore unnecessary events, this consumes additional network bandwidth and computational effort.

In the peer-to-peer form of interaction (Figure 1b), the active client maintains a separate channel with each passive client. Consequently, the event stream can also

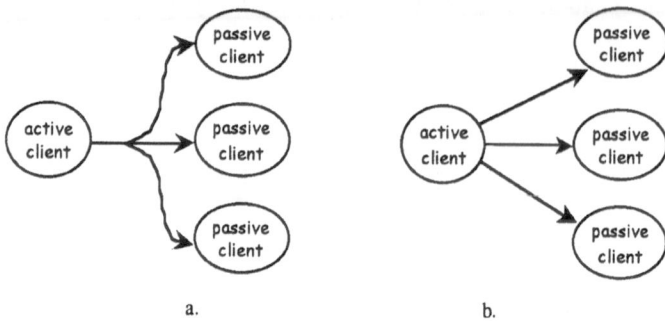

**Figure 1:** a. Broadcast mode of interaction. b. Point-to-point interaction.

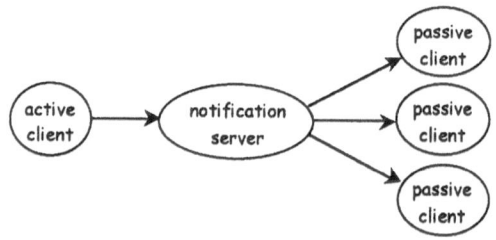

**Figure 2:** Using notification server as mediator.

be filtered on a per-client basis by the active client. This form of interaction enables each passive client to receive different rates of feedthrough, but at the expense of some fairly complex filtering mechanism at every active client.

## 2.2 Interaction With Notification Server

The presence of the notification server allows both broadcast and point-to-point mode of interaction (Figure 2). The notification server is the central point of contact between the active clients and the passive clients. The active clients send the changes to the notification server (broadcast) and it in turn can act as the mediator to adjust the rate that each passive client receives the updates independently (point-to-point).

The notification server does not necessarily have to forward the changes to each passive client at the same rate that it received it from the active client. The pace of feedthrough between the active client and the notification server will therefore differ from that between the notification server and the passive client. So, in order to obtain the right pace and the right granularity of the changes, the clients will have to negotiate with the notification server.

For example, at a user level, mailing lists distribute messages to subscribed users each time they hit the server. In contrast, moderated lists may send digests to users every month.

A bespoke notification server may have an in-built knowledge of the suitable pace of feedthrough required. But in general, the information as to what pace of low-level events is required to achieve appropriate user-level feedthrough will not reside in the notification server; the clients must communicate that information to the notification server.

## 3  Impedance Matching Policies

Impedance matching embodies both the volume of updates and the rate at which the updates are notified to the users (Ramduny et al., 1998). The feedthrough demands can therefore be reduced by:

- Sending updates less often (pace impedance).

- Sending less in each update (volume impedance).

Pace impedance deals with the frequency or the rate of notification while volume impedance influences the amount of updates that is transmitted to the user. A reduction in the rate of notification and in the volume of changes sent to the users can in fact cause an implicit gain on the resources. But this calls for a certain amount of filtering to be carried out.

### 3.1  Pace Impedance

The rate at which updates are sent out can be reduced by:

**Sending information less often:** The updates are buffered and communicated to the users when it is more convenient to them. All the information gets sent, including details such as the header, destination and so on. Only the rate at which the information is sent is affected.

**Sending chunks of information:** The information is sent in chunks to improve the overall performance. The size of the chunks or the frequency at which the chunks are transmitted can be reduced. This may cause a loss of information in some cases, but can be advantageous for lowering network overheads. For instance, message headers need not be transmitted each time messages are broadcast.

### 3.2  Volume Impedance

In addition to pace impedance, the volume of updates can be adjusted to make it more manageable to the users. The desire to reduce network bandwidth already puts some constraints on what users can see and how often they see them. Depending on the task, the amount of information sent across could be dropped to a minimum level and yet still be acceptable to the users. Users could thus receive a faster response time and the application could cope with high network traffic. However, this should not jeopardise the quality of information broadcast.

One example of this is the use of flags marking new or changed material. Flags convey awareness information at a reduced level of detail. By their very nature they are low volume, but also extreme timeliness is rarely critical.

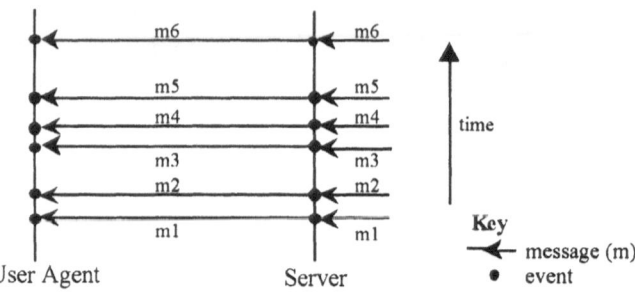

**Figure 3:** Time-space diagram without impedance matching.

## 3.3   Impedance Matching vs. QoS

Quality of Service (QoS) (Rada, 1995) ensures that the network channel has sufficient quality available to provide a better service for data transmission. This is crucial for maintaining a continuous transmission of audio, high-bandwidth video and multimedia information. QoS caters for delays and any necessary adjustments caused by the variable latency of the received data. QoS-based models also support the self-pacing of real-time data thus enabling data to be transmitted without any distortion.

When QoS is applied, for instance in the transmission of video images, the images are sent in chunks to reduce the frame rate, thus acting as a form of pace impedance. The images are also very often compressed and sent at a lower resolution and this is similar to volume impedance. So both pace and volume impedance matching can be seen to be a form of QoS. However, whereas most systems based on QoS are concerned with achieving minimum standards of throughput, the main motivation behind impedance matching is to determine whether the service can be limited to fit the data at our disposal.

## 4   Exploring Pace Policies

For the following discussion, we will assume a simple client-server mode of interaction, where user agents send messages to each other through a central server. Messages sent across the network are usually transmitted as events at the lower level. We will explore the different ways of obtaining pace impedance and show their effects on the flow of events through the use of time-space diagrams (Lamport, 1978).

Figure 3 shows the ordering of events on a time-space diagram. The horizontal direction represents space whereas the vertical direction indicates time in ascending order, with later events being shown higher than earlier ones. The dots represent events and the horizontal lines represent messages (*m*). Note that any latency in the network itself is not shown, as this is not a significant feature in the examples considered below.

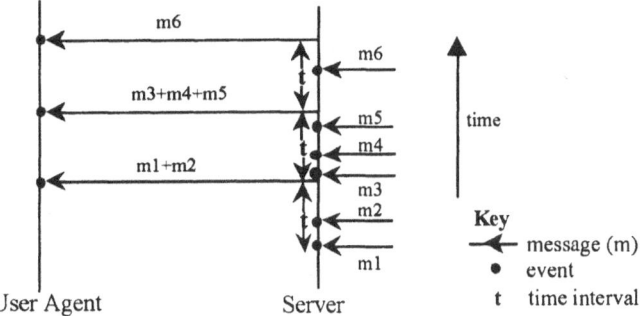

**Figure 4:** Time-space diagram with fixed time interval.

If the network connection between the client and the server is instantaneous, Figure 3 shows the ordering of events when no impedance matching is applied. The server forwards each message it receives following an event immediately to the user agent.

As pace impedance is about sending information less often, one could ask the question: how often should the messages be transmitted? Surely, there must be some kind of event that acts as a trigger, which causes the messages to be sent. The potential triggers for pace impedance are: the time factor, the volume of the message and the size of the message.

## 4.1 Fixed Time Interval

The client receives messages after every fixed time interval ($t$). The messages are buffered at the server-end until time $t$ is reached, in which case the messages are transmitted to the client in a single stream.

In Figure 4 for example, the first message stream consists of both messages m1 and m2 but only m6 is sent out in the third message stream. Because the time interval is fixed, the client can in fact poll the server. A classic example occurs in a mail system, where the client polls for changes from the mail server at regular intervals.

## 4.2 Time Delay

This option varies slightly from the previous one. Instead of sending events after every fixed time interval, an event is only generated after a time delay is reached. So, when the server receives the first message, it starts the timer and the messages are buffered until a certain delay ($\delta$) is reached, after which all the messages received are transmitted in a single stream to the user agent. The timer starts again when the next message hits the server as shown in Figure 5.

Unlike the previous case, this option is more server-based in that the server takes the initiative to generate events. The clients rely on the server to push messages towards them, as they have no knowledge of when the server actually starts counting the delay.

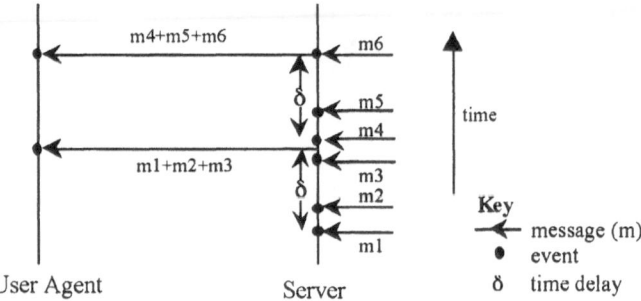

**Figure 5:** Time-space diagram with time delay.

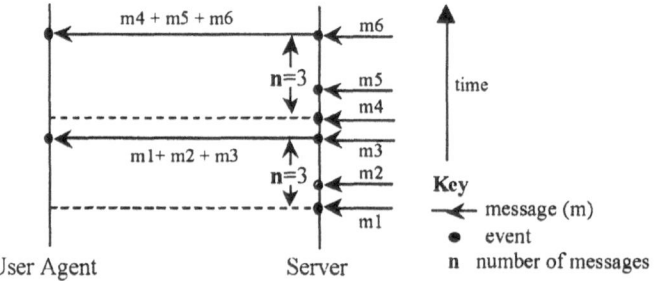

**Figure 6:** Time-space diagram with volume of messages.

## 4.3 Volume of Messages

In this case, the volume of the message acts as the trigger. The server buffers the messages until a maximum number of outstanding messages have been received, which are then sent out to the client in a single stream. Figure 6 shows the user agent receiving an event after the server has received a maximum of three messages.

This mode of pace impedance could be found in a shared text editor where it is not always effective to transmit all the keystrokes. The server could wait until a maximum number of keystrokes are received before sending them.

## 4.4 Message Size

With this option, the server forward messages to the clients once a maximum size is reached, for it is not always effective to send several gigabytes of messages. Figure 7 shows how the server send messages to the client in a single stream, once the maximum limit (max) has been reached. If the size of the message is below the maximum value, the message is kept in a queue and subsequent messages are added onto it until (max) is reached.

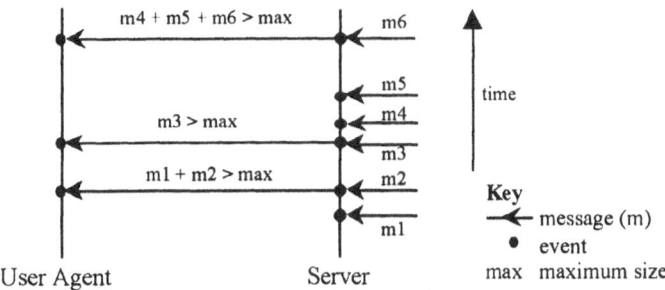

**Figure 7:** Time-space diagram with message size.

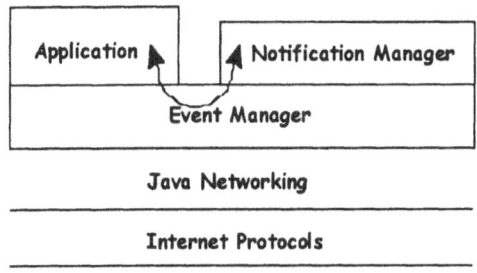

**Figure 8:** GtK infrastructure.

# 5 Getting-to-Know Notification Server

The GtK server is built over several layers of custom and standard infrastructure, as shown in Figure 8.

At the base lies the standard low-level Internet TCP/IP protocol accessed via Java networking classes.

On top of these there is a custom event management layer which supports directed message delivery between agents on different physical machines.

Finally, GtK itself uses the event manager to receive notifications about changes from active clients or information servers and then passes on the notifications about those events to the passive clients.

## 5.1 Messaging and Event Layer

The event management layer implements a distributed asynchronous messaging protocol giving GtK a uniform, generic location-independent event model. Whereas TCP/IP gives point-to-point messaging between the application processes, the Event Manager allows point-to-point asynchronous messaging between different communication objects in the same or in different address spaces. All messages and events are of the simple form:

```
sender reference : recipient reference : event_type : data
```

Applications add their own semantics for the uninterpreted ASCII data but utility classes are provided to enable standard argument marshalling.

Although the implementation of the event management layer is in Java, an ASCII protocol has been developed for message passing instead of using Java's Remote Method Invocation (RMI). This was due to several reasons. Firstly, at the time the development was started, Java RMI did not have solid foundations. Secondly, RMI is synchronous and thus does not fit closely to our preferred asynchronous event model for distributed agents (for various reasons, but mainly because our model is closer to the way modern UI code works). Thirdly, RMI depends on Java serialisation, which in our experience is not robust in Web environments, where different versions of the Java code may co-exist. Finally, the use of an ASCII based asynchronous messaging protocol makes it easier to add non-Java clients and servers.

## 5.2 Notification Manager

The distributed object layered infrastructure enables the Notification Manager to know about every other object. The Notification Manager can be controlled directly through message calls or remotely via the messaging layer. It uses the same event model as the messaging infrastructure, but also allows optional translation of event types.

The Notification Manager handles the three main functions of the notification server:

**Add interest:** Tells the server that a specific network object wants to know about specific events for a second network object.

**Remove interest:** Tells the server to cancel some or all of the interests for a given object.

**Tell all:** Asks the server to broadcast an event to all interested objects.

The above three functions together with a few additional housekeeping operations allow the expression of a wide range of different application specific notification strategies. They are similar to the facilities offered by the Java AWT Observer/Observable classes and AWT 1.1 event listener model except that these Java events are limited to a single Java process.

GtK maintains an interest table, which keeps a list of interested clients for specific objects. Each object in the interest table has one or more recipients as shown in Figure 9.

The interest table is updated based on the functions 'add interest' and 'remove interest'. When an object asks GtK to 'tell all', GtK first matches the event type and objects with the interest table and then passes on the event (with optional type translation) to all the interested clients.

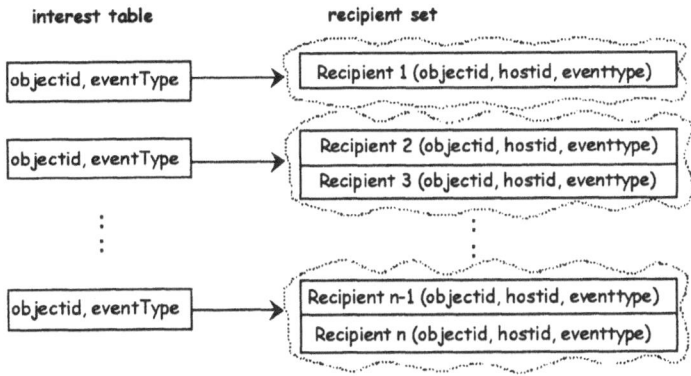

**Figure 9:** Relationship between interest table and recipient set.

## 5.3 Physical Location

GtK requires that the data invokes the 'tell all' function to inform clients of any updates. Unlike NSTP (Patterson et al., 1996), GtK is only loosely coupled to the data repository. GtK knows that data objects exist and that other objects are interested in them but it has no other application knowledge. Similarly, the data objects have to inform GtK by using 'tell all', but they need not be aware of other remote or local interested objects. GtK thus achieves a separation of concerns between the notification server and the data repository.

GtK can run in the same address space as the data objects, on the same server or on a completely different server. In addition, the separation of concerns implies that GtK can support several heterogeneous data sources, potentially on different physical servers.

## 6 Augmenting GtK for Impedance Matching

In this section, we will briefly describe how our separable notification server GtK has been augmented to provide pace impedance using some of the principles discussed in Section 4. Although impedance matching emerges from an abstract notion, it has been implemented in GtK to investigate its actual behaviour on a practical level (Ramduny, in preparation).

The pace of feedthrough can be reduced by:

- setting a certain limit (be it fixed or variable) on the volume of updates; and

- setting a time interval between the propagation of the updates.

## 6.1 Pace Parameters

Two pace parameters have therefore been defined:

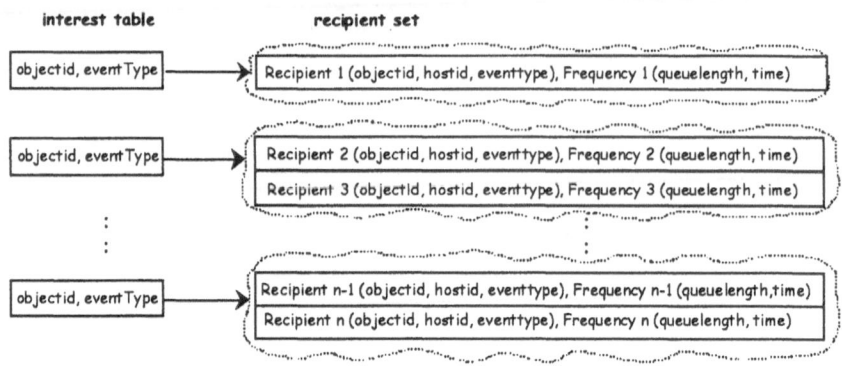

**Figure 10:** Relationship between interest table and recipient set with pace impedance.

```
queueLength // length of queue
```

queueLength allows a client object to specify the maximum number of messages or events that can be placed in a queue before they are passed on to the client (volume trigger, Section 4.3).

```
time // duration
```

time enables a client object to specify the maximum delay on events before they are passed (time interval trigger, Section 4.1).

These are combined into a single data structure:

```
Frequency = ( queueLength : time )
```

The default value for queueLength is 0, which implies an empty queue. The default value for time is −1, which denotes infinity. For example, a Frequency of (0,3) indicates that messages are buffered and sent out every 3 seconds whereas a Frequency of (10,−1) implies that messages are sent out in batches of 10.

The need to support impedance matching brings about certain changes to the main functions of GtK. In addition to keeping track of an object and its recipients, the interest table now has to be aware of each recipient's frequency (Figure 10).

## 6.2   Event Queue Management

For each recipient, a queue is maintained of outstanding events. New events are timestamped and added to the rear of the queue. Events are flushed and delivered to recipients at appropriate times depending on the pace parameters.

Events are flushed from the queue when either:

a. *current-queue-length* > *value-set-for*-queueLength.

b. *current-delay* > *value-set-for*-time.

where *current-delay* = ( *current-system-time − time-first-event-was-queued* ).

Case a is triggered when an event is added to the queue. Case b requires an alarm process to be set in the server. Conceptually there is one alarm for each non-empty queue, which is set to flush the queue at:

( *timestamp-of-the-first-event-in-the-queue* + time )

In the actual implementation, only one alarm process is used and set to the closest of the relevant alarm deadlines. This is reset when events are added to an empty queue or after the queue is flushed due to the previous alarm.

## 6.3 Altering Pace Parameters

In order to provide an acceptable pace of feedthrough that matches the users' task at hand, clients should be able to adjust the rate at which they receive updates from the notification server.

A client object can therefore change the frequency with which it wants to be notified of any updates by sending a *change-frequency* event together with the new values for queueLength and time. This will also alter the frequency of each recipient for that client object.

Note that different interface objects may require different pace of feedthrough. For example, focus objects such as the top-most window typically require a faster rate of feedback from background or iconised windows. Therefore GtK allows the setting of frequency parameters on a per object basis. Furthermore, the required pace will vary dynamically, for example, when a new object is made visible or a window is popped to the front. This is why GtK separates registering interest, typically once per object, from setting frequency which may happen repeatedly.

## 7 Discussion

The implementation of impedance matching generates some outstanding issues and these are discussed below.

### 7.1 Impedance Matching in VR

The notion of impedance matching can be found in other systems. Although the mechanism adopted in such cases is not explicitly called impedance matching and it has been employed to achieve different purposes, it does satisfy a similar functionality.

The collaborative model of awareness based on the spatial interaction of objects (Benford & Fahlén, 1993) depends on concepts of aura, nimbus and focus. Aura is a volume in space that delimits the presence of a particular object. Focus represents the objects in space that a user is interested in while nimbus represents the space controlled by those objects. The quality of information transmitted is said to depend on the level of awareness a user has of an object and this is negotiated through focus and nimbus. The role of the focus and nimbus are in fact similar to that of the focus objects. The closer the focus and nimbus, the greater is the level of awareness, hence the higher is the quality of information transmitted.

This model has been augmented with third party objects (Benford et al., 1997), which use aggregation to perform volume impedance in collaborative virtual environments, whereby a reduced level of detail is presented to the users without sacrificing the quality of the information. In order to manage the volume of data in such a complex environment, objects are grouped together and aggregate views of those objects are provided which expand further when they are selected (Ingram et al., 1996).

Recent work has considered ways of making delays explicit to users of Collaborative Virtual Environments (CVE), for example showing ghosts of past locations and predictions of current locations of remote objects (Vaghi, 2002). The current implementation on the HIVE CVE system Greenhalgh et al. (2000) is using full fidelity information but it seems likely that scaleable implementation will require pace management.

## 7.2   Impact of Rich Media

Although not discussed in this paper, our applet-based real-time Web conferencing application implemented using GtK (Ramduny, in preparation) only allows information to be exchanged in a textual mode. However, some chat systems like ICQ[1] also enable users to exchange communication verbally via voice-over-IP through the use of Internet phone such as BuddyPhone[2]. It is therefore essential that the rate at which information is exchanged through the different channels be kept in synchronicity to avoid a breakdown in communication.

When users talk through the phone while typing, the granularity of feedthrough becomes very fine-grained — character level instead of words or sentences. Consequently, the task of matching the rate of feedthrough between the two channels is not trivial. Furthermore, the introduction of additional media such as real-time graphics and video adds more demands on the resources and thus make the provision of feedthrough even more problematic.

Impedance matching is therefore required to manage the rate of feedthrough between the different channels. Some systems already provide a form of impedance matching to cope with the demands on bandwidth. For example, in media space systems such as Rave (Gaver et al., 1992) the video transmission is kept to a low volume and a low pace until a user actually clicks on the video, in which case the rate of feedthrough increases.

The solution adopted in Xerox Portholes (Dourish & Bly, 1992) makes use of frame-grabbing software for each media space and then distributing low-resolution digital images.

Similarly, in NYNEX Portholes (Lee et al., 1997), the WebCam operates at a slow rate but the images are transmitted at full speed. An integrative view of a particular group is represented through a matrix of still video images, which are snapped periodically for instance after every five minutes.

## 7.3   Ordering of Events

A major problem that impedance matching gives rise to relates to the ordering of events. Collaborative systems produce a large number of events of different kinds from several users at varying times. The order in which the events are broadcast

---

[1] http://web.icq.com/
[2] http://www.buddyphone.com/

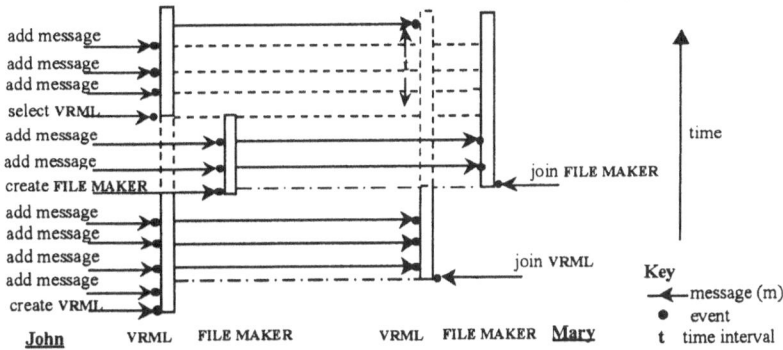

**Figure 11:** Timing diagram with point-to-point ordering of events.

may be critical in maintaining the cooperative activity. If users do not receive the events in the right order, they can easily get confused and in the worst case, they may abandon the task completely.

Let us consider the effect of impedance matching on the flow of events in a conferencing system. Figure 11 illustrates the point-to-point ordering of events between two users, John and Mary chatting on two conferences, VRML and FILE MAKER.

Starting with the lowest event, the timing diagram shows that John first creates the VRML conference and adds some messages to it. Mary joins the VRML conference shortly after. John and Mary receive an instant feedthrough of each other's messages at that point, as they are both focused on the same conference.

John goes on next to create the FILE MAKER conference, which Mary joins later. FILE MAKER now becomes the focus for both participants and conversations exchanged at that level have a higher pace of feedthrough than those in VRML.

At some stage, John decides to go back to the VRML conference while Mary is still active on the FILE MAKER conference. John now receives an instant feedthrough of all the messages added to the VRML conference but Mary only gets a set of buffered messages at a regular time interval (*t*). Given the different rates of feedthrough for the VRML conference, the order in which John and Mary receive the messages may differ and therefore run the risk of becoming inconsistent. The problem is amplified if there are some semantic dependencies between the messages.

A possible solution to deal with the inconsistent ordering of messages is to take a selective stance and delay all the messages until a certain time is reached and then send them out in the right order. But this measure will raise additional issues at the user interface level.

In a non-interactive system, this is only a problem if there are dependencies between the computational objects receiving the events and there are known ways of detecting this (Lamport, 1978). However, in interactive systems there are additional dependencies, as the user can see the effects on different objects, but the computer regards them as being distinct.

# 8  Summary

The central point of this paper is the analytic framework for impedance matching, which can be applied to augment other notification mechanisms or build new notification servers over different low-level messaging infrastructures. GtK is largely an example to show that these principles for notification server design can be achieved in a practical implementation.

We have explored the issue of pace impedance matching — the use of the notification server as an intermediary to match the required pace of updates of a passive client with the supplied rate of the active clients. Different parameters for regulating pace were considered, based on both time delay and number of outstanding updates.

Our experimental notification server, Getting-to-Know, is a 'pure' separable notification server that also supports pace impedance matching through maximum delay time and queue length parameters. Although not described in this paper, the practicality of the approach has been further explored by using GtK to build an example real-time conferencing system. To our knowledge, GtK is the only extant notification service embodying true separability from data and pace impedance matching.

Volume impedance matching is essential for controlling the quality/fidelity of notified information and it can be largely met by having different forms of application-specific, low-granularity update events. We have not dealt with this in any detail here but more generic approaches to this issue can be a valuable extension to our work.

# References

Benford, S. & Fahlén, L. (1993), A Spatial Model of Interaction in Large Virtual Environments, *in* G. de Michelis, C. Simone & K. Schmidt (eds.), *Proceedings of ECSCW'93, the 3rd European Conference on Computer-Supported Cooperative Work*, Kluwer, pp.109–24.

Benford, S., Greenhalgh, C. & Lloyd, D. (1997), Crowded Collaborative Virtual Environments, *in* S. Pemberton (ed.), *Proceedings of CHI'97: Human Factors in Computing Systems*, ACM Press, pp.59–66.

Dix, A. J. (1992), Pace and Interaction, *in* A. Monk, D. Diaper & M. Harrison (eds.), *People and Computers VII (Proceedings of HCI'92)*, Cambridge University Press, pp.193–208.

Dix, A. J. (1994), Computer-supported Cooperative Work: A Framework, *in* D. Rosenburg & C. Hutchison (eds.), *Design Issues in CSCW*, Springer-Verlag, pp.9–26.

Dourish, P. & Bellotti, V. (1992), Awareness and Coordination in Shared Workspaces, *in* J. Turner & R. Kraut (eds.), *Proceedings of CSCW'92: ACM Conference on Computer Supported Cooperative Work*, ACM Press, pp.107–14.

Dourish, P. & Bly, S. (1992), Portholes: Supporting Awareness in Distributed Work Groups, *in* P. Bauersfeld, J. Bennett & G. Lynch (eds.), *Proceedings of CHI'92: Human Factors in Computing Systems*, ACM Press, pp.541–7.

Gaver, W. W., Moran, T., MacLean, A., Lövstrand, L., Dourish, P., Carter, K. & Buxton, W. (1992), Realizing a Video Environment: EuroPARC's RAVE System, *in* P. Bauersfeld, J. Bennett & G. Lynch (eds.), *Proceedings of CHI'92: Human Factors in Computing Systems*, ACM Press, pp.27–35.

Greenhalgh, C., Purbrick, J. & Snowdon, D. (2000), Inside MASSIVE-3: Flexible Support for Data Consistency and World Structuring, *in* E. Churchill & M. Reddy (eds.), *Proceedings of the Third International Conference on Collaborative Virtual Environments (CVE 2000)*, ACM Press, pp.119–27.

Ingram, R. J., Benford, S. D. & Bowers, J. M. (1996), Building Virtual Cities: Applying Urban Planning principles to the Design of Virtual Environments, *in Proceedings of the ACM Symposium on Virtual Reality Software Technology*, ACM Press, pp.83–91.

Lamport, L. (1978), "Time, Clocks, and the Ordering of Events in a Distributed System", *Communications of the ACM* **21**(7), 558–65.

Lee, A., Girgensohn, A. & Schlueter, K. (1997), NYNEX Portholes: Initial User Reactions and Redesign Implications, *in* S. C. Hayne & W. Prinz (eds.), *Proceedings of International ACM SIGGROUP Conference on Supporting Group Work, Group'97*, ACM Press, pp.385–94.

Patterson, J. F., Day, M. & Kucan, J. (1996), Notification Servers for Synchronous Groupware, *in* M. S. Ackerman (ed.), *Proceedings of CSCW'96: ACM Conference on Computer Supported Cooperative Work*, ACM Press, pp.122–9.

Pausch, R. (1991), Virtual Reality on Five Dollars a Day, *in* S. P. Robertson, G. M. Olson & J. S. Olson (eds.), *Proceedings of CHI'91: Human Factors in Computing Systems (Reaching through Technology)*, ACM Press, pp.265–70.

Rada, R. (1995), *Interactive Media*, Springer-Verlag.

Ramduny, D. (in preparation), Frameworks for Enhancing Temporal Interface Behaviour through Software Architectural Design, PhD thesis, Staffordshire University.

Ramduny, D., Dix, A. & Rodden, T. (1998), Exploring the Design Space for Notification Servers, *in Proceedings of CSCW'98: ACM Conference on Computer Supported Cooperative Work*, ACM Press, pp.227–35.

Vaghi, I. R. (2002), Augmenting the Virtual: Model, Architecture and Techniques for the Representation of Delay-induced Phenomena in CVEs, PhD thesis, University of Nottingham.

# Multiple Viewpoints On Computer Supported Team Work: A Case Study On Ambulance Dispatch

## Ann Blandford, B L William Wong[†], Iain Connell & Thomas Green[‡]

*UCL Interaction Centre, 26 Bedford Way, London WC1H 0AP, UK.*
Email: *{a.blandford, i.connell}@ucl.ac.uk*

[†] *University of Otago, Box 56, Dunedin, New Zealand.*
Email: *william.wong@stonebow.otago.ac.nz*

[‡] *University of Leeds, Leeds LS9 2JT, UK.*
Email: *thomas.green@ndirect.co.uk*

A novel usability evaluation technique, Ontological Sketch Modelling (OSM), was applied to the analysis of systems used within a complex work setting, namely emergency medical dispatch. OSM focuses on the structure of the domain in question and the devices which are applied to that domain, in order to reason about the quality of fit between the two. This analysis shows how OSM can be used to identify misfits between domain (here incidents, ambulance calls and real-time call processing by ambulance service staff) and device (the computer aided dispatch system) in real work settings. We show how OSM can aid additional reasoning about the way in which a new or proposed computer system can both support and enhance existing work structures. The analysis presented here also yields important insights into both the still-developing OSM and the structure of emergency medical dispatch systems.

**Keywords:** usability evaluation, emergency medical dispatch, conceptual model, domain model, OSM.

# 1 Introduction

There is still a shortage of effective techniques that are suitable for analysing the systems used within a complex work setting. On the one hand, techniques based on approaches such as activity theory and distributed cognition yield valuable insights, but at a level of description that is not readily translated into implementation requirements. On the other, formal approaches that model tasks or systems provide a clearer bridge to requirements and implementation, but often do not scale well to complex systems. Approaches that bridge this gulf are gradually emerging — for example, Cognitive Work Analysis (Vicente, 1999) and the Resources Model (Wright et al., 2000). Ontological Sketch Modelling, (OSM) (Blandford & Green, 2001a), the approach presented here, also aims to bridge this gulf, focusing particularly on the users' conceptualisation of the domain in which they are working, the device representation(s) that support that work, and the quality of fit between the two. OSM is still under development; it is described briefly below. Here, we report on its application within the Central Ambulance Control room (CAC) at the London Ambulance Service (LAS). A secondary outcome of this work is a focused account of the work of ambulance control and the systems currently used to support that work.

OSM focuses on the structure, or ontology, of the domain and devices under consideration. By simultaneously modelling both the users' view of the domain and the devices that support work in that domain, the quality of fit between devices and users is revealed. As implied in its name, OSM is a *sketchy* approach to modelling; that is: we are investigating the value and limitations of models that are not constrained to be complete or necessarily consistent. This contrasts with most formal modelling techniques, which demand of the analyst that the resulting model should be both consistent and complete — a demand that appears to have limited the uptake of modelling in practice.

Models can be seen either as predictive tools, usually highly formalised, or as less formal, insight-bringing abstractions for assessing a design from a particular viewpoint. OSM belongs in the latter class. In developing a new approach to modelling, there are many key questions to be addressed:

- What is the core ontology of the model to be?

- How is the modelling technique to be applied?

- What kinds of insights does it afford (whether through the process or the product of modelling)?

Established usability evaluation techniques often miss the point that what makes a tool difficult to learn and use is the number of novel concepts to be acquired before productive work is possible. OSM successfully revealed such problems in two contexts studied earlier, namely drawing tools (Blandford & Green, 1997) and diary use (Blandford & Green, 2001b), domains in which tasks are frequently ill-structured. Ambulance dispatch represented an interesting domain because it contrasts with personal tools such as drawing packages and diaries on many important dimensions:

- Team working.

- Sub-domains that need to be described separately.

- Much information that is essential for participants, but not changed by them.

OSM describes *concepts* (entities and attributes that are significant in both the domain and the device), the actions that change the state of entities and attributes, and important relationships between entities, attributes and actions. Problems of misfit become apparent as the model is constructed. Both existing work concepts and existing support systems are taken into account. This contrasts with an approach such as contextual design (Beyer & Holtzblatt, 1998), which considers existing systems including work concepts and support systems, but does not explicitly consider the quality of fit between the two.

Constructing an OSM model involves developing a (semi-formal) description of the users' conception of their work system. This is done by role: if several individuals perform the same role, the aim is to construct a general model that captures the key features of their shared conceptualisation, rather than focusing on individual differences. The users' model is described in terms of entities and attributes (see Table 1 for an example), and the analyst may add annotations that expand on the key entities and attributes. This model is derived from an analysis of qualitative data from users — see Section 2 for an example of the kinds of data used. In parallel, a model of the device is developed, by reference to existing implementations, documentation, specifications, or other appropriate device descriptions. Again, entities and attributes are described and, in this case, information about actions is also included. These are actions that create or delete entities, and set or change attributes. The analyst is also invited to add annotations. In some cases — though this is not considered further here — there may also be concepts that are 'device-private', which the user needs to know about but cannot easily access or change.

Sources of misfits include key user concepts that are not represented by the device (forcing users to find workarounds) and device concepts that are not a natural part of the users' model (forcing users to make explicit or be aware of information that is not key to their conceptualisation). Misfits of the first type can be translated into design requirements that such concepts should be represented at the interface; misfits of the second type may indicate that the device representation needs to be restructured (to better fit the users' conceptualisation) or that device concepts need to be more clearly represented to the user (so that the users' conceptualisation can better adapt to them). A more detailed classification of misfits and account of their implications for design is under development.

In applying OSM to the LAS our aims were, firstly, to assist ongoing development work by gaining a better understanding of the domain, and, secondly, to prompt reflections on the OSM technique itself. We expected the modelling to be difficult, since ambulance dispatch is oriented towards procedures rather than conceptual structures, but were interested to see what it would yield. In practice, the analysis yielded important insights, about both OSM and the structure of emergency medical dispatch.

## 1.1   Central Ambulance Control at LAS

London Ambulance Service is one of the largest in the world, receiving an average of 3200 calls per day. The city is split into 7 sectors, each of which is managed by a sector controller with a team of support staff. Each sector team manages the work of about 35 ambulances, operating out of, on average, 10 ambulance stations. This is a much larger scale than any other ambulance service in the UK; for example, the metropolitan service described by Martin et al. (1997) receives 'hundreds' of calls per day rather than thousands.

The control room is organised into two physically separate sections, for call taking and dispatch. In the call taking area, there is one call supervisor's desk and 24 call takers' positions. Six to eight of these positions are dedicated for doctors' urgent calls. There is little communication between call takers: each is essentially 'on their own', although backup services are available when needed. The dispatch area is primarily organised around the seven sector desks, which are physically distributed around the room to mirror the layout of the city. Additional desks around the periphery of the room perform particular dedicated tasks such as managing the HEMS (Helicopter Emergency Medical Service) resources, dealing with vehicles that are off the road and providing the overall supervision for the room.

At each sector desk, there is a team of three or four people: the sector controller, who usually performs the role of 'allocator', deciding what resources (ambulances and other vehicles or personnel) to send to each incident; the radio operator, who maintains radio contact with crews on the road; and one or two telephone dispatchers who communicate with ambulance stations, hospitals and others (e.g. the Metropolitan Police or members of the public) by telephone. Although radio operators and telephone dispatchers are widely regarded as "doing the same function" — that is, dispatching vehicles to incidents — the different technologies they use have a strong influence over their actual roles. In addition, each has specified additional duties; in particular, the radio operator acts as a 'second in command' to the sector controller. The existence of so many clearly defined roles contrasts with the Services described by both Martin et al. (1997) and McCarthy et al. (1997), where there are between one and three main roles.

To set the context for this work and describe the basic functionality of the system being analysed, we present a brief history of developments within LAS.

## 1.2   LAS: A Brief History of System Development

Although London Ambulance Service has moved towards automating many aspects of operations, it has not progressed as far in this direction as many other Services. LAS achieved a certain notoriety when one attempt at computerisation failed in 1992, resulting in a blaze of negative publicity. While that failure is the most well known, it was not the first.

There have been many analyses of the failure (Page et al., 1993; Benyon-Davies, 1995; Finkelstein & Dowell, 1996), and those findings will not be repeated here. Following the major failure, LAS reverted to a manual (paper-based) system, used until 1996. It then adopted a new approach to computerisation, based on evolutionary design and implementation, involving users within the design lifecycle and employing a very small team of developers in-house. LAS went on to win an award[1] for their subsequent slower introduction of a computerised system for call-taking (Fitzgerald, 2000), in which call takers typed up details as the calls were being taken. As soon as the relevant sector could be identified (matching the address that had been entered against a computer-based gazetteer), the information was transmitted to the sector desk so that the allocator could start planning what resources to send. When the call was complete, the call details were automatically printed out on a 'ticket' at the sector desk. The allocator acknowledged receipt of the printed ticket, then whoever had dispatched a vehicle to the incident acknowledged that dispatch. At that point, the computerised 'ticket' would disappear from the display, although it could be recalled by entering the Computer Aided Dispatch (CAD) Number corresponding to the call. The sector staff could view various screens of information, of which the two most important were an overview screen listing all outstanding jobs (except non-emergency calls for which the scheduled time of arrival was more than an hour ahead) and a screen giving details of one call.

Further management of the call was done manually, using the paper tickets. The management of tickets centres around the 'activation file', or 'allocator's box'. This is a slotted metal box with each slot corresponding to a vehicle in the sector. The ticket assigned to a vehicle, representing the job to which it is currently assigned, is kept in the relevant slot. The ticket faces forward while the vehicle is on the call, and is reversed when the vehicle is returning to station but 'free'. The box sits between the allocator and radio operator, where either may easily access it.

Various new developments have recently been introduced, and more are ongoing. Some of the most significant changes have been as follows:

**Printing on station:** Until early 2001, all information about a call was communicated by telephone to the crew on station. Allocators can now send tickets to be printed at the station, and the telephone dispatcher can simply call to alert the crew to the arrival of a ticket and confirm which crew will be attending the call.

**Automating prioritising of calls:** Until Spring 2001, call takers followed a flip card-based manual procedure for taking call information. This is known as AMPDS: Advanced Medical Priority Dispatch System. Then ProQA, a computerised version of AMPDS, was installed. This included automatic coding of determinants, codes that categorise the incident type in detail. The installation was done in-house, integrating the system with data from the existing CAD system. Allocators can now access additional information about each incident, and the system bars allocators from dispatch acknowledging a job until they confirm that the ProQA information has been given to the crew.

**Mapping:** Automatic Vehicle Location System (AVLS) equipment has been fitted in all vehicles. In November 2001, the system was extended to present graphical information about the locations of vehicles and incidents on sector desks.

---

[1] British Computer Society Excellence Award, see www1.bcs.org/docs/01000/1097/pastwin.htm

## 2 Method

Data collected in LAS is being analysed in various ways, for example Wong & Blandford (2001), including the OSM analysis presented here. The data was collected from staff in LAS over an extended period of time, from August 2000 to September 2001. Consequently, the data covers a period when substantial system changes were introduced; however, it does not cover the introduction of the mapping system, which is the most substantive development in terms of information presented to sector teams. Data collection focused on the roles of staff working in the control room, but also included others:

- Early on, several members of senior management were informally interviewed, to establish their perceptions of key issues in system development. This helped to establish the context for the work.

- Internal LAS documents, including an internal audit report that analysed the roles of the various groups of staff within CAC, were studied. This helped identify the 'front', or official, version (Goffman, 1959) of what staff were expected to do and how their performance was assessed.

- Thirteen 1-hour interviews were conducted using the Critical Decision Method, in which staff recall details of a particularly memorable past incident (Wong & Blandford, 2001). Participants were 6 allocators, 5 radio operators and 2 telephone dispatchers. This provided data on major incidents (the kind that are, fortunately, rare) and staff's accounts of how they deal with them.

- 16 observation sessions with individual members of staff were conducted in a style similar to Contextual Inquiry interviews (Beyer & Holtzblatt, 1998), such that staff were observed working, and asked about features of that work when they had quiet moments between activities. Each session lasted between one and two hours. 5 call takers, 4 allocators, 4 radio operators and 3 dispatchers were observed. This provided data on routine operations; no major incidents were observed.

- Additional members of staff were interviewed and observed to help set the context of the work; this included a two-hour interview with a key member of the system development team and a day out with a crew.

- At three points during the study, our findings to date were formally presented to staff representatives and management, both to inform LAS of our results and also to verify those findings (by soliciting feedback on any inaccuracies that were detected).

The OSM analysis has been conducted by working through data (notably LAS documentation and transcripts of interviews and observations), identifying key concepts — entities and attributes — that appear in multiple sources or that are clearly important (according to the context in which the appear), plus relationships between those concepts and actions that change the state of the system. For simplicity, we model the system as if it were static, incorporating all the developments outlined above *except* the introduction of mapping.

## 3 Analysis

We structure the OSM analysis around the different roles played within CAC. However, first we outline some of the core components of a high-level system model. That is: there is a model of the system that a member of the general public would not be aware of, but that is a core part of the domain model for all workers in CAC. This model is very similar to that of systems implemented by other ambulance services, for example Martin et al. (1997). Space does not permit a full presentation of the model, but the core entities we can distinguish are as follows:

- Call types: there are three types of call, namely emergency ('999'), urgent (typically requested by doctors, for the patient to be transferred within the next two hours) and 'white', or 'Patient Transport System' calls, which are generally dealt with separately.

- All emergency calls have an AMPDS level allocated, representing the priority of the call. These levels are generally referred to as 'red', 'amber' and 'green'.

- Call tickets for emergency and urgent calls are all indexed by Computer Aided Dispatch Numbers (CAD Nos).

- The city is divided into physical and logical sectors, as described above.

- 'Virtual ambulance' identifiers relate a physical vehicle (with a fleet number) to a call sign which identifies both the station out of which it works (e.g. C5) and vehicle number (e.g. 01). The call sign generally identifies a particular crew for any given shift.

More details of the domain model are discussed below, as we present details of each role. The computer-based implementation (the CAD system) includes:

- Electronic tickets, which may be shown, listed, accessible by any individual, and may be complete or incomplete.

- The details of individual calls, as discussed below.

- Pending call list (shown on the allocator's screen).

- Information on nearest ambulance stations and hospitals.

There are constraints on this system: in particular, only one electronic ticket can be viewed at one position at one time; only certain roles can access or update particular information; information can only be updated on the electronic tickets while it is incomplete, and only by call takers.

For illustrative purposes, we present detailed extracts from the OSM model for the call taking role. Space does not permit full presentation of the model for other roles, so we discuss the most important points that emerged from modelling.

| Entity | Notes |
|--------|-------|
| Call | The call is a domain object, which is not 'known' to the computer system. |

| Attribute | Notes |
|-----------|-------|
| Incident or query? | Incidents have call records; queries have to be dealt with on a one-by-one basis. The most common queries are about estimated time of arrival (ETA) of an ambulance. |
| Chief complaint | The chief complaint determines what questions are asked. For some calls, the call taker stays on the phone and gives pre-defined medical advice on care of the patient. |
| Caller features | Calls from the police or a doctor's surgery are sometimes treated slightly differently from calls from the public. |
| Instructions to caller | May include pre-determined care information for the patient until the ambulance arrives, or instructions to prepare something (e.g. note of GP) for the crew. |

**Table 1:** The core attributes of a *call* (as a domain concept).

## 3.1   The Model of the Call Taker

The role of the call taker is primarily to take details of emergency calls and enter them in the computer-based form (or ticket). Questions are asked according to the AMPDS protocol, which is based on the chief complaint. Of the four roles considered, that of call taker is the least complicated. The call and its attributes are summarised in Table 1, and the corresponding device concept (also called a 'call' by staff, but referred to here as a 'call record') is outlined in Table 2.

The location of an incident is important; this may include information on the major road from which a minor road leads, or detailed landmarks for a call from a large place (e.g. Heathrow airport). There are two reasons for this focus on location. The first is that the computer-based gazetteer needs to be able to match the address to a map reference which determines the sector to which the call information is sent and which is also a key component of the directions given to crews. The second is that call takers seem to form a picture of the situation in order to get enough information for the crew to be sure of locating the incident quickly.

AMPDS is central to the way call takers work. Once they have identified the location to their satisfaction, they work through the chief complaint and other information in the prescribed order, asking only questions they expect the caller to be able to answer (depending on whether or not the caller was on scene at the time of the incident and how well (s) he knows the patient(s)). Call takers are aware that the determinant derived from AMPDS (e.g. 27D1S = serious stabbing) is matched by the system to ratings (e.g. 'red 3'), but many of them are unaware of how this information is subsequently used: "There's only red, amber and green. I don't think they take much notice of the other numbers, do they?"

Call takers are generally aware of other key domain concepts, such as tickets and sectors, but these have little impact on their work.

| Entity | Add by | Delete by | Notes |
|---|---|---|---|
| Call Record | Opening new record | Not possible | Call records are created for calls reporting (or giving up-dated information about) incidents. |

| Attributes | Set by | Change by | Notes |
|---|---|---|---|
| CAD Number | Set automatically by system | Not possible | Each call for the day has a unique CAD number. Numbers start from 1 at midnight. |
| Caller's number | May be transmitted automatically by exchange or entered manually | Overtype | |
| Caller's sex | Enter M / F | Overtype | |
| Caller's relationship to patient | Type in | Overtype | May be unrelated; may even be elsewhere — e.g. a care service. |
| Address information (of incident) | Typed in | Overtype | If the gazetteer does not recognise the information, there is extended dialogue between caller and call taker to re-formulate the address. |
| Map reference | Automatically generated by gazetteer when address is recognised | Not possible | See comment above. Many staff are dependent on the system to provide this information. |
| Phone number for incident | Typed in | Overtype | Only if different from caller's number. |
| Patient's age | Typed in | Overtype | Caller may not know accurately. |
| Patient's sex | Enter M / F | Overtype | |
| Chief complaint | Selected from list | Re-select | Initiates AMPDS protocol: determines which further questions are asked (there are 32 possibilities). |
| Conscious? Breathing? Alert? | Select y / n / unknown | Re-select | Call takers sometimes have low confidence in the response as terms are hard to understand. |
| Determinant | Select from series of lists | Re-select | Questions are pre-determined, depending on chief complaint. |
| Access information | Type in | Overtype | Call taker tries to ensure crew have good information for reaching the patient. |
| Safety information | Type in | Overtype | There may be reason to have concern for the safety of a crew. |
| Call category | Set by system based on determinant | Not possible | Of little relevance to call takers. |

**Table 2:** The core concepts of a *call record* (as entered into the CAD system).

There are no essential constraints or relationships that impact on the work of call takers. Because the CAD system is tailored to the call taking function, and much of the call taker's job is determined by the system, there is a good fit between system and role.

## 3.2   The Model of the Telephone Dispatcher

The primary role of the dispatcher is to dispatch crews from stations to calls at the request of the allocator. A secondary task specified in the Dispatch Audit Report is to maintain accurate vehicle availability records.

There are clear procedures to follow in giving out call information. When the dispatcher is asked to send a vehicle to a job, the job is referred to simply by CAD number, and the information is taken from the corresponding ticket. The ticket is usually on the screen, rather than on paper. The dispatcher is responsible for noting which crew from a station has responded to a call, and whether or not there is a paramedic in the crew. There is a good fit between the system and the task of giving out call information, but a less good one for the task of recording which crew has gone, because the dispatcher cannot enter information on the electronic ticket, and must note it on a separate form until the paper ticket appears.

One important attribute of call information for the dispatcher is how much of it has been communicated to a crew before they have left the station (if the call taker has not completed the call, which is common). The dispatcher has to mark on the paper ticket any information not yet given out, so that the radio operator can update the crew before they arrive on scene.

Dispatchers occasionally check the computerised list of nearest stations to check that they have heard the instructions correctly (if the station is nowhere near the incident, they may have misheard either the station name or the CAD number). Apart from this, the system is used primarily to retrieve electronic tickets before they have been printed in order to confirm the details to the crew.

As well as the tasks for which there are clear procedures, dispatchers are involved in various other tasks involving the telephone. These include:

- Taking calls from crews about various matters such as broken down vehicles.

- Calling hospitals to try and locate any crew that has 'gone missing', or to alert them to a 'blue call' (a very serious injury) that will require a trauma team to meet the ambulance when it arrives.

- Calling back to the address from which a 999 call had originated to get more precise directions on how to find the building.

In all of these cases, the dispatcher's role is to deliver a message, with content determined by someone else, to some destination. In order to do this effectively, dispatchers need to understand enough about the jobs of other team members to be able to make sense of sometimes cryptic messages. This role also involves some running around, as message are typically recorded on bits of paper that need to be delivered to the destination: this role in not yet well supported by the system.

Some dispatchers try to maintain a similar kind of overview of workload to allocators by typing in a succession of CAD numbers and seeing which upcoming jobs are likely to be for their sector: "Some people like to scan through them and ... I don't really worry about that." This task, while not core (it is done only at quiet times), is also not well supported by the system at present.

## 3.3 The Model of the Radio Operator

The primary role of the radio operator is to keep crews fully informed of all available information relating to calls at the request of the allocator. A secondary task specified in the Dispatch Audit Report is to maintain accurate activation files. The radio operators also receive calls from crews on the road.

The radio operator has to be aware of device concepts related to the communication medium being used — e.g. radio channels, vehicle fleet numbers and call signs, all directly represented on the radio operator's workstation: there is a good fit between this aspect of the role and the device used to support it.

One key concept the radio operator has to work with is the queue of pending calls, which is represented in two places: calls from crews appear as buttons on the screen, while calls requested by the allocator are represented by sheets of paper on the desk. At times of low workload, the existence of two streams to be integrated is unproblematic, but when workload is high, prioritisation across two sources is difficult. One extreme example is the beginning of a major incident: because radio calls are heard by all vehicles in the sector, during a major incident "they'll hear and go", and radio in, and CAC have to keep track of which crews have gone.

An additional challenge when workload is high is that crews have a concept of the radio operator as being busy or free: the only way for crews to assess this status is by the messages on the radio, so they may consider the radio operator to be free when in fact (s)he is busy in some other way — e.g. completing paper work. Radio operators may signal their status to crews by announcing "stand by unless priority". Workload problems are likely to be alleviated as more vehicles are equipped with data links, reducing the time needed for voice communications.

## 3.4 The Model of the Allocator

The obvious and most recognised role of the allocator is to allocate resources to incidents within their sector, aiming to keep within government-defined time targets. In practice, this entails many additional tasks, including:

- Maintaining adequate coverage within all areas in the sector

- Catering for the needs of crews — allocating meal breaks, organising appropriate support after crews have dealt with a difficult case (e.g. fatal road traffic accident), etc.

- Keeping track of the locations of all crews to ensure their safety and track their availability.

- Liaising with teams in other sectors and other services (fire brigade, police, etc.) to deliver the required service.

Resources need to be appropriate to the nature of the incident. Because the allocator's role involves rapid real-time decision-making (Klein, 1998), it is the one that is least well supported by the current system. Here, we outline some of the more substantial misfits between the allocator's conception of the task and the device model. The current OSM model for the allocator is 11 pages long, and therefore not included here. As with all other roles, the process of constructing the model involved working through transcripts and other allocator-related documentation, identifying core domain and device concepts and relationships between them, plus any misfits between domain and device.

### 3.4.1   Relationship between Incidents and Tickets

Of necessity, information about incidents is received — at least initially — through calls. For reference purposes, each call is allocated a CAD number, as described above. With the increasing use of mobile phones, the number of calls being received is rising rapidly: according to one member of staff, "the average six years ago was something like 2000 calls a day, maybe 2200." Now it is over 3000, and expected to rise further. It is believed that the numbers of both incidents and calls per incident are rising.

In the terminology of CAC staff, both calls and incidents are widely referred to as 'calls'. For example, one radio operator explained about "two calls which we linked to the same call ... I've had 7 or 8 bits of paper for one call". The action of deciding whether or not multiple calls refer to the same incident often involves allocators recognising superficial similarities (incident location, description, etc.) and then placing tickets side by side, maybe even showing them to a colleague, to judge the probability of them referring to the same incident. The current system provides no support for identifying duplicate calls, although it is planned as part of future developments, as described by one of the developers (here, 'RTA' is a Road Traffic Accident):

> "Since we've started using ProQA, or having determinants, there's always been the issue of what might be a possible duplicate call. Time is obviously one factor. Distance is another. The condition, or complaint, should be a key as well. But before we had determinants, all that was entered was free text, so there was no mechanism for doing a comparison. Now that we've got determinants what I'm going to do is effectively to get the users to provide me with a matrix of what are possible duplicates. Because a 29D2 might be a 29D5: an RTA vehicle vs. pedestrian as against vehicle vs. vehicle. [...] A snake bite probably is not likely to be a duplicate of an RTA. [...] We'll never make the decision automatically."

Allocators currently gather together information on an incident by grouping the paper tickets of all calls corresponding to that incident. Where information conflicts, they work with the best information available.

The current computer system does not support ticket grouping. Also, when there are multiple calls for one incident, allocators cannot clear them off their screen (until each one has been print- and dispatch-acknowledged) in order to distinguish them from calls for different incidents. One allocator, referring to the start of a major incident, described it as follows:

"Whenever something like that happens, the first call ... obviously the first call is gonna come up on the screen, and you see train crash, and you first think to yourself, is it real, is it not? Then you flick back to the first screen, and the screen's full with calls, so maybe you think, this is a real one. [ ... ] Well when they are on my screen, I press F1 to view the calls [ ... ] and I'll view it and I go "That's the same". Flick on through it, "That's the same", 'cos they have all got a train crash or the same location, but in all of that I might have had someone in a house that has fallen down the stairs, that's why it is very important to check through and make sure that the tickets are all the same."

This is an example of a misfit — in this case, between the call and the incident. The computer system only supports processing in terms of calls, and does not support either the identification of calls that relate to the same incident or the kind of grouping of information that is done using the paper tickets.

### 3.4.2 The 'Story' of One Incident

Just as multiple calls may (unwittingly) give information about the same incident, so successive calls may make reference to the same event. For example, a patient's representative may ring in again with further information, or querying the estimated time of arrival of an ambulance. Matching items to one stream of activity is poorly supported at the moment, relying largely on the memory of the allocator.

### 3.4.3 Stack of Outstanding Job Sheets

Tickets for outstanding urgent jobs are arranged on the desk in front of the allocator. Paper tickets appear to be used in preference to the computer-based tickets because they include all outstanding jobs, they can be ordered by time, and the most important information can be made permanently visible by writing it at the top. As Mackay (1999) notes in a different context, the physical actions of writing information at the top of the ticket and of manipulating tickets both appear to contribute to their effective use in supporting planning behaviour. The (partially ordered) stack of outstanding jobs is not well supported by the computer system implementation. Put another way, the allocators process emergency and urgent calls in substantially different ways, and this difference is not fully implemented within the current computer system.

### 3.4.4 A Ticket for a Vehicle

If multiple vehicles are needed for one incident, multiple copies of one ticket are printed. One ticket is then allocated to each vehicle 'slot' as it is dispatched. The location of tickets in slots serves to relate the vehicle to the incident. The act of printing out duplicate tickets helps the allocator to plan how many vehicles to send, and to track how many have been dispatched. Paper tickets are a 'mediating representation' that support allocators in their primary task of dispatching vehicles to incidents. In particular, if vehicles from another sector are being sent, tickets are physically handed from one allocator to the other, signifying a transfer of responsibility. In OSM terms, domain relationships are represented through the system as follows:

- Incidents occur in sectors, represented within the CAD system and revealed when a computerised ticket appears at a particular sector desk.

- Vehicles 'belong' to sectors, represented in the slotted box at the sector desk and also at the radio operator's workstation.

- Vehicles are sent to incidents, represented by the location of the paper ticket.

One consequence of the current implementation, with 'hard' sector boundaries, is that these cross-sector transfers cannot be easily organised until the paper ticket has been printed.

### 3.4.5   Incidents and Stations

As noted above, information on the nearest stations (and also nearest hospitals) is provided by the computer system. We have not observed this being used 'in earnest' by allocators. They appear to rely more on their knowledge of the area and of traffic patterns in the area — as well as availability of vehicles at each station — when identifying the most appropriate station from which to send an ambulance.

Because the computer system does not have information about the locations of vehicles — for example whether there are any currently at a particular station — the information about nearest stations appears to be of little value to allocators although, as noted above, it is sometimes used by dispatchers.

One of the allocators, describing a major incident, discussed details of traffic movement between a station and the incident:

> "Traffic's gonna be mayhem around the stations, even though you gotta send all them ambulances there, you know, you gotta start thinking of the time of day as well, traffic, you know, what's the best ways in and things like that."

The knowledge allocators are using when managing the allocation of resources to incidents is sophisticated, exploiting past experience, and cannot be neatly packaged in terms of easily identified parameters such as 'nearness', particularly in a complex and busy environment such as London.

### 3.4.6   Vehicles and Crews

Allocators appear to think largely in terms of unit of resources. Information about a particular crew will come in when there is an exceptional situation to handle, but generally the vehicle and crew are considered together. So, for example, an individual becoming unavailable at some time is thought of in terms of the impact that has on resources. Vehicles are also thought of in terms of their crew type — for example 'hotel crew' (i.e. paramedic crew), first responder unit, etc.— particularly in terms of their appropriateness to a particular incident. However, for 'standard' requirements, the allocator will simply request a vehicle from a particular station, or give permission for any crew from a station to have a meal break, delegating the detailed allocation to the station itself and simply noting what choice is made.

Allocators keep a paper record of crew shift times, meal times, etc. They use work-arounds like marking vehicles as unavailable if a crew needs time to recover after a difficult job. The current computer-based system provides no support for crew management.

### 3.4.7 Vehicle Locations

Experienced allocators have developed the ability to track the probable locations of the vehicles under their command — certainly in situations where they plan to intercept a vehicle on its route back to station and send it elsewhere. For example, an allocator sending an ambulance on an urgent (i.e. not emergency) call when it was part-way back from a hospital to its station explained:

> " ... if I give him a SW2 call at Mayday, I could have another vehicle come up nearer. [ ... ] So I let him get back a while into his own area, and then give him the call. Because between Mayday ... you've got Mayday and you've got Thornton Heath. He has to go through Thornton Heath, then he goes through Norbury, then he goes that way, then they go Lower Streatham, to Streatham Vale End, then they come up to Streatham Hill. So when they get up near that area ... it's just by judgement, of knowing your areas."

As noted above, mapping has recently been introduced, so that this information is readily available to allocators, but was not at the time of this study: at that time, this could have been viewed as a misfit between the computer system and the information needed. Whether allocators shift to using the external representation of vehicle locations, or whether they will continue to work with their ability to track this information mentally, is a question for further research.

### 3.4.8 The Allocator's Mental Picture and Level of Cover

Experienced allocators have a very detailed knowledge of their area. They know without looking how many vehicles are normally based at each station, where normal stand-by points are, where stations are, which hospitals normally have particular facilities. When they come on duty, they simply have to adapt their general knowledge to local variations — for example "that'll be a vehicle down". While on duty, they are updating their mental picture, or situation awareness (Wong & Blandford, 2001), with real-time information such as the locations and availability of particular vehicles. In maintaining their mental pictures of their sector, allocators ensure that all areas within the sector have adequate cover. Selection of ambulance(s) for a particular incident is made with this in mind. During a major incident that draws all vehicles from an area to one spot, other ambulances are moved in to provide cover. Again, the recently introduced mapping system should help allocators rapidly check that cover is being maintained.

Another aspect of the 'big picture' is keeping an overview of new incidents in the sector. Allocators flick rapidly between overview and detail screens to see the details of a call while also maintaining an overall picture of the level of demand within their sector. The current computer implementation does not indicate the arrival of a new call while the allocator is viewing the details of a call — this can only be seen when in overview mode. A revised implementation would ideally address these twin needs of needing overview and details in a seamless way.

# 4 Discussion and Conclusions

Modelling the LAS with OSM has successfully generated many insights into the quality of fit between each group of workers and the supporting computer systems. While in many cases a good fit was found, in some cases the fit was less good; for example we have discussed eight important features of the allocator's task that are poorly supported by the current implementation. As noted above, however, the computer support system is still evolving, so it will be possible to address these issues as part of the ongoing development work.

Using OSM also allows comparison between different work groups, e.g. allocators and call takers. Not surprisingly, nearly all important concepts are used by the allocators; call takers share the smallest subset of those concepts, but the set that is best matched by the currently implemented computer system. The remaining two groups, telephone dispatchers and radio operators, gave us a surprise. Although they are described as 'doing the same job', these two groups share a relatively small set of key concepts with each other, though each shares a substantial set with the allocator. The existing computer implementation supports dispatchers and radio operators reasonably well, but supports allocators less well. Overall, the current system works well because the paper system is manipulated expertly by highly skilled individuals.

We believe it unlikely that these insights could have been obtained from analysis techniques based more directly on tasks, procedures and actions. In this case, for roles other than call-taking, the lack of computer-system-related actions rendered the explicit description of actions largely fruitless. Although most of the work of ambulance dispatch consists of standard physical actions which can indeed be modelled using traditional task-centred approaches — making telephone calls, handing over pieces of paper, etc.— modelling these actions reveals little about how well the computer and other systems support the primary tasks of the staff. As in most complex work domains, the prescribed and implemented systems work well for standard tasks, but various workarounds have evolved to deal with unusual situations, so that *in practice* work flows efficiently, effectively and reliably.

The exercise has also increased our knowledge of OSM and its applicability. In the first place, we have learnt that the technique successfully scales up from our earlier domains of study (drawing tools and diary systems) to large, multi-person work systems. Moreover, the investment of effort was not unreasonably high. Whereas it would have taken weeks to produce a fully formal model of this domain, if it were possible at all, the OSM model was created in a few days. The approach of sketchy modelling does, subjectively, appear to yield useful results for reasonable effort.

We were particularly pleased to find that sub-systems of the LAS, reflecting the different roles, could successfully be separated out for analysis. Inevitably problems of boundary demarcation and inclusiveness arose: for example should we model roles within the organisation as part of the system? Should we model the HEMS desk or other specialist desks? We invariably opted for the simpler approach. However, as a sketchy approach to modelling, OSM would allow either decision to be taken.

Unlike the domains previously studied, ambulance dispatch contains plentiful many-to-many relationships between domain terms and concepts. As noted above, the term 'call' can refer to at least three different concepts: the actual telephone call, the electronic record of that call, or the incident to which a call refers. Similarly, 'red' is used to refer to a category of call (highest priority), to the colour of a ticket (which means 'emergency' rather than 'urgent' or 'patient transport'), or to the underlining on a ticket to show information that has not yet been communicated to a crew ("it's got red on it"). Conversely, the highest priority of call is often referred to as 'category A' (rather than 'red'). Consequently, extracting concepts from verbal protocols was far from straightforward, and required validation with LAS staff. Once noted, this was readily accommodated in the OSM model.

Overall, our first large-scale exercise with OSM has proved very successful. Modelling the domain and device in terms of entities, attributes, actions and relationships has proved feasible, and has yielded a model that helped provide useful insights on the domain.

Ongoing work is focusing on refining the model, clarifying the approach to modelling, testing in other domains (with other groups of users and developers) and developing tool support for model building.

## Acknowledgements

We are very grateful to all staff in CAC and elsewhere in LAS who gave time to contribute to this study, and particularly to Avril Hardy, Development Manager for CAC, for comments on an earlier version of this paper. The work has been supported by grants from Middlesex University and EPSRC (GR/R39108).

## References

Benyon-Davies, P. (1995), "Information Systems 'Failure': The Case of the London Ambulance Service's Computer Aided Despatch Project", *European Journal of Information Systems* 4(3), 171–84.

Beyer, H. & Holtzblatt, K. (1998), *Contextual Design: Defining Customer-centered Systems*, Morgan-Kaufmann.

Blandford, A. & Green, T. R. G. (2001a), From Tasks to Conceptual Structures: Misfit Analysis, *in* J. Vanderdonckt, A. Blandford & A. Derycke (eds.), *Proceedings of IHM-HCI'2001, Joined Conference on Human–Computer Interaction: Volume 2*, Cépaduès-Editions, pp.113–6.

Blandford, A. E. & Green, T. R. G. (1997), OSM: An Ontology-based Approach to Usability Evaluation, *in* E. O'Neill (ed.), *Proceedings of Workshop on Representations*, Queen Mary & Westfield College, pp.82–91.

Blandford, A. E. & Green, T. R. G. (2001b), "Group and Individual Time Management Tools: What You Get Is Not What You Need", *Personal and Ubiquitous Computing* 5(4), 213–30.

Finkelstein, A. & Dowell, J. (1996), A Comedy of Errors: The London Ambulance Service Case Study, *in Proceedings of the 8th International Workshop on Software Specification & Design (IWSSD-8)*, IEEE Computer Society Press, pp.2–4.

Fitzgerald, G. (2000), *IT at the Heart of Business*, Vol. 1 of *The IS Management Series*, BBC Books.

Goffman, E. (1959), *The Presentation of Self in Everyday Life*, Doubleday.

Klein, G. A. (1998), *Sources of Power: How People Make Decisions*, MIT Press.

Mackay, W. (1999), "Is Paper Safer? The Role of Paper Flight Strips in Air Traffic Control", *ACM Transactions on Computer–Human Interaction* **6**(4), 311–40.

Martin, D., Bowers, J. & Wastell, D. (1997), The Interactional Affordances of Technology: An Ethnography of Human–Computer Interaction in an Ambulance Control Centre, *in* H. Thimbleby, B. O'Conaill & P. Thomas (eds.), *People and Computers XII (Proceedings of HCI'97)*, Springer-Verlag, pp.263–81.

McCarthy, J. C., Wright, P. C., Healey, P., Dearden, A. & Harrison, M. D. (1997), Locating the Scene: The Particular and the General in Contexts of Ambulance Control, *in* S. C. Hayne & W. Prinz (eds.), *Proceedings of International ACM SIGGROUP Conference on Supporting Group Work, Group'97*, ACM Press, pp.101–10.

Page, D., Williams, P. & Boyd, D. (1993), *Report of the Inquiry into the London Ambulance Service*, South West Thames Regional Health Authority.

Vicente, K. J. (1999), *Cognitive Work Analysis: Towards Safe, Productive and Healthy Computer-based Work*, Lawrence Erlbaum Associates.

Wong, B. L. W. & Blandford, A. E. (2001), Situation Awareness and its Implications for Human–Systems Interaction, *in* W. Smith, R. Thomas & M. Apperley (eds.), *Proceedings of Australian Conference on Computer–Human Interaction OzCHI 2001*, IEEE Computer Society Press, pp.181–6.

Wright, P. C., Fields, R. E. & Harrison, M. D. (2000), "Analysing Human–Computer Interaction as Distributed Cognition: The Resources Model", *Human–Computer Interaction* **15**(1), 1–41.

# Design Process

# Pattern Languages in Participatory Design

## Janet Finlay, Elizabeth Allgar, Andy Dearden[†] & Barbara McManus[‡]

*School of Computing, Leeds Metropolitan University, Beckett Park, Leeds LS6 3QS, UK.*

Tel: *+44 113 283 2600*

Email: *{j.finlay, e.allgar}@lmu.ac.uk*

[†] *School of Computing & Management Science, Sheffield Hallam University, Sheffield S1 1WB, UK.*

Tel: *+44 114 225 2916*

Email: *a.m.dearden@shu.ac.uk*

[‡] *Department of Computing, University of Central Lancashire, Preston PR1 2HE, UK.*

Tel: *+44 1772 893288*

Email: *bmcmanus@uclan.ac.uk*

In recent years the Human–Computer Interaction community has witnessed a growing interest in the use of design patterns and pattern languages, a representation for design knowledge based on the work of the architect Christopher Alexander. In this paper, we re-examine Alexander's work, highlighting his participatory approach to design, his use of patterns in design generation and his ethical commitment to designing life-enhancing artefacts. Based on this review, we report on three studies exploring the use of pattern languages as tools to support a participatory approach to interactive systems design. Our results suggest that pattern languages can enable users to participate in a generative design process but that issues of form and facilitation need careful consideration.

**Keywords:** pattern languages, participatory design, Christopher Alexander.

# 1    Introduction

In recent years the Human–Computer Interaction (HCI) community has witnessed a growing interest in the use of design patterns and pattern languages, a form of representation for design knowledge based on the work of the architect Christopher Alexander (1979; 1977). Much of this interest has been inspired by the perceived success of the software engineering community in applying the concept of design patterns. Indeed, the parallels between architectural and interaction design, with their common concern for the design of the human environment, are arguably closer than those between architecture and Software Engineering, suggesting the benefits to HCI may be even greater. For software engineers, the main purpose of patterns has been to share successful solutions within the profession (Gamma et al., 1995). In HCI, the emphasis has been the same, as is evident from the definition generated at the INTERACT'99 patterns workshop:

> "The goals of an HCI pattern language are to share successful HCI design solutions *among HCI professionals ...*" (Borchers, 2001, p.39, our emphasis)

Alexander (1979, p.247) described a pattern as:

> " ... a three part rule, which expresses a relation between a certain context, a problem and a solution."

An example of a pattern is 'Sitting Wall', for which the problem and solution are given:

> **"In many places walls and fences between outdoor spaces are too high; but no boundary at all does injustice to the subtlety of the divisions between the spaces.**
>
> ... (body of pattern omitted)...
>
> Therefore:
>
> **Surround any natural outdoor area with low walls, about 16 inches high, and wide enough to sit on, at least 12 inches wide."** (Alexander et al., 1977, Pattern 243, author's emphasis)

The patterns are organised into a hierarchy with high-level patterns addressing problems such as the size and distributions of cities, moving down through patterns about civic arrangements, to patterns for individual buildings and individual rooms. Each pattern includes links to its parents and children within the hierarchy. By traversing the hierarchy, the user of the language is supported in 'generating' complete designs, but the solutions offered are generic rather than specific instantiations. According to Alexander:

> "Each pattern describes a problem which occurs over and over again in our environment, and then describes the core of the solution to that problem, in such a way that you can use this solution a million times over, without ever doing it the same way twice" (Alexander et al., 1977, p.x).

In this paper we re-examine the writings of Christopher Alexander and we explore the implications of his work for pattern language research in HCI. We begin by drawing out three key dimensions in Alexander's original work: his commitment to empowering users to participate in design, his notion of design generation and his requirement for life enhancing outcomes. We compare these to participatory design values in HCI. We then report on three studies in which we investigate the use of pattern languages in terms of these criteria. Finally, we highlight some factors which seem to be significant if we are to develop and use pattern languages in HCI in a way which reflects the criteria embodied in Alexander's work.

## 2 Alexandrian Principles

As we have noted, Alexander did more than propose a method to encapsulate good practice and facilitate reuse amongst colleagues. He saw pattern languages as a means of generating living structures that would improve the lives of the people who used them and a means of giving users control of these designs. Here we examine in more detail three related criteria that Alexander saw as central: empowering users to participate in design, generative design and life enhancing outcomes.

### 2.1 Empowering Users to Participate in Design

Alexander saw the issue of user participation in design as more than just good practice or political imperative, but as essential to successful building:

> " ... it is virtually impossible to get a building that is well adapted to these needs if the people who are the actual users do not design it." (Alexander et al., 1975, p.42)

His pattern language was therefore addressed to users, not design professionals. User participation is more than simply asking users to indicate their requirements or preferences: it is enabling users to actively and directly design their own spaces. Pattern languages were the means Alexander proposed for supporting users to do this. This emphasis is also important in participatory design in HCI. Greenbaum & Kyng for example, identify the need for a switch in focus:

> "...from users as passive participants in systems design to active user-designer cooperation." (Greenbaum & Kyng, 1991, p.14)

Alexander explicitly rejected the view that people do not know what they need or that professionals know best, often an objection given to supporting full participation in design:

> "Over and over again, we found that the families did understand, deeply and concretely, what they needed; while the arrogant views of the bank, of the public officials, that they knew what was good for the families, or that only 'architects' were competent to decide such questions, were pompous and absurd." (Alexander et al., 1985, p.204).

Not only do people know their needs but participation in design is intrinsically good, contributing to the sense of ownership and satisfaction that people have in the thing constructed (Alexander et al., 1985, p.32ff). The need for a sense of ownership is also relevant to the acceptance of interactive systems (Muller et al., 1997).

Alexander described a process for using pattern languages in housing design (Alexander et al., 1985), and discussed how different families used the same pattern language to develop very different designs. Patterns were adopted in varying degrees and interpreted in various ways, demonstrating the flexibility that can come from pattern-based design:

> "Even when people do not agree with the version of a pattern that is stated in a pattern language, the pattern still gives them the opportunity to consider the relationship between the elements mentioned; and whether they choose the 'book' version or their own version, it helps them to define this relationship ... " (Alexander et al., 1985, p.190)

Here the emphasis is on the pattern language as a catalyst for discussion and development of design ideas, not as something that constrains design activity in a specific direction.

In spite of the obvious parallels between Alexander's use of pattern languages and participatory design of interactive systems, the majority of HCI pattern languages still focus primarily on communicating design information between professionals. Borchers (2001) sees patterns as a means of communicating among team members coming from different disciplines. This may include users but it is not made explicit and he does not describe any specific examples where end-users participated in the design process. Tidwell (1999) specifies that her patterns are intended for novice designers, along with implementers, testers and managers of design teams, but end users are not included in her list. Erickson (2000), however, views patterns and pattern languages as a means of allowing egalitarian communication, a lingua franca, between *all* stakeholders in a design project. The importance of developing shared language between users and designers has also been noted by researchers in participatory design in HCI (Ehn & Kyng, 1991).

However the potential benefits of patterns to participatory design go beyond enabling effective communication between stakeholders. We contend that we should move closer to a genuinely participatory design practice: one goal of an HCI pattern language should be to empower users to *make design decisions*, cf. Bravo (1993). Patterns encapsulate design knowledge in a way that should be understandable by the user but generic, not constraining the user to a particular instantiation of the solution. Unlike guidelines, which may be too prescriptive, or principles, which can often be too abstract, patterns provide generic solutions supported by example instantiations. Users are also encouraged to contribute their own patterns and help evolve the language, cf. Greenbaum & Kyng (1991). Alexander consistently used pattern languages to enable people to participate in the design of their own homes and buildings, giving them the support to make meaningful decisions. To date, little attention has been paid to such a participatory use of pattern languages in interactive systems.

## 2.2 Generative Design

Patterns to Alexander were a component of a generative design process. Each pattern contributes to the generation of the larger system. The concept of a language is therefore important — not just individual patterns — and the language as a whole must generate coherence not just "some unrelated good ideas" (Alexander, 1996, p.7)[1]. Architectural development is, by necessity, piecemeal, but each act of design should contribute to the whole:

> "When you build a thing you cannot merely build that thing in isolation, but must repair the world around it, and within it, so that the larger world at that one place becomes more coherent, and more whole ..."
> (Alexander et al., 1977, p.xiii)

Part of this process is diagnosis. By evaluating an existing environment against the patterns, a 'map' of the 'health' of that environment is established (Alexander et al., 1975; Alexander et al., 1987). So patterns can be used to assess existing designs or partial designs as well as, or as part of the process of, generating new designs.

This 'piecemeal' design approach was in direct contrast to the long-term urban design plan (which failed to adapt to changing requirements) or to the independent building development (which took little account of its context). In this, Alexander was proposing not only a method but a paradigm shift — both a new way of thinking and a challenge to existing methods. He addressed not just building a house, but the political, organisational and environmental consequences of design. His methods attempted to put human dignity and well being at the centre of design, above all other considerations. This led him, at times, into conflict with the existing practices in his profession, for example, by promoting a decentralised, locally adaptive design approach.

It may be that we also need to consider our basic assumptions and processes: do our current approaches to interface design and engineering even allow for such a genuinely human-centred stance, let alone facilitate it? Can they allow adaptation to situations and context? This political dimension of design is also a focus of participatory approaches (Bannon, 1995).

## 2.3 Life Enhancing Outcomes

In 1996, Alexander delivered the keynote address at OOPSLA (Alexander, 1996) and gave to the software engineering community his assessment of their use of the pattern approach. His address made it clear that his emphasis was not on communication and reuse within a professional community but on generating living structures that were in the hands of their users. He emphasised this ethical focus or 'moral component' as he called it: his aim was to make a good environment, one which enhanced the lives of those who used it, and he questioned whether software engineers had addressed this issue. Such an ethical dimension is fundamental to Alexander's pattern approach in architecture:

---

[1] Alexander (1979, p.187) makes the link between pattern languages and Chomsky's notion of generative grammar.

"We have tried to construct a housing process in which human feeling
and human dignity come first ..." (Alexander et al., 1985, p.16).

Alexander (1979) talked of the "Quality without a Name", the essential quality of
an artefact which makes people feel more 'whole' through their interaction with it.
There has been some discussion as to what this might equate to in HCI: the suggestion
of 'Transparency' (Borchers, 2001, p.36) is perhaps more a property that may lead
to this quality, than the quality itself; 'engaging' (Pemberton, 2000) is getting closer
but still focuses on the system itself. Maslow (1970) identifies 'wholeness' as a
component of highest-level human need. Wholeness, in his terms, incorporates a
sense of unity and integration and is an essential component of self-actualisation.
Systems that promote this are not simply transparent or engaging but in some way
work towards this integration. In short, we are designing systems and processes that
should have a positive and integrative effect on people's lives.

Alexander judged patterns by this criterion of wholeness. He evaluated his
pattern language in action, using it to enable people to design neighbourhoods,
schools, houses and university campuses. He then assessed people's reported
sense of 'wholeness' in relation to different artefacts. This dimension has been
acknowledged by a number of proponents of HCI patterns (Bayle et al., 1998;
Tidwell, 1999) but has not been demonstrated or evaluated in practice. However,
again, it is central to participatory design philosophy (Greenbaum & Kyng, 1991).
As designers, we should seek to engage with these ethical issues in our design work
and strive towards systems and processes that enhance the lives and work of those
who engage with them.

## 3   Investigating Pattern Languages in Participatory Design

The three criteria identified from the writings of Alexander were key to his work
in the field of architecture, but do they transfer to other areas and, in particular, to
our use of patterns in HCI? Can users be empowered through patterns to participate
actively in generating designs for the systems with which they will live and work?
And, if so, does such design result in 'life-enhancing outcomes' both in terms of
users' perceptions and in the quality of the resulting systems? We have carried
out a series of empirical studies, which form a preliminary exploration of users'
application of, and response to, a selection of different pattern languages. Our
aim was to determine whether pattern languages can be empowering, generative
and produce life-enhancing outcomes outside of the domain of architecture. Before
considering the results, we discuss briefly the languages we used and the process we
employed for each study.

### 3.1   Pattern Language Development

We have used three different pattern languages in our studies to date. The first
language was taken from Borchers (2001), and focuses on the creation of blues
music. Our second language was concerned with the design of travel booking Web
sites. Our third language focused on the domain of online learning (including both
pedagogical and HCI design issues). Each of the last two languages were derived
from existing pattern collections (Bergin, 2001; Tidwell, 1999; Borchers, 2001;

Orme, 2001; van Welie, 2001; Coram & Lee, 1996). These were adapted to reflect the domains in question and to ensure internal consistency within the resulting language.

The patterns were formatted in a style based on that used by Alexander, consisting briefly of: a name and reference number; a picture showing an example of the pattern; a paragraph to set the context; three 'diamonds' marking the start of the problem; a concise problem statement (emboldened); the body of the problem, including the empirical background (the motivation for the pattern) and the forces involved in the resolution of the problem; a solution (emboldened and preceded by 'therefore'), including a diagram; another three 'diamonds' to mark the end of the problem; a paragraph indicating how this pattern relates to other 'lower' patterns in the pattern language. We chose this format to mirror Alexander's patterns and to avoid the potential distraction of including headings and additional information (Borchers, 2001).

The patterns were organised according to a staged view of Web site development, covering high level structures, navigation and layout through to low level design detail. The pattern language used for the third study also included a group of pedagogical patterns to design the task activities. New patterns were written where existing patterns could not be found to cover a particular issue. Existing patterns were adapted so that the illustrative examples used were relevant to the domains. An example of a pattern included in both languages is 'Step by Step', from which the problem and solution are shown:

> **"Certain aspects of the Web site need to be conducted in a sequence of steps for the operation to be performed successfully. The user needs to start at the beginning of the process and work through all steps to successfully complete the transaction. The user cannot start the process part way through.**
>
> . . . (body of pattern omitted). . .
>
> Therefore:
>
> **Develop a series of interlinking pages, which act as a series of steps leading to completion of the operation. Ensure that the user is aware of their whereabouts within the process at all times, and that they have the option to exit and back track as required."**

This pattern adapts the 'Wizard' pattern from the Amsterdam collection (van Welie, 2001) and Tidwell's (1999) 'Step-by-step Instruction'. Each language was indexed by a graphical 'map' and/or a structured list of patterns.

## 3.2 Facilitation Process

For each study we adopted a 'facilitation' approach, based on Alexander's housing construction project in Mexicali (Alexander et al., 1985), where he advocates making design into a collaborative activity, with an 'Architect-builder' helping the 'family' to design and build their own house. In this process, the user is active in the creative and decision making processes but is aided both in using the language and in executing ideas by the 'Architect-builder'. The 'Architect-builder' was reflected in our studies by the use of a 'Designer-facilitator', who was able to assist the users in negotiating the pattern language and in creating instantiations of their designs. However, it was the user-designer who made the ultimate decisions.

The patterns in each case were presented as a flexible resource and users were encouraged to use them in whatever way they found helpful. The physical design of the languages reflected this flexibility, allowing patterns to be browsed, read sequentially or spatially organised and manipulated. Each pattern was printed on a double-sided A4 sheet and the language was held in a loose-leaf binder, allowing users to remove and reorganise patterns as they wished.

## 3.3   Study 1: The Blues Pattern Language

In the first study we examined an existing pattern language, Borchers' blues domain language (Borchers, 2001). Although not an HCI language, it is an example of a 'user-centred' language from a domain outside architecture. The blues language was interesting to us for two reasons: it is addressed to 'users' wishing to 'jam' blues music, rather than to professionals, and it is a small but coherent language with a generative purpose. We wished to see whether such a language would support our criteria of empowering users to generate 'design' (in this case, music), with life-enhancing outcomes. We therefore used it with a small group of musician-users, including both classically trained (non-blues) pianists and blues players with little traditional training.

User 1 was a 10-year old, qualified to Grade 3 as a pianist[2] with some musical theory. User 2 was also qualified to Grade 3 as a pianist, had reasonable ability as a guitarist and had been playing musical instruments for thirty years, including blues and jazz. User 3 was a pianist qualified to Grade 5 (theory and practice) with twenty-five year's experience but no knowledge of blues. User 4 was an experienced but unqualified banjo player of more than forty years, with a limited knowledge of piano playing and very limited theory.

The activity took place over the course of one day. Each user was given the eleven blues patterns to work with and allowed as much time as they needed. Users 1 and 3 were interviewed and asked to generate some blues music. Users 2 and 4 took part in a detailed interview only, as their blues skill was pre-existing.

### 3.3.1   Summary of Observations

The pattern language required reasonable domain knowledge of musical terminology, but with that understanding, the patterns were empowering in Alexander's sense of the word. Both of the non-blues musicians were able to understand the blues concepts and use the language to generate blues music. User 1 could recount most of the patterns and was able to 'jam' a simple blues tune on the piano using four patterns. User 3 could understand and explain all the patterns in the language and 'jam' a simple blues tune using them.

User 2, an experienced blues player, suggested that the pattern language communicated the basic knowledge needed, and would help novices to learn blues.

---

[2]Musicians in the UK sit practical and theoretical examinations from Grades 1 to 8, where Grade 8 (practical) is considered a suitable level of competence for those wishing to study for a music degree at University.

He felt that the patterns gave blues players a way of developing their own style rather than simply copying that of someone else. The other experienced blues player was less enthusiastic. He did not find the patterns easy to follow saying that when he played the blues, he did "what felt right to fit in with the rest of the band".

We were unable to evaluate the inherent quality of the resulting musical contributions. However, the evident pleasure on the face of our first user when he produced a blues tune, and his enhanced confidence in his music, which later enabled him to join with others in a blues session, are outcomes which seem to reflect the Alexandrian concept of wholeness. On the other hand the other non-blues player was less comfortable with the patterns approach and felt that her technical production of blues music was simply 'following rules'.

These results are by no means conclusive but gave us an initial indication that pattern languages may be useful to users outside of the domain of architecture. However, we still needed to explore the participatory use of pattern languages in an HCI domain.

## 3.4 Study 2: The Travel Booking Web Site

Our second study focused on the use of a pattern language for rail and air travel booking Web sites. The pattern language, comprising 23 patterns, was developed specifically for the study. We chose a restricted domain for the design study as this limited the domain knowledge required both within the pattern language, and by users. This enabled us to work with users with a range of experience, including complete Web novices. We were looking for evidence of the three criteria previously discussed and any factors that may be important to the success of a pattern-based participatory design process.

Design exercises were conducted with six users ranging in experience from a retired non-web-user to a trainee Web designer. Users were asked to develop a paper prototype for a travel Web site using the pattern language. They were told that following the patterns was not compulsory, and that the illustrations shown were examples only and not definitive 'best practice'. The sessions lasted between 1 and 2 hours and were videotaped, and participants were interviewed following the task. We discuss our results in terms of our three criteria.

### 3.4.1 Empowering Users

All the sessions resulted in feasible design sketches, at varying levels of detail. The process enabled novice users with no experience of Web design to participate in the design of a Web site. More experienced designers indicated that the language had supported their design activity, for example, by highlighting elements that would otherwise have been missed. In addition, with all users, the language became a vehicle for discussion between the facilitator and the user-designer. All users challenged the patterns, in a variety of ways, including rejecting the recommended solution within an individual pattern; proposing alternative solutions for a particular problem; questioning assumptions about functionality embedded within the pattern; and raising issues that the language did not address. For example, one user suggested the value of showing a choice of possible 'closely matching' flights in response to an initial query. Suggestions of this kind might be used to further enhance and develop the language. This approach is consistent with Alexander's view that ultimately pattern languages are shared cultural artefacts that should develop and grow in the hands of users (Alexander, 1979, p.241–2).

On the other hand, two of the novice users seemed to treat the patterns as 'correct' answers, rejecting their own ideas when they were in conflict with the pattern. This was less in keeping with Alexander's view that users should adapt patterns to their own needs. It is clear, therefore, that facilitation is important. The role of the facilitator, however, is not to make decisions, but to guide the user through the process and encourage them to take control. During the exercises there were transitions in the locus of control of the drawing process, of the sequencing of design questions, and of the handling of the patterns. These transitions tended towards the users gradually taking more control, raising the question of how such transitions can be effectively enabled.

### 3.4.2  Generative Design

All users produced partial designs that were internally coherent, with both layout and navigational elements. However, our results highlight three issues that may be significant in developing an effective, generative process.

Firstly, the role of the facilitator in guiding the users through the language and highlighting the relationships between patterns was crucial to the generative design process. The inter-relationships between patterns within the language may otherwise not be appreciated and utilised.

Secondly, the form of the patterns was significant. Some users focused exclusively on the illustrated examples. Others used the examples together with the emboldened problem and solution texts. No users acknowledged using the supporting text, although two users read through the patterns in full in advance of the session, and another spent the first 23 minutes of the session reading the patterns. This focus suggests that the choice of examples is critical. One of our users commented that he would begin by considering a range of examples by visiting multiple Web sites. Another user questioned whether the full pattern form was necessary, suggesting that just the problem and solution might be appropriate.

Finally, the form of the pattern language as a physical artefact was important. Our patterns were presented as unbound single A4 sheets. We observed users browsing the set, searching the set for a specific remembered pattern, example or diagram, and organising the set spatially. The spatial organisation reflected either a sense of 'ownership' or an attempt to group related patterns. The physical form of the pattern language must facilitate these activities and we should be careful not to discard the physical affordances of separate paper presentation, for example by binding the pattern language into a book, or presenting it via a computer screen.

### 3.4.3  Life-enhancing Outcomes

The level of development of the paper prototypes was insufficient to make claims about the quality of the products from this exercise. The designs were paper-based sketches developed in a short time and some appear to be closely derivative from the examples used to illustrate the patterns. However, all users expressed satisfaction with the process and felt that the use of the patterns had enhanced their understanding of Web sites and Web design. We consider the third criteria more fully in our next study.

## 3.5 Study 3: Online Learning Web Site

Our third study is an ongoing investigation of the use of pattern languages in the design of online learning Web sites. Our pattern language included 39 patterns representing the educational domain and the Web design.

We conducted the study with six users, three male and three female, ranging in age from early twenties to mid fifties. Two users were students (undergraduate and postgraduate); four were teaching staff, two of whom were also studying for a taught higher qualification. Four had computing or technology-related backgrounds; two were from arts disciplines. All but one had some experience of Web page design. However, with one exception, this was at a basic level (designing single pages using simple tools). All were confident Web users and three had experience of using web-based learning environments. None were familiar with patterns.

Each user was asked to design a Web site to support students learning oral presentation skills. A designer-facilitator, familiar with the pattern language and Web design, guided the user-designer by indicating the stages of the design process and suggesting patterns that might be relevant to each phase. However, it was made clear that the use of patterns was not compulsory. User-designers sketched their design ideas on paper with accompanying notes. These initial sessions lasted 1–2 hours and were videotaped. Users were interviewed immediately following the session.

The designer-facilitator then used the sketches to produce a computer-based 'mock-up' of the design. Three of the users took part in an iterative design session to further develop their designs from these mock-ups.

Again we discuss our findings in terms of the criteria previously identified.

### 3.5.1 Empowering Users

All users were able to develop a viable design using the patterns approach. All were positive about the process by the end of the session, although all also admitted that they initially found the exercise difficult and in two cases 'stressful'. However, this eased in all cases as they became used to the process.

The pattern language also enabled the facilitator to structure the collaborative session, ensuring a coherent and systematic process. The structure of the session reflected the organisation of the pattern language, suggesting that this too is important to a successful participatory process.

Again users used the patterns to explore the design space. Even users with some experience of Web design indicated that the patterns gave them new ideas and helped them organise their thoughts. One of the more experienced users felt the pattern language helped him design more quickly and reliably. Again, users challenged the patterns and suggested potential patterns that were missing from the language, for example, accessibility issues. This mirrors our experience with the travel pattern language and is consistent with Alexander's view of pattern languages as evolving artefacts.

However, it became clear that some users tended to rely on the patterns. One user spoke of 'trusting the patterns' and several others indicated that their confidence in their design was due to the fact that the patterns were 'correct'. This has important implications for the development and validation of pattern languages. If users are going to be able to rely on the pattern languages, we have a responsibility to ensure they represent reliable claims about design.

### 3.5.2   Generative Design

Some evidence of the generative nature of the pattern language is seen in the fact that users modified their ideas according to what they saw in the patterns, resulting in complete designs that they acknowledged they would not have created on their own. Where the patterns challenged their prior experience or beliefs they used the pattern as a focus for negotiation and discussion. Interestingly, although the users were designing for a specific task, the designs produced were all very different, suggesting that the patterns do enable users to develop solutions that are adapted to their own requirements and expectations.

In most cases users worked with the patterns systematically, following the links to ensure that they had considered all the issues relevant to that part of the design. Several users expressed a sense of completion or closure at the end: the design was complete because they had worked through the pattern language:

> "It does feel that when you have designed the pages that it actually means something because all the criteria associated with it have been addressed."

As with the travel Web site study, facilitation was critical. Several users expressed the view that they couldn't have done the exercise without the facilitator, and all confirmed the importance of this role, the following comment being typical:

> "At first there was a lot of information and it was important to have you [the facilitator] there for guidance and reassurance."

This suggests that pattern languages should be used within a collaborative design context rather than given to users to work with alone. However, once users established a better understanding of the pattern language, they were more inclined to select patterns without the facilitator's advice. One user stated:

> "Towards the end, once I got used to using the links to go to different patterns, it's quite useful for checking you have got all the bases covered for each aspect."

The form of the language and the patterns were again found to be important. There was some confusion over the status of the illustrations and examples, with one user finding them "too restrictive" indicating that he was viewing them as the suggested solution. When asked what they found most useful about the patterns, all users highlighted either the example illustration or the bold solution text, although they had all browsed the pattern text. Some felt that the patterns contained too much detail and should be restructured to highlight the key information (one user suggested, for example, placing the solution text first). However, in the follow-up exercise, users paid more attention to the detail in the patterns and the cross referencing between patterns, with one commenting:

> "[in the second session] I read the middle sections more and I did look more at ... where it suggested to go next."

This suggests that users' needs may change as they become familiar with the patterns, and the form should support this.

As before, the patterns were used in different ways. Some users took them out of the folder and organised them spatially. Some used the structure in the folder to keep track of them. Some did both, removing those that were considered to be most important and using these to index the remaining. Flexibility in the organisation and the form of the pattern language is therefore key.

### 3.5.3 Life Enhancing Outcomes

All users enjoyed the process and found it rewarding. Several users expressed a sense of satisfaction on completing their design, feeling that the pattern language had led them through a complete process. One user, who was initially sceptical about the online learning application, ended the session by saying:

> "This has actually helped me ... I've been trying to design my own Web site for years ... "

once again suggestive of a life-enhancing outcome. Another user asked to use the pattern language to help him design further learning materials for his teaching, indicating that he found the approach particularly helpful.

In this study we carried out an additional design session with three users, which enabled us to see the level of design produced after 2–3 hours of work with the patterns. The results are encouraging. All three users completed a Web site design covering at least one detailed learning activity. The designs included multiple Web pages and decisions had been made on layout, navigation and low level design details such as colour and icon design. All the designs were internally consistent and reflected the HCI 'good practice' embodied in the patterns. The users expressed satisfaction with the process and with their designs. Further work is required to fully develop these designs and evaluate them in use.

However, the users' designs also enabled us to see shortcomings in the pattern language. For example, one user had chosen to place navigation controls at the bottom of a screen, in spite of the danger that this will scroll off the screen in some configurations. The patterns did not consider this issue, an omission that needs to be rectified. The use of the language can therefore direct its development and evolution.

## 4 Conclusions and Future Work

We have identified three criteria that reflect Alexander's priorities in the development and use of the pattern language approach, namely, empowering users to participate in the design process, design generation and life enhancing outcomes. We have conducted three studies to assess the viability of pattern languages to support these criteria in HCI design. Our results are promising and suggest that pattern languages have a role to play in participatory design; that they can be generative; and that they can lead to positive results both in terms of the user's sense of satisfaction with the process and the resulting designs. We were encouraged to find regularity in response among our users across both of the design studies, in spite of their varying experience and the different applications. However, a number of issues require further research, relating to the pattern language itself and the design process that incorporates it:

1. Firstly, there is the issue of the structure and format of the patterns. Our results suggest that users do not find the Alexandrian format particularly useful. Alternative formats need to be evaluated with users, including 'cut down' versions and more flexible formats. We need to experiment with different forms while still maintaining the distinctive essence of the patterns. The role of the illustrations also needs to be considered. We need to evaluate alternative approaches, including providing multiple example illustrations, interactive examples and use of demonstrations (such as videos of use).

2. Secondly, we need to consider how we develop pattern languages. Alexander viewed pattern languages as fluid and evolving through use. In our studies we saw how this might happen through negotiation and discussion with users and through the evaluation of resulting artefacts. However, we also have a need to validate our patterns, as our evidence suggests that users rely (heavily) on them in the design process. We therefore also need to look for external evidence that our pattern languages reflect reliable design knowledge. The content of pattern languages could usefully be informed by drawing upon other efforts to collect and formulate HCI design knowledge to support re-use, e.g. claims (Sutcliffe, 2000).

3. Thirdly, we need to investigate further the issue of the quality of the outcomes. Alexander was seeking the "Quality without a Name". If we are also to seek to achieve life-enhancing outcomes then we need to consider how to evaluate this quality. Existing usability evaluation methods may go some way towards it but they do not address the user's sense of wholeness, which is so central.

4. Finally, if we are to use pattern languages successfully in participatory design we need to consider how and where they will fit into the wider design context. How much of the design process can they support and which elements? Can they be integrated in a process with other established methods such as task analysis? Can we formalise the facilitation process?

Our ongoing work is to investigate these issues with more users and over a longer time frame. We are revising the online learning pattern language from our experiences in this work and will develop and use it with a broader range of educators and students in real design activities. However, our results to date leave us optimistic that pattern languages will be able to contribute effectively to participatory design practice.

## Acknowledgements

We acknowledge the support of our respective institutions; the work of Kay Plowman in originating the travel booking pattern language; and the valuable contributions made by our participants.

## References

Alexander, C. (1979), *The Timeless Way of Building*, Oxford University Press.

Alexander, C. (1996), The Origins of Pattern Theory, the Future of the Theory and the Generation of a Living World, Keynote speech at ACM Conference on Object-Oriented Programs, Systems, Languages and Applications (OOPSLA'96), transcript available at http://www.patternlanguage.com/archive/ieee/ieeetext.htm.

Alexander, C., Ishikawa, S., Silverstein, M., Jacobson, M., Fiksdahl-King, I. & Angel, S. (1977), *A Pattern Language*, Oxford University Press.

Alexander, C., Neis, H., Anninou, A. & King, I. (1987), *A New Theory of Urban Design*, Oxford University Press.

Alexander, C., Silverstein, M., Angel, S., Ishikawa, S. & Abrams, D. (1975), *The Oregon Experiment*, Oxford University Press.

Alexander, C with Davis, H., Martinez, J. & Corner, D. (1985), *The Production of Houses*, Oxford University Press.

Bannon, L. (1995), "The Politics of Design: Representing Work", *Communications of the ACM* **38**(9), 66–8.

Bayle, E., Bellamy, R., Casaday, G., Erickson, T., Fincher, S., Grinter, B., Gross, B., Lehder, D., Marmolin, H., Moore, B., Potts, C., Skousen, G. & Thomas, J. (1998), "Putting it all Together: Towards a Pattern Language for Interaction", *ACM SIGCHI Bulletin* **30**(1), 17–33.

Bergin, J. (2001), Fourteen Pedagogical Patterns, Available at http://csis.pace.edu/~bergin/PedPat1.3.html.

Borchers, J. (2001), *A Pattern Approach to Interaction Design*, John Wiley & Sons.

Bravo, E. (1993), The Hazards of Leaving Out the Users, *in* D. Schuler & A. Namioka (eds.), *Participatory Design: Principles and Practices*, Lawrence Erlbaum Associates, pp.3–11.

Coram, T. & Lee, J. (1996), Experiences: a Pattern Language for User Interface Design, Available at http://www.maplefish.com/todd/papers/experiences/Experiences.html.

Ehn, P. & Kyng, M. (1991), Cardboard Computers: Mocking-it-up or Hands-on the Future, *in* Greenbaum & Kyng (1991), pp.169–96.

Erickson, T. (2000), Lingua Francas for Design: Sacred Places and Pattern Languages, *in* D. Boyarski & W. A. Kellogg (eds.), *Proceedings of Designing Interactive Systems: Processes, Practices, Methods and Techniques*, ACM Press, pp.357–68.

Gamma, E., Helms, R., Johnson, R. & Vlissides, J. (1995), *Design Patterns: Elements of Reusable Object-Oriented Software*, Addison–Wesley.

Greenbaum, J. & Kyng, M. (eds.) (1991), *Design at Work: Cooperative Design of Computer Systems*, Lawrence Erlbaum Associates.

Maslow, A. (1970), *Motivation and Personality*, third edition, Harper and Row.

Muller, M. J., Haslwanter, J. H. & Dayton, T. (1997), Participatory Practices in the Software Lifecycle, *in* M. Helander, T. K. Landauer & P. V. Prabhu (eds.), *Handbook of Human–Computer Interaction*, second edition, North-Holland, pp.255–97.

Orme, D. (2001), Website Patterns, Available at http://c2.com/cgi-bin/wiki?WebsitePatterns.

Pemberton, L. (2000), The Promise of Pattern Languages for Interaction Design, Available at http://www.it.bton.ac.uk/staff/lp22/HF2000.html.

Sutcliffe, A. G. (2000), "On the Effective Use and Reuse of HCI Knowledge", *ACM Transactions on Computer–Human Interaction* 7(2), 197–221.

Tidwell, J. (1999), Common Ground: A Pattern Language for Human-Computer Interface Design, Available at http://www.mit.edu/~jtidwell/common_ground_onefile.html.

van Welie, M. (2001), Amsterdam Collection of Patterns in User Interface Design, Available at http://www.welie.com/.

# Provoking Innovation: Acting-out in Contextual Scenarios

## Steve Howard, Jennie Carroll, John Murphy[†], Jane Peck[†] & Frank Vetere

*Department of Information Systems, The University of Melbourne, Australia.*

Tel: *+61 3 8344 9249*

Email: *{showard, jcarroll}@unimelb.edu.au, fvetere@staff.dis.unimelb.edu.au*

[†] *Novell PTY Ltd, Richmond, Melbourne, Australia.*

Tel: *+61 3 9224 2000*

Email: *{john.murphy, jane.peck}@ctp.com*

**Scenario-based design typically involves stakeholders in 'walking through' textual vignettes of usage situations. We propose an alternative that increases stakeholder immersion in, and enriches the contextual aspects of, the scenarios. Our approach develops 'contextual scenarios' (bare, skeletal scenarios that describe context rather than information about actors and their goals) on the basis of rich descriptions of current practice. Contextual scenarios are then 'acted-out' during participatory design sessions. The approach facilitates the co-evolution of the artefact and situation of use. Such co-evolution we argue is critical to use-centred innovation.**

**Keywords:** scenario-based design, contextual scenarios, acting-out, performance.

# 1   Use-centred Innovation and Scenario-based Design

This paper proposes an approach to identifying opportunities for innovation arising from user needs and contexts of use, rather than advances in technology. The approach draws on scenario-based design, participatory design and theatrical performance. The essence of the approach lies in establishing a tension between an emerging artefact and a situation of use, then manipulating and examining that tension through theatrical performance. The design discourse that occurs in parallel with the performance aims to both dissolve the tension through innovating the artefact, and also to understand the impact that the artefact will have on the situation of use. In this paper we describe the method, and provide anecdotal views of its effectives from the perspectives of the stakeholders involved.

Design for innovation necessarily involves a departure from current practice. Developers of innovative products who wish to work in a use-centred fashion need support in envisioning future situations of use, the needs implicit in those situations and the form and function of appropriate technological responses. In essence, such designers need support in examining hypothetical human–computer interactions; hypothetical because the situations of use will be brought into being partly as a consequence of technological innovation. Bødker & Christiansen capture the situation well when they note that designers:

> "Find themselves caught in a dilemma between awareness of tradition and orientation towards transcendence: on the one hand starting out from the praxis and history of users in question, on the other hand making sure that something qualitatively new gets shaped in the process." (Bødker & Christiansen, 1997)

Provoking innovation in a use-centred fashion requires that the designer walks an imaginary line between current experience and expectations of the future. In this paper we describe a scenario-based approach that assists designers in co-evolving their understanding of both the technology and its situations of use, and in understanding the reciprocity that exists between the two.

Scenarios are 'sketches' of use (Carroll, 1995; Rosson & Carroll, 2000) that capture the context within which a system is used, the human actors involved and their objectives, the sequence of relevant actions and contingent outcomes. Though they can take many forms (e.g. storyboards, formal symbolic representations) typically they are encoded as textual 'vignettes', capturing a few moments in a user's life. An example of a scenario is shown in Figure 1.

Note that in Figure 1 the description of events is rich and multidimensional, including temporal issues (e.g. Friday afternoon, 4pm), roles and personalities, personal concerns (e.g. Francesca's concern that her mother is annoyed at her late homecoming) and current technological issues (e.g. the failure of the answer machine to bring the dialogue to closure by telling Francesca that the message to her boss had been received). The ability to include inherently human issues (e.g. high-level concerns, personality clashes) distinguishes scenarios from requirements as discussed in other literatures, for example Hsia et al. (1993).

> Francesca has a chest infection and is sitting on the tram travelling to her GP. It is 4pm on Friday afternoon. Expecting to be at her GP's for some time, she starts to worry. She should be at work at the moment, and has not been able to contact her boss to tell her that she is ill. She has left a message on an answering machine but is not sure that her boss has received the message. She is due to join friends tonight at the Pink Dragon, but now is not sure she'll get there in time if seeing her GP takes too long. Because of this she hopes her friends will stay there until she arrives, otherwise she will spend the evening alone. Also, one of her friends is expecting her to bring along a copy of her University assignment, which she was to collect from her tutor this afternoon but she did not manage to get to University either. On the bright side, her mother does not know where she is and so she escapes an interrogation for last night's 4am homecoming!

**Figure 1:** Example problem scenario.

---

Scenarios have been used throughout the software development lifecycle for a variety of purposes. Hsia et al. (1993) demonstrated the use of scenarios for identifying software requirements, and their use by the human–computer interaction community has extended to understanding system use, recording design rationale and managing debate over 'context' and its influence on artefact design (Rosson & Carroll, 2000). Discussion of scenarios is also common in the object-oriented design community, along with the related concept of use cases — see, for example, Jacobson (1995).

In discussing the benefits of a scenario driven approach, Carroll (2000; Rosson & Carroll, 2000) argues that scenarios:

- Promote both reflection about users and an orientation to work throughout design.

- Allow progress to be made in design deliberation without forcing a commitment to a particular design model early in the process.

- Support the consideration of many, often opposing, needs and priorities.

- Record and help integrate the evolving vision for the system.

However, traditional use of scenarios tends to be somewhat removed from the situatedness of activity when trying to understand interaction with innovative or non-existing products. Typically, scenarios are 'walked through', an analytical process relatively insensitive to complex and unpredictable contextual influences. Most classes of technological innovation, e.g. mobile and ubiquitous computing especially, need support in understanding contextual influences. We propose using participatory design techniques to supplement scenarios. These techniques help users or their representatives take a more active role in scenario-based design and help the design team situate the design activity in a rich use context.

We are inspired by the ongoing work of the GO Project at Helsinki University of Technology[1]. The objectives of GO are to implement a wireless network and to investigate the use of wireless Internet devices. GO is a three-year project (1999–2002), which is exploring a wireless infrastructure in the campus area of Helsinki University of Technology. This infrastructure provides a test bed for investigating mobile ('nomadic') Internet use of the future.

The GO group are blending ethnographically oriented observations with active user participation (Iacucci et al., 2000). The project began, intentionally, with no focus on any particular design or practice. The type and capabilities of personal devices had to be co-developed with future services. Scenarios were used as a means of envisioning future use situations.

'Role Playing' and 'Situated and Participative Enactment of Scenarios' (SPES), techniques developed in the GO project, provided a platform that helped the designers and the users discover new scenarios. The role-playing games were structured so that participants could play roles or act as themselves in given situations. The players imagined what kind of devices or services could support their mobility and communication, and they discussed and acted out their ideas. The SPES technique involved researchers following users in their normal lives and identifying opportunities for innovation. For example, a participant would imagine that he had headphones so that he could listen to music through his 'magic device' while doing mundane tasks. With SPES, the users were able to envision and enact scenarios in micro, local and remote mobility.

The significant results of role-playing games were not so much the ideas of services and devices — these roughly corresponded to established ideas of future products. The most significant results concerned the context of use of the new device and the details that became explicit in the game scenario. For example, the devices were used to organise shared taxis after the pub closed. This was rarely done in reality, but the new devices made such a practice possible.

Similar work combining theatre techniques with participatory design includes the focus troupe (Salvador & Howells, 1998; Sato & Salvador, 1999) and Strom's (2001) work on using mobile devices as props during role-playing.

We seek to extend this work in three significant ways:

- Much current work uses surrogate users as actors in the enactment sessions but it is clear that this is problematic. To quote from the GO project:

    "Sensibility and understanding are necessary not to put users in uncomfortable situations, and social and dramaturgical skills are important to encourage the user enactment." (Iacucci et al., 2000)

    Our process includes the use of actors trained in improvisation and a theatre director who facilitates the process. We hypothesised that trained actors would be more able to explore the interesting issues and problems as they unfold in the acting-out sessions as they have 'automated' the processes of improvisation found so difficult by surrogate users. Clearly this would come

---

[1] See http://go.cs.hut.fi/

at a cost- it is an open question as to the extent to which the 'character' adopted in the acting-out is a valid model of the intended users. We will return to this issue later.

- The form factors used in the GO project were chosen arbitrarily and frequently users were asked to imagine the form factor that the technology would adopt. In other work (Strom, 2001) current mobile devices have been used as the prop for the role-playing. We expected that the nature of the form factor would exert considerable influence over the participatory design sessions. We conducted an expert panel (with representation from both industrial and research organisations) that identified candidate form factors for mobile devices (our technological focus in this work), including Implements (e.g. IT enhanced pens), Accessories (e.g. rings, clothing, brooches), Handhelds (e.g. PDA devices, mobile phones) and Tablets (e.g. wireless A4 size LCD displays). Our approach uses such form factors as props to focus the improvisation and we hypothesised that this would constrain the innovation that took place to 'plausible fictions', rather than the science fictions that sometime emerge from role-plays.

- Finally, though we see our approach as fundamentally scenario-based, our scenarios differ in both role and form from typical use. Rather than being textual vignettes that are walked-though, our scenarios have to seed mini-performances. Metaphorically, instead of scenarios taking the form of short stories, they take the form of mini-stage directions. We call such scenarios 'contextual scenarios' and importantly they do not contain detailed descriptions of user characteristics and goals, instead tending to load on rich descriptions of the context within which users will act. We hypothesised that this would allow us to discover activities and goals that did not currently exist and did not appear in the scenarios; activities and goals that are brought into being through the interaction between context and user activity (i.e. acting-out). More is said later on contextual scenarios.

In the next section we discuss our approach in detail, focusing on the interplay between technology and situations of use that is central to our view of innovation.

## 2 Acting-out In Contextual Scenarios

### 2.1 Overall Approach

We blend ethnomethodological studies of current practice with acting-out using contextual scenarios. Figure 2 presents our view of the acting-out scenario-based design process.

At the heart of the approach is the *'performance'*. Here actors integrate the contextual scenarios and props to act out imaginary situations of use. Prior to this the design team and/or the actors select a *'prop'*. Props are not simply taken on face value, rather they are 'fleshed out' by the design team, suggestions are made as to what the props can accomplish, the functions they possess and the forms they may take (weight, size, shape, battery life, robustness, etc.). Further, the performance

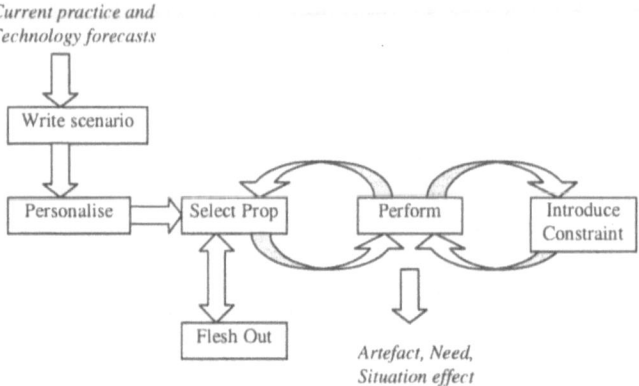

**Figure 2:** Our current view of scenario-based envisionment through acting out.

does not proceed uninterrupted until the actor feels it is complete or otherwise stops. Rather, the design team is able to interject with *'constraints'* drawn from the scenarios. Typically such constraints increase the stakes (the importance of achieving the goal) or introduce hurdles for the actor to overcome ('do it faster', 'juggle more conflicting goals', etc.). It is during that interplay between a filled-out prop and contextual constraints that opportunities for innovation are often seen.

In our case, the scenarios were seeded by ethnomethodological studies of current practice, discussed in detail by Carroll et al. (2001), Carroll et al. (2002) and Howard et al. (2001). Importantly, rather than the study of current practice limiting innovation, we have found it critical to grounding the innovation process in usage and use situations. *Scenarios* are written by the design teams to reflect their design priorities and previous ethnomethodological work, however they are *'personalised'* by the actors. We are indebted to our actors for teaching us the importance of the actor taking ownership of the scenarios. This process involves the actor entering the role described loosely in the scenario and can be achieved through a variety of means, including imagining people one knows as secondary actors in the events, or imagining similar situations that the actor is familiar with.

This paper will focus on the interplay between the prop and the constraints that takes place during the performance. In the remainder of this section we describe contextual scenarios, discuss the prop and its role in envisionment and characterise our use of constraints. In the next section we will attempt to provide some general principles for managing props and introducing constraints during acting-out sessions.

## 2.2   Contextual Scenarios and Current Practice

Table 1 illustrates a contextual scenario taken from our research notes. The table recasts the scenario of Figure 1.

Contextual scenarios can be characterised in terms of the following classification:

| Category | Example Elements | Contextual Scenario |
|---|---|---|
| Theme | Fragmentation, Social management, Lifestyle organiser | |
| Who? | Age, Culture, Experience with technology, Knowledge of the situation | Francesca, a 1st year university student |
| How and when? | Situation state, Temporal constraints, Goals | Goal — satisfy competing goals |
| Who else? | Role | Parents, doctor, lecturer, friends |
| How and when? | Temporal constraints | Within the next $x$ mins |
| Why? | Entertainment (group), Work, Education, Transit | Submit assignment, organise friends to meet tonight, talk with parent, doctor |
| Where? | Location (Physical, Social, Environmental, Technological) | Alone on public transport in transit to doctor or university, depending on timing |
| What with? | Implement, Accessory, Handheld, Tablet | Hand held |

**Table 1:** Problem scenario recast as a 'Contextual Scenario'

---

**Theme:** The general theme, derived from our ethnomethodological work, characterising the Francesca scenario is Fragmentation. Fragmentation of Francesca's life between family, friends, employers and university requires support for social management and lifestyle organisation.

**Who:** Each scenario has a primary actor (Francesca in this case). Depending on the design problem, it may be necessary to characterise the primary actor in terms of gender, age, culture, experience with technology, knowledge of the situation, interpersonal knowledge, etc.

**How and when:** The primary actor brings goals and intentions to the situation, and the situation occurs at a point in time, or in relation to other events. It may be necessary to describe the situation state, relevant activities, any temporal constraints, necessary outcomes or goals. Though we resisted providing detailed information about actors and their goals, we show later that this was problematic.

**Who else:** Scenarios may also have secondary actors (in Francesca's case the GP, her friends, mother, etc.).

**How and when:** as with the primary actor, secondary actors may have goals and their activities exist in a temporal context

**Why:** scenarios have an overall purpose that is super-ordinate to the goals and intentions of the individual actors. These might include shopping, entertainment (group), leisure (solo), rest and sleep, work, education, transit, social interchange, security, etc.

**Figure 3:** Sample props used in the research: cycling jacket, pizza box, balsa wood 'hand held', spectacles and various wearables.

**Where:** importantly scenarios take place in a physical, social and digital context. Contextual scenarios may be rich in descriptions of such factors.

**What with:** We include as part of our scenarios suggestions about which props or form factors to use.

Not all contextual scenarios will include all aspects of the above classification. Further, depending on need, scenarios may load more heavily on some categories than others. Note also that the contextual scenarios are skeletal, often lacking detail. This is acceptable as their goal is to seed a discussion between the actors and the designers. They are not intended to stand-alone.

We found that simple scenarios worked best. As we will note below, some of our scenarios exceeded the capacity of the actors' short-term memory in their length and complexity. Scenarios that were simple in expression but profound, potent or otherwise motivating were most effective.

## 2.3   Innovating using Props

Props focus the design sessions on plausible fictions, the props representing form factors that can embody innovation. Props can be suggested by designers who are interested in exploring specific devices or, as in our case, derived more systematically through consulting experts about the likely forms (size, weight, power, etc.) that will be possible in the next 5 or 10 years.

Props 'push' design innovation through their triggering and constraining affect on the performance. Figure 3 illustrates some props used in the current research.

## 2.4   Innovating using Constraints

We use constraints to 'close down' or 'open up' the design space. Constraints 'pull' design innovation through their ability to block user activity or increase the stakes on successfully completing the activity. Table 2 illustrates some constraints used in the Francesca scenario, again taken from our research notes. For example, Francesca's goal was to satisfy competing needs for her time and effort. In this case

| Category | Contextual Scenario | Constraints |
|---|---|---|
| Who? | Francesca, a 1st yr university student | |
| How and when? | Goal — satisfy competing goals | Ass deadline 1day -> 5 mins<br>Deadline flexible -> firm<br>Consequence trivial -> critical |
| Who else? | Parents, doctor, lecturer, friends | Alone -> Crowd<br>Others tolerant -> objecting (to voice interaction with device) |
| How and when? | Within the next $x$ mins | Consequence of error trivial -> critical |
| Why? | Submit assignment, organise friends to meet tonight, talk with parent, doctor | |
| Where? | Waiting on public transport in transit to doctor or univ. depending on timing | From tram -> library, or café, or bedroom |
| What with? | Hand held | Change prop from accessory -> handheld -> tablet<br>Change prop from working -> not working |

**Table 2:** Constraints as used in the Francesca Contextual Scenario.

we manipulated the time available (by moving the assignment deadline from 1 day to 5 minutes), the flexibility of the deadline (moving the deadline from flexible to firm) and increasing the stakes for a late submission (by increasing the penalty incurred). According to the focus of the design discourse, each category may have associated constraints.

It is important to note that, though we do specify constraints in advance of the performance, we remain open to discovering and using new constraints as the performance unfolds. Further, we would rarely use all the constraints specified in a given session. Performances are draining for all concerned and it is easy to be too ambitious in estimating how much can be covered.

Introducing a constraint has the effect of re-starting the performance, or part thereof. For example, the designers might suggest to the actor that a certain scene be replayed but with more urgency, or in the light of a malfunctioning device, or in a different location. Our experience suggests that trained actors are able to refocus and replay effortlessly and that this greatly assists the participation of the designers in the performance. To our surprise, we have also observed that few rules are required regarding who can talk and when. Quickly a culture of 'act-react' grows that provides sufficient space for both actors and designers to yield flowing participatory design sessions.

Talking about the impact of being interrupted by the design team, an actor noted:

"It was better when we were being interrupted and when there was a short ... the focus was shorter because it was continually being stimulated by externals, by different people's ideas. I preferred that because I felt that I was more on a journey with you rather than sitting there and trying to find my way through a journey I just did not know."

Without such interaction and interruption, our actors felt they were carrying too much of the burden of needs discovery and innovation alone.

## 2.5   *Interrogating the Actors*

Acting-out in contextual scenarios is a stop/start process that interleaves theatre with participatory design. Frequently participatory design input takes the form of question asking (directed at the actor initially and then to all present). Example questions might include,loosely taken from Norman's (1986), Approximate Theory of Action:

- How did you know what you could do? How did the device make its functionality clear to you?

- How did you know how to do that? What control and display mechanisms did the device provide you with?

- Having acted on the device, how did you know what had happened?

- How did you know you had achieved your objective?

Such questions move the design discourse away from generalities about the form factor, and its interaction with the situation of use, toward detailed user interface design issues such as visibility, affordances and feedback.

## 3   Guiding the Process

Section 2 briefly described our approach. In this section we discuss some of the key choices faced in implementing the approach as they relate to the prop and constraints.

## 3.1   *Choosing and Enriching the Prop*

### 3.1.1   *Choosing the Prop*

The prop has a large influence over the performance and design discussion that follows. Different form factors afford very different interactions and interrelate with situations in very different ways. Therefore care needs to be taken over their selection. In particular we consider:

- How many props should be used? Typically we used a single prop during each performance, though exceptions to this occur. Multiple actors engaged in a social scenario may each require a prop. In this case there is an opportunity to provide the actors with very different form factors (e.g. a bracelet and an A4 tablet) and examine, for example, UI rendering across different platforms. Alternatively, scenarios that are acted out in-situ (for example, on location in supermarkets, or in transit on a tram) give designers the opportunity to examine interaction between the device and the physical, social and digital context. In these cases the environment becomes a secondary prop. For example, one of our scenarios concerned shopping (see Figure 4) and the

**Figure 4:** Constraining the Acting-out (Actor holding prop).

acting-out took place on a busy suburban shopping strip. Another focused on a young person alone at night in an unknown town. We were exploring safety appliances. The design discussion incorporated innovations that related to ambient lighting hidden in brick walls triggered by an appliance held by the user. The walls that surrounded the performance (which took place in an oppressive alleyway) became part of the prop and hence part of the solution.

- Should actors select the props freely or be directed by the designers? Clearly designers may have interests in a specific form factor that dictates the choice of the prop. However by the time props are selected actors are immersed in the scenario and we have found it rewarding to allow actors to self-select. Discussion can then take place that illuminates the actor's rationale for the choice of form factor.

- What form should the prop take? As shown in Figure 3, we used lo-fidelity props. Alternatives exist, ranging from no prop at all (in which case the acting sessions would be similar to mime theatre) through to fully functioning appliances (in which case we'd expect the acting-out to resemble scenario-based user interface evaluation). We focused on lo-fi props as our primary interests were with the form factors, and their interaction with situations of use, rather than design detail.

- When should props be chosen and introduced? We see value in selecting props after the scenario has been introduced and personalised, and then examining the rationale behind prop selection. We recognise however that props will often be a given in many design processes. As mentioned above, there may also be value in running through a performance without a prop prior to prop selection.

### 3.1.2 Fleshing Out

Just as contextual scenarios are 'personalised', props must be fleshed-out. Fleshing out involves providing the prop with functions or constraining its capabilities. Actors

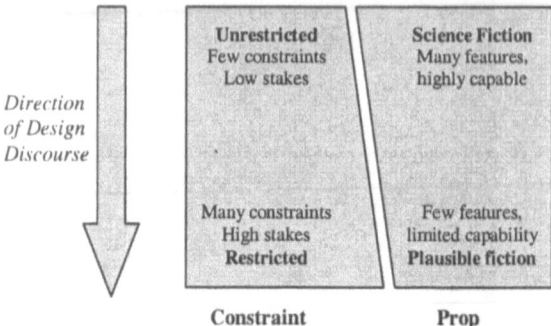

**Figure 5:** Relations between Design Discourse and the Constraint/Prop space.

call this process 'creating a motivated or endowed object' or 'accumulating creative detail' and it is a major route via which designers can influence the theatre that follows. In particular we consider:

- Quantity and complexity of endowments:  Initially we tried to limit the endowments, suggesting only one function for the prop, or describing its features in very simple terms. However we gained more value from enriching the prop and allowing the actors to self-select functions and facilities (which they held in memory), as they needed, in the context of the performance. The process was as follows (with quotes in italics, taken from our research tapes):

  - Actor or designer selects prop(s):

    Actor: "I'm looking at the props table and thinking what is going to suit my needs?" Chooses a wristwatch type appliance to help him buy a present for his girlfriend.

  - In a 'Round Robin' fashion, each member of the design team is asked to describe a feature or capability of the appliance (e.g. weight, network connectivity, specific function):

    Director: "You can experience the product through it. If it's a CD you can hear it"
    Designer 1: "There is a little puffer that delivers smell"
    Designer 2: "You can zoom in and out on the display"
    Designer 3: "Colour and movement can be seen, video"
    Designer 4: "You can watch her open her gift before its received and you can see her reactions"
    Designer 5: "It allows privacy"
    Designer 1: "It melts if touched by rain", etc.

  - The actor is told that these suggestions need not all be used and that they are not necessarily equally useful or important.  The actor can use features and capabilities as they see fit during the performance. Discussion regarding the rationale for the choice, and how that feature or function relates to activity, is encouraged throughout the performance.

This process produces for the actor a 'toolbox' of options that are evaluated and extended during the performance.

- Top down or bottom up? We have explored starting the performance with an unrestricted 'magical thing' (Iacucci et al., 2000) that can do 'anything you want it to' and slowly restricting the features and functions, and examining the effects of these restrictions on successive performances. We have also worked bottom up, selecting a restricted form factor, carefully limiting its capability at first, and then through each successive performance removing those barriers. Both of these approaches provide insight. It is difficult, in the top down approach, to know just where 'top' is. Conceptually, it is possible to start somewhere in the middle, and constrain the process downwards, thus missing the real opportunities for innovation. Of course, the bottom up process may not get to the top, but you do get as far as the creativity of the team allows! This is reflected in Figure 5 where over the course of the design discourse, the prop is moved from science fiction (where the prop is endowed with many highly capable features) to plausible fiction (where the features of the prop, whilst not currently available, are conceivable using current or nearly current technology and are mapped more closely to the need to overcome the barriers contained in constraints).

## 3.2 Managing the Constraints

### 3.2.1 Top Down vs. Bottom Up

As with the prop, we have explored introducing constraints top down (where the actor has freedom in the situation and that freedom is systematically withdrawn) and bottom up (where the actor is heavily constrained initially, but given increasing freedom during successive performances). Actors report that they find it easier to work top down, that it is more difficult to cast off constraints than it is to work around them as they are imposed. Clearly, the heart of our entire process lies in understanding the reciprocity between the props and constraints, and so any process considerations (such as top down or bottom up) for the constraint should go hand in hand with similar considerations for the prop. Again, this is reflected in Figure 5 where early in the performance (or design discourse) constraints are few and unrestrictive, and the costs of failure (the stakes) are low. As the performance proceeds constraints are introduced, the actor is intentionally restricted and the stakes are raised. This is done to stress the actor-artefact interaction, and forces the design team to innovate in order to overcome the hurdles that are being imposed.

### 3.2.2 Quantity and Complexity of Constraints

Surprisingly, given our experience with props and their complexity, we found it necessary to provide simple, single story contextual scenarios. The Francesca scenario reproduced and discussed above exceeded the actors' capacity to remember, recall and manipulate the events. If, as with Francesca, the scenarios necessarily have to include competing and interacting events and tasks, these should be broken down and introduced piecemeal.

Designers should expect scenarios to change during personalisation, and should monitor that those changes do not detract significantly from the desired goals.

### 3.2.3   Origin of Constraints

Our contextual scenarios and constraints are drawn from detailed studies of current practice, reported in Carroll et al. (2001), Carroll et al. (2002) and Howard et al. (2001). As stated earlier, we believe studies of current practice are necessary in providing the use-centredness of innovation, even though we recognise that current tasks, users, goals, etc. will necessarily be radically changed by the innovation.

### 3.2.4   Who Chooses the Constraint?

Constraints are partly specified prior to the process, and partly emerge naturally during the performance. Though designers take the primary role in introducing constraints we have not found it necessary to delimit this in any way, and often actors will both uncover a constraint and suggest its resolution quite naturally, for example:

> "Now what would I do if the screen blanked out? I guess I'd turn it to audio."

### 3.2.5   When and How?

After establishing the performance and when the actors are comfortable, we introduce constraints. Typically constraints are introduced one at a time, and at periods in the performance where the 'technology' and its effects on the performance appeared to be understood. Introducing rigorous constraints early or too frequently typically overloads the actor and brings the performance to a halt. Constraints that are introduced prior to the actor personalising the scenarios shift the focus of the performance to overcoming the barrier by 'playing the prop'. This is consistent with our finding that actors preferred a top down approach to constraint introduction.

## 4   Critique and Next Steps

We have presented a scenario-based design approach that is novel and productive. It is distinguished by its use of actors rather than users or surrogate users, the concept of contextual scenarios, and the exploration of the interrelations between technology (props) and situations of use (constraints) during acting-out.

Though we viewed what we were doing as creating a type of 'theatre of innovation', the actors felt quite differently. One stated:

> "Acting is about experience. As an actor you jump in and grab things from your life and in the process of experiencing something you also get an experience and you take an audience on that. This isn't about that. It's about trying something, it doesn't work, banging your head, trying something else to stimulate a beat."

The actors were clear that new skills and a new perspective were involved. The actors were conscious that they were not being asked to take the designers on 'an experience', or convincingly portray character and consequently they were puzzled for some time as to what was expected of them. Another commented:

> "Its unusual when you are up there (on stage), and I'm feeling sorry for you guys (the designers) having to watch this, and you're writing things down! What are you writing down!?"

Asking actors to provide designers with an enactment of a scenario, and to put aside their usual concerns for dramatic tension, characterisation and emotional integrity, should not be done lightly! Though our rationale for using actors was that users and surrogate users lacked dramaturgical skills, the skills actors posses and their view of performance and theatre, needs tailoring before they are effective in acting-out scenarios.

Finally, a word on contextual scenarios. Our intent was to create scenarios rich in context and lacking detail about the actors' goals. This was not entirely successful. As one actor states:

> "Objectives are the engine in the car. Once that's established you can chuck obstacles (i.e. constraints) and actors will strive to overcome them."

During the process we had to strengthen our goal statements, at the risk of closing down goal discovery. Our hypothesis that providing the actor with a context would be reason enough to act was incorrect.

Our current and future activities are focusing on:

- Building a tighter link between the rich data on the current situation and contextual scenarios. We are concerned that some of the observations we made in the field did not find their way into the acting-out sessions.

- Informing innovation with trends in technology. We want to better understand how to seed contextual scenarios and props with technological forecasts without turning the acting-out sessions into slaves of those forecasts.

- We want to study 'performance' in detail, and better under its weaknesses, for example its difficulty in capturing long-term changes in behaviour.

- We continue to work on constraints, and heuristics for their identification and management during acting-out.

- We want to improve our understanding of how to make use of the context that appears in contextual scenarios during the acting-out sessions. We are concerned that too much of the acting-out we observed happened as theatre, removed from the context we worked so hard to establish.

- We've got to understand the follow-through. How can the ideas generated in such design sessions best be packaged for downstream design and implementation activities?

The final word must go to our actors who raised our spirits by stating:

"To discover the future of technology you've got to let silly things happen."

## Acknowledgements

Thanks to the director and actors who taught us a lot about performance and innovation and generously gave their time and insight.

This project is being jointly funded by Novell through their Customers of the Future programme and The University of Melbourne through a MRDG Collaborative Research Grant.

## References

Bødker, S. & Christiansen, E. (1997), Scenarios as Springboards in CSCW Design, *in* G. C. Bowker & S. L. Star (eds.), *Social Science, Technical Systems and Cooperative Work: Beyond the Great Divide*, Lawrence Erlbaum Associates, pp.217–34.

Carroll, J., Howard, S., Vetere, F., Peck, J. & Murphy, J. (2001), Identity, Power and Fragmentation in Cyberspace: Technology Appropriation by Young People, *in* G. Finnie, D. Cecez-Kecmanovic & B. Lo (eds.), *Proceedings of Australian Conference on Information Systems*, Southern Cross University, pp.95–102.

Carroll, J., Howard, S., Vetere, F., Peck, J. & Murphy, J. (2002), Just What Do the Youth of Today Want?, *in* R. H. Spague (ed.), *Proceedings of Hawaiian International Conference on Systems Sciences*, IEEE Computer Society Press.

Carroll, J. M. (2000), *Making Use: Scenario-based Design of Human–Computer Interactions*, MIT Press.

Carroll, J. M. (ed.) (1995), *Scenario-Based Design: Envisioning Work and Technology in System Development*, John Wiley & Sons.

Howard, S., Carroll, J., Vetere, F., Peck, J. & Murphy, J. (2001), Young People, Mobile Technology and the Task Artefact Cycle, *in* W. Smith, R. Thomas & M. Apperley (eds.), *Proceedings of Australian Conference on Computer–Human Interaction OzCHI 2001*, IEEE Computer Society Press, pp.63–9.

Hsia, P., Davis, A. & Kung, D. (1993), "Status Report: Requirements Engineering", *IEEE Software* 10(6), 75–9.

Iacucci, G., Kuutti, K. & Ranta, M. (2000), On the Move with a Magic Thing: Role Playing in Concept Design of Mobile Services and Devices, Paper presented at the Conference 'Designing Interactive Systems: Processes, Practices, Methods and Techniques'.

Jacobson, I. (1995), The Use Case Construct in Object-Oriented Software Engineering, *in* Carroll (1995), pp.309–36.

Norman, D. A. (1986), Cognitive Engineering, *in* D. A. Norman & S. W. Draper (eds.), *User Centered System Design: New Perspectives on Human–Computer Interaction*, Lawrence Erlbaum Associates, pp.31–62.

Rosson, M. B. & Carroll, J. M. (2000), Scenario-based Usability Engineering, Notes from a tutorial given at OzCHI 2000.

Salvador, T. & Howells, K. (1998), Focus Troupe: Using Drama to Create Common Context for New Product Concept End User Evaluations, *in* C.-M. Karat, A. Lund, B. Bederson, E. Bergman, M. Beaudouin-Lafon, N. Bevan, D. Boehm-Davis, A. Boltman, G. Cockton, A. Druin, S. Dumais, N. Frischberg, J. Jacko, J. Koenemann, C. Lewis, S. Pemberton, A. Sears, K. T. Simsarian, C. Wolf & J. Ziegler (eds.), *Summary Proceedings of CHI'98: Human Factors in Computing Systems (CHI'98 Conference Summary)*, ACM Press, pp.197–9.

Sato, S. & Salvador, T. (1999), "Playacting and Focus Troupes: Theatre Techniques for Creating Quick, Intense, Immersive and Engaging Focus Group Sessions", *Interactions* **6**(5), 35–41.

Strom, G. (2001), Mobile Devices as Props in Daily Role Playing, *in* M. D. Dunlop & S. A. Brewster (eds.), *Proceedings of Mobile HCI 2001, the Third International Workshop on Human Computer Interaction with Mobile Devices*. Not yet published, paper available at http://www.cs.strath.ac.uk/~mdd/mobilehci01/procs/strom_cr.pdf.

# Haptic Interfaces

# Guidelines for the Design of Haptic Widgets

## Ian Oakley, Alison Adams, Stephen Brewster & Philip Gray

*Glasgow Interactive Systems Group, Department of Computing Science, University of Glasgow, Glasgow G12 8QQ, UK.*

Tel: *+44 141 330 4966*

Email: *{io, stephen, pdg}@dcs.gla.ac.uk*

URL: *http://www.dcs.gla.ac.uk/~stephen*

**Haptic feedback has been shown to improve user performance in Graphical User Interface (GUI) targeting tasks in a number of studies. These studies have typically focused on interactions with individual targets, and it is unclear whether the performance increases reported will generalise to the more realistic situation where multiple targets are presented simultaneously. This paper addresses this issue in two ways. Firstly two empirical studies dealing with groups of haptically augmented widgets are presented. These reveal that haptic augmentations of complex widgets can reduce performance, although carefully designed feedback can result in performance improvements. The results of these studies are then used in conjunction with the previous literature to generate general design guidelines for the creation of haptic widgets.**

**Keywords:** haptic, desktop, GUI, multi-target, design guidelines.

## 1 Introduction

There is a growing body of literature indicating that haptic feedback, or feedback that allows a user to *feel* an interface, can yield performance improvements in target acquisition tasks in GUIs. As early as 1994, Akamatsu & Sate (1994) demonstrated lower task completion times in a target acquisition task using a simple haptic mouse with adjustable friction and vibro-tactile display. In the same year, Engel et al. (1994) showed reduced error rates and task completion times using a haptic trackball with 2 degrees of freedom force feedback. Research on this topic has continued and more recently a number of researchers, e.g. Dennerlein et al. (2000), Miller &

Zeleznik (1998) and Oakley et al. (2000), have reported performance improvements attributable to haptic feedback as presented on a number of devices. In this more recent research haptic targets are typically presented as walled areas, or as wells of attractive force that actively draw the cursor towards their centre. Targets augmented in either of these ways exhibit a 'snap-to' behaviour, actively capturing the cursor as it strays over them, and requiring a user to exert effort in order to move off the target.

This research provides compelling evidence for incorporating haptic feedback into GUIs, but in fact, tells only half of the story. While there has been extensive research on the presentation of single haptic targets, there have been few investigations of more realistic scenarios incorporating multiple targets. In such situations, the influence exerted by haptic targets incidentally traversed by users as they move towards their desired destinations must be considered. The extraneous forces these widgets apply have the potential to alter the paths users wish to take, and consequently may reduce their performance and satisfaction. Indeed, this assertion is upheld in a study conducted by Oakley et al. (2001) incorporating a condition investigating a standard haptically augmented menu system.

One possible solution to this problem is to try to remove the unwanted haptic feedback by attempting to predict a user's desired destination, and applying the feedback only on this target. Such a manipulation, if successful, would serve to reduce the complexity of the multi-target case to the simplicity of the single target case, and transfer the performance benefits gained there. However, as Dennerlein & Yang (2001) point out:

> " ...only enabling one force field is an unrealistic simulation for the implementation of force-feedback algorithms. If one confidently knew the desired target, why not then select that target automatically without using the mouse?"

According to this rationale, Dennerlein & Yang are considering the implications of partially successfully target prediction systems. They describe a study presenting multiple targets to users, and manually control the number of haptic distracter targets between a user and the destination target. They reason that adjusting the number of distracter targets simulates different accuracies of target prediction. Their conclusions are mixed. They suggest that while objective measures of performance may be maintained by using partially successful target prediction algorithms, a user's subjective experience can be negatively affected.

The practicalities underpinning target prediction, however, seem more in doubt than the validity of the idea. Keunig-Van Oirschot & Houtsma (2001b; 2001a) describe several studies investigating the accuracy of prediction of the final destination of a movement given its initial trajectory. They conclude that although the creation of an algorithm to perform such a task may be possible, the parameters that control it would vary substantially from device to device and from user to user. Münch & Dillmann (1997) describe a complete system that provides not only haptic feedback in a GUI, but also a target prediction system that attempts to mediate the application of this feedback. Their target prediction system relies on both trajectory analysis and a model of application behaviour to determine user destination. They suggest that it would only be successful after a learning period for each combination of user and application.

To summarise, the literature relating to target prediction suggests that although it may be an objectively effective solution to the problems of multi-target haptic interaction, it is also a costly and underdeveloped one. Differences between individuals, devices, and even applications may be enough to render such systems useless without substantial training times. More worryingly, the evidence suggests that partially successful systems may exert a damaging influence on subjective satisfaction.

Oakley et al. (2001) suggest an alternative solution to the multi-target problem. They describe a study investigating a haptically augmented hierarchical menu system that led to performance improvements similar to those observed in haptically augmented single target interactions. They achieved this by dynamically tailoring the forces in the menu to support, and not obstruct, the motions undertaken by users. This was done through the modification of the magnitude of the force applied (which was in the form of a walled area) through the application of two simple rules. Firstly, when a user was moving slowly the maximum force exerted by a target was reduced. This enabled users to move from one menu item to an immediately adjacent one without being hindered by strong forces. Secondly, when a user was moving rapidly, which in a menu system tends to occur either horizontally or vertically, the forces that opposed that motion were reduced, while the ones that supported it were maintained. Effectively, as a user moved horizontally in the menu, only the vertical forces that aided that motion were presented, and vice versa. This allowed users to move across, or along, menu items at speed, gaining the benefits of forces supporting, without the cost of those obstructing, these actions. The results of the study showed that the condition incorporating these dynamic forces bettered a purely visual condition with no haptic feedback by reducing errors, and a condition incorporating the same haptic feedback, without these adjustments, by lowering task completion times, and reducing subjective workload.

Here we extend these ideas by describing two studies applying this kind of dynamic haptic feedback to different multi-target situations. We then build on these results, in conjunction with the previous literature, to create preliminary design guidelines for the creation of complex haptic widgets.

## 2 Experimental Overview

### 2.1 Equipment

Both experiments were conducted under Windows NT and force feedback was provided by a PHANToM (from SensAble Technologies) equipped with a pen stylus featuring a button. The PHANToM (pictured in Figure 1) is a sophisticated 3 Degrees of Freedom (DoF) output and 6 DoF input force feedback device. The workspace available to participants was restricted to a narrow vertical plane, 110mm wide by 82.5mm high (matching the available graphical range of $800 \times 600$ pixels) and 20mm deep. Motion along the $x$ and $y$ axes controlled cursor position. No action was mapped to motion on the $z$ axis.

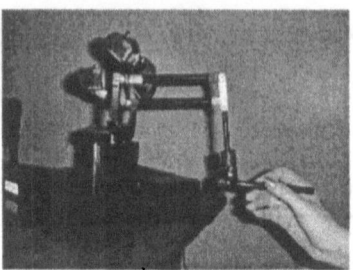

**Figure 1:** The PHANToM from SensAble Technologies.

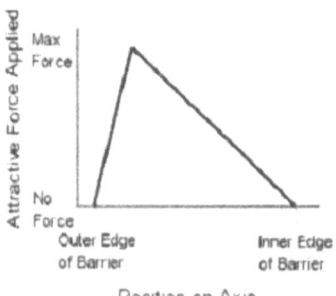

**Figure 2:** Force profile for a single haptic barrier.

## 2.2   Haptic Feedback

There were two types of haptic feedback used in these studies: Standard Haptic and
Adjusted Haptic. The first of these comes in the form of simple two-dimensional
haptic barriers. To enable these barriers to reside next to one another they had a
simple force profile ensuring that either side of the barrier returned to zero force.
Four of these barriers arranged to enclose a rectangular area served to produce a
haptified target. The force profile of a single barrier is shown in Figure 2. One
consequence of this implementation is that the corners of targets are subject to more
substantial forces, as barriers in both $x$ and $y$ dimensions independently contribute
force. This problem was partially resolved by capping the maximum exerted force
to the maximum for a single barrier, but the corners of a target still consisted of
larger areas of the maximum force. This makes diagonal motion more difficult than
either horizontal or vertical motion. The maximum magnitude of the haptic barriers
differed between the two studies: in the first it was 0.25N, in the second 0.65N. This
algorithm has similar properties to those used in other studies of haptified targets;
moving over a target causes a user to be pulled into its centre, and leaving a target
requires overcoming the barrier forces surrounding it.

   The Adjusted Haptic feedback was based on the Standard Haptic feedback,
possessing the same basic structure and magnitude (0.25N in the first study, 0.65N

in the second). It was created by dynamically applying the following three rules to modify the maximum applied strength of the haptic barriers:

1. Reduce the maximum force applied if a user is moving slowly (beneath 2cm s$^{-1}$) to a minimum of one third of its normal value.

2. If a user is moving rapidly (above 2cm s$^{-1}$) and has only been on a target for a short time (less than 100ms) reduce the maximum applied force by a factor of two.

3. Increase the maximum force applied to three times its original amount if a user has begun to perform a click (by depressing the PHANToM's button) and reduce the force back to normal levels when the click is completed (by releasing the button).

The rationale for these choices is that the first will enable users to easily move to adjacent items, the second will facilitate rapid unobstructed movements and the third will increase the likelihood that a clicking action, once begun, will be successfully completed. All transitions between different force magnitudes were gradual, so as not to disrupt users, but took place extremely rapidly. This was made possible due to the PHANToM's native 1000Hz update rate.

## 2.3 Experimental Design and Participants

Both studies had the same basic design. Both incorporated three conditions: Visual, Haptic and Adjusted. No haptic feedback was present in the Visual condition. The Haptic condition included the Standard Haptic feedback on each target, while the Adjusted condition featured the Adjusted Haptic feedback.

The first study involved eighteen participants, the second twelve. No participants performed in both studies. The majority of the participants were computing science students, the rest were experienced computer users. No participant had more than trivial previous experience with haptic interfaces. Both studies featured fully balanced repeated measures experimental designs; each included six order conditions. Each order condition was completed by three participants in the first study, and two participants in the second study. Practice in all three conditions in both studies took place immediately before the experiment began and always occurred in the same order as the presentation of conditions in the experimental session.

## 2.4 Measures

Both studies were subject to the same basic range of subjective and objective measures. Subjective assessment was achieved through the application, after the completion of each condition, of a modified version of NASA TLX (Hart & Staveland, 1988), an established measure of workload. Standard TLX questionnaires consist of the following six scales: Mental Demand, Physical Demand, Time Pressure, Effort Expended, Frustration Experienced and Performance Level Achieved. We included one extra factor: Fatigue Experienced. We feel that this is an important additional factor to consider with regard to haptic interfaces.

Objective measures in both studies included task completion time and a detailed taxonomy of errors. Both studies were essentially target acquisition and selection tasks, and in this situation we consider an error to have occurred when a user moves over the desired target and then off it again without completing the selection process. These errors fall into the following categories:

1. A *slide over*, which occurs when the user simply moves over the correct button, and then off it, without making any attempt to select it. This is arguably part of the normal targeting process.

2. A *slip off* (Brewster, 1998) which is more serious than a slide over and which occurs when a user initiates the selection process by (at least) depressing the PHANToM's button, but then moves off the target before releasing the PHANToM's button. In this case the target is not activated, although the visual feedback received is typically the same as for a successful operation.

3. A *miss* which is a selection of the wrong target. In this category we include failed attempts to select the wrong target; situations in which a user begins to select an inappropriate button, but then fails to complete this action by performing a slip off.

## 2.5   Hypotheses

Both studies shared similar hypotheses. We predicted that the Haptic condition would show fewer errors than the Visual condition (as the haptic walls make staying on a target easier), at the cost of an increase in time, workload and possibly slide over errors (as the walls make movement more difficult). We hypothesised that the Adjusted condition would combine the positive aspects of both the other conditions, yielding low task completion times, low workload and a low occurrence of errors.

## 3   Experiment 1

### 3.1   Task

This study involved the evaluation of a haptically augmented toolbar. Each button in the toolbar was 22 pixels square visually and 3.025mm square haptically. The toolbar consisted of twenty-five buttons arranged in a square configuration, and is pictured in the centre of Figure 3. The visual representation and behaviour of the toolbar was based on the toolbars that appear in existing GUIs. Moving over a button led to it visually highlighting; depressing the PHANToM's button led to the display of a different highlighted state; releasing the PHANToM's button completed the interaction. To ensure a wide variety of approach angles to this toolbar, it was placed in the centre of the eight large start points, each identified by a number and positioned at 45° intervals around it. Each trial involved moving over a specific start point identified in an instruction panel on the far right of the screen. When this occurred, a picture of the target button was displayed in the instruction panel. Selecting this button in the toolbar completed the trial, and caused a new start point to be displayed.

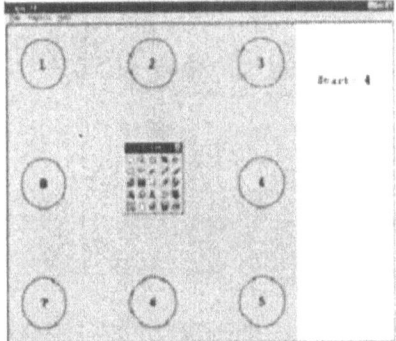

**Figure 3:** Screenshot of haptic toolbar study.

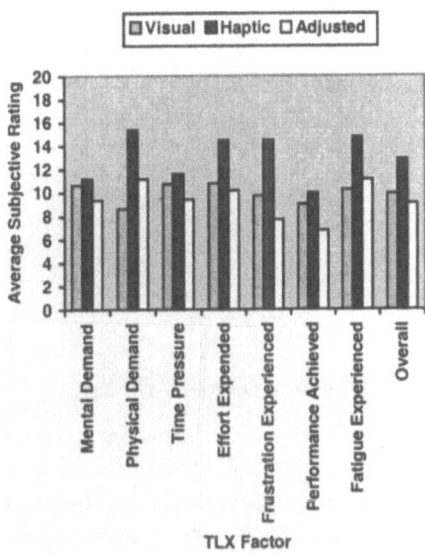

**Figure 4:** TLX rating for Study 1.

Given eight start points and twenty-five targets, there were two hundred trials in the experiment: one instance of every possible combination. These were displayed in a random order. Task completion time was measured from the moment a participant left the start point until the successful selection of the appropriate button.

## 3.2   Results

All analyses of subjective measures, time and errors were conducted using repeated measures single factor ANOVA and post hoc t-tests, using Bonferroni confidence

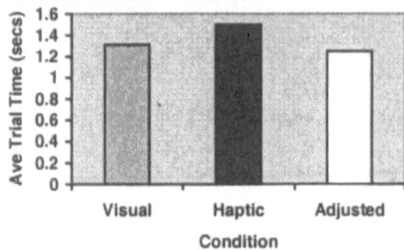

**Figure 5:** Average task completion time in Study 1.

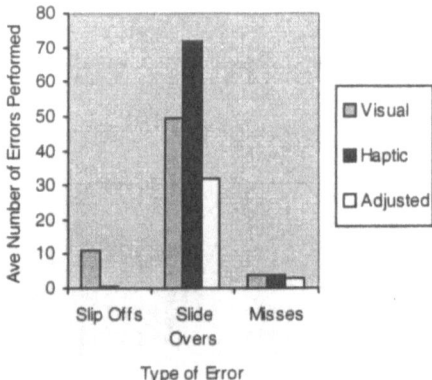

**Figure 6:** Errors recorded in Study 1.

interval adjustments. Results from the TLX questionnaire are presented in Figure 4, adjusted so that higher ratings consistently indicate higher workload. Overall workload was significantly higher in the Haptic condition than in the Visual and Adjusted conditions (both $p < 0.001$). The Haptic condition was rated significantly more taxing than the Adjusted condition in all individual scales (all at $p < 0.01$) except Time Pressure, and more demanding than the Visual condition in all factors (all at $p < 0.01$) bar Time Pressure, Performance Achieved and Mental Demand. There were no significant differences between the Visual and Adjusted conditions in any aspect of the subjective measures.

The timing data are presented in Figure 5. No significant difference in task completion time was found between the Visual and Adjusted conditions, while both yielded significantly faster times than the Haptic condition (both $p < 0.01$). Error data are presented in Figure 6. The Adjusted and Haptic conditions produced significantly fewer slip offs than the Visual condition (both $p < 0.01$). The Adjusted condition also yielded significantly fewer slide overs than the Visual and Haptic conditions (both p < 0.01), and the Visual condition fewer than the Haptic (p < 0.05). Finally, there were no significant differences in the number of misses.

## 3.3 Discussion

In this study, the experimental hypotheses were upheld: the Adjusted condition combined the favourable aspects of both other conditions. It attained the low error count apparent in the Haptic condition and the rapid task completion time present in the Visual condition. The Haptic condition was more subjectively taxing than the other two conditions. These results support those reported in Oakley et al.'s (2001) study of a haptically enhanced menu. The standard haptic feedback that is effective in a single target situation results in a performance hit when applied in a situation incorporating multiple targets. Appropriately adjusted haptic feedback, however, can lead to performance benefits in these complex environments.

# 4 Experiment 2

## 4.1 Introduction

This second study was related to the first, and involved the haptic augmentation of icons spread across a canvas; a typical cluttered desktop. From the perspective of creating haptic augmentations there are several key differences between a group of icons and the buttons on a toolbar. Most importantly, groups of icons, unlike toolbars, do not possess a highly structured and rigid spatial arrangement. There is no guarantee that a target will be adjacent to another, and even adjacent targets tend to be separated by bands of empty space. A second difference is simply one of size — icons are much larger that buttons on a toolbar, and are spread over a greater area. Consequently, it may be reasonable to expect that the speed at which users move may also alter from that used when interacting with a toolbar. These factors seem likely to exert some influence on the effectiveness of haptic augmentations, and we sought clarification as to what this might be.

## 4.2 Task

The graphical representation of the icons was 32 pixels square, while the text underneath spread further than this (up to 52 pixels). The haptic representation encompassed both these areas and was slightly larger than the graphical representation at 7.7mm, or 56 pixels, square. This discrepancy is due to the fact that the icons were sensitive to selection events occurring slightly beyond the range of the graphical representation of the widget, and the area of the haptic target was made to match this active range. This behaviour is typical of icons in windowing systems. Clicking once on an icon caused it to highlight (if it was not already) and double clicking activated the icon. Both highlighting and activation were triggered in response to the depression of the controller button, rather than the release. The user was not able to move the widgets.

Thirty icons (including the target) were present on the screen at all times, and each trial in the study involved moving over a single, stationary start point (positioned in the centre bottom of the screen) and then moving to and double clicking on a specific icon. The position of each icon was randomised on the

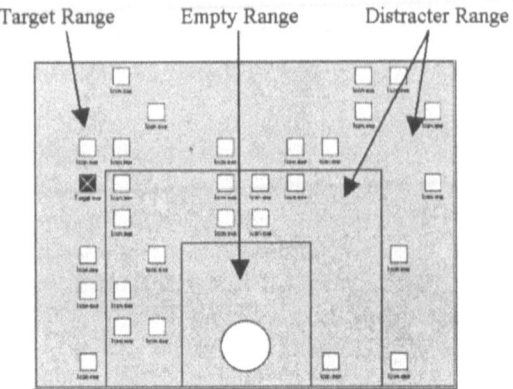

**Figure 7:** Screenshot of haptic icons study.

completion of each trial within the bounds of the following three restrictions. Firstly, a 12 by 9 grid of valid icons positions was used to ensure that the targets appeared neatly arranged in rows and columns. This grid also ensured that there was always a 1.375mm (or 10 pixel) space between adjacent targets. Secondly, no icons were ever positioned near the start point (it resided at the centre bottom of a four icon by four icon gap in the grid). Finally, the active target, the one that participants had to select, was constrained to appear outside of a larger 8 by 6 gap around the start point. These manipulations ensured that targets could never intrude on the start point — users always began a trial in a haptically empty space — and increased the likelihood that users would have to traverse distracter targets in order to reach their desired destination. Figure 7 is a screenshot of the experiment, labelled to indicate these positioning constraints. As we were not interested in the cognitive search time involved in locating the target icon, we used only two, very distinct, graphical representations for the icons; the target was a red cross, the distracters were yellow circles. Each condition in the study involved two hundred trials. Task completion time was measured from the moment a participant left the start point until the successful selection (double click) of the target icon.

## 4.3 Results

All analyses of subjective measures, time and errors were conducted using repeated measures single factor ANOVA and post hoc t-tests, using Bonferroni confidence interval adjustments. The TLX results are pictured in Figure 8, adjusted so that higher ratings always indicate a higher workload. Few significant differences were revealed between the three conditions. The Adjusted condition yielded significantly improved ratings of Effort Expended and Performance Level Achieved when compared to the Visual condition (respectively $p < 0.05$ and $p < 0.01$), and significantly reduced Frustration Experienced when compared to the Haptic condition ($p < 0.005$).

The timing data are presented in Figure 9. The adjusted condition resulted in significantly faster times than either the Visual or Haptic conditions (both $p < 0.05$).

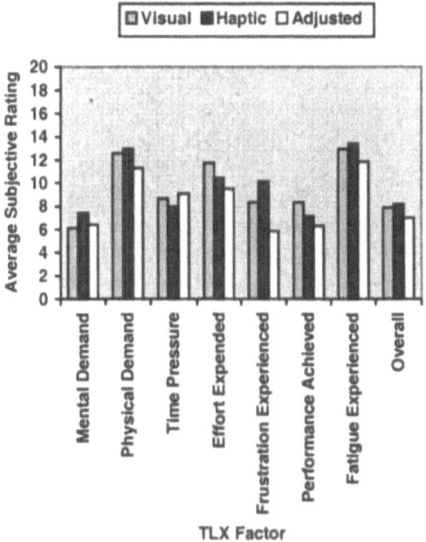

**Figure 8:** TLX rating for Study 2.

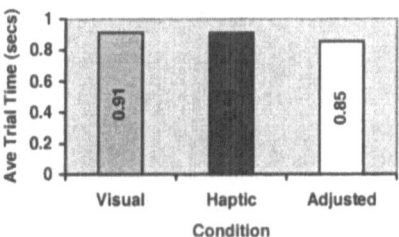

**Figure 9:** Average task completion time in Study 2.

Error data are presented in Figure 10. Fewer slip off and slide over errors are present in the Adjusted and Haptic conditions when compared to the Visual condition (all $p < 0.005$). The Visual condition, however, resulted in fewer misses than the Haptic condition ($p < 0.01$).

## 5 Discussion

The experimental hypotheses concerning the Adjusted condition were upheld. It combined the fastest task completion times with the lowest error rates, and showed a modest gain over the Visual and Haptic conditions in subjective measures. However, the Haptic condition, while exhibiting the predicted decrease in error rate compared

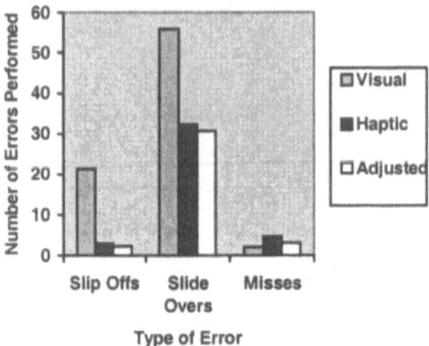

**Figure 10:** Errors recorded in Study 2.

to the Visual condition, did not produce the expected performance hit in terms of task completion time and subjective measures. As the same feedback was responsible for this performance hit in the toolbar study, this may indicate that target acquisition tasks relying on large, spatially separated targets are not sensitive indicators of the effectiveness of a haptic augmentation. Techniques that improve performance in these situations may fail in more challenging scenarios and the ability to generalise from them should be questioned. Interestingly, the Visual condition resulted in fewer miss errors than the Haptic condition. We suggest that this may be a consequence of participants getting 'snagged' on nearby distracter targets, when, without the haptic feedback, their velocity would have normally carried them over their desired target.

## 6  Guidelines for the Design of Haptic Widgets

The two studies described here, in conjunction with some of the previous literature (Oakley et al., 2001) indicate that the haptic augmentation of multiple targets with unadjusted attractive forces is at best not optimal, and at worst can reduce performance and subjective satisfaction. However, they also suggest that appropriate haptic feedback — haptic feedback that provides performance improvements at no cost — can be created through various manipulations of these haptic augmentations. Here we attempt to make explicit, to explain, the process by which these manipulations were designed. We present an initial set of guidelines for the design of effective haptic widgets to function in both single and multi target situations.

Miller & Zeleznik (1998) have previously presented three guiding principles to aid the creation of haptic widgets:

1. Haptic feedback should be used to reduce errors through guidance; provide forces to support the motions that a user is undertaking.

2. Forces applied should function as feedback; they should be based upon, but never control, a user's input.

3. Force feedback applied to a user should be over-ridable; a user should be able to pop through, or escape, from any haptically augmented area.

The guidelines we present here share similar tenets to these principals. However, we try to go further, to more precisely define the problems and solutions involved in adding haptic feedback to desktop widgets.

These guidelines are based around the idea that the force presented should support, and not oppose, a user's intent. This entails drawing a balance between allowing users to move where they want as freely as possibly, and providing forces to improve targeting and reduce errors. An advantage of these guidelines is that they do not require target prediction, a currently immature technology. A disadvantage is that they do assume that an extremely dynamic simulation controls the haptic feedback. The guidelines rely on the rapid, smooth adjustment of force magnitude according to the current state of interaction, and this flexibility may be challenging to implement on current consumer devices, such as the haptic mouse used by Dennerlein et al. (2000).

## *6.1 Guiding Strategy*

Haptic feedback has the potential to improve objective user performance in two ways: reducing the number of errors made, or decreasing task completion times. We suggest that it is more profitable to design haptic augmentations to achieve this first aim, to reduce errors. There are several reasons for this. Firstly, a reduction in errors can be linked to improvements in other metrics: it has been associated with decreases in task completion time (Dennerlein & Yang, 2001), and some studies have linked it to subjective satisfaction (Oakley et al., 2000). Secondly, to gain an increase in task completion time, users must adopt a movement strategy supported by the haptic augmentation, and there is no guarantee that this will occur. There are more assurances that forces to prevent errors will be successful. For instance, an attractive basin supports faster movement times, because targeting is simpler, and a reduction in errors, because a conscious effort is required to leave the target. However, although users may move towards the target more rapidly, this is a choice they make. The decrease in errors, on the other hand, is simply a property of the attractive forces applied over the target.

## *6.2 Choice of Haptic Augmentation*

Widgets augmented with attractive basins or haptically walled areas have typically provided the best performance improvements (Oakley et al., 2000). However when designing the haptic feedback for a widget, it is also important to consider its shape, and the likely path a user will take over it. For instance, when using these standard targeting augmentations in conjunction with square or rectangular widgets, diagonal motion is more difficult than horizontal or vertical motion. This may have an impact on performance and subjective satisfaction.

## *6.3 Interaction between Force Strength and Widget Size*

The maximum strength used for any widget, or set of widgets, should be dependent on both the size of the widgets and density of the arrangement that they are presented in. As the toolbar study described in this paper indicates, a dense arrangement of small widgets requires small forces, as large forces will severely hamper motion from one widget to an adjacent one. Also motions over small, well packed widgets are likely to be slower, as only a short distance must be travelled. Consequently small forces are sufficient to aid targeting. Correspondingly, large, spatially separated widgets suit much stronger forces, as illustrated in the second study presented here. With the absence of nearby widgets, the presence of these stronger forces is less likely to be disruptive. Also users often approach large spatially distributed widgets at considerable speed. Thus, targeting benefits are likely to be maximised by increasing the strength of the forces applied, to match the increase in approach speeds.

## 6.4   *Range of Useful Force Magnitudes*

The literature suggests that the maximum strengths of haptic targets should be in the range of 0.25N (used in the toolbar study here) to 0.8N (Dennerlein et al., 2000). There is little research indicating whether these figures would be device dependant, and it is worth noting that for use in multi-target situations, feedback of these magnitudes will typically need to be adjusted as described later in these guidelines. Maximum applied strength is also likely to be highly dependent on individual differences. In any real system, it would be essential that maximum strength be user configurable. We suggest however, that the general strength ratios between different sizes and densities of widgets would stay more or less the same across users; irrespective of the maximum strength a user chooses, the proportions between the magnitude of the forces applied over a large target, and of that applied over a small target seem likely to remain the same.

## 6.5   *Exploit Patterns of User Behaviour*

The haptic feedback present on a widget should capitalise on patterns of motion afforded by that widget. This is often related to the shape of the widget. In Oakley et al.'s (2001) study of haptically augmented menus, they exploited the fact that motion in a menu typically occurs either vertically or horizontally to provide only supportive forces. Given the similar shape of the widgets, this same manipulation has the potential to apply to scrollbars. The scrollbar could exert strong targeting forces as a user moves along its length, but fade out these forces when a user attempts to move off it, in a direction perpendicular to its length. In a scrollbar it may also be appropriate to increase the strength of the targeting forces with increased speed along the scrollbars length.

## 6.6   *Exploit Widget Behaviour*

Widget behaviour can also often be exploited to increase the effectiveness of a haptic augmentation at no cost. In both studies reported in this paper the Adjusted conditions incorporate haptic feedback designed to aid the completion of an action that has been begun. The strength of the haptic walls increases when a user begins to select a target, and reduces to normal levels on the completion of that selection. A similar strategy could be applied to any widget interaction that incorporates more than a single explicit stage. Beginning the interaction could trigger a change in the haptics, such as an increase in magnitude, designed to support the interactions successful completion.

## 6.7  Dynamic Response to Slow Movement

Force should vary according to speed: slow motions require low forces. In situations incorporating densely packed widgets this is especially important. It is hard to traverse from one widget to an adjacent widget when opposed by even a relatively low force. Users often end up moving further than they intended, 'popping through' the target widget onto one beyond it. They are then faced with the same task again — moving to an adjacent widget. This can lead to very frustrating interactions, and is arguably the biggest problem with multi-target haptic widgets. Varying the applied force such that slower motions are opposed by lower forces can overcome this problem, allowing users to move freely, while still providing a sufficiently strong force that accidental movements off a target are prevented. The strength of force required to support targeting clearly reduces in tandem with a reduction in the speed at which a user is moving, and to produce effective multi-target haptic augmentations it is essential to capitalise on this fact.

## 6.8  Dynamic Response to Rapid Movement

Equally, an extremely rapid motion over a target typically indicates that it is not a user's final destination, and thus requires the application of low forces. Users do not want to be impeded by widgets that are nowhere near their final destination. Again this is especially important in situations where there is a high density of widgets. In these situations it is likely that a user will traverse over numerous irrelevant widgets before reaching his or her desired target. One mechanism to achieve this is that used in the studies described here, where weaker forces are applied during the first 100ms that a user is over a widget. A disadvantage of this manipulation is that it may decrease the effectiveness of the behaviour observed by Dennerlein & Yang (2001) in which users throw themselves at speed towards a haptic target, relying on the forces it exerts to halt them. Reducing these forces for the first few moments that a user is over a target may make it less effective at capturing a rapidly moving user.

## 7  Conclusions

We have presented two studies investigating the use of haptic feedback to support targeting tasks. Both studies indicate that the best performance can be gained through the application of carefully designed haptic feedback, which is dynamically responsive to current states of interaction and directly measurable aspects of user behaviour (such as velocity). Following on from these studies, we have produced preliminary guidelines to make explicit the reasoning behind the design of the successful feedback, and to allow others to apply these techniques in different situations. While we focus on augmenting standard GUIs, we suggest that the findings, and guidelines, presented here may have further applicability. Many fish-tank VR systems incorporate both haptic feedback and interface widgets, and the research described here will translate easily to these systems. Other uses may include haptics systems for scientific visualisation, or for visually impaired people. In both these scenarios users are often required to explore complex arrangements of haptic targets. Applying the techniques outlined in these guidelines could make these tasks simpler and less demanding.

## Acknowledgements

This research was supported under EPSRC project GR/L79212 and EPSRC studentship 98700418. Thanks must also go to the SHEFC REVELATION Project, SensAble Technologies and Virtual Presence Ltd.

## References

Akamatsu, M. & Sate, S. (1994), "A Multi-modal Mouse with Tactile and Force Feedback", *International Journal of Human–Computer Studies* **40**(3), 443–53.

Brewster, S. A. (1998), "The Design of Sonically-enhanced Widgets", *Interacting with Computers* **11**(2), 211–35.

Dennerlein, J. T. & Yang, M. C. (2001), "Haptic Force-feedback Devices for the Office Computer: Performance and Musculoskeletal Loading Issues", *Human Factors* **43**(2), 278–86.

Dennerlein, J. T., Martin, D. B. & Hasser, C. (2000), Force-feedback Improves Performance for Steering and Combined Steering-targeting Tasks, *in* T. Turner, G. Szwillus, M. Czerwinski & F. Paternò (eds.), *Proceedings of the CHI2000 Conference on Human Factors in Computing Systems*, CHI Letters **2**(1), ACM Press, pp.423–9.

Engel, F. L., Goossens, P. & Haakma, R. (1994), "Improved Efficiency through I- and E-Feedback: A Trackball with Contetual Force Feedback", *International Journal of Human–Computer Studies* **41**(6), 949–74.

Hart, S. & Staveland, L. (1988), Development of NASA-TLX (Task Load Index): Results of Empirical and Theoretical Research, *in* P. Hancock & N. Meshkati (eds.), *Human Mental Workload*, North-Holland, pp.139–83.

Keunig-Van Oirschot, H. & Houtsma, A. J. M. (2001a), Cursor Displacement and Velocity Profiles for Targets in Various Locations, *in* C. Baber, M. Faint, S. Wall & A. Wing (eds.), *Proceedings of Eurohaptics 2001*, University of Birmingham Education and Technology Research Group, pp.108–12.

Keunig-Van Oirschot, H. & Houtsma, A. J. M. (2001b), Cursor Trajectory Analysis, *in* S. A. Brewster & R. Murray-Smith (eds.), *Proceedings of Haptic Human–Computer Interaction (HHCI 2000)*, Vol. 2058 of *Lecture Notes in Computer Science*, Springer-Verlag, pp.127–34. Available electronically from http://www.informatik.uni-trier.de/~ley/db/conf/hhci/hhci2000.html.

Miller, T. & Zeleznik, R. (1998), An Insidious Haptic Invasion: Adding Force Feedback to the X Desktop, *in* M. Beaudouin-Lafon (ed.), *Proceedings of the 11th Annual ACM Symposium on User Interface Software and Technology, UIST'98*, ACM Press, pp.59–64.

Münch, S. & Dillmann, R. (1997), Haptic Output in Multimodal User Interfaces, *in* A. R. Puerta & E. Edmonds (eds.), *Proceedings of the 2nd International Conference on Intelligent User Interfaces (IUI'97)*, ACM Press, pp.105–12.

Oakley, I., Brewster, S. A. & Gray, P. D. (2001), Solving Multi-target Haptic Problems in Menu Interaction, *in* J. A. Jacko & A. Sears (eds.), *Companion Proceedings of*

*CHI2001: Human Factors in Computing Systems (CHI2001 Conference Companion)*, ACM Press, pp.357–8.

Oakley, I., McGee, M., Brewster, S. & Gray, P. D. (2000), Putting The 'Feel' Into 'Look And Feel', *in* T. Turner, G. Szwillus, M. Czerwinski & F. Paternò (eds.), *Proceedings of the CHI2000 Conference on Human Factors in Computing Systems, CHI Letters* **2**(1), ACM Press, pp.415–22.

# Multi-session VR Medical Training: The HOPS Simulator

## Andrew Crossan[†], Stephen Brewster[†], Stuart Reid[‡] & Dominic Mellor[‡]

[†] *Department of Computing Science,* [‡] *Faculty of Veterinary Medicine, University of Glasgow, Glasgow G12 8QQ, UK.*

Tel: *+44 141 330 3541, +44 141 330 4966*

Fax: *+44 141 330 4913*

Email: *{ac, stephen}@dcs.gla.ac.uk*

URL: *http://www.dcs.gla.ac.uk/{~ac, ~stephen}*

**Virtual reality medical simulators offer the potential to provide a training environment for a novice doctor to practise skills without risk to patients. However, these simulators must be shown to provide learning before they are used in a medical training environment. This paper describes the first stage of an experiment to assess the effectiveness of the Glasgow Horse Ovary Palpation Simulator for training novice veterinary students. The performance on the simulator of a group of participants has been measured over multiple training sessions. The results show that over 4 training sessions, participants improved in their accuracy in diagnosis on the simulator while reducing the time required to make the diagnosis.**

**Keywords:** haptic interaction, force feedback, virtual reality training, medical simulation.

## 1 Introduction

There are inherent problems in training medical personnel. Serious ethical considerations must be addressed, particularly in providing training for procedures where a mistake can lead to permanent injury or can prove fatal for the patient. Traditional methods of training — such as would be provided by anatomy labs — do not provide the flexibility or realism required for training. The apprenticeship approach is most often used in both human and veterinary medicine. The student will watch many procedures performed by an experienced doctor or veterinarian before performing the procedure themselves under the expert's supervision. There is an obvious risk to the patient in this instance.

Virtual Reality (VR) simulations are increasingly being researched for use as a training tool in medicine. They have the potential to provide a safe, controllable environment for novice doctors to learn, allowing them to make mistakes without consequences to the patient. It is also possible to integrate both the anatomy and physiology, which is not possible in an anatomy lab. A wide range of reusable rare conditions and complications can be modelled and presented to a user when required. VR training also offers the possibility of providing a standardised performance rating for any user which is not possible with traditional teaching methods. Currently, a doctor's ability to perform a procedure is most often based on the number of times he/she has performed it. This may provide an inaccurate measure. By assigning tissue properties to the virtual model, and monitoring the user's actions and forces used, it is possible to objectively rate his/her performance on metrics such as tissue damage. Only through appropriate presentation of this performance feedback can users adjust their behaviour to improve performance. VR simulators are now widely thought to offer the potential of providing a new medical training paradigm. As such, commercial as well as research systems are being developed worldwide. For a simulator to become an accepted training tool, however, it is necessary to show that it improves performance for the task it is modelling.

## 1.1   Computer Haptics Overview

Computer haptics refers to interaction with a computer through the user's sense of touch. When interacting with a virtual environment such as a medical simulator using a haptic device, users can feel their interaction with the virtual objects. Current haptic devices can be separated into two categories: tactile and force feedback. Tactile technologies (such as a Braille device) stimulate the skin to generate the sense of contact with an object. Force feedback devices stimulate the kinaesthetic system, restricting the motion of users by applying forces to the fingers, hand or body.

An example of a high-resolution force feedback device is the PHANToM from SensAble Technologies (Massie & Salisbury, 1994). The PHANToM allows a user to interact with a virtual environment through a single point. The user can move freely in 6 degrees of freedom ($x$, $y$, $z$, roll, pitch and yaw). The device can also provide 3 degrees of high-resolution force feedback to resist or assist motion in the $x$, $y$ and $z$ dimensions. By using the standard GHOST toolkit, geometric and VRML objects can be incorporated into a PHANToM environment to provide the touchable model. For each of these models, stiffness, friction and damping properties can be set to provide a variety of different feels.

## 1.2   Medical Simulation Overview

Virtual medical simulations are becoming more common, and as the fidelity increases, they are expected to become more widely accepted as a training aid. Flight simulations are often used as an analogy in that they provide training in a multi-dimensional, safety-critical task. Although not widely accepted for many years, improved technology has lead to more realistic simulations that have proved useful in developing, maintaining and assessing pilot skill. They have been successfully used to simulate a wide range of conditions and emergencies, while reducing the learning curve for trainee pilots by providing a safe, controllable learning environment (Rolfe & Staples, 1986).

Simulation training is not a new idea in human and veterinary medicine. Students gain experience in certain techniques through use of plastic or rubber models, but these often lack realism and provide no useful feedback to the trainee. Surgical skills can also be improved in the anatomy labs that are incorporated into the medicine and veterinary medicine courses. Again, there are problems however since cadavers are a scarce resource, and are not generally reusable. Living tissue can also have noticeably different haptic properties than cadaver tissue (Higgins et al., 1997). VR medical simulators have the potential to present anatomical and physiological information to the user simultaneously on reusable models. Simulations currently developed can be divided into those that provide training for minimally invasive surgery (MIS), surgery, or palpation procedures. MIS simulators are by far the most common (Bro-Nielsen et al., 1999; Kühnapfel et al., 1999; McCarthy et al., 1999; Sherman et al., 1999). In an MIS procedure, surgeons view their interaction with the patient through a monitor, and hence, it lends itself to a virtual simulation. The Preop endoscopic simulator (Bro-Nielsen et al., 1999) developed by HT Medical Systems is one example of a system combining a force feedback MIS training system with anatomical and physiological models. Other systems exist to simulate other MIS procedures such as arthroscopy or laparoscopy. SKATS (Arthur et al., 1999) and VE-KATS (Sherman et al., 1999) present knee arthroscopy training systems.

Surgery simulations cover a wide range of techniques using different surgical instruments. Cathsim (Barker, 1999) is an example of a commercially available training system for venipuncture. Users of Cathsim can practice inserting a needle into a virtual vein with different scenarios available. Berkley et al. (1999) present a simulation for training in wound suturing with real time deformable tissue to increase the fidelity of the simulation. Simulation for cutting procedures in particular present problems as models need to be dynamically adjustable, to allow incisions. Delp et al. (1997) have developed tissue cutting and bleeding models for this purpose.

The development of a palpation simulation presents different problems than a surgery simulation. During surgery, a medical practitioner interacts with the patient through surgical instruments, so the quality of haptic feedback from the tissue to the surgeon is degraded. Palpation, however, involves the medic interacting directly with skin or tissue. The development of palpation simulators tends to be less common, although palpation is an important technique for the diagnosis of many conditions. Two recent examples come from the Human Machine Interface Laboratory at the CAIP Center at Rutgers University. They have developed a simulation using the Rutgers Master II for training in palpation for the detection of sub-surface tumours using experimentally based force-deflection curves (Dinsmore et al., 1997). They also present a prostate simulator developed using the PHANToM, which can model several different prostate conditions.

One of the most important aspects of a virtual training system is that a user can be given a standard performance rating for the procedure performed. Determining

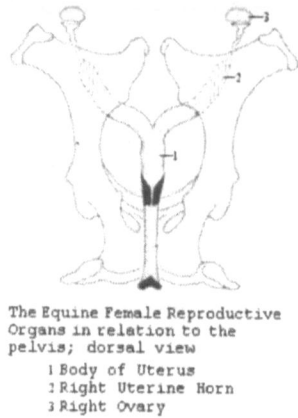

The Equine Female Reproductive
Organs in relation to the
pelvis; dorsal view
1 Body of Uterus
2 Right Uterine Horn
3 Right Ovary

**Figure 1:** Dorsal view (from above) of the reproductive system of a non-pregnant mare.

---

the performance in a medical procedure is difficult however, since it can be a complex, multi-dimensional task with many different outcomes — not just success or failure. Metrics will depend on the training task performed. Gorman et al. (1998) suggests the following metrics for a task involving driving a simulated needle through a target overlaying a blood vessel: time on task, accuracy, peak force applied, tissue damage, surface damage, and angle error. However, they note the difficulty in calculating tissue or surface damage accurately. For a palpation simulator where the user may wish to examine the whole of an object for specific shape or surface properties, accuracy and angle error may not be so relevant. Particularly in training for diagnosis, metrics can be very high level. For example, in Glasgow University's Horse Ovary Palpation Simulator (HOPS) (Crossan et al., 2000), users palpate the ovaries for a follicle to diagnose the stage of ovulation of the horse. The users might be asked "Does a follicle exist on either ovary, and if so, what size is the follicle". Systems exist to allow user performance to be stored over many training sessions (Bro-Nielsen et al., 1999), such that any trends of improvement or otherwise can be noted. This could eventually lead to an objective method of certification of medical trainees (Higgins et al., 1997). O'Toole et al. (1997) present a study suggesting that experienced surgeons perform better than novice surgeons on the metrics defined on their surgery simulator.

## 2 Horse Ovary Palpation

During an ovary examination, the vet inserts a gloved hand into the pelvic area of the horse through the rectum. The vet must search through the pelvic region of the horse for the uterus. The ovaries are attached to the uterus, and each can be found by following either the left or right uterine horn (see Figure 1). This is difficult since the vet must perform this search through touch alone. It usually requires several attempts before an inexperienced student can locate an ovary. Once located, the vet will cup the ovary with one or more fingers, and palpate it using his/her thumb. In particular they will look for any abnormalities in the shape or surface properties of the ovary, and through experience, will be able diagnose different conditions through touch alone. For the purposes of the Glasgow University simulator, follicles of different sizes can be placed at different positions on the ovary models. A follicle is a roughly spherical fluid filled sac that grows on the surface of an ovary. Some of this sac exists under the surface. It will typically grow from a small size to a few centimetres in diameter. As the follicle grows, it will also tend to move towards the centre of the ovary. Depending on the size, position and feel of the follicle a vet can diagnose the stage of ovulation of the horse. There may be many follicles on each ovary, but only one follicle will eventually ovulate. Other surface features may exist on the ovary surface. A corpus luteum feels similar to a follicle and may therefore be mistaken for one. Unlike a follicle however, it is ridged around the edge. Ovarian cysts or tumours may also exist, but are less common. Below are given some typical descriptions of the common objects involved.

An ovary is a hard fibrous object. It may feel similar to many objects in the abdomen and is therefore difficult to identify. A corpus luteum is object on an ovary's surface that may feel similar to a follicle. However, unlike a follicle, it has a thick walled with a ridge. A follicle is a thin walled, soft partially submerged object on an ovary's surface. Horse veterinarians were closely involved when developing the shape and haptic properties for the virtual ovaries.

The core skills involved in this procedure are location and identification of the ovaries, and recognition of surface features on the ovaries. Ultrasound scanning is now often used to identify the surface features. However, the Glasgow University Veterinary School still considers palpation as an important technique for students to learn.

Students are expected to participate in training outwith the Glasgow veterinary course. Approximately five percent of all students will get placements in an equine practice. This is one of the most useful ways of gaining experience in equine welfare. However, particularly for an invasive procedure such as ovary palpation, a student may still not get a chance to examine a horse. A veterinarian is often paid for the time spent performing examinations, and clients may be unwilling to pay for the time it would take to teach a novice. A horse owner is also unlikely to allow an inexperienced student to examine his/her horse, as there is the possibility of causing injury.

## 3   Multi-Session Training Study

A previous study has shown that over one training session, participants trained using the HOPS simulator perform no worse on specimen ovaries than participants trained using traditional methods (Crossan et al., 2000). In this case, performance was based on the correct location and sizing of a follicle on the specimen ovaries. This study also showed that there was a low percentage of correct identification in both cases (~11% correct), which suggests current methods of teaching can be improved upon. This experiment will build on the previous work with the HOPS simulator by examining the effect on performance of multiple training sessions.

## 3.1 Hypotheses

### 3.1.1 Hypothesis 1

The independent variable for Hypothesis 1 is the quantity of haptic training that the participants receive. The dependent variable is the performance level on the virtual ovaries. Performance is defined by the number of follicles that have been placed correctly on an ovary, and the correct sizing of these follicles.

The performance level of the participants on the simulator will significantly improve with an increasing number of training sessions.

### 3.1.2 Hypothesis 2

The independent variable for Hypothesis 2 is the quantity of haptic training that the participants receive. The dependent variable is the time taken to complete the examination of the ovaries. The time required to complete the task will significantly decrease as the participant receives more simulator training.

### 3.1.3 Hypothesis 3

The independent variable for Hypothesis 3 is the quantity of haptic training that the participants receive. The dependent variables are individual workload, confidence and overall workload when examining the virtual ovaries.

The measured individual workload factors when examining the virtual ovaries will significantly decrease as the participants receive more simulator training. Participants' overall workload will significantly decrease while confidence will significantly increase.

## 3.2 Participants

One group of participants was involved in the experiment. The group consisted of second year veterinary students at Glasgow University Veterinary School who have learned the theory of ovary palpation from lectures but have no practical experience of in-vivo ovary palpation through university teaching. There were eight participants — seven female and one male. All were regular computer users, but none had any previous exposure to the PHANToM.

## 3.3 Experimental Set-up

Participants interacted with the HOPS environment using a PHANToM 1.5 from SensAble Technologies with the standard thimble attachment. The simulation was run on a 700MHz dual-processor PC. The equipment for the experiment was set up as shown in Figure 2. The participants wore headphones to mask noises produced by the PHANToM motors.

## 3.4 Design

### 3.4.1 Training

As participants had no previous exposure to the PHANToM, they took part in an initial training session immediately before the first haptic training session. This training stage was designed to familiarise users with interacting with a three dimensional environment using the PHANToM. They were each presented for five minutes with a standard environment supplied by SensAble Technologies that allowed participants to interact with movable boxes. Participants could both feel their interactions through

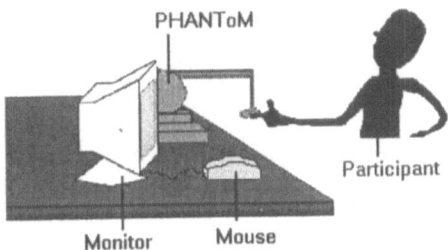

**Figure 2:** The experimental set-up used. Participants interacted through the PHANToM. Ovary models and PHANToM interactions were not displayed to the user on-screen, while the mouse was used to start and stop examinations.

the PHANToM, and see their interactions on the screen. The participants were then presented with an environment containing a haptic only representation of two spheres. In this condition, they could not see the spheres or the PHANToM cursor on the screen.

Initially the size of the spheres varied. Each participant was asked to state whether the left or right sphere was larger or they were equal size using touch alone. A random selection of each of these cases was presented to participants to explore until they reach an appropriate level of performance. There was no time limit for the exploration, but participants proceeded after answering five cases correctly.

A similar training session was provided for training in softness discrimination using the PHANToM. The same environment containing two spheres was used although the size of the spheres remained constant while their softness was varied. Participants stated whether the left or right sphere was softer, or whether they were of equal softness. Once again there was no time limit, and the participant proceeded after answering five cases correctly.

These training stages were only presented to the user before the first experimental session. They were designed to provide some initial familiarisation of the PHANToM as well as training in size and softness discrimination, and locating objects though touch alone. These skills were important for the experimental task.

In addition to the above training, users were presented with a visual and haptic representation of the HOPS environment (shown in Figure 3) before each experimental session. The participants were asked to explore the plain environment — no surface features — for five minutes.

### 3.4.2 Task

All participants were presented with the same thirty-two ovary cases over the four training session, but in counterbalanced orders. There were four orders of presentation with two participants being presented with each ordering. In one experimental session, participants were each presented with eight ovary cases. Also, in each experimental session, the total number of follicles in all cases was kept constant at seventeen. For each case, participants were told that there were zero, one

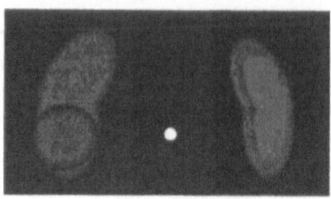

**Figure 3:** The Horse Ovary Palpation Simulator. This environment consists of a left and right ovary. On the bottom half of the left ovary, a spherical follicle can be seen. The user's cursor is shown as the sphere in the centre.

or more follicles present on either ovary and were allowed five minutes to explore the environment while identifying all follicles. Identification involved positioning the follicle on the left or right ovary, the front or back of the ovary, and top or bottom half of the ovary. Once identified, participants were asked the size of the follicle. They were told that the follicles would either be 2cm, 3cm or 3.5cm in diameter. Participants started and stopped each case using the mouse. If a case was explored for five minutes, he/she was alerted that his/her time for examining the current case was finished and was allowed to proceed to the next case.

Time measurements were taken for each case. As timing information would be affected by the number of follicles found in a case, there were equal numbers of cases of equal complexity in each experimental session. Therefore, there were two one-follicle cases, three two-follicle cases and three three-follicle cases presented in each session.

Participants were asked to complete a NASA TLX workload evaluation form after each experimental session had ended. Four such experimental sessions spaced a week apart were performed by each participant. Participants were not told if their answers were correct or incorrect at any time during the experiment. This was to ensure that measured confidence values were not affected by results, and that all training was as a result of time spent using the simulator.

## 3.5 Results

Correctness data for positioning the follicles is shown in Figure 4. Results were analysed using GLM ANOVA tests. Increasing the number of training sessions was found to have a significant effect when comparing mean accuracy in placing follicles on the ovaries over the four training sessions ($F = 4.27$, $p < 0.02$). Post hoc analysis using Tukey tests show a significant difference in performance in Session 1 and Session 3 ($p < 0.04$) and Session 1 and Session 4 ($p < 0.03$). Although a slight performance increase can be seen in Figure 4 between Sessions 3 and 4, this difference is not significant.

Similar analysis was carried out on follicles that were correctly positioned and sized over the four training sessions. The results over four training sessions are shown in Figure 5. GLM ANOVA analysis shows a significant performance difference as training progresses ($F = 7.28$, $p < 0.021$). Post hoc analysis using a Tukey test revealed that there were significant differences between performance in

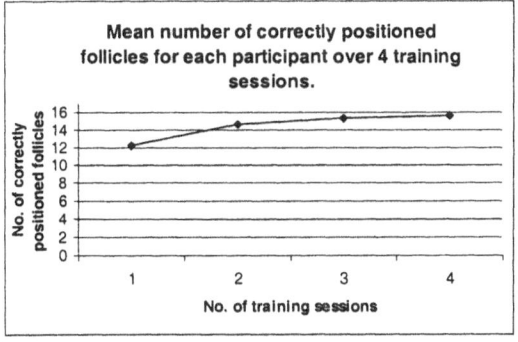

**Figure 4:** Average number of correctly positioned follicles for all participants over four training sessions. There were 17 follicles in each session.

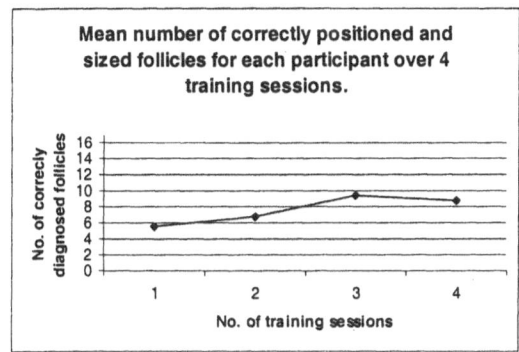

**Figure 5:** Average number of correctly positioned and sized follicles for all participants over four training sessions. There were 17 follicles in each session.

Sessions 1 and 3 (p < 0.003), Sessions 1 and 4 (p < 0.02) and Sessions 2 and 3 (p < 0.04). Although a slightly decrease in performance can be seen in Figure 5 between Sessions 3 and 4, this difference is not significant.

The results of the timing data are shown in Figure 6. Timing data was again analysed using a GLM ANOVA test. The results show a significant decrease in time taken to complete the task as training progressed (F = 10.64, p < 0.001). A post hoc Tukey test revealed a significant decrease in time taken for the task during Sessions 1 and 2 (p < 0.05), Sessions 1 and 3 (p < 0.03), Sessions 1 and 4 (p < 0.001), and Sessions 2 and 4 (p < 0.05). Again, although time taken to complete the task decreases between Sessions 3 and 4, this difference is not significant.

The results gathered from workload analysis are shown in Figure 7. It is important to note that for 'Performance Achieved' and 'Confidence Level', lower score indicates better perceived performance or confidence.

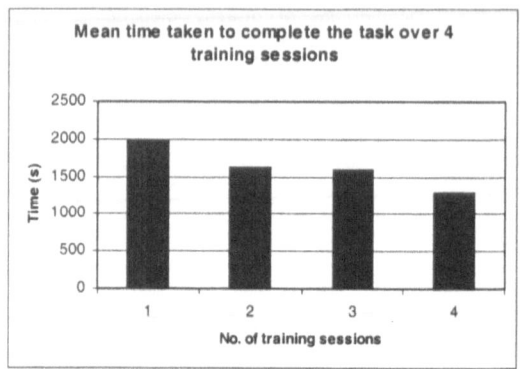

**Figure 6:** Mean time to complete task over all training session for all participants to complete the task.

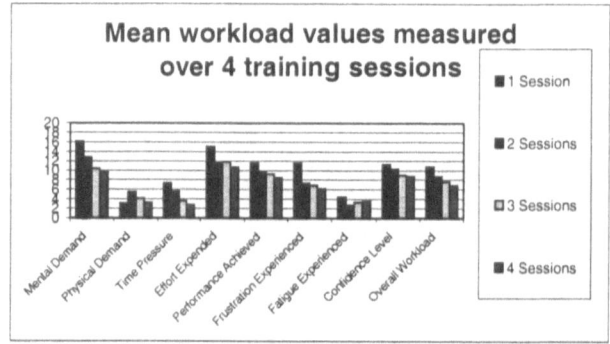

**Figure 7:** Average workload for all participants shown over 4 training sessions. Performance achieved and confidence level are such that a lower value indicates better perceived performance or confidence.

A GLM ANOVA suggests that there is no significant decrease due to participants completing multiple training session ($F = 2.38$, $p = 0.098$). GLM ANOVAS on the individual factors suggest that the only workload factor significantly affected by multiple sessions is 'Mental Demand' ($F = 3.80$, $p < 0.03$). The post hoc Tukey test showed a significant decrease in 'Mental Demand' is shown between Sessions 1 and 4 ($p < 0.03$).

## 4 Discussion

Hypothesis 1 has been supported by the results. As the number of experimental sessions increased, a significant increase in performance was also noted when examining both correctly positioned, and correctly positioned and sized follicles. For correctly positioned follicles, this difference was significant between Sessions 1 and 3, and Sessions 1 and 4. The fact that no significant performance difference was shown between Sessions 2, 3, and 4 suggests that the training benefits of multiple sessions in placing follicles may be levelling off after two or three sessions. Results suggest that sizing the follicles proved a more difficult that required more training. Significant performance differences were noted between Session 1 and all other sessions as well as between Sessions 2 and 3. This suggests that participants were still learning, and improving performance during the third training session. There is a slight decrease in performance between Sessions 3 and 4, but this is not significant. This may indicate that the performance improvements due to time spent on the simulator had levelled off by the fourth session.

Hypothesis 2 has also been supported by the results. Significant decreases in time were shown between Sessions 1 and all other sessions, and Sessions 2 and 4. This difference is emphasised by the fact that examination times were capped at five minutes for each case. The majority of examinations not completed in five minutes occurred in the first week. Again, there was no significant time difference noted between Sessions 3 and 4. This may suggest that participants would not become much faster with more training. The timing data combined with the performance data shows that as participants received more training, they were able to complete the task in less time without having a detrimental affect on performance.

Hypothesis 3 was not supported by the data. There was no significant mean overall workload differences noted throughout the four training sessions. Although no significant decrease was noted, there was a general downward trend noted which may become significant after more training sessions. Similarly, although there was a general increase in confidence noted throughout the training sessions, these increases are not significant. The increase suggests however that a significant result may be possible with more training sessions. For each of the individual workload factors, only 'Mental Demand' showed a significant decrease throughout the training sessions. The perceived 'Mental Demand' for Session 4 was significantly less than the perceived 'Mental Demand' for Session 1. This may correspond to the fact that the participants were performing better at this stage, and taking less time to complete an examination.

## 5 Future Work and Conclusions

The results described above are the first stage in an experiment to assess the usefulness of HOPS as a training tool for veterinary students. The results show that as participants received more training on the simulator, their performance in diagnosing the condition of the ovaries improved, while time taken to make the diagnosis and overall workload for the task decreased. The next stage of the experiment will measure how closely these improvements translate to improvement in performance in the real life ovary examination procedure. The experiment will involve 2 groups: the same group of participants who performed the experiment described above, and a group of participants who have similar background knowledge but have had no haptic training. The performance of each group will be measured on the same set of specimen ovaries as used in student anatomy laboratories. The hypotheses tested will be that the group who have received haptic training will diagnose follicles on the ovaries more accurately, while taking significantly less time. It is hypothesised the haptic training group will show higher confidence levels and lower overall workload than the no training group.

These results have provided an encouraging basis for the future experiment described. They have demonstrated that learning takes place in the HOPS simulator environment over several training sessions. The next stage of the experiment will demonstrate whether or not these improvements carry through to the real life procedure.

## Acknowledgements

This research was funded by the Faculty of Veterinary Medicine at Glasgow University. Thanks must also go to the SHEFC REVELATION Project, SensAble Technologies and Virtual Presence.

## References

Arthur, J. G., McCarthy, A. D., Wynn, H. P., Harley, P. J. & Barber, C. (1999), Weak at the Knees? Arthroscopy Surgery Simulation User Requirements, Capturing the Psychological Impact of VR Innovation through Risk-based Design, *in* A. Sasse & C. Johnson (eds.), *Human–Computer Interaction — INTERACT '99: Proceedings of the Seventh IFIP Conference on Human–Computer Interaction*, Vol. 1, IOS Press, pp.360–6.

Barker, V. L. (1999), Cathsim, *in* J. D. Westwood, H. M. Hoffman, R. A. Robb & D. Stredney (eds.), *Proceedings of Medicine Meets Virtual Reality*, IOS Press, pp.36–7.

Berkley, J., Weghorst, S., Gladstone, H., Raugi, G., Berg, D. & Ganter, M. (1999), Fast Finite Element Modeling for Surgical Simulation, *in* J. D. Westwood, H. M. Hoffman, R. A. Robb & D. Stredney (eds.), *Proceedings of Medicine Meets Virtual Reality*, IOS Press, pp.55–61.

Bro-Nielsen, M., Tasto, J. L., Cunningham, R. & Merril, G. L. (1999), Preop Endoscopic Simulator: A PC-based Imersive Training System for Bronchoscopy, *in* J. D. Westwood, H. M. Hoffman, R. A. Robb & D. Stredney (eds.), *Proceedings of Medicine Meets Virtual Reality*, IOS Press, pp.76–82.

Crossan, A., Brewster, S. A. & Glendye, A. (2000), A Horse Ovary Palpation Simulator for Veterinary Training, *in* M. Harders & S. Huber (eds.), *Proceedings of PURS 2000*, Hartung-Gorre, pp.79–86.

Delp, S. L., Loan, P., Basdogan, C. & Rosen, J. M. (1997), "Surgical Simulation: An Emerging Technology for Training in Emergency Medicine", *Presence* **6**(2), 147–59.

Dinsmore, M., Langrana, N., Burdea, G. & Ladeji, J. (1997), Virtual Reality Training Simulation of Palpation of Subsurface Tumors, *in Proceedings of Virtual Reality Annual International Symposium*, IEEE Computer Society Press, pp.54–60.

Gorman, P. J., Lieser, J. D., Morray, W. B., Haluck, R. S. & Krummel, T. M. (1998), Assessment and Validation of a Force Feedback Virtual Reality Based Surgical Simulator, *in* J. K. Salisbury & M. A. Srinivasan (eds.), *Proceedings of Phantom User Group '98*, MIT Press, pp.27–9.

Higgins, G. A., Merrill, G. L., Hettinger, L. J., Kaufmann, C. R., Champion, H. R. & Satava, R. M. (1997), "New Simulation Technologies for Surgical Training and Certification: Current Status and Future Projections", *Presence* 6(2), 160–72.

Kühnapfel, U., Çakmak, H. K. & Maaß, H. (1999), 3D Modeling for Endoscopic Surgery, *in Proceedings of the IEEE Symposium on Simulation*, pp.22–32.

Massie, T. H. & Salisbury, K. (1994), The Phantom Haptic Interface: A Device for Probing Virtual Objects, *in Proceedings of the ASME Winter Annual Meeting, Symposium on Haptic Interface for Virtual Environments and Teleoperator Systems*, pp.295–302.

McCarthy, A., Harley, P. & Smallwood, R. (1999), Virtual Arthroscopy Training: Do the Virtual Skills Developed Match the Real Skills Required?, *in* J. D. Westwood, H. M. Hoffman, R. A. Robb & D. Stredney (eds.), *Proceedings of Medicine Meets Virtual Reality*, IOS Press, pp.221–7.

O'Toole, R., Playter, R., Blank, W., Cornelius, N., Roberts, W. & Raibert, M. (1997), A Novel Virtual Reality Surgical Trainer with Force Feedback: Surgeon vs. Medical Student Performance, *in* J. K. Salisbury & M. A. Srinivasan (eds.), *Proceedings of Phantom User Group '97*, MIT Press, pp.73–5.

Rolfe, J. M. & Staples, K. J. (1986), The Flight Simulator as a Training Device, *in Flight Simulation*, Cambridge University Press, pp.232–49.

Sherman, K. P., Ward, J. W., Wills, D. P. M. & Mohsen, A. M. M. A. (1999), A Portable Virtual Environment Knee Arthroscopy Training System with Objective Scoring, *in* J. D. Westwood, H. M. Hoffman, R. A. Robb & D. Stredney (eds.), *Proceedings of Medicine Meets Virtual Reality*, IOS Press, pp.335–6.

# Memorable Systems

# An Investigation of Memory for Daily Computing Events

## Mary Czerwinski & Eric Horvitz

*Microsoft Research, One Microsoft Way, Redmond, WA 98052, USA.*

Tel: *+1 425 703 4882*

Email: *{marycz, horvitz}@microsoft.com*

URL: *http://research.microsoft.com/users/marycz*

**In pursuit of computational tools for augmenting computer users' abilities to interleave multiple tasks, we examined computer users' ability to identify and recall computing events deemed to be important, both with and without supportive reminder tools. Memory for events occurring during computer sessions was studied both 24 hours after an initial taped session and again after a one-month period of time. Results show that memory for important computing events is fragile and that software tools could be used to augment users' memories of how they have spent their time while computing. In addition, we observed that approximately half of the events that users identified as important could be identified automatically with available computational methods, and an attempt was made to characterise the nature of the remaining events. Finally, in a probe of alternate designs for reminding systems, we found that users typically preferred to see snapshots of their computing events in a prototype reminder system, without audio, as opposed to a full video version of an event reminder system.**

**Keywords:** reminder systems, memory augmentation, free recall, memory prostheses, empirical findings.

## 1 Introduction

Today's software systems and applications provide few tools for the resumption of suspended tasks. Typical pressures and distributions of tasks and communications rarely allow users to complete a single project without interruptions, and later restarts, of tasks. Portfolios of projects and goals across business and personal life require users to manage multiple suspensions, resumptions, and interleavings of efforts. The computational and graphical capabilities of personal computers hold great opportunity for assisting users with the management of multiple, interleaved tasks. However, to date, computers, and related technologies, have largely amplified the problem. Personal computers provide users with a tantalising means for initiating multiple projects and for collecting large quantities of interrelated data and resources associated with different projects. Computers have evolved into both a general work palette, providing a one-stop shop for multiple projects, as well as a networked communication and information-tracking tool. Thus, the quantity of interleaved projects and of notifications occurring during ongoing work continues to increase. As common examples, the popularity of email and instant messaging challenges users with handling an ongoing stream of notifications, most of which may be unrelated to the task at hand. The recent blossoming of cellular phone usage, the continuing growth of wireless computing and handheld devices has ensured that users can be contacted — and disrupted — almost anywhere at any time. Recent research has demonstrated that such ubiquitous notification can be costly in that interruptions, they provide distract users from ongoing tasks (Czerwinski et al., 2000; Maglio & Campbell, 2000; McFarlane, 1999).

Our research is motivated by our belief that personal computers provide an unprecedented opportunity to augment users' abilities to suspend and return to tasks, whether the suspension is induced by external disruptions or the result of the user-directed shifting among multiple tasks. The goal of building *memory-augmentation systems* to help users to remember and, more generally, to reinstate tasks initiated earlier, following some period of time after a disruption, can be decomposed into several subproblems. The subproblems include:

1. The automated recognition of critical events and content associated with a task.

2. The presentation or display of components of previously suspended events or content in a manner that efficiently reminds and updates users about suspended tasks.

The experiments and results described in this paper probe aspects of both subproblems.

In this paper, we review our efforts to characterise the nature of memories that users would most benefit from being reminded about. We attempted to focus our attention on the most important events to attempt to capture and to later remind users about. We framed our pursuit of these events with the question: Of the set of events in users' daily computing lives that they tend to wish to recall at a later time, which subset of events do users tend to forget? By focusing on the subset of events that are both *deemed as important and tend to be forgotten*, we seek to triage engineering efforts to build an augmented memory system. We hoped that such a framing of high-payoff reminders might assist us to better characterise the informational and contextual properties of the most useful reminders.

We also present experiments that probe the relative effectiveness of alternate approaches to reinstating memories of prior context via different methods for rendering previously captured events and interactions. The results on high-payoff events and on the best approach for rendering memory-jogging content provide information about two critical challenges on the path to building effective automated memory augmentations systems.

## 1.1   Related Work

Related research on reminder systems includes investigation of 'prospective' memory (McDaniel & Einstein, 1993; Eldridge et al., 1992; Ellis & Nimmo-Smith, 1993; Harris, 1984; Kvavilashvili, 1992; Lamming & Newman, 1992; Sellen et al., 1996; Terry, 1988; Wilkins & Baddeley, 1978). The study of prospective memory has been distinguished from traditional research on memory in cognitive psychology in that cues for retrieval are largely self-generated (one must remember to remember), and that the events to be remembered are intentions or plans to perform some action in the future. In traditional memory research, cues for retrieval typically are generated by the researcher and the memory is for events or relationships learned in the past over a very short time period in the laboratory. Prospective memory failures have been shown through diary studies to be a serious problem as reported in the daily lives of knowledge workers (Eldridge et al., 1992; Terry, 1988), yet very little is known about the mechanisms for bringing intentions to mind, nor how technology could be used to reduce forgetting.

A recent observational study performed by Jones et al. (2001) highlighted the severity of the problem of getting back to information that users had discovered previously, and the lack of existing tool support in today's software. The study explored the myriad of ways that users attempt to keep Web information available for future reference. Documented strategies included emailing useful links to one's self or others for easy access via the email inbox, pasting the Web information into documents, printing out Web pages, saving Web pages to one's hard drive, and adding the URL as a link on a personally maintained Web page. They found that the 'reminding' value of any one of these methods depended greatly upon a user's habits. For instance, if a user triaged their email inbox on a routine basis, the reminding value of emailing a Web link to oneself is likely to be high. However, if the inbox is overloaded with email, the value of that method is likely to be low. Interestingly, browser bookmarks, a feature designed explicitly to help remind users of their important Web content, were not observed to be used by the individual participants in the study, and the authors therefore concluded that bookmarks have a low reminder value. In order to boost the reminder value of bookmarks, the authors suggested integrating bookmarks into existing hierarchical organisers, such as the email folder hierarchy or the hierarchy of the file system. In addition, they suggested that bookmarks should include a better reminding function, including why the Web page was relevant to the user, perhaps the context in which is was originally found, and what actions remain to be taken with the information contained on the Web page.

Lamming et al. (1994) studied the usefulness of a video diary as a memory prosthesis to help knowledge workers remember work activities that were intended for the future. They demonstrated that their participants indeed forgot quite a bit about their daily activities, and that video could be useful in aiding recall of past accomplishments and future intended activities. Full video was employed as the source of reminders in this study. We find it unlikely that knowledge workers would take the time to skim through full video in order to recall past or future activities or intended behaviours. Nevertheless, the idea of capturing user activities and allowing the user to replay brief snapshots of their activities in some summarised or abstracted form could serve as the basis for a useful type of reminder system. We were inspired by this idea in the prototypes used in our study.

Renaud (2000) provided a mini-review of how interruptions wreak havoc with users' primary tasks. She pointed out that warnings can help, but that they come at a cost; many users don't necessarily go back to the primary task, or they return only after a significant delay. Renaud's discussion appears to assume that users perform tasks in a linear manner, rather than addressing the broader, common challenge of multitasking. She suggests that imagery and pictorial presentations are superior to verbal representations in aiding memory. Renaud also classifies interruptions into multiple categories. She describes visualisation for context-reinstatement and reminding that attempts to support users' 'limited, sequential information processing abilities'. She argues that a reminder system must be an 'extra'-application, easily interpretable, and linked to explanations of system states and actions. She attempts this in her system design by melding 'UI sequences', selections made by the user in the user interface, to request/response sequences. Her visualisation has two main components. First, there is a session history window that chunks actions into 3 groups: current, groups of 10s, and groups of 100s, with the current category as default. A textual explanation window below the clustering of actions contains a set of explanations for the system actions that are currently selected. Second, there is a 'replay my actions' feature, which can perform replay actions from the beginning to the end of a system session or walk through the last $n$ actions. Renaud performed a user study examining error messages and observed that users used the system to determine how to recover from errors (in the study, users had to remember system parameters entered in order to recover). Renaud focused on error recovery, rather than on the challenge of reinstating rich context after an interruption or remembering an intended activity — functionalities we desire in a reminder system.

Altmann & Gray (2000) emphasize dynamic task environments in their research, in which users have to update their task continually with new instructions. An example environment included a fighter-plane cockpit. Their results demonstrate that new instruction updating depends on forgetting old instructions, and they study how forgetting places constraints on how the new information is encoded. They label this process 'preparing to forget'. Altmann & Gray describe and then test key assumptions of 'functional decay theory'. Their data shows that, after an initial encoding phase, there is a relatively stable use phase, in which activation for an item or instruction must begin to decay (preparing to forget). In other words, after initial encoding of new instructions, a user will operate optimally if she allows those instructions to slowly decay from memory. They demonstrate, using their serial-attention paradigm, that functional decay theory can predict many aspects of how users really handle constantly updating instructions. They observe how long it takes to prepare to forget (focusing on 1 item for about 5 seconds requires an initial 1 second of encoding prior to those 5 seconds). They conclude by stating that, within dynamic task environments, if users do not have enough time to pay attention to an update and do not have enough time to let a previous task item fade from memory, situation awareness can degrade 'catastrophically'. Relating this finding back to prospective memory, a user cannot attend to a future behaviour if the previous task is still requiring attentional resources in short-term memory. This would appear to be an important principle to keep in mind when designing technology to augment users' memory for their computing work.

Some recent work has investigated software support for users' task flow or for contextual awareness. Most of this research has either focused on visualisation of calendar events or the desktop, or augmenting the user's memory via a combination of intelligent agents and wearable computers.

Lamming & Flynn (1994) developed Forget Me Not, designed as part of a wearable computing system. The system's purpose was to continuously log a user's physical context over time so that personal event retrieval could be easily accomplished at a later time. The context saved includes information about the user in both the physical and virtual worlds. Memory-aid systems like Forget Me Not tried to help with everyday memory problems such as recalling a name or finding a document. The system created autobiographies for users by capturing who they met, where they went, who they phoned, and other contextual data. The authors based their system on the concept of episodic memory, the theory that we organize part of our memory about the past into episodes (Tulving, 1983), and that the location, who was there, etc., are strong episodic cues for retrieval from long-term memory. An example of how Forget Me Not might be used includes the scenario of a user asking a note-taking application to retrieve notes from a previous meeting with the person currently co-located with the user. This prior research comes the closest in spirit to the work we are carrying out on memory augmentation, though we are extending our notions of event tracking to include thematic content as well as episodic.

The Remembrance Agent (RA) (Rhodes & Starner, 1996) also helped play the role of a memory augmentation agent by continuously displaying information relevant to the current physical context of the user. The RA differed from Forget Me Not in that it looked at and retrieved specific textual information rather than automatically summarising the user's actions and context. RA augmented memory by autonomously presenting previous email and notes relevant to current email written by the user. Although the goal of the RA system was to remind users of potentially forgotten information, it made no attempt to discern whether or not those documents were truly likely to have been forgotten. In addition, the system required users to manually determine which documents were stored in the database for future retrieval. Another wearable reminder system, named Memory Glasses (DeVaul et al., 2000), uses time, location, and activity to guide its delivery of reminders to its user. It focuses on the user's context and uses sensors (a camera and a microphone) to determine the user's activity (e.g. engaged in conversation, walking, etc.). If a contact is physically near someone wearing Memory Glasses, and has a profile that matches one or more of the wearer's interests, the system can alert the wearer to that effect. Interests are limited to names, personal interests and hobbies.

Rekimoto et al. (1998) has implemented what he refers to as "time machine computing". In this work, a user is provided with access to visualisations of what one's computer desktop looked like, at any point in time in the past, or even in the future. With this 'time-travelling' desktop, it is argued that a user no longer needs a folder hierarchy. If a document is deleted from the desktop, the user can always time travel back to the date when the document was being used and retrieve it again. The basic idea is that when you travel back in time you can see the items that were open on the desktop when you were using that document of interest, thus helping you to reinstate the original past context of use for that document. One important aspect of the system is that the user can leave 'reminders' to herself in the future. Although the idea is interesting, we questioned whether views of the top-level desktop alone were sufficient to reinstate context of use for many documents and tasks. We hoped to identify what it was about users' desktops that they found important in a reminder system through a study in which users' desktops were recorded and then prototypes were examined and evaluated for their usefulness. The concept of the 'time machine' metaphor influenced our thinking about this problem, and in our user research we strove to understand whether or not simply capturing the state of documents and information on the desktop would provide enough contextual information to significantly enhance users' work flow and multitasking.

Despite the recent emergence of research on memory augmentation tools, users today have few tools that can assist with the remembering of tasks and content. However, researchers have found that users often develop practices with existing commercially available systems and applications to support memory needs. As an example, studies have recently shown that an email mailbox is often used as an informal to-do list (Gwizdka, 2000; Jones et al., 2001). Users will send themselves email to remind themselves of events of deliverables at a later date. One study of email tool usage showed that when reviewing their email, people often 'flagged' messages that contained to do items in order to create a visual reminder (Gwizdka, 2000). In a related study we found that multiple inbox rules and strategies are leveraged to perform this reminder function, from altering the colour of items to moving them to semantically labelled folders to using flags (van Dantzich et al., submitted). Of course, just as with paper, these inbox reminder strategies do not proactively remind users as to their upcoming action items, so the inbox must be triaged continually. In addition, the manner in which these reminders are displayed in order to help the user remember what the reminder pertains to, its priority and context, needs to be scrutinised. Ideas for displaying such information were generated over the course of this research and will be described in a later section of the paper.

Our primary goals with this research are twofold: to determine what information computer users want to remember for future use but are likely to forget, and to construct meaningful prototypes for how to display that information to a user in a meaningful way. The area of focus for this research in the long-term is epitomised by Figure 1.

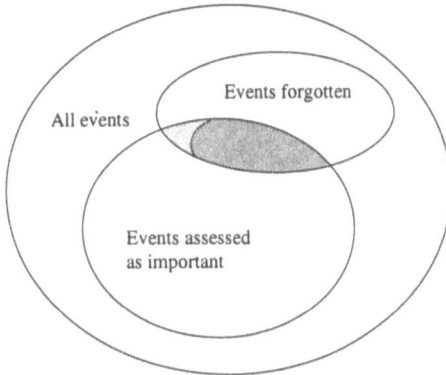

**Figure 1:** Characterisation of event subsets. We are interested in identifying and characterising events that are both assessed as important and that are forgotten (shaded regions at the intersection). The darker region represents the large portion of events that are important and forgotten that can be sensed with current event technologies.

## 2 Experiment 1 — Personal Desktop Reminding

Based on the earlier work by Sellen et al. (1996), we decided to start with an in situ study of what users truly remember about desktop computing events, what they consider to be important for future awareness, and how they tend to refer to those events.

### 2.1 Participants

Eight participants (one female), aged 31–55, all research colleagues, agreed to participate in this experiment. Research colleagues were chosen for this initial study because of the invasiveness of the data collection; we planned to capture their daily lives on video, and to potentially include email, phone,hallway and instant message communications. None of the participants knew the questions motivating the study. As this study was considered a pilot study investigating memory for computing events, the sample size was purposefully small. Larger sample longitudinal studies are currently underway in our laboratory.

### 2.2 Methods and Procedure

Participants were scheduled for one-hour taping sessions, and were told that the video camera would probably not be close enough to capture enough detail to read their email but that regardless the content would be considered confidential. After initial camera setup, instructions to ignore the camera, and to behave as normal as possible while going about their daily research activities, approximately 50 minutes of taping was performed. For three of the participants (the first three), the experimenter was in the room with the participant, and could therefore move the camera and follow the participant around as appropriate. For the final five participants, a tripod was acquired and used in order to remove experimenter from the room so as to allow the participants to behave as naturally as possible, despite being taped. A Panasonic digital video camera equipped was used to perform the video recording.

Exactly 24 hours after the recording session, and once again exactly one month after the recording session, participants were sent an email questionnaire asking them to recall freely the events that had occurred during the taping session, for their estimates of how long these events lasted, and the order in which they occurred. In addition, they were asked to indicate which events were 'higher-level' types of events, as opposed to subtasks within a goal. Users were not informed ahead of time about the existence or nature of the 24-hour and 1 month free-recall challenges. After the initial 24-hour free-recall information was received from the participants, the experimenter sat down with them individually for a half-hour video annotation session. For this session, the participants reviewed their videotapes and provided verbal commentary along with the timestamp at which the event occurred from the video camera. Subjects were told to imagine that they were reviewing their tape with an eye toward "designing a personal desktop video reminder system", so that they could have access to *important* events that happened during that hour of taping. Participants were told to pay particular attention to key or important events that they might want to have access to in the future. The experimenter captured this commentary in her notes along with the timestamps from the video camera. This annotation session always took place within 24–48 hours of the original taping session.

Two prototypes were built from the verbally annotated videotapes. The first prototype design, which we call *PersonalStreams*, shows short video clips of the events that users' identified as important events to be stored for future access when they had reviewed their videos. Each clip varied in length depending on what the user described as important, with a 2 second fade out and in of the next clip. The second style of prototype is referred to as *PersonalStills*, because only one representative still was captured from each video clip used in the PersonalStreams prototype. To explore the benefits or lack thereof of audio in these prototypes, we designed the PersonalStills prototypes to be silent, unless a key interaction was occurring off screen (e.g. a hallway conversation took place and there was no still to represent this). This was only necessary once for 2/8 participants. PersonalStreams always contained the audio that had occurred during that particular clip. On average, the PersonalStreams prototypes were 4 minutes and 44 seconds long, while the PersonalStills were on average 2 minutes and 51 seconds long (both compressed from a 50 minute session).

Because we wanted each of the prototypes to have similar duration and tempo, we needed to determine a length of a video segment that was acceptable, or a pace that felt right. In the end, we decided to base our design heuristics on the second participant's (S2's) video segmentation, as he was the most mobile. S2 often got up from his desk during the videotaping, moving from one colleague's office to another. Other times he would go to his whiteboard, or move his chair between his various computers. In order to capture the event information called out by this participant, the pace for PersonalStreams need to be more fine-grained than for the other participants. Therefore, we designed the PersonalStills prototype for S2 and then replicated that time sequencing in each of the other prototypes to maintain some consistency. Each of the stills is therefore four seconds long, including the two second display of the still, and one second each for fade in and out. We placed one second of 'black' in between each of the stills. In determining the timing on the video segments, we were dependent upon the movement of the participant, letting their annotated actions set the length for how long the scene should run. Our design heuristic for the PersonalStreams prototype was to give the user enough time in each video segment of the prototype to see the key events that they annotated for us during the video review process. The one constant with the video segments was that there was always one second of 'black' in between each of the segments in a PersonalStreams prototype. All prototypes were played back to participants using the Microsoft Windows Media Player, version 7.0.

After receiving email about the 30-day free recall phase of the study, participants were shown their prototypes for the first time and asked to view them twice. The first viewing was simply to watch the video. The second viewing was for participants to point out events represented in the prototypes that they had since forgotten but were reminded of by the video. Order of presentation was counterbalanced so that three participants saw the PersonalStills prototype first, and three saw the PersonalStreams prototype first. (Unfortunately, for 2 participants, the original session video quality was so low at times due to poor auto-focus behaviour of the camera, that only the PersonalStills prototype could meaningfully be edited). User satisfaction data was collected as well as comments and improvement suggestions about the first prototype from users before moving to the 2nd prototype.

## 3 Results

### 3.1 24 Hour Free Recall and Time Estimation

Analysis of the free recall and time estimate data within 24 hours of the initial session taping showed that participants recalled an average of 17.88 events, with a range of 5 to 40 events freely generated from memory. These data are shown in Figure 2. Participants were asked to earmark which events they thought were high level events in these free recalls, and an average of 4.63 events were called out as such (range = 2 to 8 high level events). Interestingly, on average there was one false memory (a description of an event that actually did not appear on their videotapes, given their own annotations of the tapes) per free recall summary (range = 0 to 4, mode = 0). The false memories were typically common activities that a participant usually performed at that time of day, possibly inserted because the participant had forgotten what really happened at that time. Perhaps even more surprising is the amount of overestimation observed with regard to the actual amount of time associated with events; on average participants overestimated event times by 144.9%. Finally, we found that the correlation between the order in which events were listed and their actual temporal order was quite high, r = 0.77.

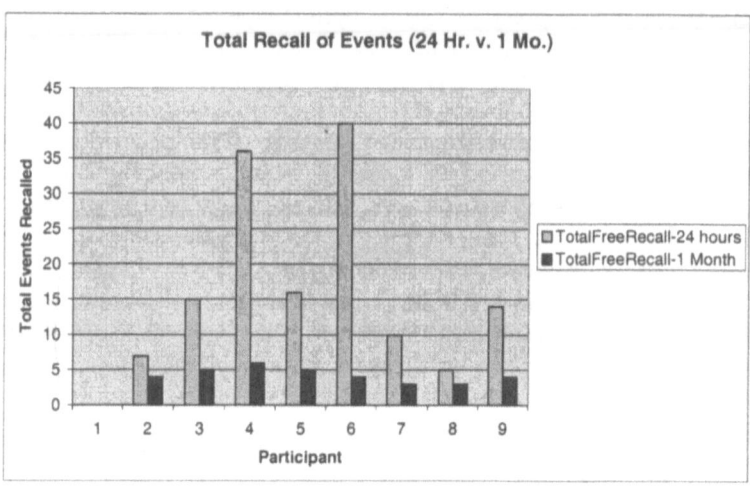

**Figure 2:** Total events recalled at one day and one months.

After the free-recall data was received, participants viewed their videotapes and provided verbal commentary, as described above. On average, 40.25 (range = 9 to 69) events were provided via verbal commentary by participants, providing a ratio of 0.45 of free recall/video recall events, or just under twice as many events recalled when watching the video. However, most of these events turned out to be 'lower-level' events, since on average participants commented that there were only 4.75 higher-level events (i.e. events that they would truly want to have access to in the future) during the video recalls, which is a ratio of 0.98 of free recall/video recall of the higher-level events. In other words, participants had a fairly good memory for the important computing events that they would want to remember in the future after only 24 hours have gone by.

## 3.2 One Month Free Recall and Time Estimation

On average, participants only recalled 4.25 events from the taped session one month later, a significant drop in event free recall from the first 24 hours, $t(7) = 3.08$, $p < 0.01$. This drop over time is shown in Figure 2. The comparison of the number of events freely recalled both after 24 hours and then one month later and the events annotated in the video 24 hours after taping is shown in Figure 3. The decrease in free-recall memory was not at the expense of new, false memories interfering with memory for events, as the average number of false memories dropped to 0.31 (range = 0 to 1, mode = 0), an improvement over the 24-hour free-recall performance. It also would appear that one's memory for task durations gets more accurate with some lapse of time-participants still overestimated durations one month later, but only by 26.82%, on average, though this large drop did not reach statistical significance. There was another striking decline highlighted in the one-month free recall data, memory for the temporal order of events dropped to a correlation of

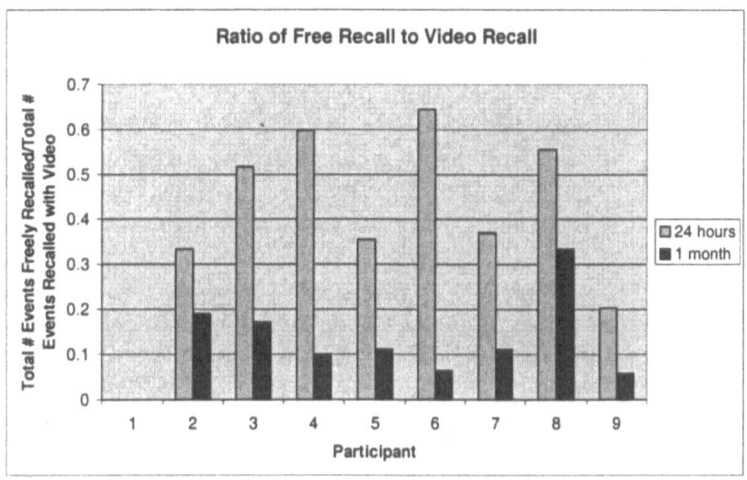

**Figure 3:** Ratio of free-recall to video-supported recall of events.

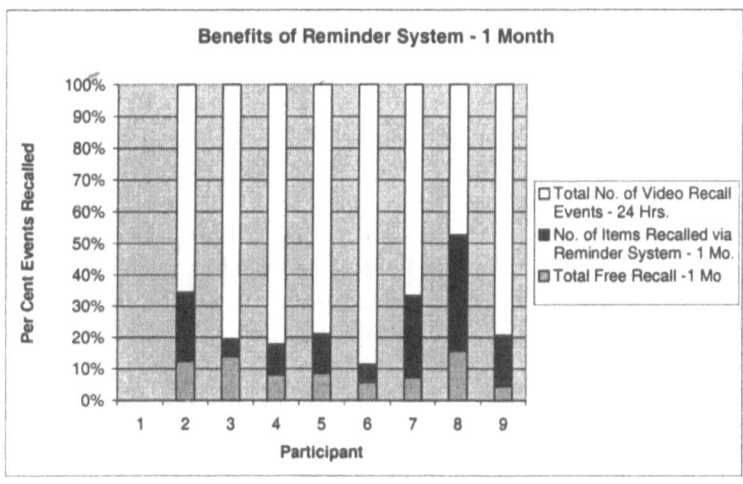

**Figure 4:** Boost in recall associated with use of the reminders at 1 month.

0.356, a borderline significant drop when compared to the 24-hour data, $t(7) = 1.96$, $p = 0.09$. No other differences between the 24-hour and 1-month free recall data were significant.

After the one-month free-recall data was received, participants reviewed their PersonalStreams and PersonalStills prototypes. Regardless of which reminder system was viewed first, participants remembered an average of 7.3 events after viewing the prototypes that they had not remembered in their free recall summaries, this was a borderline significant increase in event recall, $t(7) = 1.89$, $p = 0.07$. All users benefited from the reminder prototypes, though they varied greatly in how much benefit each individual derived. One participant recalled over 50% of the desktop events one month later with the reminder system, while another participant just barely remembered more than 10% of the events even with the reminder system. Figure 4 shows the overall benefits of the reminder prototypes for each participant one month after the initial desktop videotaping.

We did not have enough participants to examine the effects of the order of use of the PersonalStills and PersonalStreams. However, we did collect preference and satisfaction measures for each prototype that a participant viewed. Four out of six participants that received both PersonalStills and PersonalStreams prototypes preferred the PersonalStills version for its subtlety and brevity.

## 3.3   Event Identification

Event-recognition technology available today can be harnessed to identify a significant quantity of the events considered to be important by subjects. The identifiable events, which we refer to as *directly observable* events, include information about the applications that are being used or switched to and from, 'patterns' of behaviour, like reading and deleting email or editing a text document, and debugging and compiling code. These events and richer patterns of behaviour can be detected in a straightforward manner by an event monitoring and abstraction system similar to ones developed for user modelling (Horvitz et al., 1998) or situation-assessment applications (Horvitz et al., 1999).

We found that 43% of the events identified as important by users in this study could be detected by an event monitoring system similar to that described by Horvitz et al. (1998). The system could be also be used to recognise, and store for later reminders, 22% of the 56% of the important events that had been forgotten by users within 24 hours. Events that would be challenging (though not impossible) for a system to identify include the motivations behind various patterns of behaviour. Many times the user would describe the motivation behind a task switch or a behaviour as the key piece of context that would help make sense of the computing event at a later time. Although user modelling applications have been making strides in reasoning about the hidden goals and needs of users, we believe that providing a means for users to efficiently annotate context in real-time or soon after interactions would be valuable in memory augmentation systems. Methods for creating annotations about context should include easy-to-use methods for capturing voice and textual comments. Such user annotation can be extended with automated event monitoring and abstraction to enhance future retrieval.

## 3.4   What Made People Forget Things?

Many participants reported that they forgot events that happened to them frequently, or on a daily basis. It makes sense that less important events or more mundane, frequently occurring events tend to be forgotten easily. S2 stated it best:

> "Things that are in my day-to-day script don't necessarily get included during the free recall exercise. I included the 'relative offsets' or information that was strongly emotional."

In addition, participants described 'broadcast' events as being relatively less important to keep track of mentally, e.g. group email announcements were deemed less important than information that came directly to them. Finally, as reported in the memory literature, performing very similar tasks prior to the videotaped event or directly after the videotaped event interfered with the ability to freely recall events without the prototypes. Therefore, it would appear that the desktop reminder system would be especially useful to users who tend to perform the same kinds of tasks repeatedly over relatively long time frames, for example, software developers working on large, complex systems or knowledge workers creating distinct, but similarly structured documents.

## 3.5 Participants' Design Ideas and Preferences

Several users shared comments and opinions about the optimal design of an intelligent reminder system. S1 said that the stills were not as 'noisy', and that, qualitatively, he liked the stills much better than the full video. The stills were brief and tended to have better video quality because of the hand held camera used for taping. However, we note that S1 forgot several events and the stills were not sufficient for reminding him; he caught singular events with the stills but could not make out 'back and forth' events, like an error he encountered that required him to go back and forth between two applications. S2 said that with stills he could not tell exactly what he was doing. He used the mouse movement and pointer as a clear indicator of what he was doing in the videos, especially when there were a lot of windows open. He also said he needed the audio; even hearing the key clicks was informative for him. S5 preferred stills but agreed that the audio was often more helpful than the video. S4 and S7 said they had more time to examine the events in the stills prototypes than in video, though S7 commented that the video provided more continuity. In video, however, both participants thought there was too much focus on the action, but they said that the action was not necessarily important for remembering context. S6 and S7 thought a 'semantic zoom' approach would fit their requirements best. They suggested having something like a knob that first shows you still images plus some textual description of the event, but as you turn the knob you move closer and closer to veridical video and audio of the event. S6 insisted that the video would have to be very high quality in order to discern exactly what was being typed on the computer. S6 thought that seeing content being typed in documents and email was crucial for remembering context. S7 agreed, stating that many applications are purposefully designed to look alike, so being able to zoom in to the textual level of detail is very important. S6 requested the ability to stop the video at any point in time and to be able to navigate efficiently directly to that application, from the place where he was in the video (e.g. reinstating the application or system context with associated operational state). These qualitative remarks correspond fairly well with findings reported previously by Tse et al. (1998), wherein it was found that users could extract gist information from multiple streams of fairly rapid video display throughput (up to 3 frames per second for three simultaneous slide show displays), but that this high level of data throughput was 'overwhelming' from a user perception point of view.

# 4 Discussion

We recorded a one-hour segment of desktop computing tasks from eight participants with an eye toward designing a prototype system that could remind users what they doing, or intended to do. As it was not clear at the start of this project what a user would remember and forget from that hour of recording, we collected their free recalls of the one-hour segment at both 24 hours after the initial taping and one month later. Very few psychological studies have investigated human memory for computing events, *in situ*, over this length of time. In addition to the free recall tasks, participants in this study verbally annotated their videotaped sessions for us so that we could make note of key events and other items of interest identified by the participants. Based on these highlighted events, we built the PersonalStreams and PersonalStills video prototypes for each individual participant, using Microsoft's Media Player as a nominal user interface for interacting with the content.

We observed that, after one month's passage of time, users forgot a significant number of events that they had deemed as important for remembering later during the original recording sessions. In addition, we found that users initially had an excellent memory for the temporal order of events, but this knowledge decayed significantly over time. We observed that the video reminder prototypes were able to augment the user's memory sufficiently about important events and about event ordering. Users remembered significantly more information after viewing the prototypes than they could generate on their own. In addition, they were reminded of the true sequence of events, which often allowed them to make better sense of their past activities.

Although participants preferred the PersonalStills prototype more than the PersonalStream prototype, some participants insisted that audio, and to some degree, video, would be required in order to remember certain events, and especially sequences of events. Based on our debriefing sessions with participants, we now believe that a combination reminder system would be ideal.

We are pursuing the augmentation of memory in several ways. On the design front, we are pursuing prototypes that provide users with a temporally linear or hierarchical list of thumbnails with textual headings of major events. We are interested in the value of audio and video playback as options for the encoding of events. Based on feedback about the prototypes studied in this paper, we believe that a user-interface metaphor similar to that provided by typical VCR or media players could suffice. In essence, participants only used the Play, Pause, Stop, Rewind and Fast Forward options to review their reminder prototypes. However, other navigation and indexing tools may be of value. As an example, one participant suggested that it would be valuable to have the ability to 'jump back in time' to their document or application while viewing the video or still, and we will consider this a possible feature to add in future versions of our prototypes as well.

We also found that there is 'low-hanging fruit' on the front of automation; a significant number of the events deemed as important can be detected by an event monitoring system available today. A reminder system limited to such events could be valuable in augmenting users' memories of important events. However, we suspect research will be required to limit the number of encoded events captured to the ones deemed as useful or appropriate by users, so as to minimise overloading users with too many events. We found that not all important events and context could be detected easily by current event systems. Approximately half of the events highlighted by the study participants contained a high-level intention or goal, as opposed to the application or document that they were using. These higher-level events could be supported by a reminder system if the user were provided with a means for efficiently editing or refining initial suggestions of event activity that might be provided by an automated system. Whatever the mechanism provided to support these types of events, the user interface affordance must be fairly 'lightweight', so that the user could easily leave a simple reminder notation with the system prior to a task switch or in the face of an interruption.

In summary, we have reviewed several new findings in this paper on memory for events in an office setting. First and foremost, we have detailed the nature and amount of forgetting that typically occurs over the course of a day or a month about common computing events. Secondly, we have attempted to characterise the aspects of those events that an automated system would be able to identify. We also described user-interface controls that will likely be necessary in a system that can augment users' memories for typical computing events. Finally, we have provided preliminary evidence that video-based (either full or stills) reminders can significantly enhance computer users' memories for their daily tasks, especially after a full month's passage of time. We are continuing research on systems for augmenting memory, with longer-term, *in situ*, computing scenarios and with richer, more intelligent software reminders.

## Acknowledgements

Special thanks to the participants of this study, who volunteered to be videotaped and kindly provided hours of recall data.

## References

Altmann, E. M. & Gray, W. D. (2000), Managing Attention by Preparing to Forget, *in Proceedings of the IEA2000/HFES2000 Congress*, Human Factors and Ergonomics Society, pp.152–5.

Czerwinski, M., Cutrell, E. & Horvitz, E. (2000), Instant Messaging: Effects of Relevance and Time, *in* S. Turner & P. Turner (eds.), *Proceedings of HCI'2000: Volume 2*, British Computer Society, pp.71–6.

DeVaul, R. W., Clarkson, B. & Pentland, A. (2000), The Memory Glasses: Towards a Wearable Context Aware, Situation-appropriate Reminder System, In CHI2000 Workshop on Situated Interaction in Ubiquitous Computing.

Eldridge, M., Sellen, A. J. & Bekerian, D. (1992), The Range, Frequency and Severity of Memory Problems at Work, Technical Report EPC-1992-129, EuroPARC.

Ellis, J. A. & Nimmo-Smith, I. (1993), "Recollecting Naturally-occurring Intentions: A Study of Cognitive and Affective Factors", *Memory* 1(2), 107–26.

Gwizdka, J. (2000), Timely Reminders: A Case Study of Temporal Guidance in PIM and Email Tools Usage, *in* G. Szwillus, T. Turner, M. Atwood, B. Bederson, B. Bomsdorf,

E. Churchill, G. Cockton, D. Crow, F. Détienne, D. Gilmore, H.-J. Hofman, C. van der Mast, I. McClelland, D. Murray, P. Palanque, M. A. Sasse, J. Scholtz, A. Sutcliffe & W. Visser (eds.), *Companion Proceedings of CHI2000: Human Factors in Computing Systems (CHI2000 Conference Companion)*, ACM Press, pp.163–4.

Harris, J. E. (1984), Remembering to do Things: A Forgotten Topic, *in* J. E. H. . P. E. Morris (ed.), *Everday Memory, Actions and Absent-mindedness*, Academic Press, pp.71–92.

Horvitz, E., Breese, J., Heckerman, D., Hovel, D. & Rommelse, D. (1998), The Lumiere Project: Bayesian User Modeling for Inferring the Goals and Needs of Software Users, *in* G. F. Cooper & S. Moral (eds.), *Proceedings of the Fourteenth Conference on Uncertainty in Artificial Intelligence*, Morgan-Kaufmann, pp.256–65.

Horvitz, E., Jacobs, A. & Hovel, D. (1999), Attention-sensitive Alerting, *in* K. B. Laskey & H. Prade (eds.), *Proceedings of the Fifteenth Conference on Uncertainty in Artificial Intelligence*, Morgan-Kaufmann, pp.305–13.

Jones, W. P., Bruce, H. & Dumais, S. T. (2001), Keeping Found Things Found on the Web, *in* H. Paques, L. Liu & D. Grossman (eds.), *Proceedings of ACM's CIKM'01, the Tenth International Conference on Information and Knowledge Management*, ACM Press, pp.119–26.

Kvavilashvili, L. (1992), "Remembering Intention: A Critical Review of Existing Experimental Paradigms", *Applied Cognitive Psychology* **6**, 507–24.

Lamming, M. & Flynn, M. (1994), Forget-me-not: Intimate Computing in Support of Human Memory, *in Proceedings of FRIEND21, International Symposium on Next Generation Human Interface*, pp.125–8. Also available as Xerox EuroPARC Technical Report TR 1994-103, http://www.xrce.xerox.com/publis/cam-trs/html/epc-1994-103.htm.

Lamming, M. & Newman, W. (1992), Acitivity-based Information Retrieval: Technology in Support of Personal Memory, *in* F. H. Vogt (ed.), *Information Processing '92: Proceedings of the 12th World Computer Congress*, Vol. 3, ElSc, pp.68–81.

Lamming, M., Brown, P., Carter, K., Eldridge, M., Flynn, M., Louie, G., Robinson, P. & Sellen, A. J. (1994), "The Design of a Human Memory Prosthesis", *The Computer Journal* **37**(3), 153–63.

Maglio, P. P. & Campbell, C. S. (2000), Trade-offs in Displaying Peripheral Information, *in* T. Turner, G. Szwillus, M. Czerwinski & F. Paternò (eds.), *Proceedings of the CHI2000 Conference on Human Factors in Computing Systems*, *CHI Letters* **2**(1), ACM Press, pp.241–8.

McDaniel, M. A. & Einstein, G. O. (1993), "The Importance of Cue Familiarity and Cue Distinctiveness in Prospective Memory", *Memory* **1**(1), 23–41.

McFarlane, D. (1999), Coordinating the Interruption of People in Human–Computer Interaction, *in* A. Sasse & C. Johnson (eds.), *Human–Computer Interaction — INTERACT '99: Proceedings of the Seventh IFIP Conference on Human–Computer Interaction*, Vol. 1, IOS Press, pp.295–303.

Rekimoto, J., Ayatsuka, Y. & Hayashi, K. (1998), Augment-able Reality: Situated Communication through Physical and Digital Spaces, *in Proceedings of the Second International Symposium on Wearable Computers (ISWC'98)*, IEEE Computer Society Press, pp.68–75.

Renaud, K. (2000), Expediting Rapid Recovery from Interruptions by Providing a Visualization of Application Activity, *in* C. Paris, N. Ozkan, S. Howard & S. Lu (eds.), *Proceedings of Australian Conference on Computer–Human Interaction OzCHI 2000*, IEEE Computer Society Press, pp.348–55.

Rhodes, B. & Starner, T. (1996), The Remembrance Agent: A Continuously Running Automated Information Retrieval System, *in Proceedings of the First International Conference on The Practical Application of Intelligent Agents and Multi-agent Technology (PAAM '96)*, pp.487–95. Available at http://web.media.mit.edu/ rhodes/Papers/remembrance.html.

Sellen, A. J., Louie, G., Harris, J. E. & Wilkins, A. J. (1996), "What Brings Intentions to Mind? An In Situ Study of Prospective Memory", *Memory* **5**, 483–507.

Terry, W. S. (1988), "Everyday Forgetting: Data from a Diary Study", *Psychological Reports* **62**, 299–303.

Tse, T., Marchionini, G., Ding, W., Slaughter, L. & Komlodi, A. (1998), Dynamic Key Frame Presentation Techniques for Augmenting Video Browsing, *in* T. Catarci, M. F. Costabile, G. Santucci & L. Tarantino (eds.), *Proceedings of the Conference on Advanced Visual Interface (AVI'98)*, ACM Press, pp.185–94.

Tulving, E. (1983), *Elements of Episodic Memory*, Clarendon Press.

van Dantzich, M., Robbins, D. C., Horvitz;, E. & Czerwinski, M. (submitted), Scope: Providing Awareness of Multiple Notifications at a Glance, Paper submitted to the Conference on Advanced Visual Interfaces (AVI2002).

Wilkins, A. J. & Baddeley, A. D. (1978), Remembering to Recall in Everyday Life: An Approach to Absent-mindedness, *in* M. M. Gruneberg, P. E. Morris & R. N. Sykes (eds.), *Practical Aspects of Memory*, Academic Press.

# How People Recognise Previously Seen Web Pages from Titles, URLs and Thumbnails

## Shaun Kaasten[†], Saul Greenberg[†] & Christopher Edwards[‡]

[†] *Department of Computer Science*, [‡] *Department of Psychology, University of Calgary, Calgary, Alberta, Canada T2N 1N4.*

Tel: *+1 403 220 6087*

Email: *saul@cpsc.ucalgary.ca*

**The selectable lists of pages offered by Web browsers' history and bookmark facilities ostensibly make it easier for people to return to previously visited pages. These lists show the pages as abstractions, typically as truncated titles and URLs, and more rarely as small thumbnail images. Yet we have little knowledge of how recognisable these representations really are. Consequently, we carried out a study that compared the recognisability of thumbnails between various image sizes, and of titles and URLs between various string sizes. Our results quantify the trade-off between the size of these representations and their recognisability. These findings directly contribute to how history and bookmark lists should be designed.**

**Keywords:** history system, bookmarks, Web browsers.

## 1 Introduction

Web browsers supply various features to help people revisit their previously seen pages. These are typically some variation of a Back button, history, and bookmark facility. Excepting Back, which draws the page directly in the browser window, all facilities represent the page by some abstraction in an ordered or hierarchical list: by its title, or its URL, or more rarely as a miniature thumbnail.

Titles and URLs, of course, differ from what people see on the rendered page, and consequently they may encounter difficulties finding and recognising the exact page they want to revisit. Titles, usually extracted from the HTML <Title> tag, are fraught with complications. They are often missing, are inaccurate or completely

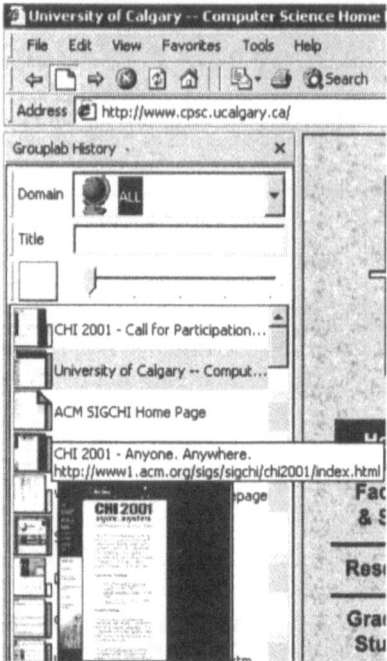

**Figure 1:** Our experimental system.

wrong, or identify the site it came from but not the page, or do not match the text actually seen at the top of the Web page (Cockburn & Greenberg, 1999). URLs are similarly problematic: while they do sometimes give a human-comprehensible descriptive path and label of the current page, they are often cryptic, especially when dynamically generated by a Web server (Cockburn & Greenberg, 1999). Additionally, because both URLs and titles can be long, most browsers will truncate them to fit within the (usually narrow) size constraints of the history or bookmark facility.

Some researchers (including ourselves) suggest that small image thumbnails of captured pages are better representations (Ayers & Stasko, 1995; Cockburn et al., 1999; Hightower et al., 1998; Kaasten, 2001; Kaasten & Greenberg, 2001; Robertson et al., 1998; Woodruff et al., 2001; Suh et al., 2002). Even though they are small and of low image fidelity, they are direct representations of what the user actually saw. However, thumbnails suffer problems as well. For example, while small thumbnails allow for many to be presented in the list, this compromises their fidelity and thus their recognisability (Cockburn & Greenberg, 1999).

We know that a revisitation system needs to display pages in a way that makes the pages easy for users to recognise. Yet we have little formal knowledge of how well people recognise Web pages by title, or URL, or thumbnail. Thus designers have created revisitation systems via hunches, guesswork, or by just copying what was done before. In our own work, for example, we are designing a system that combines Back, History and Bookmarks into a single model (Figure 1) (Kaasten, 2001; Kaasten & Greenberg, 2001). A sidebar lists pages as low-fidelity thumbnails and truncated titles, while a page's full title, URL, and high-fidelity thumbnail are shown in a pop-up window that appears when the user hovers the mouse pointer over an item in the list. Yet this seemingly simple system prompted several design uncertainties: how large should thumbnails be, should titles vs. URLs be used, how should titles or URLs be truncated to fit into the list, etc. Surprisingly, there are almost no studies excepting our own investigating thumbnail vs. title vs. URL use in Web browsing, but see Czerwinski et al. (1999) for their evaluation of thumbnails and text in a 3D environment.

Consequently, we decided to examine experimentally how well people recognise previously seen Web pages from their titles, URLs and thumbnails. After stating four specific research questions, we describe our experimental design. We then present our results along with their implications to the design of revisitation systems.

## 2 Research Questions

This study investigates how well people recognise pages they have previously seen when shown representations of these pages as titles, URLs and thumbnails at various sizes. The study frames the following four research questions.

### 2.1 Question 1: Thumbnail Recognition and Size

*Are thumbnails recognisable? What is the trade-off between recognition vs. thumbnail size? What makes them recognisable?*

We need to know how often people recognise a page by its visual appearance, and what parts of its visual features (text, fonts, layout, etc) contribute to its recognition. However, thumbnail image size (i.e. pixels/image) is obviously an important factor (Cockburn & Greenberg, 1999). The larger the thumbnail, the more it will resemble the page the person actually saw, and the more likely the person will recognise it. Yet there is a trade-off between thumbnail size and the number of thumbnails that can be displayed in the modest screen space typically allocated for a revisitation list. If the thumbnails are very large, the page may be recognisable but the person will be able to see only a few items in the list at a time. Finding off-screen items requires scrolling, which is tedious. If the thumbnails are too small, the person will see many of them at a glance but will also find it difficult to recognise the page from its tiny graphic: its text, embedded images and even its typographic structure may be illegible. Also, revisitation lists often collect thumbnails of pages from the same site; if these pages have a consistent visual look, people may not be able to discriminate between them because subtle differences between pages will not be discernible (Cockburn & Greenberg, 1999).

To make thumbnails useful, this first research question searches for a reasonable trade-off that balances thumbnail recognition with space demands: at what size thresholds do thumbnails have a reasonable chance of being recognised?

| Method | a) Example Title | b) Example URL |
|--------|------------------|----------------|
| Right | University of Calgary — Comput... | http://www.cpsc.ucalgary.ca/gr... |
| Middle | University of C...ience Home Page | http://www.cpsc...ouplab/software |
| Left | ...y — Computer Science Home Page | ...ucalgary.ca/grouplab/software |

**Table 1:** Truncation examples showing only 30 letters of a title and URL.

## 2.2 Question 2: Title Recognition and Size

*Are titles recognisable? If truncated, what is the trade-off between recognition vs. title size per truncation method?*

As mentioned in the introduction, titles have many problems (Cockburn & Greenberg, 1999). This second question asks how recognisable a page is from its title. We also need to know how recognition trades off with title size. In this context, size refers to how much of the title's text is visible to the user. The problem is that most practical revisitation systems are designed to occupy a conservative amount of screen width (e.g. Internet Explorer's history bar; or our own system displayed in Figure 1), and these cannot fit long titles within the narrow column. As a result, these systems truncate titles to fit within the narrow list width.

There are three different approaches to truncating: right, middle, and left. Different browsers often use different methods. Table 1, Column a illustrates each method by example, where the title 'University of Calgary — Computer Science Home Page' is truncated to 30 letters. Notice how the title reads quite differently with each truncation method. Right truncation shows only the title's beginning, where one sees that the page is from the University of Calgary, and guesses that it has something to do with computers. Middle truncation shows only beginning and end portions, and one sees that it is from a university beginning with the letter 'C', and that it is some kind of homepage. Left truncation shows only the ending, so one sees that it is a Computer Science homepage, but not that it is from a university.

For titles to be useful, we need to know the threshold title size per truncation method that offers a reasonable chance of page recognition.

## 2.3 Question 3: URL Recognition and Size

*Are URLs recognisable? If truncated, what is the trade-off of recognition vs. URL size per truncation method?*

The same trade-off we see in title sizes also applies to URL sizes, and Table 1 Column b illustrates how the left, middle, and right truncation methods are applied to a URL truncated to 30 characters. Again, each method hints at different aspects about the page-that it is from the University of Calgary in Canada (right truncation), that it refers to software (middle truncation), and that it is the software portion of the GroupLab research group (left truncation).

## 2.4 Question 4: Distribution of Title and URL Sizes

*What is the distribution of title and URL sizes from pages typically found on the Web?*

We would expect both titles and URLs between random Web pages to vary greatly in their size. Some will be short, and should easily fit in even a narrow revisitation list, while others will be very long. If most titles/URLs are short then truncation is not that important. If they are long, we can expect much truncation. What we need to know is the distribution of title and URL sizes if we are to place answers from Questions 2 and 3 in context.

## 3 Method

We designed a controlled study to answer the above questions. For each subject, we collected a list of their recently visited pages. We analysed the title and URL length distribution of these pages (Question 4), and then showed the subject a succession of representations of his/her previously visited pages. We first displayed each representation at a tiny size (i.e. image size for thumbnails, string length for titles/URLs). We then gradually increased this size until the subject could describe the site from which the represented page came from, and then which specific page it represented. Thus we probed for the size threshold at which representations became recognisable (Questions 1–3). Finally, we asked people to evaluate the correctness of their responses.

### 3.1 Variables

Independent variables were the *representation type* shown to the subject (thumbnail, title, URL), and for titles and URLs the *truncation method* (right, middle, left). The main dependent variables were two *size thresholds*: first where the subject could identify the Web site and second where they could identify the exact page. Another dependent variable was the *correctness of the identifications*, as rated by the subject. This number of correct pages yields an overall indication of each representation's recognisability. Qualitative data were the subjects' *written descriptions* about how they were able to identify the page.

### 3.2 Subjects

We recruited 20 paid 2nd year or higher computer science students, all practised Internet users. As this group is likely proficient at recognising pages by URL vs. other groups, they provide a 'best-case' scenario for URL effectiveness.

### 3.3 Stimuli

We wanted to test subjects' recognition of their previously visited pages. This implies two study phases: *priming* where the subject looked at a chosen set of Web pages, and *testing* where the subject attempted to recognise selected pages from their representations. To reduce variability and increase repeatability, we should prime subjects with identical pages. However, finding a good set of candidate pages introduces three problems with serious implications on how we could generalise our results to browser design.

**Artificiality of page interest:** Subjects may have no personal connection with the set of pages we give them. This could profoundly affect how well (or how poorly) they remember these pages. In real use, we expect people will attend to various pages quite differently due to their immediate interest or page appeal.

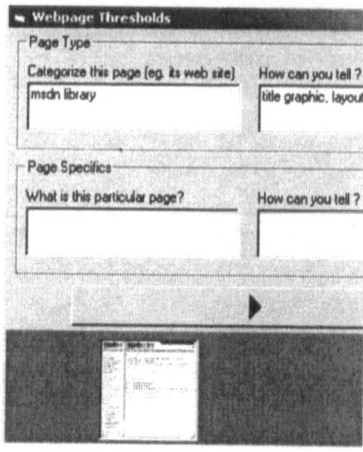

**Figure 2:** Subject pauses thumbnail growth at 36×36 and identities Web site.

**Artificiality of learning:** The way we ask subjects to 'learn' pages could profoundly affect how well they are remembered. We could present pages for a timed duration, or insist they read each page, or have them search the page. In real use, we would expect people to learn pages differently: as a function of their interest, how they read them, etc.

**Page composition:** Pages on the Web are remarkably inconsistent. In visual terms, they vary greatly in their typographic structure (use of proximity, white space, fonts, contrast), and their graphical elements (image type, quantity, size and noise such as advertisements). Similarly, pages vary greatly in how titles and URLs are composed. There are virtually no statistics that describe common page attributes. If we 'make up' our own pages, the ability of people to recognise them may have little bearing on how they recognise the perhaps quite different pages on the Web.

Consequently, we decided to use the actual pages viewed by subjects during normal browsing activity as stimuli, which means our study is a quasi-experimental design.

## 3.4 Materials

We used a high-end computer running Windows 2000 with a 17″ monitor at 1152×864 resolution with 32-bit colour. We used Internet Explorer 5 (IE-5) to display pages to the subject during a verification phase. All subjects had previously browsed the Web using IE-5 or Netscape Navigator 4.x.

For the priming phase, our *history extraction software* extracted into a file the URL, title and last-visit date of pages that an IE-5 user had visited on their machine. Our *stimuli preparation software* read in this history file, displayed each page, let the experimenters select 30 pages, and generated a high-quality thumbnail of these

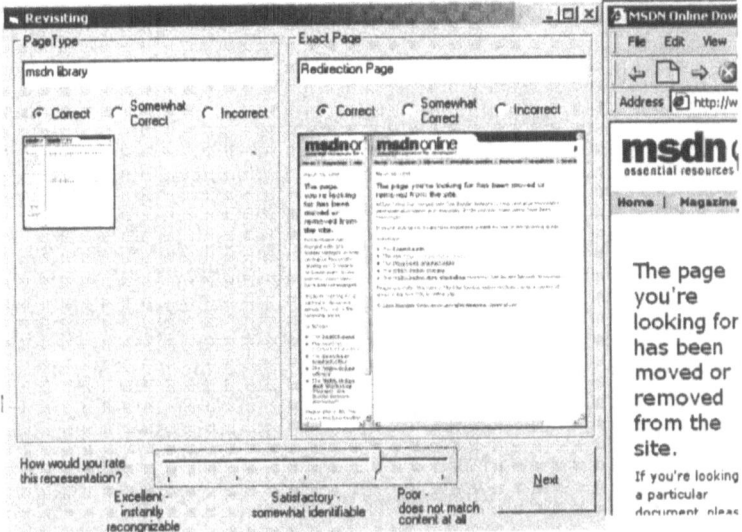

**Figure 3:** Subject verifies their choice and rates the representation.

pages. Our *stimuli presentation software* presented the stimuli to the subjects and recorded their responses (Figure 2), while our *stimuli verification software* let them verify the correctness of their responses (Figure 3).

## 3.5   Procedure

### 3.5.1   Step 1 Stimuli Preparation

First, the subject submitted their history record to us (most included pages they visited within the last 3 weeks). IE users used our history extraction software, while Netscape users invoked its history list 'save' option. Second, using the stimuli preparation software, we pseudo-randomly selected 30 pages and captured high-quality smoothed thumbnail images of them. We manually filtered out pages that would not load properly (e.g. slow and password-protected pages), 'frames' pages (which contain multiple history entries for a single page), and pages without titles. We also excluded a page if several others from the same site had already been selected.

### 3.5.2   Step 2 Stimuli Presentation

We ran a subject about 1–3 days after receiving his/her history file. The procedure for each trial began by showing the subject (using our stimuli presentation software) one of the page representations at a tiny, probably unrecognisable size. For thumbnails, this was 16×16 pixels. For titles or URLs, the initial string size was two letters. Depending on the truncation method used, this meant the subject saw the first two letters, the first and last letter, or the last two letters. Truncated URLs included their 'http://' prefixes, and we will discuss issues related to this later. We then gradually increased the representation size until the subject could just recognise the Web site the page came from. The subject would then continue until he or she could identify the specific page.

Figure 2 illustrates a moment in the thumbnail trial sequence. Previously, the subject had seen a $16 \times 16$ thumbnail image but did not recognise it. The thumbnail dimensions then grew automatically at a rate of 16 pixels every 3 seconds. This subject watched the thumbnail as it increased in size until she just recognised what Web site it came from, in this case at size $36 \times 36$ pixels. At this point, she clicked the 'play/pause' button (Figure 2, middle) to pause the thumbnail's growth. She then typed a description of the Web site (in this case 'msdn library') in the top left field labelled 'Page type', and how she recognised it in the top right field labelled 'How can you tell?' (title, graphic, and layout). Figure 2 was taken at this point. She was still uncertain about which particular MSDN page the thumbnail represented, so she pressed the 'play' button and the thumbnail continued growing. Finally, she recognised the page at size $108 \times 108$ pixels as a 'redirection page' because she could read its textual contents at this size. She clicked 'pause' and filled in this page-specific information (fields in the middle of Figure 2). She then clicked a 'next' button (not shown) to proceed to the next trial page.

The sequence for the textual representations was similar, except the text replaced the thumbnail image in Figure 2. The title or URL was initially truncated to display only two letters using one of the left, middle or right methods, and this text size then grew by two letters every 3 seconds.

The subjects saw 30 different pages; thus they had 30 trials. Each trial used only a single page and representation. Trials alternated through thumbnail, title, and URL. Titles and URLs alternated between right, middle and left truncation.

### 3.5.3   Step 3 Stimuli Verification

After completing all 30 trials, the verification process began. Using the stimulus verification software, subjects went through their responses to see if they correctly identified the pages. For each page, we showed the subject the form in Figure 3 (left window), as well as the actual Web page at full size in the IE-5 browser (right window). This form displayed that page in the representation they saw at the two sizes he/she indicated as just being able to recognise the Web site (left side) and exact page (right side). The subject used this form to indicate if his/her answers were correct, somewhat correct, or incorrect (top). The subjects used the same form to rate how well the representation 'captured' the page (bottom). For titles and URLs, this rated the non-truncated title/URL, not just the portion that he or she saw before answering. For the thumbnail, the question referred to the page concept rather than its size — does the 'look' of the full sized page, as seen in the browser, give a good indication about its content?

## 4   Results and Discussion

### 4.1   Thumbnail Recognition and Size

Research Question 1 asked about the trade-off between recognition vs. thumbnail size.

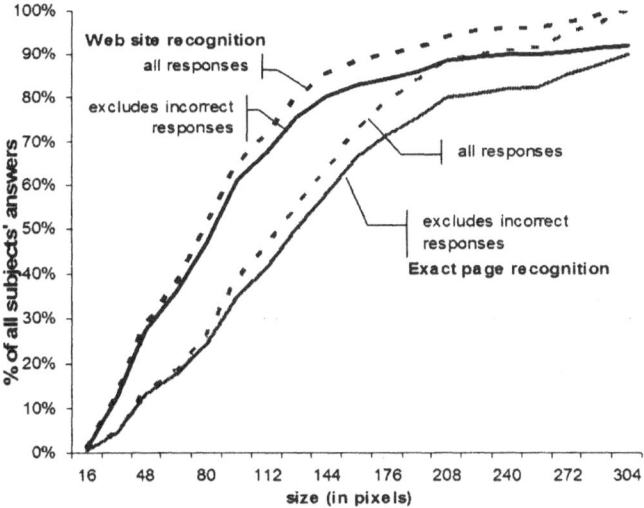

**Figure 4:** Running sums of thumbnail stop sizes.

### 4.1.1   Results

Figure 4 plots the threshold thumbnail sizes where people were able to just recognise the Web site (top 2 lines) and the exact page (bottom 2 lines) as cumulative distributions. We call these recognition points the 'stop sizes'. Each point gives the running sum of all previous points. The dotted lines plot all responses, which we include for comparative purposes. The solid lines exclude incorrect responses — this measure shows only responses that were rated 'Correct' or 'Somewhat correct' in Step 3 — and are thus a reasonable measure of thumbnail recognition. This measure will form the basis for our discussion.

### 4.1.2   Discussion

All subjects tried to recognise the thumbnail images by the time it reached $304 \times 304$. In total, they rated only ~10% of their guesses as completely incorrect. This 90% success rate means that (not surprisingly) people are fairly good at recognising pages from their visual images if they are appropriately sized.

More specifically, Figure 4 provides a cost–benefit guide of the recognisability of a given thumbnail size. We premise this on the (reasonable) assumption that showing a person a thumbnail at one particular size is equivalent to the cumulative effects of seeing the thumbnail at all of its smaller sizes. That is, a larger thumbnail will be at least as recognisable as all of its smaller versions. For example, if we wanted at least 60% recognition of Web sites by thumbnails, we would need a thumbnail sized at least $96 \times 96$ pixels or less. Choosing this size also means that people will recognise the exact page only ~35% of the time.

To ease comparisons, we establish benchmarks for recognition that will allow us to directly compare and make recommendations for thumbnail, title and URL

| Recognition rate | Thumbnails | | Titles | | | | | |
|---|---|---|---|---|---|---|---|---|
| | Web site | Exact page | Web site | | | Exact page | | |
| | | | Right | Middle | Left | Right | Middle | Left |
| Minimal: 15% | 32×32 | 48×48 | 6 | 8 | 9 | 12 | 12 | 12 |
| Low: 30% | 48×48 | 80×80 | 8 | 12 | 12 | 18 | 16 | 18 |
| Medium: 60% | 96×96 | 144×144 | 15 | 20 | 18 | 39 | 30 | 28 |
| High: 80% | 160×160 | 208×208 | 25 | 42 | 28 | — | 46 | 50 |
| Maximum | 92% | 90% | 92% | 87% | 93% | 75% | 83% | 80% |

| Recognition rate | URLs | | | | | |
|---|---|---|---|---|---|---|
| | Web site | | | Exact page | | |
| | Right | Middle | Left | Right | Middle | Left |
| Minimal: 15% | 8 | 14 | 11 | 15 | 16 | 14 |
| Low: 30% | 11 | 20 | 17 | 25 | 22 | 19 |
| Medium: 60% | 16 | 29 | 25 | 43 | 34 | 30 |
| High: 80% | 34 | 43 | 42 | 58 | 65 | 50 |
| Maximum | 92% | 87% | 92% | 83% | 82% | 88% |

**Table 2:** Recommendations for sizes of thumbnails and titles and URLs at various benchmark recognition rates.

size. We will set the benchmarks as 15%, 30%, 60% and 80% for minimum, low, medium, and high recognition levels respectively. We also include a 'maximum' which indicates the percentage of pages correctly recognised. Of course, developers can choose their own benchmarks, where they can look up particular sizes directly in Figure 4.

Table 2 tabulates these benchmarks. For example, the table (and Figure 4) suggests that if space is very tight, the minimum useful size for a thumbnail is ~32×32 pixels for identifying Web sites, and ~48×48 pixels for identifying exact pages. If space demands are somewhat less stringent, low recognition (~30%) is achieved with ~48×48 pixels for Web sites and ~80×80 pixels for exact pages. For medium recognition (60%), we need 96×96 pixels for Web sites and 144×144 pixels for exact pages. Finally, for high recognition (80%), we need 144×144 pixels for Web sites and 208×208 pixels for exact pages. The maximum recognition we could achieve with even larger thumbnails is ~90%.

## 4.2 Thumbnail Features

Research Question 1 also asked what makes thumbnails recognisable at given sizes.

### 4.2.1 Results

Each time the subjects made a guess at the Web site or exact page, they specified the predominant features that influenced their guess (Figure 2, top). These comments invariably dealt with the following visual attributes:

**Colours:** Background and font colours for the page.

**Text-related:** Legible text from the title or secondary titles on the form. This can be graphical (as in a banner).

**Image-related:** A distinctive image on the page.

**Layout-related:** Distinctive formatting of page elements.

We categorised the subjects' answers into these attributes and counted how often they occurred. When subjects mentioned more than one attribute, we counted them in multiple categories. When identifying Web sites, we found that 'early' identifications ($<64\times64$ pixels) were primarily due to gross page features such colours or layout. Between sizes $64\times64$ and $96\times96$, all four attributes were roughly mentioned at par. From $100\times100$ pixels up, text and to a lesser extent images predominated. This makes sense: while text and image fidelity increased at these larger sizes, gross features such as layout and colours would not change much.

The importance of text is even more evident in the exact page identifications. While layout and colour are somewhat important at small thumbnail sizes, nearly all 'late' identifications ($100\times100$ pixels and larger) mentioned text-related attributes. Yet we see from Figure 4 that only a modest number of exact page identifications took place with thumbnails smaller than $100\times100$. Thus subjects needed larger thumbnails, and the vast majority of identifications were based on reading text-related cues. In fact, subjects mentioned text 90% of the time whenever they identified the exact page, compared to ~30% for layout and image-related attributes, and 12% for colour (these do not sum to 100% because people can list multiple attributes). Thus we conclude that subjects relied heavily on reading text inside the thumbnail. Of course, this implies that the thumbnails were large enough for the subjects to read the text.

### 4.2.2 Discussion

These results suggest what thumbnail cues enable recognition. Very often, subjects identified Web sites by small thumbnails (less than $96\times96$ pixels) through its colour and layout rather than details. This is likely because many Web sites have a distinctive 'look' that can be recognised in a small image icon. Yet for identifying exact page, being able to read some of the page's text was clearly important[1]. What is likely is that a page's surrounding colours, page layout and images provide the context and redundancy to make the site recognisable, while dominant text pinpoints the exact page.

These results have implications for Web site and page design. First, they re-enforce the value of repeating colour/layout/images across pages, for pages become recognisable as coming from a particular site. Second, if thumbnails become an important interface feature then page designers should be encouraged to use large title and banner font sizes that are visible in small thumbnails (Woodruff et al., 2001).

---

[1] We could argue that using a thumbnail to display text defeats its purpose of using graphics, for instead we could simply display the text, at a font size that is much easier to read than in a shrunken graphic. However, the text that dominates a page and therefore its thumbnail is often different from the page's technical title.

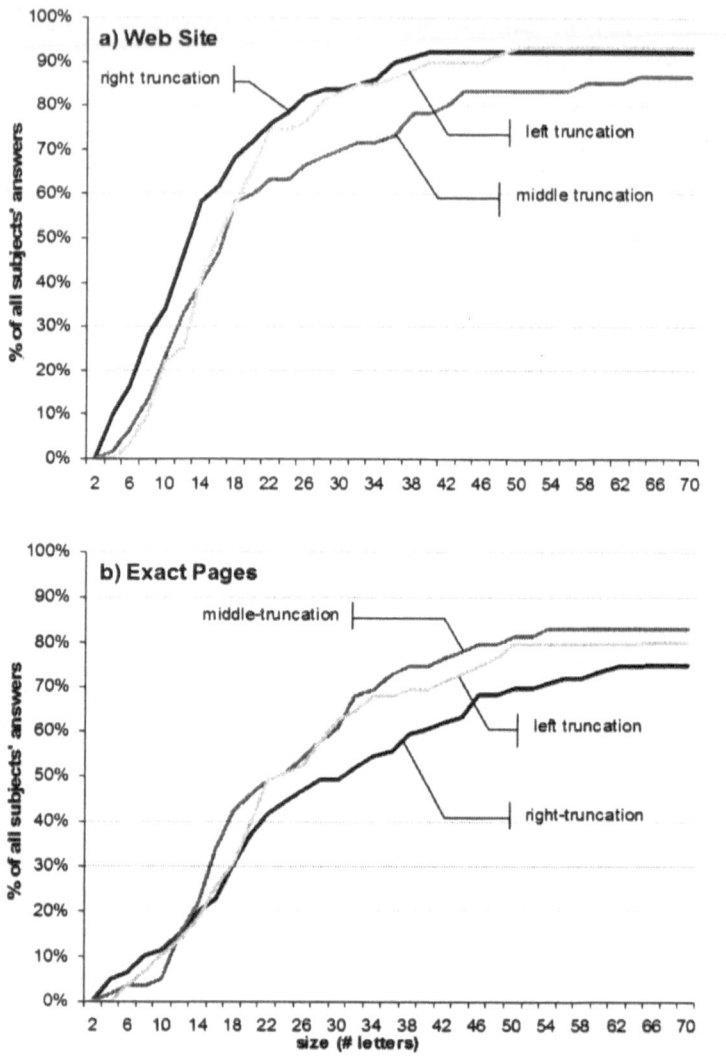

**Figure 5:** Running sums of title stop sizes.

## 4.3  Title Recognition and Size

Research Question 2 asked about the trade-off between recognition vs. title size per truncation method.

### 4.3.1  Results

Similar to Figure 4, Figure 5 plots the stop-size distributions as a running sum for each of the title truncation methods when identifying Web sites (Figure 5a) and exact pages (Figure 5b). For clarity, we only graph and discuss data that excludes incorrect responses. Table 2 tabulates this data using our benchmarks.

### 4.3.2 Discussion

Ignoring size, people managed to correctly identify the Web site between 87–93% of the time, and the exact page between 75–83%. When size is taken into account, we see that right truncation stood out as best for Web site identification (Figure 5a). This is not surprising; many titles begin with the Web site name, as in 'University of Calgary, Department of Computer Science — Research' and the right-truncation method reveals this beginning portion.

For identifying the exact page, the discerning portion appears at the end of the title, as revealed by both the left and middle truncation methods. Thus, right truncation fairs poorly compared to the other two methods (Figure 5b). Except at very low sizes, middle truncation is slightly favoured over left truncation for identifying the exact page, as seen in the running sums of Figure 5b. This suggests that both prefix and suffix slightly re-enforce recognition. Invariably, people need to see more letters of the title for identifying the exact page than the Web site. For example, comparing the best-performing truncation methods between Figures 5a & b at 26 letters, we see that right-truncation gives us 82% recognition for Web sites, while middle truncation gives only 54% recognition for exact pages; indeed we have to double the title length to 52 to bring the exact page recognition rate to 82%.

As before, these distributions allow us to make recommendations for designing a revisitation list based on titles, as tabulated in Table 2. For example, for medium (60%) recognition, we need 15–20 letters (depending on the truncation method) for Web sites, and 30–39 letters for exact pages. Unfortunately, no truncation method stands out as best for both Web sites and exact page identification.

## 4.4 URL Recognition and Size

Research Question 3 asked about the trade-off between recognition vs. URL size per truncation method.

Before answering this question, we should mention that we included the standard 'http://' prefix in the URLs we presented to subjects as done in several existing history systems. Unfortunately, this meant that subjects shown the right and middle truncated URL did not see any useful portion of the beginning URL until after the 7 letters in 'http://'. In hindsight, we should have filtered off this prefix e.g. by showing 'www.ucalgary.ca...' instead of 'http://www.ucal...'. (The same argument is not true for the 'www.' extension as it often differentiates intranet from internet pages). Consequently, we corrected our results. First, we subtracted 8 letters from the right truncation size (because we increased the size in multiples of two, we could not subtract exactly 7 letters). Next, we subtracted 4 letters from the middle truncation size as this method reveals both the suffix and prefix: while not a great solution, it is close enough for comparative purposes. We use and discuss only these corrected data in this paper.

### 4.4.1 Results

Similar to Figure 5, Figure 6 illustrates the stop size distributions as a running sum for each of URL truncation method when identifying Web site (Figure 6a) and exact page (Figure 6b). Table 2 tabulates these results.

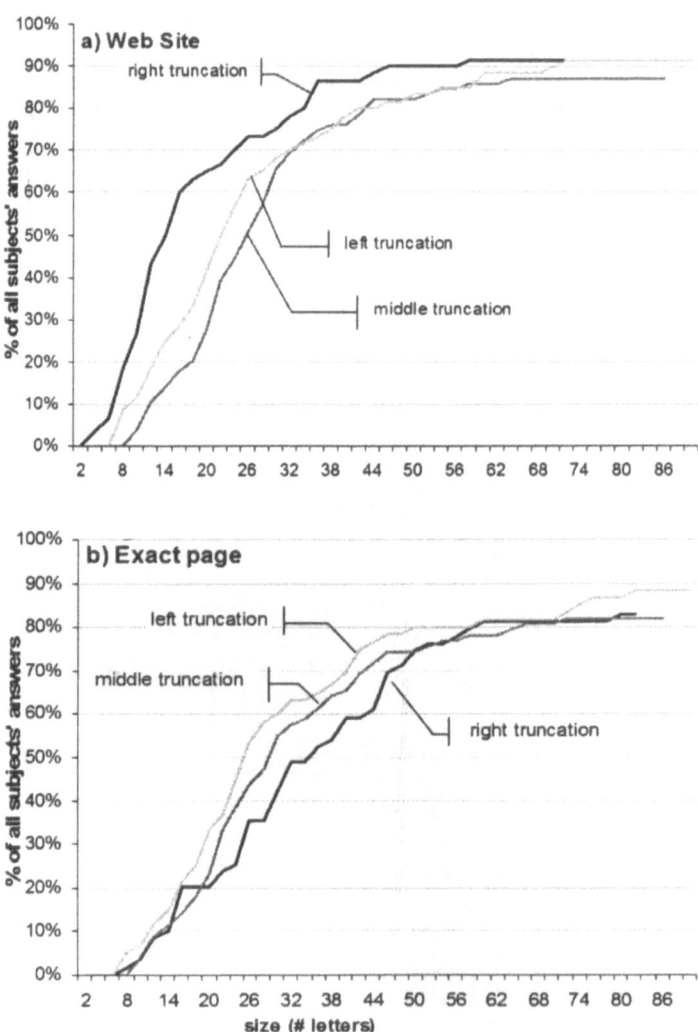

**Figure 6:** Running sums of (corrected) URL stop sizes.

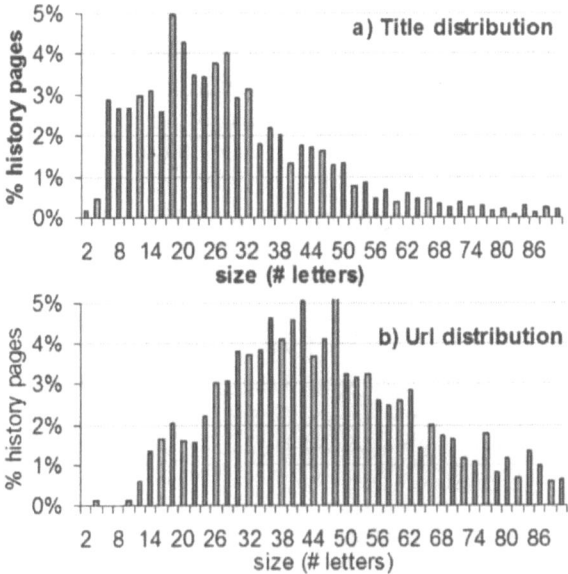

**Figure 7:** Distribution of title and URL lengths.

### 4.4.2    Discussion

Ignoring size, people managed to correctly identify the Web site from its URL between 87–92% of the time (which is comparable to titles), and the exact page between 82–88% (which is better than titles). When size is taken into account, we see that the right truncation method stood out as best for Web site identification (Figure 6a). This is expected, as the Web site name is often reflected within its URL prefix e.g. www.ucalgary.ca for the University of Calgary. For identifying exact page, the left truncation method proved best. This too makes sense as the suffix is often a meaningful label for the exact page.

## 4.5    Distribution of Titles and URLs on the Web

Research Question 4 asked about the distribution of title and URL sizes of pages typically found on the Web.

### 4.5.1    Results

We analysed the 9200 pages that comprised all submitted history records. First, 30% of all pages did not have titles (remember that we excluded these from the set shown to subjects). We then plotted the title size frequency distribution of the remaining pages (Figure 7a) and the URL size distribution of all pages (Figure 7b). For pages with titles, the mean title length is 31. For all pages, the mean URL length is 40 (standard deviation = 22 for both).

### 4.5.2   Discussion

30% of these pages did not have titles. This is much higher than a recent finding that only 5% of pages lack titles (Cockburn & McKenzie, 2000). It could be that our logs included title-less pop-up advertisement windows often raised as a side effect of visiting a page. Clearly, this needs more study. Still, we can conclude that the overall recognition of pages by its title is between 5–30% worse than shown in Figure 5 and Table 2, as a title cannot be displayed if it is missing.

Ignoring pages without titles for now, the distributions in Figures 7a & b inform us about how many titles and URLs would be truncated if the revisitation could only display a certain number of letters. For example, if the system could only display the first 20 letters, then only 55% of the titles and 8% of URLs will fit completely (these are calculated as the running sum of all size frequencies). Thus, users will have to make decisions based on incomplete information for almost half of the items for titles, and for almost all the items for URLs. This suggests that our concerns in this study about the effects of size and truncation are valid.

## 4.6   Correctness / Error Rates

As a side note, we elaborate how often subjects correctly identified pages by thumbnails, titles, and URLs. Recall that we asked subjects to validate their Web site and exact page guesses by scoring them as incorrect, somewhat correct, or correct (Figure 3, top). We aggregated these responses for the three different title and URL truncation methods into 'Titles' and 'URLs' categories.

### 4.6.1   Results

Statistically, there was no difference between the different error rates of the various representations (ANOVA $p > 0.05$, $F = 1.21$) for identifying Web sites. However, subjects had fewer errors with thumbnails than with titles or URLs when identifying exact pages (ANOVA $p \leq 0.05$, $F = 12.21$).

Subjects proved quite accurate at identifying the Web site for all representations, where they rated fewer than 10% of their answers being incorrect, another 10% as partly correct, and fully 80% as completely correct. For exact page identifications, subjects had a similar accuracy of 80% correct when using thumbnails. However, they were less accurate when using titles and URLs to identify the exact page: only 60% were completely correct.

### 4.6.2   Discussion

Thumbnails of Web pages prove to be a reasonably accurate way for people to identify both the Web site and the exact page. This supports the hypothesis that thumbnails are a useful representation for revisitation systems. It also suggests that our standard history lists that use only titles and URL representations are not as effective as one would like. If users only have a 60% chance of recognising the exact content from a title or URL in the history list, they may not be motivated to invest the extra work it takes to operate the list (opening, scrolling, closing) in order to track down a page. Simply put, it is not worth the effort to switch to a list containing items where there is only a 60% chance that the desired page will be recognised.

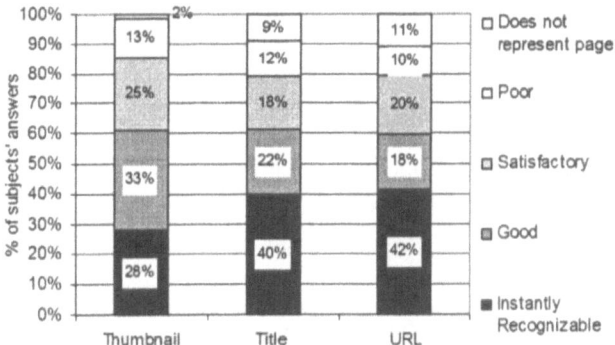

**Figure 8:** Subjects' rating of thumbnails, titles and URLs.

## 4.7   Subjects' Representation Ratings

Each subject used the 5 point scale in Figure 3 (bottom) to rate how well the thumbnail, title or URL representation 'captured' the content of the page.

### 4.7.1   Results

Figure 8 shows the results, converted to percentages. Subjects rated 15% of the thumbnails and 21% for both titles and URLs as poor or worse representations. Only 2% of thumbnails were in the 'does not represent the page' category when compared to 10% for titles/URLs. On the other side, all representations had ratings of ~60% in the good or higher category, but there were fewer thumbnails in the instantly recognisable category.

### 4.7.2   Discussion

These results suggest that thumbnails are a slightly better representation than titles or URLs. While thumbnails have marginally less instant recognition, they received generally better overall ratings. Titles are even worse than shown here because this data only includes pages with titles. We could safely assume that the extra 5–30% of pages without titles would be in the worst category.

## 5   Conclusion

In this paper, we contribute hard data valuable for the design of revisitation systems. The data directly compares URLs and titles, and shows that both have reasonable recognition rates. Because we cannot realistically show long titles and URLs in our revisitation system, the data tabulates the trade-offs between truncation methods on page recognition, e.g. Figures 4 & 6 and Table 2. Designers can use these to predict the consequences of using particular space-conservative displays. We also examine the recognisability of thumbnails. While they currently appear only in research systems, we have shown that people feel they are good representations of pages, and that they can accurately recognise the page they represent at particular sizes. We also showed that people mainly use a thumbnail's colour and layout to identify its

Web site, and the thumbnail's dominant text (legible only at larger sizes) to identify its exact page. However, text becomes legible only at larger sizes.

These results are also important for Web page designers, for it is in their best interest to design pages that can be effectively recognised and therefore revisited easily. Web pages should have short but well named titles. The URL site and file name should be descriptive yet not long. For thumbnail images, pages throughout a single Web site should have a consistent layout and colour scheme. As well, a text banner should be large enough to be visible in a modest-sized thumbnail, e.g. as in Woodruff et al. (2001).

Of course, more work needs to be done. First, this study looked at thumbnail recognition *in isolation* from one another. Yet in actual practice, a history list (as in Figure 1) will comprise many thumbnails, where similar-looking thumbnails for a site are likely located near each other. We believe these clusters will make thumbnails even more recognisable, meaning that our results likely suggest the 'worse case' of recognition. A next study should examine this. Second, although our study used actual pages visited, we did not separate peoples' recognition of familiar vs unfamiliar pages. In practice, we expect frequently visited pages will be more recognisable and we should test this. Third, we need to investigate the interplay and thus recognition between combined thumbnail/title/URL representations, as in the integrated history system shown in Figure 1. We expect the redundancy between representations will likely improve recognisability even further.

Finally, we need to redesign our system in Figure 1 to use these recommendations, deploy it to end-users, and evaluate its effectiveness in actual use. In our own experiences using this system, we have found the thumbnail-based integrated history system incredibly helpful, to the point where we find it quite painful to switch back to the normal history system provided by Internet Explorer.

## References

Ayers, E. & Stasko, J. (1995), Using Graphical History in Browsing the World Wide Web, *in* I. Goldstein & A. Vezza (eds.), *Proceedings of the 4th International World Wide Web Conference*.

Cockburn, A. & Greenberg, S. (1999), Issues of Page Representation and Organisation in Web Browser's Revisitation Tools, *in* J. Scott (ed.), *Proceedings of OzCHI'99 The Ninth Australian Conference on Computer–Human Interaction*, IEEE Computer Society Press.

Cockburn, A. & McKenzie, B. (2000), "What Do Web Users Do? An Empirical Analysis of Web Use", *International Journal of Human–Computer Studies* **54**(6), 903–22.

Cockburn, A., Greenberg, S., McKenzie, B., Smith, M. & Kaasten, S. (1999), WebView: A Graphical Aid for Revisiting Web Pages, *in* J. Scott (ed.), *Proceedings of OzCHI'99 The Ninth Australian Conference on Computer–Human Interaction*, IEEE Computer Society Press.

Czerwinski, M. P., van Dantzich, M., Robertson, G. & Hoffman, H. (1999), The Contribution of Thumbnail Image, Mouse-over Text and Spatial Location Memory to Web Page Retrieval in 3D, *in* A. Sasse & C. Johnson (eds.), *Human–Computer Interaction —*

*INTERACT '99: Proceedings of the Seventh IFIP Conference on Human–Computer Interaction*, Vol. 1, IOS Press, pp.163–70.

Hightower, R., Ring, L., Helfman, J., Bederson, B. & Hollan, J. (1998), Graphical Multiscale Web Histories: A Study of PadPrints, *in* K. Grønbæk, E. Mylonas & F. M. Shipman (eds.), *Proceedings of the 9th ACM Conference on Hypertext — Hypertext'98*, ACM Press, pp.58–65.

Kaasten, S. (2001), Designing an Integrated History/Bookmark System for Web Browsing, MSc Thesis, Department of Computer Science, University of Calgary.

Kaasten, S. & Greenberg, S. (2001), Integrating Back, History and Bookmarks in Web browsers, *in* J. A. Jacko & A. Sears (eds.), *Companion Proceedings of CHI2001: Human Factors in Computing Systems (CHI2001 Conference Companion)*, ACM Press, pp.379–80.

Robertson, G., Czerwinski, M., Larson, K., Robbins, D., Thiel, D. & van Dantzich, M. (1998), Data Mountain: Using Spatial Memory for Document Management, *in* M. Beaudouin-Lafon (ed.), *Proceedings of the 11th Annual ACM Symposium on User Interface Software and Technology, UIST'98*, ACM Press, pp.153–62.

Suh, B., Woodruff, A., Rosenholtz, R. & Glass, A. (2002), Popout Prism: Adding Perceptual Principles to Overview+Detail Document Interfaces, *in* L. Terveen & D. Wixon (eds.), *Proceedings of CHI2002 Conference on Human Factors in Computing Systems, CHI Letters* 4(1), ACM Press, pp.251–8.

Woodruff, A., Faulring, A., Rosenholtz, R., Morrison, J. & Pirolli, P. (2001), Using Thumbnails to Search the Web, *in* J. A. Jacko & A. Sear (eds.), *Proceedings of CHI2001 Conference on Human Factors in Computing Systems, CHI Letters* 3(1), ACM Press, pp.198–205.

# MATI: A System for Accessing Travel Itinerary Information using Mobile Phones

## Masood Masoodian & Nicholas Lane

*Department of Computer Science, The University of Waikato, Private Bag 3105, Hamilton, New Zealand.*

Tel: *+64 7 838 4978*

Fax: *+64 7 858 5095*

Email: *m.masoodian@cs.waikato.ac.nz*

URL: *http://www.cs.waikato.ac.nz/~masood*

**Travellers usually carry some kind of a printed travel itinerary which list various information related to their trip, such as flights and hotel bookings, in a tabular form. Often the only observable relationship between different activities listed on a conventional itinerary is that the activities follow one another sequentially in time. Various computer-supported travel itinerary visualisation systems have been developed in recent years to allow making references between different events on an itinerary easier. Unfortunately, all of these visualisations rely on a large computer display, and as such, aren't suitable for travellers without continuous access to computers. We have developed a system called MATI, which allows access to personal travel itinerary information using Wireless Application Protocol (WAP)-enabled mobile phones. This paper describes MATI, and identifies some of the design issues that had to be resolved during its development.**

**Keywords:** mobile computing, information visualisation, mobile phones, handheld devices, Wireless Application Protocol (WAP), travel itinerary.

## 1 Introduction

Over the last few years the popularity of small handheld computing and communication devices has achieved a phenomenal growth. In no other area this growth has been more spectacular than in that of mobile telephony. Mobile phones have become common every day devices in many parts of the world. For instance, it is reported that in some Scandinavian countries more than 60% of the population own a mobile phone (Björk et al., 1999).

Despite this popularity, the current growth of the mobile phone industry is far less impressive than once predicted by some. It is, however, believed that the current growth will accelerate rapidly in the near future (Buchanan et al., 2001). It is also commonly accepted that the lack of useful services, as well as the high cost of accessing available services have often been the reason for the slower rate of growth for mobile phones.

New services are being developed by the industry to expand the use of mobile phones beyond their current use for simple audio communication. One particular field in which mobile phone services are likely to have the greatest impact is that of travel and tourism.

Other handheld devices such as PDAs have already been utilised for delivery of context-aware information to users. For instance, GUIDE (Cheverst et al., 2000) was developed to provide different types of context-aware information to visitors of a city, information such as the nearest cheap hotel, the next performance at a local theatre, and so on. HIPS (Broadbent & Marti, 1997; Marti et al., 2001) is another similar system which allows delivery of context-aware information within a particular location (e.g. a museum).

In this paper we discuss the development of a system called MATI which allows access to personal travel itinerary information using mobile phones. MATI provides access to textual and graphical visualisations of travel itinerary using the Wireless Application Protocol (WAP) (Varshney & Vetter, 2000; Väänänen-Vainio-Mattila & Ruuska, 1999; Wireless Application Protocol Forum Ltd, 2002).

Mobile phones, like most other small handheld devices, have limited screen real estate and restricted input capabilities. Therefore, one of the challenges faced by the research presented here has been in devising new visualisation techniques to allow useful presentation of complex graphical information on small display area of a typical mobile phone.

Our knowledge of the design issues related to development of interfaces for small devices, sometimes referred to as the 'baby faces' (Marcus et al., 1998), is limited at present. It is hoped that the discussion of some of the design decisions made during the development of MATI will provide guidelines for development of future systems requiring presentation of complex information on small displays.

## 2   Visualisation of Travel Itinerary Information

The travel itinerary of a trip plays an important role in facilitating organisation and scheduling of the activities relating to the trip. The itinerary is generally created before the trip starts, and subsequently may be modified during the trip. A travel itinerary is often in a tabular form, listing related travel events in a sequential date and time order. Travellers usually carry a printed version of their itinerary during the course of their travel which can range from a simple trip to a complicated one spanning over several weeks or months. These kinds of tabular itineraries are often less than satisfactory to carry, use, or change and update specially during a long travel which may include several flights, transport or accommodation bookings, meetings and other events.

One of the main problems with conventional travel itineraries is that they do not always provide an overview of the relationship between various events of a trip. The only relationship which can be viewed in a standard travel itinerary is that various events follow one another sequentially in time. For instance, for a particular trip it might be easy to check whether Sydney is going to be visited before Los Angeles or not, but it may be a bit more difficult to find out quickly if a hotel stay in Sydney is longer or shorter than a hotel stay in Los Angeles. Similarly it may be very difficult, or nearly impossible, to find out the arrival time in Sydney based on the local time of Los Angeles after a long flight from Los Angeles to Sydney. Information such as these are often needed by travellers when for instance they need to contact someone at a city which is in a different time-zone or on the other side of the international dateline.

## 2.1   Graphical Travel Itinerary

Graphical visualisations have been devised to represent the concept of passage of time (Plaisant et al., 1996), train timetables (Tufte, 1983) or air travel (Tufte, 1990; Pu & Faltings, 2000). Most of these representations, however, either don't address the issue of travel over different time-zones, or only deal with travel between two locations, without the possibility of including other intermediate locations.

An ongoing research project at the University of Waikato has focused on developing novel computer supported travel itinerary visualisations tools which provide better access to itinerary information. This project has also investigated various aspects of the collaborative activities of travel agents and their clients during the course of a travel arrangement. A Collaborative Information Gathering (CIG) tool has been developed to assist travel agents with the process of creating a travel itinerary with their clients remotely over the Internet (Apperley et al., 2000). A major component of the CIG software is a graphical travel itinerary visualisation, which allows travel agents and their clients to graphically, as well as textually, create, edit, and view travel itineraries synchronously and asynchronously over the Internet.

Figure 1 shows an example round trip between Perth, Australia, and London, UK, with stops in Sydney and Los Angeles. The vertical axis is in time-zone units, showing the time difference between various locations, as well as the international dateline when necessary. The vertical axis also shows the names of the cities which are either destinations or transit points along the way.

The horizontal axis, on the other hand, shows the normal progression of time at a particular location. From this axis it is possible to see for instance how long a flight has taken, or how long a hotel stay is. When a travel crosses the international dateline, the difference between days on different hemispheres is shown along the top and bottom lines of the visualisation.

Using these two different time scales it is possible to compare the time of various events across different time-zones. A horizontal black line depicts a stay event in a location, while the upward and downward lines show travel eastward, or westward respectively. The dark and light shaded stripes show the 12-hour night and day periods while midnights and mid-days are marked with a dark grey or a white diagonal line.

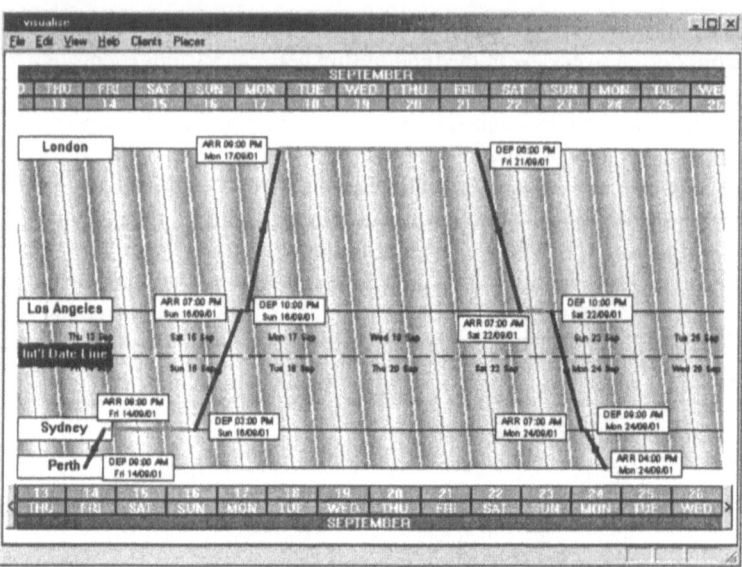

**Figure 1:** Travel itinerary visualisation showing a return trip between Perth, Australia and London, UK.

The CIG system also provides mechanisms for collection of information from different online sources around the world such as the Web sites of airlines and hotels. This information can be automatically entered into the system, and later on accessed through the interface by clicking on different travel events represented on the visualisation.

## 2.2 Mobile Access to Travel Itinerary

An evaluation of the CIG visualisation has shown that it solves many of the problems associated with a tabular form of travel itinerary (Thomson & Apperley, 1999). However, an important limitation of this visualisation tool is that it requires a large display screen, such as that of a desktop computer or a laptop.

Although the use of the CIG system allows an easy way of generating and editing a travel itinerary before the start of a trip, it is not very suitable for use by travellers during their actual trip. At present the likely users of the CIG system have to do one of the following:

1. access their itinerary over the Internet, whenever possible, using a standard computer;

2. save it on a portable computer and carry it with themselves; or

3. print and carry a paper copy of the itinerary.

There are numerous problems with these forms of access which make the system less likely to be used by travellers. These problems can be summarised as:

- The itinerary should be readily portable: access to itinerary information using a computer connected to the Internet (as in Case 1) makes it difficult, or often impossible, to reach important information when the traveller is rushing from one place to another (for instance to catch a flight).

- The itinerary should be modifiable: in Cases 2 and 3 where the itinerary is saved or printed, if for any reason changes are needed to be made to the itinerary during the trip then the initial itinerary becomes inaccurate and obsolete. Anyone who travels regularly would be well aware of the fact that such changes in travel events are not uncommon these days when delays in flights and train schedules are often likely.

- All the travel itinerary information should be accessible: in Case 3 where the itinerary is printed the user looses the ability of accessing relevant information by clicking on different travel events on the visualisation. This type of accessibility is important because much of the information about the events isn't directly shown on the visualisation. For example, information about a particular hotel stay might include the phone number and address of the hotel which aren't shown on the graphical visualisation.

It is clear that an appropriate solution to all these problems could be found by investigating the possibility of the use of some kind of an Internet-enabled mobile device which can provide remote access to travel itinerary information.

Regardless of the choice of the target mobile device there are important design challenges that need to be addressed first. As mentioned earlier these challenges are related to providing useful visualisation of complex information on small display screens, which all the handheld devices inherently suffer from at the present. This is particularly true of the mobile phones that despite having the smallest screens are most likely to be adopted as a suitable technology for delivery of itinerary information due to their widespread popularity.

Addressing these types of visualisation challenges is the focus of the research presented here. The rest of this paper describes the development of a series of visualisations suitable for mobile phone technology. Some of the solutions to the problem of showing the complex CIG visualisation on a small mobile phone display are highly relevant to other information visualisation challenges faced by developers of software for similar technologies.

## 3   Itinerary Visualisation on Small Screens

The graphical travel itinerary visualisation of CIG is too complex to be displayed effectively on the small display of a typical mobile phone. It is necessary to modify the visualisation by making it less complex, while at the same time keeping its most essential features.

The itinerary visualisation can be modified in a number of ways to make it more suitable for a small display area. Two of these are:

- Simplifying the visualisation.

- Providing a section-by-section view of the simplified visualisation.

## 3.1   Simplifying the Visualisation

The CIG visualisation combines and presents a range of itinerary related information to the users. Some of this information, however, is more critical to providing a general understanding of the itinerary than the others.

Clearly the main feature of the CIG visualisation is that it allows the users to get an overview of the events of a trip in relation to one another. In contrast there are other features, which although useful, play a less important role in the effectiveness of the visualisation.

It is therefore possible to remove some information from the visualisation without greatly affecting its usability while at the same time achieving some degree of simplicity. In particular the visualisation can be simplified by:

- Changing the vertical axis by abbreviating the names of the cities.

- Placing the cities across the vertical axis relative to one another rather than accurately reflecting their time-zone differences.

- Changing the horizontal axis by only showing the start and end dates and times for the trip.

- Dividing the horizontal axis into equal steps rather than always showing the exact number of days and nights.

It is on the other hand important to show the relative length of travel and stay events as accurately as possible, because their visual relationships are important to the effectiveness of the visualisation.

## 3.2   Providing a Section-by-Section View

It has already been mentioned that providing the users with an overview of the whole travel itinerary is an important aspect of the graphical visualisation. Hence it is necessary to allow users to get an overview of the travel itinerary visualisation for the duration of the entire trip in a simplified form, and then allow them to zoom-in and view parts of the itinerary in more detail, with the option of moving horizontally or vertically to view different sections of the itinerary.

A natural way of zooming-in would be to give the users the option of viewing the itinerary in a monthly, weekly, or daily scale. In the zoom-in mode the user could either start at the beginning of the trip, or the current point in time (which the system is ware of), and then view the itinerary for the previous or next month, week, or day depending on the selected zoom scale.

The users could also be given an event-based form of zoom-in functionality, where it is possible to move between various travel events in a graphical form and view their details individually. This form of zoom-in can be combined with the time-based zooming in months, weeks, or days.

Unlike the horizontal movement, the vertical movement between different sections of the itinerary in a zoom-in mode seems to be less useful. The vertical axis gives the relative location of the cities in relation to different time-zones. However, as pointed out earlier, this axis can be simplified to show the cities in relation to one another rather than their accurate time-zones. This will make it possible to list them on the vertical axis one after the other. In this form it will be possible to represent the fact that for instance Sydney is in a time-zone ahead of Perth by showing Sydney ahead of Perth on the vertical axis without showing how many time-zones there are between Sydney and Perth.

In many travel situations the number of cities visited is small and manageable. This means that it is often possible to fit the abbreviated names of the cities along the vertical axis without the need for a zoom-in function vertically. The situation where it is not possible to fit all the destination cities along the vertical axis is a problem which will be discussed later in this paper.

There is also some evidence from the relevant literature (Buyukkokten et al., 2001) which points out to the fact that requiring both horizontal and vertical scrolling on a small display to allow viewing of large amount of information can be disorienting to the users.

## 4   MATI Prototype

The widespread popularity and availability of mobile phones makes them ideal tools for delivery of travel related services. Mobile phone technologies such as WAP (Varshney & Vetter, 2000; Väänänen-Vainio-Mattila & Ruuska, 1999; Wireless Application Protocol Forum Ltd, 2002) are already being used for delivery of travel and business oriented services.

Until recently WAP has been viewed by many as a de facto standard for providing Internet-based services to most handheld devices, including mobile phones, PDAs, and palmtops (Björk et al., 1999). The reason for popularity of WAP is because it allows access to documents written in WML (Wireless Mark-up Language) over the Internet using WAP-enabled devices.

WML is really a simplified version of HTML that made the World Wide Web so universally accessible. Unlike HTML though, WML is perhaps too restrictive to be useful in general. These restrictions coupled with the high cost of using WAP have made it a less than satisfactory technology to use.

Future technologies such as 3G are at present being developed and promoted by various organisations[1] including the World Wide Web Consortium (2002). These new technologies are supposed to remedy some of the shortcomings of WAP, and hopefully facilitate better delivery of services to mobile devices in a less costly fashion.

Despite these limitations WAP seemed like a suitable technology that could be adopted as the basis for the initial development of a prototype system to access travel itinerary information using mobile phones. A prototype system called MATI (Mobile Access to Travel Itinerary) has now been developed to access the CIG visualisation over the Internet. Although MATI currently relies on WAP, the underlying visualisation concepts developed during this research are expected to be useful for devising future systems which may be based on more sophisticated technologies than WAP.

---

[1] See for example Ericsson Australia's http://www.ericsson.com.au/technologies/3g Web page.

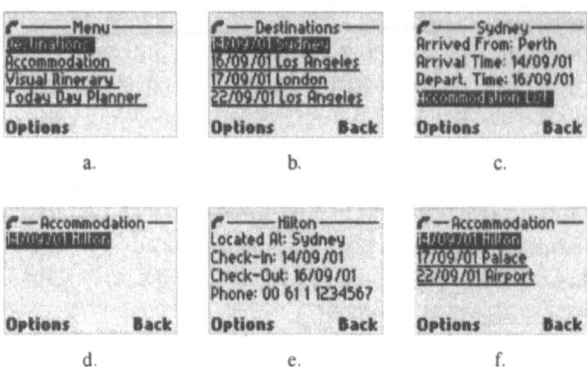

**Figure 2:** a. The main menu of MATI. b. Destination list of the whole itinerary. c. Information relating to a particular destination. d. Accommodation list for a particular destination. e. Information relating to a particular hotel. f. Accommodation list of the whole itinerary.

MATI is designed to provide access to a simplified version of the CIG visualisation, based on the criteria discussed in previous section. MATI allows the users to access travel itinerary information in two different modes, textual and graphical.

## 4.1   Textual View

Textual view of the travel itinerary information is the simplest kind of view that MATI provides. Figure 2 shows several sample pages accessed via MATI. All of these pages relate to the example CIG itinerary visualisation shown in Figure 1. As Figure 2 shows, in textual view, MATI allows the users to access the list of all the destinations of an itinerary (2a), from which a user can select a particular destination (2b) to find out information related to that destination (2c), for instance all the hotel bookings related to that city (2d) or details of a particular hotel (2e).

MATI supports user access to some information via different paths. For example, one can access the information about a hotel booking either by following the path described above (2a, 2b, 2c, 2d, 2f) or directly via the list of all the hotels (2a, 2f, 2e).

Furthermore, as the textual view provides more details about all the events of an itinerary, it can also be accessed through the graphical view which aims to support an overview of the itinerary rather than its specifics.

## 4.2   Graphical View

Graphical view of MATI is based on the requirements discussed earlier. Figure 3 shows a number of pages related to our example itinerary. The users of MATI can select different levels of zooming for viewing an itinerary (3a). It is possible to either get an overview of the entire itinerary (3b), or a specific time period (3c) from which the user can access previous or next consecutive time periods (3d, 3e). The users can also jump directly to a weekly (3f) or monthly view.

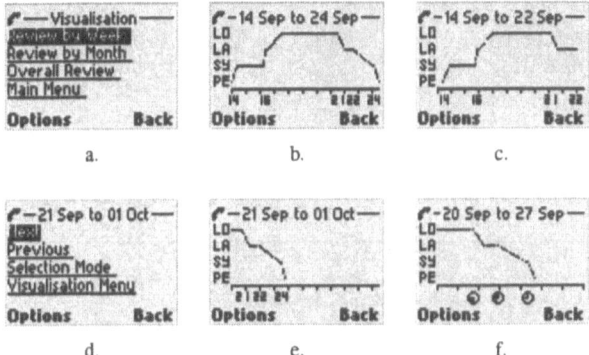

**Figure 3:** a. Menu for different levels of viewing. b. Overview of the whole itinerary. c. The first 9 day period of the itinerary. d. Menu for selecting the next or previous period. e. The next 9 day period of the itinerary. f. A weekly view of the itinerary.

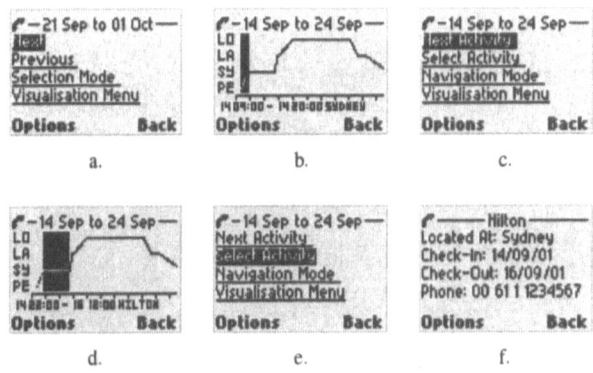

**Figure 4:** a. Switching from the navigation to selection mode. b. The current travel activity. c. Menu for selecting the next or previous activity. d. The next activity. e. Selecting an activity for more information. f. Details of the current activity.

It is important to note that the amount of information related to various events that MATI provides in graphical view changes depending on the zoom level selected by the user. For instance, when a period of time selected by the user is sufficiently small enough, MATI shows the hours of the day during which different events are going to take place using a simple clock-face system in 3-hour day and night slots (3f). On the other hand, if the selected time period is large, only the dates of the days in which events occur are shown (3b).

If the users require further information about the itinerary events they can access these via the textual view. One way of accessing textual information has already been demonstrated (Figure 2). Another interesting way of accessing textual information is through the graphical selection mode.

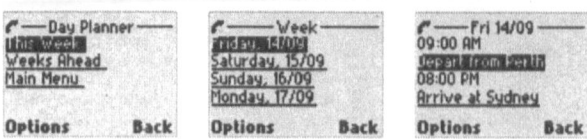

**Figure 5:** a. The day planner menu. b. The next 7 days (this week). c. Events relating to a selected day.

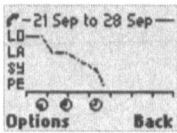

**Figure 6:** Itinerary view starting from today's day.

Figure 4 shows how the users can change from graphical navigation mode to graphical selection mode (4a), allowing them to step through different events (4b, 4c, 4d) and select to view information relating to the current event (4e, 4f). It is also possible to switch back from selection mode to navigation mode (4c or 4e).

Another way of selecting events for accessing more detailed information is by using the day planner (Figure 5). This method allows the users to rapidly move between different weeks of an itinerary (5a), followed by choosing the relevant day (5b), and subsequently selecting the desired event (5c).

MATI also utilises information about the current date and time to filter irrelevant itinerary events. For example, the users can activate the time awareness future of MATI so that the system only gives the itinerary information that are going to happen in the future, ignoring all the past events. Figure 6 shows the entire relevant itinerary when the current date is set to 21 September.

## 5  System Architecture

MATI has been developed as an extension to the CIG system. The CIG software itself is based on a client/server style architecture (Apperley et al., 2000). All the components of the CIG software communicate with one another through a central hub (Figure 7). The system supports several different types of visualisation tools, one of which is the time-line visualisation described earlier. These visualisation tools interact with one another by sending and receiving data in the form of 'travel events', which are single itinerary components such as a flight or hotel stay. The travel events are also stored at a central database which can be queried by the visualisation tools through the central hub.

As far as the CIG system is concerned MATI is just another visualisation tool which queries the central database for travel events. At the user's end, on the other hand, MATI interacts with the mobile phone through a WAP gateway.

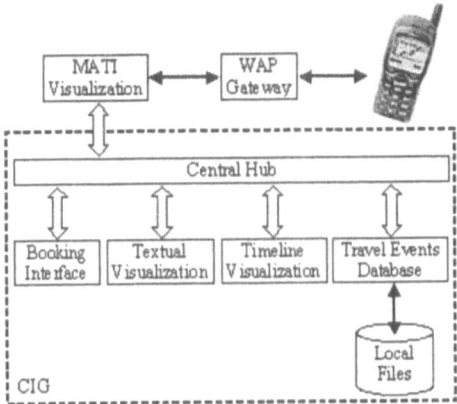

**Figure 7:** Architecture of MATI.

When a user connects to MATI through the gateway, the user's mobile phone queries are sent by MATI via the central hub to the travel events database. MATI then converts the results of the queries which it receives from the database into either WML cards (for textual information) or WBMP (Wireless BitMaP) images (for graphical information). These WML cards or WBMP images are then sent to the mobile phone through the gateway and are displayed to the user.

# 6 Evaluation

At present our knowledge of the usability of small screens is generally based on the research done in the 1980s when there was a considerable interest in using miniature displays in ATMs, typewriters, photocopiers and so on (Buchanan et al., 2001). Majority of the recent research on small displays have mainly focused on issues relating to presentation of textual material such as Web pages. In fact, most of the research has concentrated on presentation of lists or navigation of textual content (Buchanan et al., 2001).

Clearly there is a need to investigate the usability of small screens for presentation of graphical information. So far those who have done some research in this field have looked at the use of small displays for presenting photographs and images (Rist, 2001).

It is therefore important that the design and development of systems such as MATI are closely guided by empirical studies that test their effectiveness in real-life situations. It is also hoped that such evaluations will contribute to an understanding of a diverse range of unknowns about graphical information representation on small screens.

As part of this process of evaluation, a small in-house study of MATI was conducted to identify and resolve any major usability problems before doing a major user evaluation. It is, however, important to note that these evaluations were done

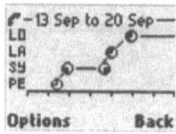

**Figure 8:** Clocks showing each event's start and end time.

---

using the SmartPhone WAP Emulator[2] rather than real mobile phones, mainly due to the high cost of using WAP at present.

This evaluation has shown several limitations of the horizontal view of travel itinerary. One such limitation is associated with showing the names of the destination cities on the vertical axis. Currently if there are a handful of destinations then their names can be shown in abbreviated form. However, as the number of cities increases this solution becomes less suitable because it is not then possible to fit all the names in a small space. Indeed the abbreviations themselves may end up being the same for different city names.

A solution to this problem is to show the city names on the visualisation graph itself rather than on the vertical axis. However, our evaluation of the use of clock-faces for representing travel events' time (Figure 6) has demonstrated that clock-faces are more useful if they are shown on the visualisation graph where events change from one to another (Figure 8). We have decided to use the intersection point between the events for clock-faces rather than the city names.

An alternative solution to the above problem is to use time-zone names rather than individual city names to represent a number of destination cities which fall in the same time-zone. For instance rather than showing both Melbourne and Sydney, the system may only show E-AU to represent Eastern Australia. This solution is only used when there isn't enough space to show all the cities; otherwise the individual city names are shown in abbreviated form.

Another perceived difficulty with the use of the current visualisation is that mobile phones often allow going back and forth between the screens using the up and down buttons or a scroll button. To use the up and down motion to move left and right between various time periods in a zoom-in mode seems to be less natural than expected. This problem can be solved by rotating the visualisation from a horizontal view to a vertical view.

A revised version of MATI has now been developed to allow users to select between the horizontal and vertical views of the itinerary visualisation. The new version also includes a number of other features some of which have been discussed here.

A major user study of MATI has also been undertaken to compare the graphical and textual visualisations. The results of this study, although failed to demonstrate any clear advantages of graphical visualisation over the textual one, indicated that the two visualisations were complementary to one another in their presentation of

---

[2]SmartPhone WAP Emulator is available at http://www.yospace.com/

itinerary information. It is expected that the use of the systems and its effectiveness will improve over time, as the users get more familiar with the graphical visualisation and are able to interpret the information presented in it more easily and accurately.

## 7 Conclusions

The emergence of handheld computing devices, with their limited display capabilities, has generated interesting information visualisation challenges which must be addressed by HCI researchers and practitioners. These challenges are by no means new, and in many cases can be compared to those faced in the past by researchers dealing with the development of systems such as ATMs. There are however a range of new services and applications for which these modern mobile devices are being designed, each with their own new visualisation requirements.

This paper has described one such system which has been designed to allow access to graphical travel itinerary information using mobile phones. It is clear that over the next few years the handheld computing technology will evolve rapidly. Despite these advances, however, it is still likely that the visualisation techniques such as those developed during this research will benefit other systems where it is necessary to provide access to complex graphical information using similar devices with small display area.

## Acknowledgements

The CIG visualisation system described in this paper was developed as part of a collaborative information gathering research project funded by the Foundation for Research, Science and Technology, through Public Good Science Fund (grant number UOW808). The authors would also like to acknowledge the contributions of the other members of the CIG research team.

## References

Apperley, M., Fletcher, D., Rogers, B. & Thomson, K. (2000), Interactive Visualisation of a Travel Itinerary, *in* V. Di Gesu, S. Levialdi & L. Tarantino (eds.), *Proceedings of the Working Conference on Advanced Visual Interfaces*, ACM Press, pp.221–6.

Björk, S., Holmquist, L. E., Redström, J., Bretan, I., Danielsson, R., Karlgren, J. & Franzén, K. (1999), WEST: A Web Browser for Small Terminals, *in* B. Schilit (ed.), *Proceedings of the 12th Annual ACM Symposium on User Interface Software and Technology, UIST'99, CHI Letters* 1(1), ACM Press, pp.187–96.

Broadbent, J. & Marti, P. (1997), Location Aware Mobile Interactive Guides: Usability Issues, *in* D. Bearman & J. Trant (eds.), *Proceedings of the Fourth International Conference on Hypermedia and Interactivity in Museums*, Archives & Museum Informatics, pp.88–98.

Buchanan, G., Farrant, S., Jones, M., Marsden, G., Pazzani, M. & Thimbleby, H. (2001), Improving Mobile Internet Usability, *in* V. Y. Shen, N. Saito, K. T. Yung, M. R. Lyu & M. E. Zurko (eds.), *Proceedings of the Tenth International World Wide Web Conference (WWW10)*, ACM Press, pp.673–80.

Buyukkokten, O., Garcia-Molina, H. & Paepcke, A. (2001), Accordion Summarization for End-game Browsing on PDAs and Cellular Phones, *in* J. A. Jacko & A. Sear (eds.),

*Proceedings of CHI2001 Conference on Human Factors in Computing Systems, CHI Letters* **3**(1), ACM Press, pp.213–20.

Cheverst, K., Davies, N., Mitchell, K., Friday, A. & Efstratiou, C. (2000), Developing a Context-aware Electronic Tourist Guide: Some Issues and Experiences, *in* T. Turner, G. Szwillus, M. Czerwinski & F. Paternò (eds.), *Proceedings of the CHI2000 Conference on Human Factors in Computing Systems, CHI Letters* **2**(1), ACM Press, pp.17–24.

Marcus, A., Ferrante, J. V., Kinnunen, T., Kuutti, K. & Sparre, E. (1998), Baby Faces: User-interface Design for Small Displays, *in* C.-M. Karat, A. Lund, B. Bederson, E. Bergman, M. Beaudouin-Lafon, N. Bevan, D. Boehm-Davis, A. Boltman, G. Cockton, A. Druin, S. Dumais, N. Frischberg, J. Jacko, J. Koenemann, C. Lewis, S. Pemberton, A. Sears, K. T. Simsarian, C. Wolf & J. Ziegler (eds.), *Summary Proceedings of CHI'98: Human Factors in Computing Systems (CHI'98 Conference Summary)*, ACM Press, pp.96–7.

Marti, P., Pucci, F. & Rizzo, A. (2001), "External Aids for Social Memory", *Information, Communication & Society* **4**(2), 261–73.

Plaisant, C., Milash, B., Rose, A., Widoff, S. & Shneiderman, B. (1996), Lifelines: Visualizing Personal Histories, *in* G. van der Veer & B. Nardi (eds.), *Proceedings of CHI'96: Human Factors in Computing Systems*, ACM Press.

Pu, P. & Faltings, B. (2000), Enriching Buyers' Experiences: The SmartClient Approach, *in* T. Turner, G. Szwillus, M. Czerwinski & F. Paternò (eds.), *Proceedings of the CHI2000 Conference on Human Factors in Computing Systems, CHI Letters* **2**(1), ACM Press, pp.289–96.

Rist, T. (2001), A Perspective on Intelligent Information Interfaces for Mobile Users, *in* M. J. Smith, G. Salvendy, D. Harris & R. J. Koubek (eds.), *Proceedings of the 9th International Conference on Human–Computer Interaction (HCI International '01)*, Lawrence Erlbaum Associates, pp.154–8.

Thomson, K. & Apperley, M. (1999), Developing a Graphical Timeline Representation for a Travel Itinerary, Working Paper 99/15, Department of Computer Science, The University of Waikato.

Tufte, E. R. (1983), *The Visual Display of Quantitative Information*, Graphics Press.

Tufte, E. R. (1990), *Envisioning Information*, Graphics Press.

Varshney, U. & Vetter, R. (2000), "Emerging Mobile and Wireless Networks", *Communications of the ACM* **43**(6), 73–81.

Väänänen-Vainio-Mattila, K. & Ruuska, S. (1999), "Design: Designing Mobile Phones and Communicators for Consumer Needs at Nokia", *Interactions* **6**(5), 23–6.

Wireless Application Protocol Forum Ltd (2002), What is WAP and WAP Forum?, http://www.wapforum.org/what.

World Wide Web Consortium (2002), Mobile Access: Working Towards Seamless Web Access from Mobile Devices, http://www.w3.org/Mobile.

# User Interface Design as Systems Design

## Harold Thimbleby, Ann Blandford, Paul Cairns, Paul Curzon[†] & Matt Jones[‡]

*UCL Interaction Centre, 26 Bedford Way,*
*London WC1H 0AP, UK.*
Email: *{h.thimbleby, a.blandford, p.cairns}@ucl.ac.uk*

[†] *Interaction Design Centre, Middlesex University,*
*London N14 4YZ, UK.*
Email: *p.curzon@mdx.ac.uk*

[‡] *Department of Computer Science, University of Waikato,*
*Private Bag 3105, Hamilton, New Zealand.*
Email: *always@acm.org*

When designing complex systems, it is standard systems engineering practice to carefully design the interfaces between subsystems. Yet when designing human–computer systems, the interface between human and system is not usually thought through in such terms. Instead, the human is often given wide access to arbitrary parts of the system, and the result is a complex human–computer system that fails in various ways.

We illustrate this argument with a case study of a public walk-up-and-use rail ticketing system. We show that the interaction imposed on the user is inappropriate to the user's task needs; we show how user interface problems arise through access to organisational conventions that are of little interest to users. Furthermore, the wide interface is beyond the resources of the rail organisation to manage.

Conversely we show that an interface designed to hide irrelevant complexity (exactly as one would do approaching user interfaces as a systems engineering design problem) can have a beneficial impact on the user experience, including improving the reliability of the total system.

**Keywords:** design, graphical user interfaces, interaction design, personal technologies, public user interfaces, system complexity, systems engineering, walk up and use.

# 1  Introduction

Standard good HCI practice is to find out about user tasks as one of the first steps in design, otherwise it is tempting to start design from the functionality provided by (or planned to be provided by) the system. The system functions may interact in interesting and complex ways, but the HCI issue is to support the user task, rather than give access to the underlying system *per se*. One of the most successful user interfaces to general purpose systems is the graphical user interface, and its success in providing access to PC functionality means it is frequently a candidate for use in other applications, which are supposed to support much simpler tasks; the same is true of Web-style user interfaces, which provide such easy access to the world they 'must' provide easy access to simpler systems! Unfortunately neither a GUI nor a Web-style interface constrains the designer much, and does not motivate finding a clear view of the task, because it is possible to support almost any functionality and hence almost any task.

This paper argues that proper design, based on well-known systems engineering principles, can transform the user experience by hiding irrelevant complexity. We support our abstract discussion with a case study of rail ticket vending machines as an example of complex public technology, but the principles underpinning the discussion apply very widely across a range of technologies and contexts of use. We show how appropriate design can eliminate conventional user interface problems for the task in hand, including problems of implementation quality. We will see, further, that having eliminated conventional problems, latent issues become salient: user acceptance now depends on solving less technical but more social problems.

## 1.1  The Abstract Systems Design View

Many goals cannot be achieved by simple systems. Most interesting systems involve people interacting with each other and often with complex computer systems, and all within some bigger system that is intended to achieve goals such as "staying in business, whilst adhering to regulatory and legal requirements." It is well known that interacting subsystems can exhibit complex behaviour that no subsystem alone may be able to exhibit, such as deadlock, livelock, non-determinism and feature-interaction (multiple features combining in unexpected and usually unhelpful ways). In the specific case of human–system interaction, there are particular problems such as closure errors (including post- and pre-completion errors), which are psychological representations of the abstract system concepts like deadlock.

To avoid such undesirable problems arising in new systems it is crucial that the interfaces between subsystems are well-defined and understood and, moreover, simple. An interface specifies how subsystems interact with each other, and a good interface deliberately hides details that are irrelevant. Once interfaces are well-defined, it is possible to change subsystems (for instance, to make them more efficient) without detriment to the overall system behaviour, provided the interfaces are maintained. In fortuitous cases, of course, one may improve systems by changing interfaces, but in practice it has been found that carefully managing the separation of concerns of different subsystems through well-defined interfaces is crucial to successful design. More importantly, when interfaces are well defined, it is possible to reason clearly about a subsystem without having to know everything about all other subsystems: because their details are hidden, their details are irrelevant. Conversely, many system failures can be attributed to circumventions (be they accidental, overlooked or in hindsight unwisely exploited), of what were supposed to be well-defined interfaces. These systemic issues are no less true of human–system or human–computer interaction than of conventional technical systems engineering.

The value of good interfaces between subsystems has been known for a long time (Parnas, 1972). However this knowledge has not been extended to user interface design; for example, a comprehensive textbook on software engineering (Sommerville, 2000) includes a thorough discussion of interface design but the chapter on user interface design does not take a systems approach, being entirely conventional user-centred design.

Typically the interface between the human and the technical system — the *user interface* — is deeply entangled with the internal details of the system. *This is exactly the wrong way to do it.* User interfaces are often designed to control as many features of the system as possible, so this entanglement is inevitable. Indeed there is a line of thought within HCI (Norman, 1986) that one central role for the user interface is to communicate the underlying system model to the user. Interfaces are also deeply entangled with the social, perceptual and cognitive details of the human: hence the lively debates about design, colour, screen layout, culture, and so forth. These issues have a significant impact on the success of the combined human–system. It is a truism that there are no easy design solutions, and one often has to build prototypes and iterate design to identify feasible improvements.

In human–computer systems, there are usually many parallel interfaces (in the systems sense). For example, if interaction using the primary interface deadlocks, there may be interfaces available that support 'reset', 'cancel' and 'timeout': and these operations may be initiated by other subsystems in the computer or in the user (or even bystanders helping the user). Users, of course, usually reflect on their behaviour and can walk away or take other action. In some contexts, avionics being a case in point, with hard real time constraints, the design of the control interfaces is very difficult if they are not to create, rather than solve, further problems of interaction. There is a great deal of interest in designing systems so that users' awareness of interaction (and likely consequences) does not lead to panic or other extreme actions outside the specification the primary interfaces.

Technology is changing, and ideas about the best ways of designing user interfaces are also changing. For many tasks, GUIs are easier to use than command lines, and for a while they have been the best way of interacting with general purpose PCs. We have excellent visual computing skills, and GUIs exploit these skills — e.g. recognising overlapping windows (Friedhoff & Peercy, 2000) — to raise the level of complexity that is easy to interact with. However, the recognised strengths of GUIs do not mean they are best in general. Indeed, because GUIs are so good, they can give the surface impression of providing good solutions while actually forcing the interaction to an inappropriate level.

## 2   Case Study

Many cities world-wide depend on public walk up and use ticket vending machines for the smooth running of their transportation infrastructure. As a case study, we take a ticket machine installed in early 2001. The machine is a realistic representation of the state of the art in walk up and use technology[1] and is used by the public to undertake real and important daily tasks. Ticket machines are a serious application to study: not only do they raise revenue for operators, but difficulties with them can mean users miss trains and have their lives disrupted, which has a further impact on others. There is also a 'problem amplification': not only do individual users have problems, but when they do, they delay people waiting in the queue behind them. A point a rail employee made to us was that passengers have to learn how to use the ticket machine while they are trying desperately to *use* it to get a ticket before their train comes.

The ticket machine considered here has numerous user interface problems; thirty years of relevant usability research and practice has had very little obvious impact on its design, even though incorrect operation of the machine can result in the user being unable to travel or being fined for travelling with incorrect tickets. An alternative view is that the designers are concerned with usability, but that they are only empowered to address surface-level usability concerns (such a colour and button layout) rather than the complex usability concerns that might be regarded as systems engineering. The design well illustrates the endemic poor usability in the current every-day computing infrastructure, and the lack of impact of deep usability concerns on designers, manufacturers and those charged with installing new systems.

Although some work has been done on analysing the interactive problems of public technology, e.g. Stanton & Baber (1997), much work involves attempts at adding sophisticated interactive capabilities to ticket machines and kiosks. This work has included adding emotional avatars (Christian & Avery, 1998) and new input techniques (e.g. for sign language interaction). Our analysis suggests this approach, at least if not guided by more systems-level thinking, is misguided. Our case study shows very clearly how organisational issues cause bad user interface experiences that are not hidden from the user in conventional approaches.

### 2.1   *Methodological Issues*

The context of work studied here is enormously complex, and there is no established methodology for investigating issues such as the interaction between usability, organisational and regulatory conditions. There are also ethical challenges: if the work were commissioned by the interested parties then the independence of researchers would be compromised; conversely, those parties should have a right to answer any criticisms of their systems. We have tried to engage in discussion with the main interested parties (the manufacturers and the rail operators).

The ticket machine manufacturer has been very co-operative with us, though they work under constraints. They provide hardware to their customer's requirements. In turn, much of the hardware they use is constrained by external

---

[1]There is a difference between 'state of the art' relative to the potential of current technology and 'state of the art' *in practice* as actually used on the British national rail system. We mean the latter here.

issues, such as financial regulation beyond their control. For example, there may be a better way of users interacting with the credit card facilities, yet this is supplied as a sealed unit for security reasons, and it cannot be changed. The rail operators have declined to comment.

New evaluation techniques for difficult-to-study contexts and applications are needed (Cheverst et al., 2000). Some have further argued that the definition of 'usability' needs to be extended for these new contexts to include notions of intimacy, beauty and social acceptance (Thomas & Thimbleby, to appear). The work reported here is based partly on the experiences of the authors and exploratory investigation of the system interface, partly on periods of observation of others using the ticket machines in question, and partly on discussions with various stakeholders: users, railway staff and the hardware manufacturers. All examples discussed in the body of this paper have been witnessed by the authors or have been experienced during everyday use by at least one of them; the scenarios are not contrived.

A JavaScript simulation has been made of the ticket machine user interface that is adequate to explore the issues raised in this paper, and from which most of our claims can be double-checked. (The simulation obviously doesn't provide tickets or change.) It can be used in a browser over the Web (e.g. for evaluation) and the complete source code is available. See http://www.uclic.ucl.ac.uk/projects/tvm for the simulation, which for copyright reasons may be used for non-commercial research purposes only.

## 2.2   A Brief History of Passenger Transport Systems

Before explaining the case study further, it is helpful to briefly review the organisational history in which the user's task is situated. In the next section, we shall see how many user interface problems arise because the interface gives the user access to the intricacies of the broader ticketing system implementation; this provides the background to show, as we do later, how the interface can be narrowed to conceal this irrelevant detail.

To stay in business, transport systems must collect revenue from travellers (or from other sources, such as subsidies) and, in turn, must provide an acceptable service to those travellers to ensure repeat business. Given human nature and the unreliability of transport systems, relying on trust is insufficient: some passengers do not pay, and some modes of transport fail. Thus tickets were invented as a reliable token of the contract between passengers and transport operators. In Victorian times, railway transport became very sophisticated, and the range and type of tickets expanded. Tickets were printed on card by mechanical devices; as more uses for tickets became apparent (e.g. for distinguishing between contracts with different railway companies) different colours of tickets were introduced. And so on.

Today, over a century later, many interacting layers of complexity have been accreted. Rail companies introduced many sorts of ticket fares, depending on modes of travel, and numerous loyalty schemes — involving identity cards in addition to conventional tickets — such as discounts for family travel at certain times of day. Passengers may use credit cards to pay for tickets: these transactions are heavily regulated. In the United Kingdom another layer of complexity was introduced by the privatisation of the railway network, resulting in many competing organisations and authorities with overlapping interests.

The British railway ticketing system can seem impenetrable to passengers: there are many options and restrictions on tickets and forms of travel. In our terms, the complexity that passengers see arises because the interface between passengers, as one component of the transport system, and the railway companies, as another component of the system, has been defined so that passengers 'see' and interact with the internal complexity of the transport infrastructure. Almost all of that is irrelevant to the needs of the passenger, namely to travel economically and in good time.

Rail companies provide interfaces between passengers and the complex ticketing systems: they provide human ticket clerks. The human clerks are supposed to provide optimal ticketing (and other advice) for passenger travel requests. Unfortunately ticket clerks are an expense and managing their costs, in turn, encourages further complexity in ticketing. If clerks cannot always be present, then new forms of tickets have to be introduced (e.g. 'permits to travel'). Stations now have ticket clerks, automatic ticket machines, *and* permit to travel machines (and on major stations, like Kings Cross, there are several sorts of ticket machines to cater for different rail operators!).

There is a straightforward business case to automate the ticketing process, and there are substantial potential gains. Passengers will be pleased to have shorter ticketing queues, for instance, and rail companies will be pleased to better manage the demands on ticket clerks in order to save costs, and perhaps to improve ticket clerks' morale.

All this, the history and business case, is well known, though the systems complexity might not be widely appreciated as a highly relevant factor of user interface design.

## 2.3    The Conventional Solution

A conventional user interface design solution to rail ticketing would be to automate as much as possible of the ticket clerk's role, and automatic ticket machines have been widely used since the 1980s. Ticket machines are intended to replace the clerk for a given fraction (e.g. 80%) of passenger ticketing needs. As might be expected from our introductory comments, automating the existing interface between passenger and complex rail system cannot avoid the complexities apparent in the original interface itself, unless the specification of that interface is simplified. So, not only do we find the expected deadlock and other symptoms of bad design in our case study, we also find that the new automated system is itself só complex as to introduce its own quality control problems. It is incomplete and unreliable.

The particular ticket machine discussed here was installed on Welwyn North station (north of London's King's Cross station) in early 2001. Similar models are installed throughout the UK. The machine has a rectangular purple label saying it is "Easy to use."

ASCOM, the hardware manufacturer, has installed over 30,000 ticket vending machines around the world (http://www.ascom.com, Sept. 2001), with half still in use, handling over 40 million transactions a day. With this scale of operation any usability problems will have a huge aggregated social impact. In Britain, the 1000+

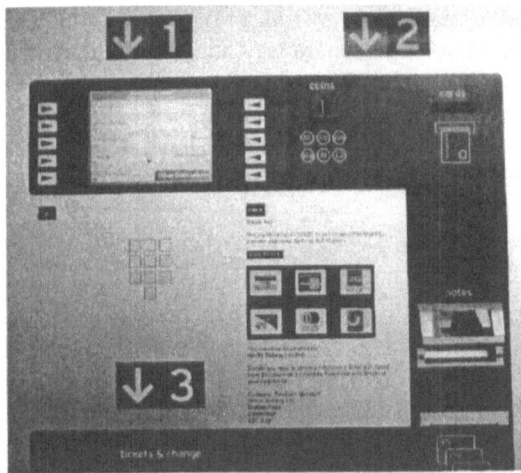

**Figure 1:** The ticket vending machine. The screen (diagonal 25cm, underneath the '↓ 1' arrow) is at eye level for a standing adult, its centre 1.47m off the ground. There are five hard buttons on each side of the display screen (looking like triangular arrows) with meanings as displayed on the screen. There are two buttons with fixed meanings, for information (blue, on the left) and for cancelling (red, on the right). There are ten unlabelled buttons beneath the display that do nothing. The user can insert coins, credit cards or paper currency (underneath the '↓ 2' arrow). A slot at the lower right, that looks like it might accept proprietary tokens, is apparently used as an alternative slot to return rejected notes. Tickets and change are obtained at the bottom of the machine, under the '↓ 3' arrow.

ASCOM machines have an annual revenue well in excess of £100 million: bad user interface design can be costly; conversely, incremental improvements to user interface design has worthwhile payoffs. If users make mistakes — even if in any one location particular types of mistake are experienced infrequently — the overall cost to rail operators will be huge. On individual stations the usability of a ticket machine has an impact on both traveller and rail staff satisfaction. There is also the knock-on loss of reputation when travellers see other users having difficulties.

## 2.4 The Ticket Machine

We now explore the design of the current ticket machine user interface: we show how user interface problems are entwined with system complexity.

Figure 1 shows the ticket machine kiosk discussed in this paper. The main buttons are on each side of the screen, and there are two permanently-labelled buttons: one for information, towards the bottom left of the screen, blue with a white italic $\boxed{i}$; and one for cancelling (towards the bottom right of the screen, in red, and labelled explicitly as $\boxed{\text{CANCEL}}$. The $\boxed{i}$ button provides help, yet there is no explanation of this (perhaps on the principle that users should recognise $\boxed{i}$ as the international standard sign meaning 'information').

The interface employs a standard desktop (GUI/Web) paradigm, but is not, in fact, one. The on-screen labels look like buttons, but do not act like them. Likely surface damage would make a touch screen unreliable (so buttons would probably still be needed). Many passengers we spoke to said they thought the screen was touch sensitive, and they found out the hard way that it has buttons off to each side. One user was observed to repeatedly press the screen; many press the screen for the final 'purchase ticket' step. The designers have applied a widely recognised interface paradigm in an inappropriate context (possibly because the early prototypes they worked on *were* GUIs on their own computers, without a representation of the final context of use).

The actual buttons are placed some distance from the screen (see Figure 1) because physically reinforcing the machine against vandalism (e.g. on unattended stations) is a major design factor: a steel frame means buttons cannot be closer. It is likely that if the screen information looked less like buttons, and were carefully aligned with the markers linking the buttons to the screen area, the mistake of thinking the screen was touch sensitive (as well as the obvious alignment mistakes) would be less likely. For instance, the rectangular button images could be changed to arrows pointing towards the buttons users must press, in forms like Purchase Ticket ⫸ and possibly animated. Whether this would be an effective idea could easily be checked by experiment, but the point is that the interface needs to be designed for the actual context of use, with all the ensuing constraints.

The top-level screen, which appears either if a user presses CANCEL or after a short time-out, provides some common destinations, such as King's Cross (a major rail terminus in central London).

## 2.5  Examples of Use

We now give a list of design and usability problems encountered with the ticket machine. The point is to illustrate how the interaction takes place at the wrong level for the user, leading to many unnecessary difficulties and breakdowns, and also to set the scene for discussing the potential advantages of solutions based on designing *system* interfaces more appropriately.

### 2.5.1  Buying a Ticket: Mismatch of Task Structures

First, we present the complex set of steps a user has to perform to achieve the most important goal: buying a ticket.

One of the authors has a routine task of buying a return train ticket for his daily work commute from Welwyn North station (in the countryside) to New Southgate station (in London suburbia). Because he is a regular traveller, he has a Network Card (a sort of loyalty card), which allows certain discounts on certain journeys.

New Southgate is not a destination mentioned on the top level screen of the ticket machine, so the user will select Other Destinations and select through the alphabet (through several screens) until New Southgate appears. If the user makes no mistakes, this takes 10 button presses.

None of the choices shown at this stage of the interaction mentions a network card discount, and one button is unused — so it would appear that all choices the machine supports must have been catered for. If the user selects the choice More Fares, they get no network card choice in the next screen either.

The first time the machine was used, it became necessary to ask for help from a rail employee, who asserted that there was a network card option. With help from the official, we persevered, and discovered that from the screen with the spare button, you could choose the Cheap Day Return option and get more options, *including* discounts. This is an example of unnecessary complexity for the user: discounts are not an after-thought, but a central part of the task of getting the most economical ticket for the journey.

However on the screen providing network card discounts, there is now no Previous Screen option, so the user cannot change any other part of their choice. The hard key called CANCEL remains, of course, but using it at this stage takes the user back to the initial screen. The key could be better called RESET or START AGAIN, as it resets the entire interaction rather than cancelling the last step (which the soft key Previous Screen does on many screens).

If the user selects Railcard discounts [2] from here, the next screen confirms that they have selected a ticket to New Southgate, but does not confirm what sort of ticket it is (is it a single, season, a return, or what?). There are two network card choices, neither of which match our user's network card. The user selects one, and is now ready to pay. The screen does not confirm what sort of ticket the user is getting, and there is no choice to return to a previous screen to revise (or confirm) any previous choices.

The user can now put in cash or cards and get the ticket. However, most of the screen stays steady as the cash is inserted, and no special feedback is given to reassure the user that cash is being entered successfully. (We have watched people insert notes, and jump around frustrated, since the machine appears to have eaten their cash but does not appear to be doing anything helpful.)

These usability difficulties indicate a lack of understanding of even the simplest user tasks (as perceived by users), or of the importance of context-relevant feedback on the state of the machine. The overall task structure reflects the complexity of the organisational task model, rather than the relative simplicity of the user's.

### 2.5.2 Inadequate Help: Inadequate System Testing

If the help button [ *i* ] is pressed when a user is trying to find network card discounts, the screen displays nonsense:

```
Help not implemented for ContextID 0011.
```

Eighteen months later, we rechecked, and found *another* screen with no help implemented for ContextID 0047! It is difficult to understand why help has not been implemented properly. As well as being a comment about bad user interface design (including lack of testing), this error is a sad comment about the quality of software development, and poor maintenance (this problem has been present, despite user interface upgrades, for over 18 months, and has survived the introduction of multi-lingual internationalisation — a process which one might have supposed would have reviewed all system texts).

The following text used to be shown when the [ *i* ] button was pressed with the machine at its top level (it is now shown a few levels down from the top level, after the user has selected their working language):

---

[2]Note the inconsistent capitalisation.

```
Using This Machine
1.         Select your destination.
2          Select the ticket type required.
3.         Select Railcard discount if applicable.
4.         Pay by card or cash.
```

The interaction designers seem to think that ticket type and railcard discount are different things — a point we return to below. This screen is only accessible at a point where the user has not yet become aware that there is a likely confusion over ticket types and discounts. As is widely recognised, users only read the manual as a last resort, and are therefore unlikely to read this information *before* starting (this information is not available later in the interaction).

The help text shown above used to be at the top level before the machine was upgraded to be multilingual, but is now three button presses down (and the simple typos are still there). Someone who needs this help will need help finding it.

In each of the four languages (English, French, German, Dutch) available at Welwyn North, one option, "Collecting pre-ordered tickets" is always presented in English. Unbelievably, its help screen (in all languages) is Help not implemented for ContextID HM08. At the time of writing, this option is not available at New Southgate at all. The simplest explanation is: either New Southgate has not been upgraded (to a faulty system), or Welwyn North had part of its help system incompletely deleted. Whatever the explanation, there is a software quality problem *and* a version control/distribution problem. (Or perhaps it is deliberate?)

We are concerned that regulations have been quietly inserted (for instance they discuss how to obtain ticket refunds for incorrect tickets issued by the machine) without telling any user. Whether the rail operators would dismiss usability problems by citing the disclaimers hidden in the user interface remains to be seen; a £5 'administrative charge' can be levied in any case — a use of regulations that permits profit from bad design.

### 2.5.3   Sometimes It Does Not Work

On several occasions, a few seconds after the ticket machine shows "insert payment" (right at the end of a 10-or-more key press interaction to buy a ticket) we have found it unable to actually issue a ticket. It just says "Your cash is being returned," when no cash has been put in the machine which can be returned! One reason for this problem is that tickets can be printed on two stocks of paper. Suppose the ticket machine has run out of normal ticket paper. The user interface is designed so that type of ticket is one of the last choices a user makes, so it is only at this stage that the machine knows whether it can print the requested ticket. If this is the case, the interaction sequence could be re-designed so that choice of ticket type is made earlier in the interaction, or the machine could display on the initial screen (just as it does when there is no change) that it has restrictions. Why not simplify the ticket regulations — which should be part of the system design. How ever one looks at it, this is a poor feature of user interaction design.

Similarly the machine sometimes will only accept credit cards (perhaps due to running out of change or the cash box being full) or will only accept coins. The user is only told this at the end of an interaction, having already spent time selecting the ticket to purchase. Worse, at the appropriate stage of the interaction, the screen briefly indicates that all payment methods are available, before removing those options that are not available. The delay in correcting the screen is long enough for a user to read it and start inserting coins or cards, no longer looking at the screen.

Sometimes the machine has limited change. It will allow a user to try and buy a ticket, and if they overpay it will return their change. Since the rail operator already has ticket credit notes, why does it not allow a user (who may well be in a rush to catch a train) at least the option of having a credit note printed?

Sometimes the machine will allow a user to get to the penultimate screen, then it displays a screen saying the fares are not available.

In all cases, the user interface is unimaginative, and not based on a clear view of the user's task and the real time pressure users work under. The user is led down garden paths, perhaps as long as 20 button presses, and is then frustrated.

### 2.5.4   Multiple Ticket Problems: The User as Enemy

Suppose the user is part of a family group and wants to buy a ticket for themself and the party travelling with them. It takes about 13 key presses to buy one ticket. Unfortunately the ticket machine then reverts to the top level screen, so it is not possible to say, as it were, "same again". Parents travelling with children cannot easily buy cheaper tickets for them. Each and every individual in a party to the same destination must repeat the whole process again. This will take a considerable time — and will provide more opportunities for errors, which in turn will increase the time required to complete their tasks.

We have been told by other passengers that buying multiple tickets using credit cards is further hampered because the machine blocks cards after repeat purchases.

The machine would have been easier to use with an Another one button ("repeat last purchase," "again"... the label needs some evaluation to be sufficiently unambiguous), properly integrated with the (existing, but not fully working) Previous Screen button, so that further tickets could be bought easily, just allowing the user to select whether the new ticket is for an adult or a child.

We understand that features like this, which make it easier for the user, also make fraud easier for thieves. Suppose a stolen credit card is being used: the Another one button would permit rapid multiple ticket purchases. From this point of view, it is important to slow down purchases! Losses from just one organised gang amounted to about £25,000 per week, so limiting fraud is a serious design concern.

Changing the ticket machine's user interaction for multiple purchases also impacts on wider issues. The ticket machine must be approved by the Rail Settlement Plan authorities (e.g. regulating how monies are divided between the numerous train operators, for instance as happens with tickets that cover surface and underground travel on different companies). New styles of dispensing multiple tickets is not just a local user interface issue; it could mean seeking new approval; this is a slow and expensive process that has to be offset against the benefits to users (and the increased revenue it may or may not generate).

As in other domains, such as computer security (Adams & Sasse, 1999), the user appears to be viewed as 'the enemy': the task is made difficult for the many to protect the organisation against the fraudulent behaviour of a few. This entrenched attitude is further exacerbated by the complexity of the change process. There has been no strategic usability thinking.

### 2.5.5   Costly Errors and Costly Tickets: Misfits with User Goals

Unlike interfacing to a human operator, mistakes cannot be rectified once a ticket is purchased.

Although the ticket machine 'knows' how ticket prices vary with the time of day, it never tells users that if they wait a few minutes, or if they travel on the next-but-one train, they can buy cheaper tickets — routine advice that human ticket offices give. (Travel before 10am is more expensive because workers have no choice but to travel at those times; tickets are cheaper later in the day when the rail company wants to attract discretionary travel.) We have found that the machine's clock is sometimes wrong (it has been up to 8 minutes slow), and it will therefore sell over-priced tickets. It is tedious for passengers that, although the last train before 10am has left and therefore it is impossible to travel before 10, the ticket machine will happily sell over-priced tickets until it thinks it is after 10.

Some cheaper tickets cannot be bought at all. The ticket machine only sells tickets from the local station. For example, if the user starts travelling before 10am, buying a ticket to an intermediate station and a continuation cheaper ticket from there (for after 10am) to the destination is something human ticket offices provide (saving about £5 on a return trip to London), but cannot be achieved from the machine.

Sometimes a traveller will want to travel as far as they can without exceeding the cash they have available (e.g. to get as close to home as possible when they don't have enough cash). The ticket machine forces a user to choose their destination first. If the destination costs more than the user has, they then have to try other sorts of tickets or other, closer, destinations. This is extremely hard to do with a ticket machine as opposed to a human ticket office (especially as destination stations are organised roughly alphabetically rather than in order along the route).

It might be better if a user could put in as much cash as they can afford for the desired destination, and then ask the machine for cheaper options (e.g. single tickets rather than returns, or for destinations one or two stations short).

The ticket machine knows the time, and gives the user cheaper ticket options when they are apparently permitted. Unfortunately if a train is running late, a user may have bought a ticket at the cheaper rate which is not permitted on the train actually used. The passenger is then subject to a supplement or penalty fare, as well as embarrassment.

In all these cases, we see a particular organisational orientation towards the user's task: the task is framed only as 'buy a ticket from this station using the next train to a specified destination station,' without any recognition that users often frame their tasks in other terms, such as 'travel from here to there within a reasonable time at low cost,' or 'travel as far as possible in that direction for the available cash.' Although simple observational studies in a ticket office or passenger interviews would establish the range of common user tasks, this might be difficult to integrate easily with the current organisational view, so the user is forced to adapt to the organisational perspective — to work at the wrong level.

## 2.5.6 Post-completion Errors

Post-completion errors occur when a user finishes their task before the interaction is complete (Byrne & Bovair, 1997). The classic example occurs in some designs of cash machines (ATMs), where a user, wanting to get cash, inserts their card, types their PIN, collects their cash, and walks away. They have finished but the machine is left holding the card. A simple redesign, widely known, does not give the user their cash until they have retrieved their card: this ensures completing the task completes the interaction.

The ticket machine suffers the same problem. On one occasion we had to wait for a woman to get her ticket, and she walked off with it. We asked her to come back and collect her change, which had dropped into the ticket slot the moment after she had turned her back on the machine. This is a standard post-completion error.

We interviewed the woman who had bought the ticket. She blamed herself for leaving her change behind. However, her task was to buy a ticket; the ticket machine gave her a ticket, so she picked up the ticket and turned away. If the train she had wanted was already at the station, she would immediately have been running towards it and not even had a chance to hear the change clunk over the noise of the train arriving. She had completed the task she had set out to do (buy a ticket) but the user interface had not finished its part of the task.

The ticket machine hardware can drop change before, or at the same time as, the ticket itself; the actual order used is a software design decision. We understand that one reason for this decision is that return tickets are printed on two separate tickets (the 'out' and 'return' parts), and the designers did not want users to leave part of the ticket behind. Leaving change till last, they must have reasoned, sometimes — when there is change! — reduces the risk of users leaving without one half of their ticket. Again, trying to improve the user experience at the machine level has implications for the wider design of the entire process: why are return tickets printed on two pieces of paper?

The problem is that the ticket machine is providing an interface to the old system. When human ticket clerks issued tickets, the advantages to the rail operator of multiple tickets might have been worthwhile compared to the trivial problems of issuing them. When the user interface of the ticket machine merely copies this procedure, it exposes the user to intricacies that are now inappropriate and indeed cause predictable errors.

## 2.5.7 Limited Awareness: Pre-completion Errors

The converse of a post-completion error might be called a pre-completion error: the interface obstructs the user completing the task.

The ticket machine sometimes displays the soft button $\boxed{\text{Purchase Ticket}}$, but when it does, it is not possible to pay. In fact, the user is supposed to press a button at this point — because the ticket machine is otherwise 'unaware' that they are trying to pay (it has no sensors on its coin and credit card slots, which could have been used to avoid the button press).

We understand that this user interface difficulty is caused by regulations: users must confirm before purchasing. One might have thought that trying to pay was tantamount to confirmation — but changing the user interface now with financial implications could require a costly new regulatory approval process. (If the financial systems were designed with usability as a priority changes would already be underway.) Of course, pressing a button called ⟦Purchase Ticket⟧ is hardly confirmation that the user wants *that* ticket.

The first time we encountered this problem, we assumed the machine was not accepting credit cards (maybe its communications line had failed) so we hunted around and found a £20 note. By the time we had correctly inserted it into the note slot, the machine had timed out. Despite the user being very active with the machine it times out, because it has no sensors to know the user is still busy with it. We have seen users walk away in disgust at this stage. (Incidentally, paying by £20 note gets, say, sixteen £1 coins as change, which takes a substantial time to drop into the ticket slot, and even longer to retrieve as the slot is an awkward 'pouch' without enough room to grab more than a few coins.)

### 2.5.8  Limited Accessibility: Identifying User Groups

Users with poor mobility have to get close to the ticket machine, and wheelchair users will find the high screen and high coin slots awkward. Blind or partially sighted users will not be helped that the buttons *always* make a beep, regardless of whether the machine is working or not. (Thus it is pointless rote-learning a sequence of button presses, since there is no way to know whether they are working.)

### 2.5.9  Bad Organisational Interface: Design for Maintainability

A discussion with a rail employee revealed he had not been trained to use the machine, let alone explain it to anyone else. The ticket machine has an internal user interface when the door is opened. There is an operator's manual, but he hasn't seen it. He has to empty the cash from the ticket machine from time to time; the first time he did this he set off police alarms, since he didn't know how to use the security interface! We understand the machine's manufacturers provide training courses but these have not been widely taken up by rail companies.

## 3  The Problem Restated

A computer system has been introduced into a complex system (i.e. the existing railway ticketing system, including its regulations) without taking the opportunity to reappraise the design of the systemic interfaces to the user. The interface design appears to be motivated by providing an 'easy to use' interface to replace the current human interface, and was thus driven by (organisational) functionality rather than by (user) task analysis.

A user interacting with the system still has to contend with all the historical intricacies of the original complex system, as well as coping with (what is for them) a new interface to the GUI — itself implemented in a confusing way. In fact, the computer ticket machine has increased the complexity of the interface to the transport system. Fixing the conventional user interface problems that have been created is a new problem, and one that is at or already beyond the limits of the designers' resources (they may not have been funded adequately to do a good job, or they may be unable to deal effectively with the complexity of the design task set them). The overall system goals have got lost in trying to solve the wrong problem at the wrong level, though nevertheless at a level that can be represented as a pushbutton graphical user interface. Unfortunately, the conventional user interface problems are quite interesting in their own right (they are also apolitical), and might divert usability professionals from tackling the bigger issues of design. It may be that, despite the new interaction problems, the automation of ticketing has obtained some gains in cost-effectiveness for the rail operators: there would then be little incentive to seek better solutions.

## 3.1 Summary of Concrete Design Problems

The following points briefly summarise higher-level issues from the discussion above.

- The software user interface encourages users to make errors of well-known and easily avoidable categories (e.g. post-completion errors), and fails at the end of interactions (e.g. when it has run out of change, or does not know fares). The user interface over-serialises: the user has to break down their task in the unpredictable order the machine specifies rather than an order appropriate for the user's specific task — the machine is not *permissive* (Thimbleby, 2001) (see also below). The user interface is misleading for partially-sighted users. (For example, the keys beep regardless of whether they do anything.) And so on.

- The user interface is inconsistent and, for example, has missing help texts. The recent introduction of multiple languages has not been checked. The quality of the user interface is very poor, and indicates the software developers are unaware of (or unwilling to apply) well-known international standards (ISO 9000 series, or ISO 13407 on user-centred design processes, etc.) and undergraduate textbook techniques. Evidently, the programmers did not comply with the British Computer Society's (2001) codes of conduct.

- In contrast, the hardware interface is very tightly constrained by concerns of vandalism, robustness and credit card security. We understand some of the hardware components (e.g. credit card verification) cannot be changed — though this is itself another usability problem, which should have been addressed much earlier.

- Rail staff have not been trained.

- The design increases rail revenue by discounting user needs. (Users who fail using it in the time available but who still travel will be fined; users who buy the wrong ticket can get no refund; and so on). Apparently, the user interface designers did not consider the users' tasks or their frequency (e.g. the machine does not support buying multiple tickets to the same destination).

- Trying to improve the user experience leads to larger issues and challenging fundamental assumptions on rail travel and regulation.

The list reflects a variety of shortcomings in the design. A motivator to improve usability could come from HCI standards produced by organisations such as the ISO.

The ticket machine has a label "easy to use". Far better, for all concerned, if this claim was validated by reference to some international standard. ISO WD 20282 is a potential candidate. The European Union is also working towards standardising presentation aspects (terminology and so on) of tourism information services. Such efforts might further improve a user's ability to understand the interface superficially. However, although conventional usability practices and standards will reduce user frustrations, we are advocating a fundamental shift in usability design. A more rigorous engineering-based design process would avoid many of them.

## 4   A Solution

The case study lists problems and attributes them largely to bad interface design. We must now turn from criticism to constructive suggestions, based on designing the interface to be as restrictive (in the system interface sense) as possible.

To summarise: the user's task is to travel; the rail operator's task is to raise revenue from passenger travel. The user can achieve their goals by getting on and off appropriate trains at the appropriate stations; the rail operator requires to know how to bill the user, where they start their journey, where they end it, and some time information (to allow for differential pricing). Conventional solutions, embedded in the historical necessity of 'ticket thinking' has led to layers of complex interactions between large inflexible (institutionalised) subsystems. For instance, as we saw, eminently justifiable (and very rigid) rules about credit card transactions have a direct and deleterious impact on the user experience. Such rules cannot easily be changed, and certainly cannot be changed within the design brief of the ticket machine design. The crucial problem is that the interface exposes the user to this unnecessary detail and complexity. Graphical user interfaces (and Web-style interfaces) are adaptable and flexible: they merely encourage this wrong level of design.

In contrast to GUIs, which have been so successful for personal computer systems, personal (small, ubiquitous, location aware, . . . ) technologies (PTs) seem like solutions looking for problems. In some sense they must be, because they are new and opening up new possibilities that have not been thoroughly explored. On the other hand, a characteristic of personal technologies is the elimination of the conventional user interface. Much interaction with personal technologies is implicit: they infer, through sensors and communications, what the user is doing. The consequence is that using PTs almost automatically restricts the interface: anything that can be inferred by the PT need no longer be part of the explicit user interface. In particular, as fewer things are explicitly mentioned in the interface, the interface necessarily becomes more permissive.

To develop a deeper understanding of the design issues, we now consider the simplest kind of PT appropriate to the ticketing task: one that simply provides user authentication, and can transmit that authentication data over a distance of, say, 3 metres. With that, we can propose a radically different kind of design solution that addresses most of the identified problems. However such a solution introduces, or rather emphasises, new issues: in hiding system complexity, issues of social complexity emerge as new usability challenges that are masked, or less central, when working with existing technologies. (In turn, 'society' can be considered a system, but to do so is beyond the scope of this paper.)

We assume the user and their PT are registered with the transport operator, with arrangements for billing (e.g. charging to the user's account, or to that of a parent under agreed conditions). There might be agreed limitations on the use of the PT to reduce the risk to the owner of the PT being stolen and used without proper authorisation. We can propose a scenario of use ...

If there are PT entry channels at stations, the user's starting station can log their entry into the system. At the destination station, the user passes through an exit channel, collecting a receipt showing the journey details and cost, so that they can check the bill when it arrives. If at any point there is a choice of a cheaper or more expensive option, this should be clearly displayed. For example, before the time when fares reduce from peak to off-peak, there should be a clear indication before the user enters the system to show that entering after (say) 9.56am will cost less than entering now. Similarly, if there are alternative train operators offering different services at different rates, there might be clear indications that the passenger is electing to use a more expensive service that will be surcharged. There would have to be additional PT detectors on such trains to bill for the higher grade service; the same principle would apply to those travelling first class. For regular commuters, there can be discounts (as currently implemented in 'season tickets,' or in other ways, such as 'rail miles' benefits).

Such a solution would address the problems identified earlier, as follows:

- There would be no end-user interface that suffers from problems such as inconsistency of interaction, spelling mistakes, missing help text, etc. A PT solution can hide a range of complexity in the existing system irrelevant to the user task: credit card equipment regulations, multiple ticket stock, adult/child distinctions, returns/singles/season tickets, change or the lack of it, penalty fares, vandalism, multiple operating companies, time restrictions, etc.

- As noted, the current hardware interface is constrained by concerns of vandalism and security. Radio transmitters can be located in less accessible places and be more easily protected against the weather. They would therefore require less servicing, and no routine servicing (such as repairing breakages, replacing ticket paper, emptying cash boxes). This would remove the need to train station staff in their maintenance.

- With radio communication with the ticket machine, any user interaction could always be completed, so there would be no risk of post-completion errors, provided the user did not have to collect anything physical from the ticket machine (e.g. a hardcopy receipt) at entry: the receipt at exit would only be for the user's records. The user task is defined by the user's actions; a family group can be detected by the system through information stored within the system (on familial relationships and ages of children).

- There would no longer be an issue of over-serialisation (non-permissiveness) of the user task, or over the system adapting to users making regular journeys.

- The system would work as well for blind and partially-sighted users as for anyone else. It would also work for less mobile users who would not need to find and get directly close to the machine itself.

- Users would be charged for the journeys they actually make, and not suffer from buying an incorrect ticket by mistake. In fact a lot of complexity has moved from the paced interactive task to an un-paced review of the bill. (There is no reason why billing companies should not compete and therefore provide a better service than the current non-competitive, uninterested in users, system aspires to.)

A PT approach is easier to implement and to design thoroughly. A major problem with conventional user interfaces is that programs are serial, but users may work out what they want to do in almost any order (hence the requirement for permissiveness noted above). Often user interfaces are badly implemented, partly because of the combinatorial interaction possibilities. In contrast, the radio protocol for a PT is very simple (above the error correction layers). The main implementation task is maintaining a database of users and billing appropriately — a task that is already performed effectively by most utility (gas, electricity, etc.) companies, and which should therefore be better understood that the current ticketing task.

From the rail operators' perspective, one of the disadvantages of PTs might be a loss of revenue from people making mistakes or buying more expensive tickets than they need to. However, it is likely that this would be more than offset by reduced costs of providing conventional tickets and reduced fraud (particularly fare evasion).

From the user's point of view, such a system presents some new challenges:

- There may be situations where the PT does not work. For example, one might be wishing to 'treat' someone else to a rail outing (for example, a children's outing): a conventional ticket would have to be bought for people not covered by PTs.

- The user may lack confidence in the system — for example, about billing or about whether they are actually authorised to travel — and, without a paper ticket, may feel vulnerable to over-charging or other error.

- Probably most fundamentally, such a solution raises privacy issues: as users are tracked through the system, their current locations may be traceable. Whether the issues are much greater for this use of PT than they are for established technologies such as mobile telephones remains to be seen.

The current ticket machines are intended to address 80% of user needs, leaving the remaining 20% to be dealt with in the traditional way by a clerk. One difficulty a user has is knowing from the outset whether their current task is an '80%' one or a '20%' one: the user may try to use the machine and eventually give up, or may go straight to the clerk, which defeats the point of providing the machines. If the same approach is taken to PTs, they are not being proposed as the total answer to all travel billing needs, but as a way of dealing with most traveller needs, while leaving some to the ticket office. The ticket office might sell 'single use' PTs or what look like traditional tickets but with embedded disposable chips.

There are two areas in which the system may break down: failures associated with users, or associated with the technical infrastructure. Currently, the rail companies can cope with passengers who have mislaid their season ticket: such passengers can formally request a refund of the fine (but only a limited number of times over the life of the season ticket). Clearly the 'non-functional PT' excuse will have to be treated equally leniently. Using network communications, the official should at least be able to check whether the passenger claiming to have left their PT at home in principle does have a PT. In the second case, where the PT infrastructure fails, simple safeguards (e.g. as are used in automatic bank transactions) can ensure the passenger is not charged, is refunded, or obtains compensation, as the case may be.

# 5 Conclusions

Despite more than thirty years of usability research, public interactive kiosks, exemplified by the ticket machine of our case study, are difficult to use, causing the public frustration and worse. We have analysed one such state-of-the-art system to show how fundamental and far reaching the problems can be.

The 'invisible computer' has become a popular slogan, and personal technologies certainly make computers invisible to users. Books have been written on the invisible computer (Norman, 1998) and on the invisible future (Denning, 2002). From our arguments it should be clear that invisible computers are a side-effect of some good design, not a cause. We want to support the user's tasks and experience, with as little irrelevant interference from the inner details and workings of the system as possible. Our approach is much deeper than just making the computer invisible: it means making unnecessary and irrelevant complexity invisible, thus making parts of the system invisible (which may imply making the computer more invisible). We support the user's task by defining the system interface, not to control the computer (as a GUI does so well) but to support the operations required by the user. In the case of travel, the user's task is obvious, and — as the case study made clear — personal technologies can directly support the user's task and almost completely hide the intricacies of the rest of the system.

*Hiding system complexity can solve or avoid conventional usability problems.* We argued this abstractly; we showed that exposing complexity in our case study led to poor user interface quality. Poor quality is due to the user interface giving the user inappropriate access to what could have been hidden parts of the rail system. We argued that hiding the intricacies of the system makes the user interface trivial to use, and we showed a practical way to do so using personal technologies.

*Personal technologies can improve user interfaces by narrowing system interfaces.* The original ticket machine is a wide and flexible interface to the rail system: System⇔User. Using a personal technology (as we described it) greatly narrows the interface and hides much system complexity: System↔PT↔User. In doing so the PT defines an interface that creates a separation of concerns that allows all interaction to be much simpler than with the original and, specifically for the ticketing system solution, for the user to interact at no time or order critical points.

*Better interfaces highlight social problems.* Having solved conventional user interface problems, social problems still remain. The simplest PT solutions raise privacy problems, which have no obvious 'solution' apart from the public becoming accustomed to the out-weighing benefits of simple and reliable technology. Developers of more complex infrastructures need to be aware of the far-reaching social implications their designs may have.

*On the basis of current implementation standards, simply getting anything to work reliably remains a problem.* The ticketing machines studied here had problems partly because they were too complex for their designer/system interface. Unfortunately many of the schemes proposed in the PT literature are also complex (e.g. requiring complex network protocols). Trying to achieve a reliable user interface may force organisations (in this case, rail operators) to re-design systems holistically, rather than just attach user interfaces.

*Good design will help transform society.* Even within the limited scope of the case study it is clear that many conventional commercial working practices (such as the use of complex fare structures) will become counter-productive as better design — perhaps driven by the simplifying technologies of PTs — become more widely taken up. Travel, in particular, gives people benefits. Users may be willing to trade the obvious increased usability for the more hidden surveillance by PTs: the PT infrastructure is likely to become much wider than transport, to provide other business or even state benefits (e.g. combining the PT with a national ID card). For international travel, now with heightened security concerns, the trade-offs are stark. The central and right concern of HCI, valuing the user, clearly now has a very important role to play in leading to a more peaceful and better world.

In short, user interface design is not about building user interfaces (such as GUIs) to an existing system, or to a computerised version of an existing system. The 'system' is much larger than the computer that may run the user interface. User interface design is about defining interfaces, in the systems sense, that appropriately support the user's tasks and which conceal everything else. Doing so may result in a specialised interface that does one or a few things well, but therefore is much easier to implement reliably and easier to achieve satisfaction for the user. Perhaps one reason why user interfaces are so bad, and have been for so long, is because user interface designers have been concentrating on solving the wrong problems.

## Acknowledgements

Harold Thimbleby is a Royal Society–Wolfson Research Merit Award Holder and acknowledges their generous support. We are grateful for some very helpful meetings with ASCOM Autelca of Gümligen-Berne, Switzerland, who manufacture the hardware but not, in this case, its software. This research was partly supported by EPSRC Grant GR/R71467/01.

## References

Adams, A. & Sasse, M. A. (1999), "Users Are Not the Enemy: Why Users Compromise Security Mechanisms and How to Take Remedial Measures", *Communications of the ACM* **42**(12), 40–6.

British Computer Society (2001), *British Computer Society Codes of Conduct and Practice.* Version 2.0.

Byrne, M. D. & Bovair, S. (1997), "A Working Memory Model of a Common Procedural Error", *Cognitive Science* **21**(1), 31–61.

Cheverst, K., Davies, N., Mitchell, K., Friday, A. & Efstratiou, C. (2000), Developing a Context-aware Electronic Tourist Guide: Some Issues and Experiences, *in* T. Turner, G. Szwillus, M. Czerwinski & F. Paternò (eds.), *Proceedings of the CHI2000 Conference on Human Factors in Computing Systems*, *CHI Letters* **2**(1), ACM Press, pp.17–24.

Christian, A. D. & Avery, B. L. (1998), Digital Smart Kiosk Project, *in* C.-M. Karat, A. Lund, J. Coutaz & J. Karat (eds.), *Proceedings of CHI'98: Human Factors in Computing Systems*, ACM Press, pp.18–23.

Denning, P. J. (ed.) (2002), *The Invisible Future*, McGraw Hill.

Friedhoff, R. M. & Peercy, M. S. (2000), *Visual Computing*, Scientific American Library.

Norman, D. A. (1986), Cognitive Engineering, *in* D. A. Norman & S. W. Draper (eds.), *User Centered System Design: New Perspectives on Human–Computer Interaction*, Lawrence Erlbaum Associates, pp.31–62.

Norman, D. A. (1998), *The Invisible Computer*, MIT Press.

Parnas, D. L. (1972), "On the Criteria to Be Used in Decomposing Systems into Modules", *Communications of the ACM* **15**(12), 1053–8.

Sommerville, I. (2000), *Software Engineering*, sixth edition, Addison–Wesley.

Stanton, N. A. & Baber, C. (1997), Rewritable Routines in Human Interaction with Public Technology, *in* E. Hollnagel (ed.), *Proceedings of ECCS'97: European Conference on Cognitive Science*, EACE, pp.20–5.

Thimbleby, H. W. (2001), "Permissive User Interfaces", *International Journal of Human–Computer Studies* **54**(3), 333–50.

Thomas, P. & Thimbleby, H. (to appear), The New Usability: The Challenge of Designing for Pervasive Computing, *in International Conference on Computer Communication*.

# Usability

# A Comparison of Think-aloud, Questionnaires and Interviews for Testing Usability with Children

## Afke Donker[†] & Panos Markopoulos[‡]

[†] *PI Research, PO Box 366, 1115 ZH Duivendrecht, The Netherlands.*
Tel: *+31 20 774 5673*
Fax: *+31 20 6905327*
Email: *afkedonker@hotmail.com*

[‡] *Eindhoven University of Technology, Den Dolech 2, 5600 MB Eindhoven, The Netherlands.*
Tel: *+31 40 247 5247*
Fax: *+31 40 243 1930*
Email: *p.markopoulos@tue.nl*
URL: *http://www.ipo.tue.nl/homepages/pmarkopo/*

The paper reports a comparative assessment of 3 usability-testing methods (UTM) involving 45 children aged 8–14 as test-users. The 3 methods were concurrent think-aloud, interview and questionnaire. These 3 UTM's require different levels of verbalisation from the children that were performing the evaluation. It was hypothesised that the age of the children, their gender, verbal competence and extroversion level would influence which method works best. The results of this study show that the think-aloud protocol helps identify most usability problems and suggests that girls thinking out loud report more usability problems than boys.

**Keywords:** usability testing, think-aloud, verbal protocol, interview questionnaire, comparing methods, methodologies, children.

# 1  Introduction

The field of human computer interaction has in the last few years shown an increasing interest in generating scientific and methodological knowledge about how best to design interactive systems for children. This paper presents an experimental study that aimed to generate sound methodological knowledge about how best to involve children as subjects in usability testing. In particular the paper reports an experiment that compared the number of problems identified by three usability-testing methods, when the test-users were children.

There is a significant body of literature on the comparative assessment of usability evaluation methods. This sub-field of HCI has been punctuated by the article of Gray & Salzman (1998) who shed a critical light on earlier published work on comparisons of usability evaluation methods. Gray and Salzman urged researchers to scrutinise their methodology and to be very cautious about the validity of their recommendations. The papers they reviewed along with the majority of such work published during the 90s, compare usability inspection methods with usability testing methods (UTMs). A major motivation for making such comparisons has been to establish the validity and efficiency of the inspection methods relative to the testing methods. (With usability inspection methods usability problems are predicted without exposing the system under test to test-users. In UTMs users or their representatives actually experience interaction with the system under test).

The main body of research on the procedures appropriate for usability testing was published in the '80s but this remains a lively research topic. Some related work is discussed in Section 3. The present paper addresses the specific question of how the instrumentation and the procedures available for usability testing affect their efficiency when the test-users are children. The purpose is to derive methodological knowledge: how should the fact that children have different capacities and different interests than adults, influence the set-up of a usability test?

Section 2 discusses related work on usability testing with children. Such work is very sparse and the practical advice offered lacks empirical validation. To our knowledge, no report exists of a systematic comparison of evaluation methods focusing on children users. Nor has there been a systematic effort to specify the method and instrumentation of usability testing for children users.

Section 3 surveys the research literature concerning the comparative efficiency of the three UTMs studied for adult test-subjects. It discusses whether we should expect these results to hold for children users, an issue investigated by the experiment presented in this paper.

Section 4 describes the experiment: the experimental design, the participants, the procedure and the results. Section 5 concludes with a discussion of the findings and pointers for future work. Section 6 presents the current conclusions.

# 2  Testing Interactive Systems with Children Users

Druin (1999) suggests that having children as test-users of technology is an established practice. However, little published work exists regarding the methodological concerns that arise when children are involved. Milligan & Murdock (1996) claim that teenagers identify more usability problems than adult users, but do not offer any empirical evidence to support their claim. Hanna et al. (1997) document practical difficulties and adaptations that need to be made to standard usability testing procedures, when the test participants are children. They touch on a wide diversity of subjects such as:

- The decoration of the room and the observation equipment used, e.g. use small microphones, don't let children face a camera or a one-way mirror.

- The behaviour of the experimenter, e.g. how to encourage the children when they fail at a task.

- The varying capabilities of children of different age-groups (e.g. give short tasks to younger children, children under the age of 2.5 cannot use standard input devices, children above 14 act as adults in a testing session).

- The behaviour of the tester and the constitution of tasks, which are defining elements of any UTM.

- How the presence of adults, parents and kin affects the performance of the children.

- How to overcome the limitations of the verbalisation capabilities of children.

This advice is rational and seems very useful to practitioners, but is not backed up by evidence other than the personal experience of the authors. While it may not be necessary to seek experimental validation of every experience-based guideline some methodological issues beg further investigation. For example, a plausible argument made by Hanna et al. (1997) is that children have a smaller attention span than adults and that they have a comparatively smaller ability to carry out tasks assigned to them at younger ages. Hanna et al. (1997) suggest more intervention by the evaluator or smaller sized tasks. However, it is still not clear what the optimal 'size' of task should be or how the intervention by the evaluator should be carried out to avoid biasing the results of the evaluation. Note that a biasing effect has been found with adult users in an experiment that only modified a sentence that described the maturity of the product to test users (Bentley, 2000). This effect could reasonably be hypothesised to be larger for children test users, especially when the evaluator would prompt them throughout their interaction with the system.

Clearly, to provide sound and generalised evidence of the effect of such factors on usability testing the issues described have to be studied separately. The research presented here focuses on the verbalisation capability of children and their extroversion. The ability of children to verbalise evolves as they grow up and at lower ages could impair their ability to verbalise usability problems. The extroversion of children may significantly affect whether they are likely to voice their thoughts about the usability problems that they experience. Extrovert children may be inclined to name more problems with a technique like talk-aloud than introvert children.

Distinguishing children with respect to their verbalisation capabilities is perhaps more meaningful than distinguishing them by their age. Arguably verbalisation capabilities directly affect the ability of a testing technique to reveal usability problems. Therefore, differences in verbalisation capabilities might confound results concerning the ability of different testing methods to reveal usability problems, established earlier with adult users.

## 3   Comparative Assessments of UTMs

Several comparative assessments of UTMs have been published. Mostly, they gauge the efficiency of evaluation methods with respect to the number of problems uncovered and the number of users involved as test-subjects. The three specific testing methods compared (think aloud, interview and questionnaire) have been compared in the past. However, slight variations in the exact evaluation procedure make the results of published work not directly comparable. Of the studies that have been done we mention the two most closely related to our study.

Ohnemus & Biers (1993) studied the effect of displacing the verbal protocol with respect to the actual interaction session. They found that retrospective think aloud reveals more usability problems than concurrent think aloud, and that delaying the retrospective analysis a further 24 hours does not impact its efficiency.

Henderson et al. (1995) compared four UTMs for adult users. Their conclusion was that a retrospective verbal protocol analysis reveals more usability problems than using logged data, post-test interviews and post-test questionnaires. They did not find any significant difference between the interview technique, the logging, and the questionnaire regarding the number of problems found. The testing techniques we studied are very similar (but not equal) to their verbal protocol, questionnaire and interview. Because of differences in verbal capabilities between adults and children we expected to find different results. We anticipated that children who are verbally more competent than their peers would find more problems using the think aloud method. We expected that children who are not very verbally competent, or who are very introvert, would find more problems using a UTM that does not require them to verbalise as much.

## 4   Report of the Experiment

Hereby, we report the comparison of three usability evaluation methods or, more accurately, three protocols for the behaviour of children during usability testing. The three methods compared are concurrent think-aloud, interview and questionnaire. In the think-aloud method, a single user is asked to think aloud while interacting with the system being evaluated. The information collected provides an account of usability problems experienced and indications as to the source of these problems. The interview procedure studied was a semi-structured interview that was executed after completing each of the evaluation-test tasks. The questionnaire was also filled-in after completing each task. The number of problems reported with these three methods was compared, and a linear regression analysis was performed to establish the effect of age, verbal competence, extroversion, gender and UTM.

### 4.1   Design of the Experiment

A between subjects design was adopted. The usability testing procedures compared were designed to be as similar as possible. The major difference between them was the level of verbalisation they required of the children. On other aspects such as the number of children involved, tester intervention during the performance of test-tasks, etc., the methods were the same. In doing so we hoped to ensure causal construct validity, which would have been endangered had we tested evaluation methods in the exact form in which they have been introduced in the literature. Such methods differ in numerous aspects, so it would have been unclear which ones cause the difference in problems found.

All evaluations were done at the schools of the children, the experimenter was present and interfered to the same extent in the different UTMs and the children were asked to perform the same 21 tasks, individually, on the same software product. This was a semi-educational game where children solve puzzles that about biological facts. The specific product was chosen after reading reviews at a Web site for parents (www.maki.nl), because a reasonable number of problems were expected.

The effectiveness of the UTMs was measured by counting the number of problems the children mentioned. Gray & Salzman (1998) object to this measure. They argue that when one usability evaluation method finds more problems than another, this could be because this method finds more real problems (hits), which would make it a more effective method, or because this method finds more non-problems (false alarms), which would make it less effective. However, Jeffries & Miller (1998) have argued that this criticism only applies to usability inspection methods. They argue that what the users experience or report as usability problems should, by definition, be considered as real problems (hits). We adopted this view, although as is mentioned in the discussion section, we cannot rule out the possibility that children will report non-existent problems.

We determined what the children perceived as problems by asking them the following questions:

- Did you need help solving the task?

- Did the computer make it easy for you to do the task?

- What, if anything, happened that you did not expect or want?

In the 'think aloud' condition, the children were asked to mention anything they might want to answer to these questions as they experienced it. In the think-aloud condition the experimenter put a sheet of paper next to the children with these questions printed on them. When they were quiet she prompted them ("keep talking", "remember the questions") and pointed to the questions.

In the structured interview condition, the experimenter asked the children the questions after each task and in the questionnaire condition, the children were asked to complete a small questionnaire containing these questions after each task. In the questionnaire the answers to the first two questions were given by circling a smiley face of the child's choice indicating agreement or disagreement with a positively phrased sentence. Hanna et al. (1997) recommend this scheme for eliciting subjective ratings from children in questionnaires. We adopted this way of getting their opinion to further reduce the verbalisation requirements.

When counting the problems everything that the children indicated they could not do without help was counted as a problem. The answers to the second of the questions above were disregarded because overall children gave very vague and ambiguous answers to this question ("kind of easy"). What we did include as problems were the things that the children did not want or expect the program to do.

The verbal competence of the children (in Dutch) was measured using four parts of the Wechsler Intelligence Scale for Children Revised (WISC-R) (de Bruyn et al., 1974). The WISC-R is a test that is used to assess the intelligence of children. It is much used because of the vast amount of information that is gathered about it, the variety of sub-tests it contains and its proven usefulness (de Bruyn et al., 1974). The four sub-tests that were used (information, understanding, similarities and vocabulary) test various capabilities, one of which is productive language proficiency, which we were interested in. Usually, the test is administered orally and individually. In this study this procedure was not followed in order to prevent children to learn from their friends that participated in the experiment before them. It was found very likely that children who do not know the answer to a question would ask the teacher or other children for information after the test and could then be overheard by other subjects. As a result we would not have tested verbal competence as much as memory and subject number. To make sure this did not happen we asked the children all to fill out a questionnaire at the same time. We also had to be confident that the children would not become frustrated as they got to the part of the test that was too difficult for them. We did not want children to be (or feel) obliged to fill out questions that they did not know the answer to. This is why we made 5 separate paper and pencil tests, one for each age group. We only included the questions that were not too easy or too difficult. To do this we used an appendix of the WISC-R containing characteristics of individual items. We excluded items that were made correctly by more then 95% of the children of a certain age and items that were made correctly by less than 5%.

The extroversion of the children was measured by letting them complete a part of the valid and standardised 'Amsterdamse Biografische Vragenlijst voor Kinderen' (Amsterdam Biographical Questionnaire for Children) (Wilde & van Dijl, 1967). This test consists of yes/ no items designed to measure how neurotically stable and extrovert children are and what test-attitude they have (self-defensive or self-critical). Twenty items were used that related to extroversion.

## 4.2  Participants

As subjects 45 children of five different grades participated in the experiment. The evaluations took place in three schools in Utrecht, The Netherlands. The children were aged 8 to 14, with a mean age of 10 years and 2 months. Seven children were later excluded from the study. One was ill and with six there were technical difficulties to such an extent that the data became useless. Thus 38 children were included in the statistical analysis, 16 boys and 22 girls.

## 4.3  Procedure

The teacher introduced the experimenter to the class and nine children from each class were selected (by the teacher or randomly). These children were first asked

| | Model | The number of problems found | | |
|---|---|---|---|---|
| | | B | SE B | β |
| 1 | Constant | 7.000[†] | 0.813 | |
| | Think Aloud | 7.500[†] | 1.447 | 0.654 |
| 2 | Constant | 8.484[†] | 0.913 | |
| | Think Aloud | 7.478[†] | 1.326 | 0.652 |
| | Gender | −3.509[†] | 1.248 | −0.325 |

**Table 1:** Summary of stepwise regression analysis for variable predicting the number of problems for children found in the product (N = 38). Note: $R^2 = 0.427$ for Model 1. $\Delta R^2 = 0.106$ for Model 2 ($p < 0.01$). [†] $p < 0.01$.

to complete the 4 sub-tests of the WISC-R (the paper and pencil version) and the extroversion items of the ABV-K. After that they were randomly assigned to one of the three UTMs and they were asked to evaluate the program individually. The other children were asked to return to the classroom until they were sent for. To counteract a possible social desirability bias (Manstead & Semin, 1996) we stressed that we wanted to find as much awkward and illogical things in the program as possible. After a short introduction, the experimenter demonstrated what children were supposed to do and the children had a chance to try it. They got some short feedback and then the real evaluation started. Children were asked to perform 21 tasks in sequence, e.g. click on the computer icon and solve the puzzle, go to the 'wet lake', put the water plant in the correct spot on the list, etc. After the evaluation, which lasted on average 45 minutes, the children were thanked for their participation. Most of them enjoyed the experiment. After all the evaluations were complete the experimenter counted the number of problems the children had mentioned. A range of problems were reported by the children, e.g. not recognising something as a control object, spelling errors that meant the answer was not recognised, not knowing how to exit a particular screen, or not understanding the instructions provided by the software. Because of the homogeneity of the problems no analysis was performed to determine differences between methods on sort of problems found.

## 4.4 Results

A linear regression analysis was performed to establish the effects of several variables on number of problems found. Age, verbal competence, extroversion, gender and UTM were entered in the analysis. Only the gender of subjects and the high verbalisation UTM (think aloud) had a significant effect. The regression model is shown in Table 1.

Post hoc tests (Bonferroni) showed that the number of problems found by the girls using the think aloud method differed significantly from the number of problems found by girls using the questionnaire (mean difference = 8.23, p = 0.004), girls being interviewed (mean difference = 9.43, p = 0.001), boys using the questionnaire (mean difference = 10.19, p = 0.008), and boys being interviewed (mean difference = 11.73, p = 0.000). No other differences were significant. The mean numbers of problems found per gender and per method are shown in Table 2.

| | Girls | Boys |
|---|---|---|
| Think Aloud | 16.86 | 11.20 |
| Interview | 8.63 | 6.67 |
| Questionnaire | 7.43 | 5.13 |

Table 2: Mean number of problems per subject, shown by gender and UTM.

## 5 Discussion

The 'think aloud' protocol uncovered significantly more problems than the other two methods. The number of problems found with the questionnaire and the structured interview did not differ significantly. We had expected the results to be different for children of different abilities (verbal competence and extroversion), but this was not the case. It could have been, however, that the children that found it difficult to think aloud tried very hard to overcome their difficulties to make the experimenter happy, another example of the social desirability bias (Manstead & Semin, 1996). However, the effort children invested does not explain why more problems are found when children use the 'think aloud' protocol. An explanation for this effect could be that talking more leads to reporting more problems. However, it could also be because the children that used the 'think aloud' protocol reported problems as they occurred, while the children that used the questionnaire and the structured interview waited with reporting the problems until the task was finished. We tried to keep the difference as small as possible by letting them report after every task and by keeping the individual tasks small, but still some children clearly forgot problems they encountered in the beginning of a task. This explanation would mean that it is best to have children report the problems they experience as they encounter them. Another solution to this problem could be to let the children perform evaluations using videotape as a memory prompt (Henderson et al., 1995). Seeing themselves perform the different tasks may help them remember the problems they encountered. Think-aloud could also be performed in this way. Ohnemus & Biers (1993) show that this form of retrospective think-aloud is more effective for adult users than our concurrent think aloud.

It might have been more effective to let the children verbalise and to have the experimenter ask them questions at the same time. Questions could be: "What did you think would happen?" or "Why did you do that?" and (very important): "Is this a problem?". This could be investigated in further research. The fact still remains that, specifically with a questionnaire, it is not possible or very time-consuming to have children report every problem as it occurs. It may also lead to non-problems being reported, because when you ask children after an event if they want to report a problem on the questionnaire, they might feel obliged to do so, even if they did not experience the event as a problem.

On average boys found fewer problems than girls. This could be because girls have less experience on computers and find using one more difficult. Whitley (1997) reports that this is in fact the case, but the difference was not very large in his study. Another explanation could be that girls do not like this kind of game. Whitley (1997) found no evidence for the hypothesis that boys like computers better than girls, but it could still be that boys just like this particular game more and that they therefore find less problems. With hindsight it appears that it would have been useful to assess the subjective usability using a questionnaire like SUMI in order to discount this latter possibility.

Ohnemus & Biers (1993) use a subjective scale for usability. Using this in the present experiment would possibly have made it easier to interpret the differences found between boys and girls. Had girls found the program less usable than boys, the results could be attributed to their lack of experience with, for instance, this kind of program. The fact that this effect is only visible in the think aloud method could then be explained by the love girls have for talking. Had girls and boys found the program equally usable, it would be more likely that girls were more honest, or more honest to this experimenter, who was female, about which problems they encountered. When a different experimenter (for instance a man) would have been present during evaluation, boys might have been more eager to mention the problems they experienced or girls may not have talked as much. Jacobsen (1999, p.51) suggests that comparative studies such as the one reported here should employ equal number of experimenters as test-users, to guard for the fact that differences found using 'between subjects' comparative studies should be attributed to the experimenter rather than the technique itself. The effect of experimenter features is something that can be investigated in further research.

As explained, a possible social desirability bias (Manstead & Semin, 1996) that could have led the children to not naming things they considered problems was counteracted by telling them we wanted to find as much problems as possible. Because of a reversed bias, it could be that the children felt compelled to name problems. They might have named things that they did not really consider as problems. In this case we might indeed have had 'false alarms'. But since all children in all conditions were biased in the same way, this does not explain why children in the think aloud condition and girls specifically find more problems than the others do.

There were some difficulties in counting problems. We counted things that did not go as expected and we encouraged children to name those things. Subsequently we classified all the things the children mentioned as problems. However, if all the things the children mentioned had gone the way they expected them to go, the game would probably not have been any fun to them. It might have been better to ask the children whether they were frustrated about what went wrong or whether they thought of it as a challenge. Kersten-Tsikalkina & Bekker (2001) propose a scheme to classify things children say about products. First they distinguish fun experiences from frustration experiences and second they propose several causes for this fun or frustration, for example control, feedback, or challenge. When children do not know which item they have to use, this is a challenge. Some challenge can be fun, but when it becomes too difficult, it can become frustrating. However, with the data we collected it is not possible to determine whether children experience something as fun or frustration.

Also, what we were interested in was the amount of information children gave us concerning their interaction with the program using different UTMS. Girls in the think aloud method name more problems than the other children do. Whether they are frustrated or having fun, a developer of software would gather more information about his product using girls and think aloud than another UTM or boys.

The results of the present study are very similar to those reported in the studies of Henderson et al. (1995) and Ohnemus & Biers (1993) for adult test users. The interview technique described in Section 4.1 was very similar to the one assessed by Henderson et al. (1995). However, the questionnaire they used was a generic user satisfaction questionnaire that has been validated empirically, while in our case a task-specific questionnaire was developed for the purposes of the evaluation study. The verbal protocol of Henderson et al. (1995) was retrospective while the present study used a concurrent verbal protocol. Ohnemus & Biers (1993) have shown that for adult users, a retrospective protocol reveals more problems than a concurrent think aloud. It would seem that the effect we found for verbal protocol might be even more pronounced had this been retrospective.

The three procedures for data collection that we compared described in Section 4.1 could be thought to interfere with the interaction itself. Henderson et al. (1995) guarded against this by ensuring that the interaction experienced was identical for all conditions studied. Of course, whether this is so, depends on the granularity of the tasks studied which was not clear in their article: at least for subjects who they interviewed after every sub-task performed, the interview itself may have influenced the primary interaction tasks.

## 6   Conclusions

The experiment reported shows that thinking aloud helps children report more usability problems than other methods. This is consistent with earlier findings for adult users. This result seems not to be affected by different verbalisation capabilities or differences in extroversion of the children.

Hanna et al. (1997) caution that young children have more trouble than adults do in verbalising their thoughts. We expected methods like think-aloud that require high verbalisation skills to be less effective for younger children or children with fewer verbalisation skills. Our expectations were not confirmed. Children seem to be highly motivated to please the experimenter, perhaps more so than adults. It seems that even when children find it difficult to do something they will try their best to do it anyway. This might explain the efficiency of using teenagers as testers, as suggested by Milligan & Murdock (1996). Topics for further research could be a comparison of the number of problems found by adults and children, or the effect of motivating children.

Girls were found to report more problems than boys during usability testing in our experiment. One might suggest that it might be better to recruit girls to test a product as they find more problems than boys do. However, providing such an advice would be premature, as Gray & Salzman (1998) have suggested. Similar studies need to be performed with more products, tested at different stages of development, with evaluations performed by children belonging to more age groups and by several experimenters of both genders who might individually exhibit different behaviours.

The study presented does though suggest that we can safely focus on verbal protocol analysis as the main vehicle for usability testing with children. In the immediate future, further evidence confirming that verbalisation capabilities and extroversion do not impact the relative efficiency of UTMs will be sought by extending the scope of the study to other ages and products.

## Acknowledgements

We acknowledge gratefully the children the students and teachers of the following schools at Utrecht: 'Dr Bosschool', 'de Spits', and 'de Panda'. We also wish to thank Nick Broers for his advice on statistics issues and Tilde Bekker for fruitful discussions on usability testing with children.

## References

Bentley, T. (2000), Biasing Web Users Evaluation: A Study, *in* C. Paris, N. Ozkan, S. Howard & S. Lu (eds.), *Proceedings of Australian Conference on Computer–Human Interaction OzCHI 2000*, IEEE Computer Society Press, pp.130–4.

de Bruyn, E. E. J., Vander Steene, G. & van Haasen, P. P. (1974), *Wechsler Intelligence Scale for Children — Revised*, Swets & Zeitlinger. Nederlandse uitgave, Verantwoording.

Druin, A. (1999), The Role of Children in the Design of New Technology, Technical Report 99-23, HCIL, University of Maryland. http://www.cs.umd.edu/hcil.

Gray, W. D. & Salzman, M. C. (1998), "Damaged Merchandise? A Review of Experiments that Compare Usabilty Evaluation Methods", *Human–Computer Interaction* **13**(3), 203–61.

Hanna, L., Risden, K. & Alexander, K. J. (1997), "Guidelines for Usability Testing with Children", *Interactions* **4**(5), 9–14.

Henderson, R. D., Smith, M. C., Podd, J. & Varela-Alvarez, H. (1995), "A Comparison of the Four Prominent User-based Methods for Evaluating the Usability of Computer Software", *Ergonomics* **38**(10), 2030–44.

Jacobsen, N. E. (1999), Usability Evaluation Methods: The reliability and Usage of Cognitive Walkthrough and Usability Test, PhD thesis, Department of Psychology, University of Copenhagen.

Jeffries, R. & Miller, J. R. (1998), "Ivory Towers in the Trenches: Different Perspectives on Usability Evaluations", *Human–Computer Interaction* **13**(3), 270–4.

Kersten-Tsikalkina, M. & Bekker, M. (2001), Evaluating Usability and Fun of Children's products, *in* M. G. Helander, H. M. Khalid & M. P. Tham (eds.), *Proceedings of International Conference on Affective Human Factors Design*, Asean Academic Press.

Manstead, A. S. R. & Semin, G. R. (1996), Methodology in Social Psychology, *in* M. Hewstone, W. Stroebe & G. M. Stephenson (eds.), *Introduction to Social Psychology*, Basil Blackwell, pp.74–106.

Milligan, C. & Murdock, M. (1996), "Testing with Kids & Teens at IOMEGA", *Interactions* **3**(5), 51–7.

Ohnemus, K. R. & Biers, D. (1993), Retrospective Versus Concurrent Thinking-out-loud in Usability Testing, *in Designing for Diversity: Proceedings of the Human Factors and Ergonomics Society 37th Annual Meeting*, Human Factors and Ergonomics Society, pp.1127–31.

Whitley, B. E. (1997), "Gender Differences in Computer-related Attitudes and Behavior: A Meta-Analysis", *Computers in Human Behavior* **13**(1), 1–22.

Wilde, G. J. S. & van Dijl, H. (1967), *Amsterdamse Biografische Vragenlijst voor Kinderen, voorlopige handleiding bij de ABV-K*, F van Rossum.

# An Eye Movement Analysis of Web Page Usability

## Laura Cowen[†‡*], Linden J Ball[†] & Judy Delin[‡]

[†] *Department of Psychology, Lancaster University, Lancaster LA1 4YF, UK.*

Tel: *+44 1524 593470*

Fax: *+44 1524 593744*

Email: *l.ball@lancaster.ac.uk*

[‡] *Enterprise IDU, Old Chantry Court, 79 High Street, Newport Pagnell, Buckinghamshire MK16 8AB, UK.*

An experiment is reported that investigated the application of eye movement analysis in the evaluation of Web page usability. Participants completed two tasks on each of four Web site homepages. Eye movements and performance data (Response Scores and Task Completion Times) were recorded. Analyses of performance data provided reliable evidence for a variety of Page and Task effects, including a Page by Task interaction. Four eye movement measures (Average Fixation Duration, Number of Fixations, Spatial Density of Fixations, and Total Fixation Duration) were also analysed statistically, and were found to be sensitive to similar patterns of difference between Pages and Tasks that were evident in the performance data, including the Page by Task interaction. However, this interaction failed to emerge as a significant effect (although the main effects of Page and Task did). We discuss possible reasons for the non-significance of the interaction, and propose that for eye movement analysis to be maximally useful in interface-evaluation studies, the method needs to be refined to accommodate the temporal and dynamic aspects of interface use, such as the stage of task processing that is being engaged in.

**Keywords:** eye movement analysis, Web page usability, performance measures.

*Now working at IBM, Winchester. Email: cowenla@uk.ibm.com. Tel: +44 1962 815 622.

# 1   Introduction

There is currently a multitude of methods available for evaluating user interfaces. These range from subjective user feedback (including interviews and focus groups), through semi-formal methods such as Cognitive Walkthroughs (Wharton et al., 1994; Preece et al., 1994) and Heuristic Evaluation (Nielsen, 1994), to more objective user testing. Although the latter is probably the most reliable evaluation technique, it remains rather limited in the amount of information it can provide about user performance. Typically the only data that are acquired via user testing are success rates and completion times for users attempting interface tasks. These data can inform designers about when the user had difficulties with the interface, but not necessarily what specific areas of the interface caused such problems.

The interest in finding objective usability evaluation methods that can pinpoint problematic features of interfaces has prompted researchers to look at how eye movements might be used to understand the way that users view, search and process information, see for example Baccino & Colombi (2001) and Crowe & Narayanan (2000). The present paper reports an exploratory experiment investigating the use of eye movement measures to evaluate Web page designs. We argue that eye movement data can augment the data obtained through user testing by providing more specific information about the user's cognitive processes — see Rayner (1995) and Henderson & Hollingworth (1999) for discussions of the relationship between eye movements and cognition.

## 1.1   What Makes Eye Movement Analysis Useful?

When an individual looks at an object, an image of the object is projected on to the retina, which is composed of light-sensitive cells that convert light into signals that can be transmitted to the brain via the optic nerve. The distribution of these retinal cells is uneven, with denser clustering at the centre of the retina than at the periphery. Such clustering causes the acuity of vision to vary, with the most detailed vision available when the object of interest falls on the centre of the retina. Outside this foveal region visual acuity rapidly decreases. Eye movements are made to reorient the eye so that the object of interest falls upon the fovea and the highest level of detail can be extracted (Gregory, 1990; Rayner & Pollatsek, 1994).

The focusing of the eye on an object is termed fixation. A fixation typically lasts about 300ms. After a fixation the eye goes through a movement — termed a 'saccade' — to fixate on another part of the same object or on a new object. Such saccades are high-speed, ballistic movements that last approximately 150–200ms from planning to execution (Palmer, 1999). During a saccade no information is obtained as perception is inhibited to prevent the viewer seeing a blur. Only when the eye is relatively still, during a fixation, can information be extracted from the display. The assumption of researchers who aim to examine eye movements in order to assess the usability of displays and computer interfaces is that the duration of fixations, and the pattern of eye movements in general, are dependent on how easy or difficult the display is to process. If the display, or any part of it, is difficult to process then fixations will be longer and there will be more fixations closer together (with relatively short saccades) than if the display is easy to process.

## 1.2 Using Eye Movements to Evaluate Interface Usability

A major problem with using eye movements to evaluate interface usability issues is that eye movement recordings provide a large quantity of raw data that can be time-consuming to analyse and potentially difficult to interpret meaningfully. In their pioneering research on eye movement analyses of interface usability, Goldberg & Kotval (1998; 1999a; 1999b; Kotval & Goldberg, 1998) proposed a set of 11 eye movement measures that they argue can make analysis more efficient and can also be automated to some extent — for full details, see Goldberg & Kotval (1998). Included in these are *spatial measures*, such as the number of backtracking saccades made on the display, which may indicate whether or not an interface matches up with a user's expectations (i.e. if a user's expectations are fulfilled then they shouldn't have to move their eyes back and forth several times across the display). Other examples of spatial measures include the total scanpath length (i.e. the total distance the eyes move around the interface), the spatial density (or distribution) of fixations on the interface, and the average saccade length or amplitude (which would indicate the extent of search, and, therefore, the quality of the layout). Goldberg & Kotval also propose a range of *temporal measures* that indicate the depth of processing required by an interface user. These include measures of the mean duration of fixations while using the interface, and the ratio of fixation to saccade duration (which indicates the relative proportions of time spent processing and searching the interface).

Goldberg & Kotval evaluated the validity of these measures by examining users' eye movement behaviour in relation to several versions of a Windows-style interface that they created in order to simulate a graphical software package. Down one side of the interface was a selection of buttons, or 'tools', that the participant was required to find whilst their eye movements were recorded. The physical grouping or appearance of the tools was varied in different experimental conditions so as to make the tasks harder or easier to perform. The difficulty of the tool groupings was assessed independently by 80 interface design experts and typical users. The investigators examined whether the proposed eye movement measures would be sensitive to the differences between the interfaces, and also whether the findings produced by the eye movement measures positively correlated with the independent usability ratings of the interfaces.

It was found that the various measures were differentially sensitive to manipulations of the experimental interface layout. So, for instance, when the physical grouping of the tools on the interface was varied, only measures of global searching behaviour tended to be sensitive because little processing was required of the tools themselves once found. However, when the tools varied in the way in which they were labelled, nearly all of the measures were seen to be sensitive to such differences, since different levels of search and processing behaviour were required by the alternative interfaces.

When the data from the measures were correlated with the independent usability ratings, all the measures indicating global search behaviour were found to have linear relationships with the usability ratings, with the best predictors of usability being the number of backtracks and scanpath duration. Indeed, an unusable interface could be predicted to necessitate scanpaths nearly 80% longer than those required by an excellent interface. Local search and processing measures (at the level of individual fixations and saccades) showed interesting patterns of sensitivity to usability. The relationships between the fixation duration and fixation/saccade ratio measures and usability were both U-shaped. Therefore, at the lowest and highest levels of usability, the measures were largest, decreasing at intermediate levels of usability. However all three local search and processing measures showed less than 50% change between the best and poorest interfaces, and, therefore, were not as sensitive to variation in usability as some of the global search measures.

## 1.3   The Use of 'Real' Stimuli in Usability Evaluation

Although Goldberg & Kotval's work motivated aspects of our present study, the experimental design that we adopted differed from theirs in several important ways. Perhaps most crucial of all were the differences between the two experiments in terms of the nature of the interfaces that were used as stimuli and the tasks that participants were required to undertake.

Looking at the stimulus issue first of all, Goldberg & Kotval created their interface designs especially for use in their experiments. Although this method of stimulus design allows for a large amount of control over variables, it is difficult to generalise findings to real interfaces designed by real designers for real end-users. Most interfaces used by people in everyday contexts have been designed for them to complete tasks that satisfy their personal goals. In the present experiment, home pages from commercial Web sites were used as stimuli, as Web design is currently of great interest to usability specialists.

Concentrating on Web interfaces in the present study made it relatively easy to obtain a selection of complementary, but real Web pages. An alternative approach to obtaining a selection of 'naturalistic' Web page designs might have been to take a single page design and to adapt it multiple times to produce different stimuli. However, as argued by Buckingham (1931) on the subject of manipulating typographical layouts for experimental purposes:

> "[the] ... separating of size of type, length of line, and interlinear spacing ... is wholly artificial." (Buckingham, 1931, p.103)

By this he meant that it is not possible, in testing visual designs, to manipulate only one variable whilst keeping all others constant.

For example, in the present situation, moving a Web page's navigation menu to different locations on the page gives one variable that can be manipulated easily: menu location. However, it is likely that other, less obvious variables, are also created when the navigation menu is moved, for example, the amount of empty space increases where the menu used to be, and the empty space is reduced in the menu's new location. Also, it may be necessary to move other items on the page in order to accommodate the new position of the navigation menu, which would create yet another variable.

The Web pages selected for the present study were homepages from four Web sites produced by an international mobile phone service provider. In each country that the company operates, there is a separate Web site. Only English-language Web sites were used: from Belgium, India, Switzerland and the UK. The Web sites were appropriate for experimental testing because they each had an individual design (page layout, content, information architecture), whilst holding constant the overall 'look' of the company's brand (e.g. the standard colour scheme, the presence of the corporate logo on each homepage, and similar subject matter and purpose). Therefore, these Web sites naturally possessed both variables that were held constant and variables that varied from stimulus to stimulus.

A second critical difference between our study and that of Goldberg & Kotval concerned the interface tasks that participants were asked to attempt. Goldberg & Kotval's participants were required simply to find, as quickly as possible, a tool on the interface. This, however, appears to be a rather simplistic and de-contextualised interface activity. Also, since the tasks were presented in the middle of the interface for the participants to read, the experiment would have taken away most of the realism of the exercise. In the present study the interface tasks were read to the participants and consisted of requests to find pieces of information of a kind that would be required by a real user of the Web site.

Another major difference between the two studies was in the way in which the eye movement measures were evaluated. Goldberg & Kotval had 50 typical users and 30 interface designers rate the interfaces for their usability and then correlated such ratings with eye movement scores. However, it is debatable whether such usability ratings are themselves valid. The 30 interface designers may well have had experience of (and possibly training in) predicting the usability of an interface, but the 50 typical users were unlikely to have had such experience or training.

In the present experiment the relative usability of the four stimulus pages was evaluated by analysing the participants' task performance independently from their eye movement behaviour. This meant that the results of the eye movement measures could then be compared with the findings from the performance measures in order to assess whether they detected the same pattern of differences between pages.

It is finally noteworthy that fewer eye movement measures were used in our study than in Goldberg & Kotval's study. Three of their measures were employed: Average Fixation Duration (a processing measure), Number of Fixations (a local search and processing measure), and Spatial Density (a global search measure). A fourth measure that they did not use — Total Fixation Duration — was employed as a global measure of the total amount of processing performed on each page, rather than just the mean amount of processing on each part of a page.

## 2 Overview of the Experimental Design and Predictions

Each of the four Web pages that we used in the experiment was presented twice to each participant. Appropriate counter-balancing was used to counteract potential order effects. On viewing a Web page, the participant was asked to find information about either using a mobile phone abroad (Task 1) or buying a new mobile phone handset (Task 2). All participants completed both tasks on all the pages.

Three hypotheses were derived for the study in relation to participants' performance data, that is, their task processing time and success rates. First, it was predicted that the four pages would differ in their support of the participants' tasks (i.e. there would be a main effect of the *Page* factor). Second, it was predicted that

Task 1 ('abroad') would be seen to be more difficult than Task 2 ('handset'), since the concept of how to go about using a mobile phone abroad would be less familiar to participants than the concept of shopping (i.e. there would be a main effect of the *Task* factor). Third, the relative difficulty of the two tasks would depend on the pages they were being performed on (i.e. an interaction would be evident between the Page and Task factors). Finally, our expectation was that some — and possibly all — of the eye movement measures should detect the differences described in the previous three hypotheses.

## 3   Method

### 3.1   Participants

Seventeen participants took part in this experiment. Their ages were classified within five-years intervals. The modal interval was 25–29, with seven of the participants within this age range. The other participants were spread across the intervals tailing off at the ends: 15–19 and 45–49. All participants either did not wear glasses or did not need them to read the displays used in the study. Approximately half the participants had taken part in eye tracking experiments previously. The participants came from a variety of professions and included students, graphic designers, writers, teachers and lecturers.

   All participants were regular Web users and all but one owned a mobile phone. English was the native language for all but two participants, and these were currently completing doctoral degrees at UK universities, having previously also studied in the UK and, therefore, they spoke and read English to a high standard. Participants took part in the study voluntarily and were typically interested in the eye tracker and wanted to watch the video of their own performance after completing the experiment.

### 3.2   Apparatus and Stimuli

Three PCs running MS Windows 98 were used to run the experiment and record data.

#### 3.2.1   Stimulus Presentation

Stimuli were presented on a Pentium II 400MHz desktop PC with 128MB RAM and 16MB display memory. The monitor had a 15″ flat LCD screen (for clarity of external video recording) with a screen area of 1024×768 pixels. The monitor was placed on a stand to raise it up so that the centre of the display was level with the participant's eyes. The keyboard was not required for the experiment and was hidden. Participants made their responses by clicking on hyperlinks with a mouse.

#### 3.2.2   Data Collection

Eye movements were recorded using SensoriMotoric Instruments (SMI)'s Head-mounted Eyetracking Device II (HED-II) with Scene Camera. The eye tracker uses two small cameras (the Eye Camera and the Scene Camera) mounted on a bicycle helmet for comfort, weighing only 450g in total. No contact is made with the participant's eye. A harmless and unnoticeable infrared light shines into the participant's eye so that the front surface of the eyeball is illuminated. This produces two effects: the bright pupil and the corneal reflection (SensoriMotoric Instruments, 1999). Because the eyeball is not a perfect sphere, the corneal reflection moves less than the pupil as the eye rotates. The image-processing software, 'iView', on the Pentium II PC (to which the eye tracker is connected), analyses the transmitted image. It computes the centres of the pupil and corneal reflection, from which it can compute the Point of Regard (SensoriMotoric Instruments, 1999) or absolute line of gaze (Jacob, 1995). The resolution of the HED-II eye tracker is better than one degree and it has a sampling rate of 50Hz. Every 20ms the eye tracker transmits the $x$ and $y$ coordinates of the participant's visual line of gaze to the iView PC for processing.

The eye movement data collected in the present study, including the $x$ and $y$ coordinates of gaze and also the processed fixations, were saved for subsequent analysis, and exported to spreadsheets. Recording of the eye movement data files had to be started and stopped manually by the experimenter. In addition, the video recording from the Scene Camera of the display the participant was viewing was also saved. A still snapshot was taken from the video so that the eye movement scanpaths could be overlaid for calculating data for the eye movement-derived Spatial Density measure. Before the experimental trials began, each participant was calibrated to the screen of the monitor on which the stimuli were to be presented. A white sheet of paper was taped over the screen, to prevent distraction by items displayed on the computer desktop. A laser pointer was used to mark nine points on the paper for the participant to fixate in turn. Participants were seated on a stable chair and a chin-rest was provided so that they could hold their head steady during the testing.

### 3.2.3 Stimuli

The four Web site homepages described in Section 1.3 were used as stimuli. Two tasks were asked of each participant on each page. Task 1 stated that: "You want to know more about using your mobile phone outside <*country name*>", whilst Task 2 stated that "You want to buy a new mobile phone *handset* from this Web site". The tasks were worded in the second person to try to encourage the participant to think of the task as their own goal. The name of the country (in which the Web site was used) was used in Task 1 rather than saying 'abroad', which could have primed participants to look for a particular term on the page. In Task 2, the word 'handset' was emphasised so that participants understood that they were looking for phones rather than whole packages and payment plans.

So as to avoid participants becoming too familiar with the pages, the order of task presentation was counterbalanced. All participants viewed the pages (labelled A to D) in the same order: A, D, B, C, D, A, C, B. Participants were allocated alternately to group 'Order 1' or group 'Order 2'. The Order 1 group received Task 1 on the first page (A), Task 2 on the second page (D), Task 1 on the third page (B), and so on. The Order 2 group received Task 2 on Page A, Task 1 on Page D, and so on. Each participant received each task once on each page but never received the same task on two consecutive pages and never received the same page without two other pages in between.

Pages were loaded prior to participants entering the room. The windows were maximised to fill the full screen and then retracted to the Windows Task Bar so that they could not be seen by the participant prior to starting the experiment. The pages were presented individually in Internet Explorer 5.5 windows so that all the animations and links worked correctly. The presentation of pages was controlled by the participant. The participant opened the correct page when asked to do so by the experimenter. The tasks were read aloud to the participant who was asked to avoid head movements (including speaking) once calibrated.

## 3.3 Procedure

It was explained to participants that four homepages from mobile phone international Web sites would be presented twice each and that for each page there would be a task to complete. They were told to complete the task by clicking on the link where the information could be found. If they had difficulty with the task they were to guess at which was the correct link. The procedure for opening and closing pages using the computer mouse was explained until the participant indicated understanding of this. The participant was shown the eye tracker and the experimenter explained what the cameras did. It was emphasised that only the eye and the stimulus display would be recorded, not the participants themselves.

After gaining consent to continue the study, the tracker helmet was placed on the participant's head and fastened, and the participant's eyes were calibrated to the display screen. Once calibrated, the participant was asked not to move, particularly during the presentation of a page. In between pages, if necessary, they could move slightly to get more comfortable. All participants were offered the opportunity to sit back for a moment half-way through the experiment.

The experimenter started the recording of the dot-overlaid scene video on the laptop and this recorded continuously until the end of the testing session. The participant was asked to open the first page. As soon as the page appeared on-screen, the experimenter started recording the eye movement data using the iView software on the iView PC (this had to be done manually by pressing a key: once to start recording and once to stop), while simultaneously starting to read aloud the relevant task. The participant could look at the page and use the mouse at any time during the presentation of the page stimulus (including while the experimenter was reading the task) and the trial was completed when they clicked on a hyperlink, whether or not it was the correct target. When the participant clicked a hyperlink, the experimenter stopped iView recording the eye movement data. At the end of the testing session, after the participant had answered each task on each of the four pages, the dot-overlaid scene video recording was stopped. The MPEG produced by the dot-overlaid scene video recording was saved, as was the eye movement data file and the associated fixations file.

## 4   Results and Discussion

Two classes of data were obtained: performance data and eye movement data. The performance data taken were Response Scores (whether or not a correct link was clicked), and Task Completion Times (how long it took the participant to complete the task — and self-terminate the trial — by clicking a link). The eye movement data involved four different measures that are described in detail in Section 4.2. With the exception of Response Scores, all data were examined statistically using analysis of variance (ANOVA). The factors in these ANOVAs were Page (within participants, with four levels: A, B, C, and D), and Task (within participants, with two levels: Task 1

| | Page A | Page B | Page C | Page D | Mean |
|---|---|---|---|---|---|
| Task 1 | 35 | 100 | 65 | 38 | 60 |
| Task 2 | 100 | 100 | 65 | 13 | 70 |
| Mean | 68 | 100 | 65 | 26 | |

**Table 1:** Percentage frequency of 'correct' responding broken down by Page and by Task.

('abroad') vs. Task 2 ('handset')). Where necessary, Simple Main Effects analyses and Tukey HSD tests were also conducted. The alpha level for all tests was set to 0.05. The data for each measure, apart from Response Scores, were tested for skew prior to analysis. As some conditions produced skew values greater than 1, the data were log-transformed. For some measures this reduced the levels of skew, but when the transformed data were subjected to ANOVA the effects revealed were similar to those obtained when analysing the untransformed data. All results that we present in this paper are, therefore, based on the untransformed data.

## 4.1 Performance Measures

### 4.1.1 Response Scores

Participants' performance was scored for each task on each page. If the link that was clicked (terminating the trial) would have provided the information required by the task then a score of 2 was given. If the link would not have provided this information then a score of 1 was given. Table 1 presents the percentage frequency of correct responding for each task on each page. This table reveals that participants performed poorly on page D and extremely well on Page B, whilst Pages A and C were intermediate. Overall, there appears to be no major effect of Task on responding, although there is some indication that Task 1 ('abroad') was slightly harder than Task 2 ('handset'). There is also a suggestion that the Page and Task factors may interact as there is a marked separation between performance levels for Tasks 1 and 2 on Page A that is not evident for other pages.

As the Response Scores represent a dichotomous dependent variable it was inappropriate to subject these data to ANOVA. Instead, the Page and Task factors were treated as predictor variables, and logistic regression was used to examine whether they were predictive of Response Score. All predictors (including the Page×Task interaction) were entered into the regression model in a single block. The variability explained by the model was good (41% – Cox & Snell $R^2$; 56% – Nagelkerke $R^2$) and the overall percentage of responses correctly predicted by the model was 80%. This represented a marked improvement on the 65% value based on the initial maximum likelihood estimation. The overall model was significant at p = 0.001 according to the Chi-square statistic ($\chi^2$ = 67.57, df = 7). The regression analysis indicated that only the effect of Page was significant (Wald statistic = 9.70, p = 0.021, df = 3), demonstrating the high predictive validity of this variable as a determinant of correct responding. In sum, the logistic regression analysis confirmed the effect of Page on Response Scores that is evident in the descriptive data presented in Table 1, albeit

|        | Page A | Page B | Page C | Page D |
|--------|--------|--------|--------|--------|
| Task 1 | 3      | 3      | 2      | 2      |
| Task 2 | 2      | 3      | 1      | 1      |

**Table 2:** Number of correct target links available on each page.

|        | Page A | Page B | Page C | Page D | Mean   |
|--------|--------|--------|--------|--------|--------|
| Task 1 | 28.112 | 13.881 | 12.623 | 15.825 | 17.610 |
| Task 2 | 14.975 | 12.269 | 11.415 | 21.277 | 14.984 |
| Mean   | 21.544 | 13.075 | 12.019 | 18.551 |        |

**Table 3:** Mean task completion time (s).

with the caveat that that the apparent Page×Task interaction was not reliable on this performance measure.

Inspection of the percentage frequency correct scores in Table 1 shows that only on Page B did all of participants correctly answer both tasks. However, as Table 2 shows, the four pages varied in the number of correct target links available. As can be seen, Page B was also the page with the most correct targets available, three for each task, suggesting that the probability of clicking the correct link depended on how many correct links were available. However, although Page A also contained three correct possible targets for Task 1 ('abroad'), the frequency of correct responding here was the lowest for that Task across the four pages. Notwithstanding the fact that this difference was not reliable in the logistic regression analysis, it does hint at the possibility that the design of a page may well 'hide' the correct responses from the user, leading to lower levels of performance. Future work could systematically manipulate the number of correct target links associated with tasks in order to examine effects on performance.

### 4.1.2   Task Completion Times

The duration of time between the page appearing on-screen and the participant clicking on a link in response to the task (i.e. task completion) was recorded. Each participant could provide a maximum of eight task times (one for each task on each page). Eleven data points were removed prior to analysis due to confounds such as the participant mishearing the task and asking for it to be repeated, or pages loading slowly or incorrectly. The mean task completion times on each page are presented in Table 3.

A 2×4 ANOVA revealed significant main effects of Page [$F(3,24) = 11.28$, $p < 0.001$], and Task [$F(1,8) = 11.29$, $p = 0.010$], as well as a Page×Task interaction [$F(3,24) = 5.57$, $p = 0.005$]. Simple main effects analyses were conducted to understand the cause of the observed interaction. It was found that on Page A — but not on the other pages — performance at Task 1 was significantly slower than at Task 2 [$F(1,14) = 21.23$, $p < 0.001$]. This suggests that on Page A, finding out about buying a new handset was better supported than finding out about taking a phone abroad. An effect of Page was found for Task 1 ('abroad') [$F(3,33) = 23.11$, $p < 0.001$] and further analyses using the Tukey test showed that performance was reliably slower on Page A than on all the other three pages. An effect of Page was also found for Task 2 ('handset') [$F(3,33) = 5.06$, $p = 0.005$] and was also further analysed using the Tukey test to show that performance was reliably slower on Page D than on Page B and Page C. Finding out about using a phone abroad was more difficult on Page A than on any other but finding out about new handsets proved most difficult on Page D.

These various Task Completion Time results were similar to the pattern of results relating to the Response Scores measure (Table 1), although this latter performance measure does not appear to have been sensitive enough to detect reliable effects for all factors. On the whole, though, it is evident that pages that produced more correct responses also produced the faster response times. Responses on Page A were more often correct on Task 2 ('handset') than on Task 1 ('abroad'). Furthermore, these responses were given more quickly on Task 2 than on Task 1, suggesting that participants had more trouble completing Task 1 than Task 2, even though there was one more correct link available for the former task than for the latter (Table 2) on Page A. The observations that performance for Task 2 was significantly slower on Page D than the other pages, and that performance of Task 1 was significantly slower on Page A than the other pages, also corroborate similar findings revealed by the Response Scores measure. Taken together, these similarities in the findings of the two measures provide a solid benchmark of the relative levels of usability of the four pages. The findings of the eye movement measures can, therefore, be compared confidently with the findings relating to these performance measures.

## 4.2 Eye Movement Measures

The measures taken of the recorded eye movement scanpaths were: *Total Fixation Duration* (the sum of all the fixation duration times whilst completing a task); *Number of Fixations* (the total number of individual fixations on a page whilst completing a task); *Average Fixation Duration* (the average duration of individual fixations on a page whilst completing a task); and *Spatial Density of Fixations* (the spatial distribution of fixations on the page whilst completing a task). Eye movements were collected at a sampling rate of 50Hz (the $x$ and $y$ coordinates of the eye's line of gaze were collected every 20ms). These gazepoint samples were processed by the iView software to form fixations and saccades. The minimum duration of a fixation was 100ms and the gazepoint could not deviate more than 40pt horizontally or vertically during a fixation[1]. Each participant could provide a maximum of eight scores for each measure, one for each of two tasks on each of four pages. Due to one participant being poorly calibrated, only 16 of the 17 participants could provide eye movement data for analysis. In addition, 15 data points (16 on the Spatial Density measure) were removed from each measure prior to analysis due to technological problems, head movement or poor calibration.

---

[1] "Gaze position in iView has no physical unit (e.g. millimetres, pixels) but is related to the calibration area settings." (SensoriMotoric Instruments, 1999). The calibration area in the present experiment was 721pt×279pt.

|        | Page A | Page B | Page C | Page D | Mean   |
|--------|--------|--------|--------|--------|--------|
| Task 1 | 23.502 | 14.880 | 14.937 | 14.904 | 17.056 |
| Task 2 | 14.674 | 12.053 | 9.829  | 17.440 | 13.499 |
| Mean   | 19.088 | 13.467 | 12.383 | 16.172 |        |

**Table 4:** Mean total fixation duration (s).

|        | Page A | Page B | Page C | Page D | Mean   |
|--------|--------|--------|--------|--------|--------|
| Task 1 | 553.50 | 488.00 | 404.83 | 434.83 | 470.29 |
| Task 2 | 487.50 | 471.33 | 394.00 | 482.50 | 458.83 |
| Mean   | 520.50 | 479.67 | 399.42 | 458.67 |        |

**Table 5:** Mean fixation durations on each page (ms).

### 4.2.1   Total Fixation Duration

The duration of all the individual fixations made on a page during the performance of a task were totalled. The mean total fixation duration can be found in Table 4. A $2 \times 4$ ANOVA was conducted and revealed main effects of Page [$F(3,12) = 5.62, p = 0.012$], and Task [$F(1,4) = 7.93, p = 0.048$]. The main effect of Task revealed that participants spent more time fixating (processing) when completing Task 1 ('abroad') than when completing Task 2 ('handset'). This suggests that Task 1 was probably more difficult to represent mentally than Task 2. A significant main effect of Task was also found in the Task Completion Times measure reported above — though in the latter it was also shown that the effect of Task interacted with the effect of Page. Within this interaction, where there was found to be a significant simple main effect of Task (though on Page A only), it was (as here) Task 1 that was found more difficult than Task 2.

The simple main effect of Page was further analysed using the Tukey test. This revealed that total fixation duration (i.e. total processing time) on Page A was significantly longer than on both Page B and Page C. The Total Fixation Duration measure is linked with the Task Completion Time measure but is not the same because the latter includes the duration of saccades as well as fixations. The Total Fixation Duration measure produced similar but not identical results to the Task Completion Time measure. It only detected differences in processing times rather than differences in overall performance (processing and searching) times.

### 4.2.2   Number of Fixations

The number of individual fixations made on a page whilst performing a task was totalled. As the $2 \times 4$ ANOVA that was conducted on these data revealed no significant effects, the mean values for this measure have not been tabulated here.

### 4.2.3   Average Fixation Duration

For each task on each page, the total fixation duration was divided by the number of individual fixations to reveal the average duration (in milliseconds) of fixations on a page whilst completing a task. The mean fixation duration can be found in Table 5. A 2×4 ANOVA revealed a single significant main effect of Page [$F(3,12) = 5.45$, $p = 0.013$]. Further analysis using the Tukey test showed that this effect was due to the individual fixation durations on Page C being significantly shorter than on Page A. This implies that Page A had a lower level of usability than Page C. Inspection of the means for each of the other measures for the main effect of Page showed Page A to consistently be the one with the lowest usability (the highest mean), except on the Response Scores measure where Page A had the second highest overall response score. However, the interaction revealed by the Task Completion Time performance measure showed that the usability of Page A depended significantly on which task was being performed on it. So although the Average Fixation Duration measure was sensitive to the general overall pattern of page means, it was not sensitive enough to detect the more complex Page×Task interaction in determining a page's level of usability.

### 4.2.4 Spatial Density of Fixations

The scanpaths of the recorded eye movements were overlaid (using the iView software) on snapshots of the display taken from the Scene Camera video. A screenshot was taken and loaded into a graphics package so that a grid, with squares measuring 30×30 pixels, could be overlaid on the screenshot of the page. The number of squares containing one or more fixations was manually counted. This number was divided by the total number of squares covering the page and then multiplied by 100 to produce a percentage. A 2×4 ANOVA revealed no significant differences in spatial coverage of fixations regardless of Task or Page, and so mean values for this measure have not been tabulated here.

## 4.3 Relative Usability of the Four Homepages

The performance measures (Response Scores and Task Completion Times) were collected to identify differences in usability (how well a page design supported the user's task) between the four pages. The more sensitive Task Completion Time measure revealed a significant interaction between Page and Task, indicating that the usability of a page depended on the task performed on it. Further investigation into the nature of this interaction showed that Page A supported the task of finding out about new handsets significantly better than the task of finding out about taking a phone abroad. This basic difference of task difficulty on Page A was reflected in an omnibus main effect of Task for the Task Completion Time measure, where the task requiring information about taking a phone abroad was significantly more difficult than the task requiring information about new handsets.

Although many of the differences in usability between individual pages were not significant, the two measures showed similar patterns of results (Figures 1 & 2; Tables 1 & 3). On the whole, Page A and Page D showed the worst usability (despite the good performances on Task 2 on Page A) while Page B and Page C showed intermediate to good usability. Most pronounced on the graphs is the difference in the performances for the two tasks on Page A. As a high score shows good usability on the Response Scores measure but bad usability on the Task Completion Times measure, the two graphs show very similar patterns of results. Therefore, it is

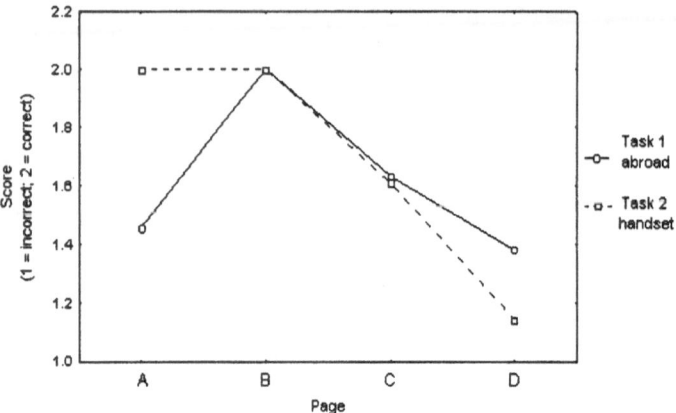

**Figure 1:** Mean Response Scores (where 2 = correct response, and 1 = incorrect response).

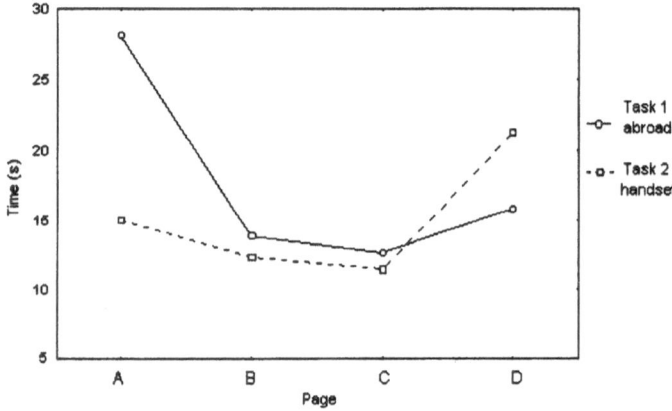

**Figure 2:** Mean Task Completion Times: Page×Task interaction [F(3,24) = 5.57; p = 0.005].

probably safe to compare the relative sensitivity of the eye movement measures with that of the performance measures.

### 4.4 The Sensitivity of Eye Movement Measures to Usability

The eye movement measures (Total Fixation Duration, Number of Fixations, Average Fixation Duration, Spatial Density) were collected in order to observe whether they were sensitive to the relative usability differences revealed by the two performance measures. Unlike the Task Completion Time performance measure, none of the eye movement measures was sensitive to the Page×Task interaction. The two time-based fixation measures did, however, detect significant main effects

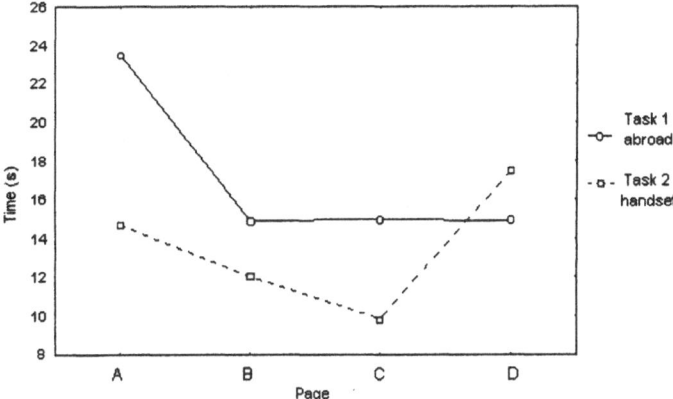

**Figure 3:** Mean Total Fixation Duration: Page×Task interaction [F(3,12) = 1.00; p = 0.426].

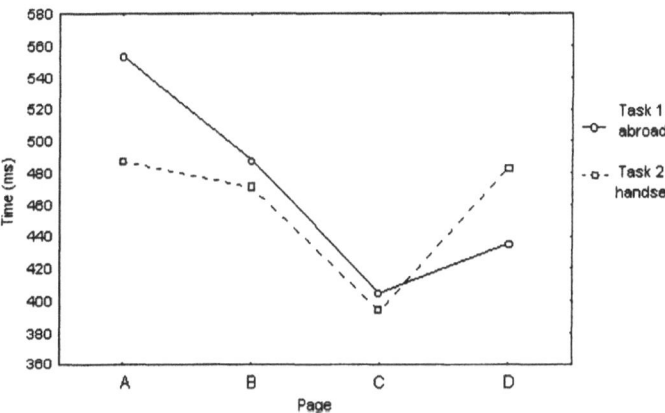

**Figure 4:** Mean Average Fixation Durations: Page×Task interaction [F(3,12) = 1.41; p = 0.287].

of Page in line with both performance measures. Total Fixation Duration showed that Page A required significantly more processing overall than both Page B and Page C; the Average Fixation Duration measure showed that Page A required significantly more local processing than Page C. A main effect of Task from the Total Fixation Duration measure did show a difference in the same direction as that found by the Task Completion Time measure: the 'handset' task was found easier than the 'abroad' task. These results from the two time-based eye movement measures, along with the similar patterns of page usability differences (Figures 1–4) suggest that the four measures (two performance and two time-based fixation measures) were detecting similar variations in usability across the four pages.

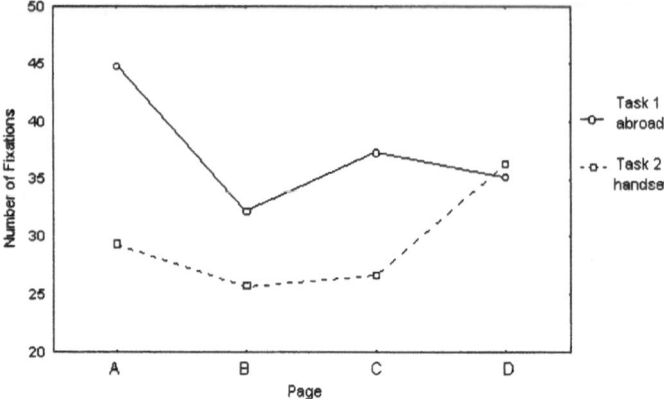

**Figure 5:** Mean Number of Fixations: Page×Task interaction [F(3,12) = 0.41; p = 0.746].

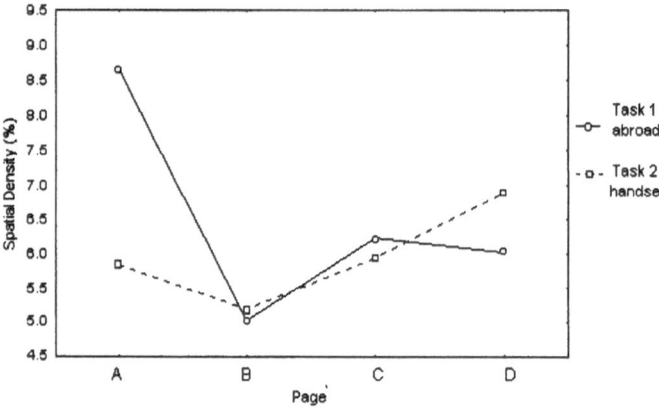

**Figure 6:** Mean Spatial Densities: Page×Task interaction [F(3,9) = 0.75; p = 0.548].

The other two measures, though not showing significant differences for either main effects of Page or Task, or for Page×Task interactions, do produce graphs (Figures 5 & 6) that are similar in shape to those produced by the results from the other measures. The eye movement measures do appear to have been able to detect the same usability differences between the pages as the performance measures. Reasons why the eye movement measures were not as reliably sensitive as the performance measures are considered in the General Discussion.

# 5 General Discussion

A number of a priori hypotheses were tested in this exploratory study. The first prediction was that the four pages would differ in their support of the given tasks. Significant main effects of Page were found in the data of both performance measures and also the two time-based eye movement measures. The second prediction was that Task 1 would be seen to be more difficult than Task 2. Significant main effects of Task were found in the data of one performance measure (Task Completion Time) and one eye movement measure (Total Fixation Duration). Our third prediction was that the relative difficulty of the two tasks would depend on the pages they were being performed on. A significant interaction between Page and Task was found in the data for the Task Completion Time performance measure. None of the eye movement measures found this interaction to be significant, but inspection of the graphs of means for each measure reveal patterns concomitant with the emergence of a Page×Task interaction effect.

Overall, our findings lend support to the view that the eye movement measures we took were sensitive to similar patterns of influence that were evidenced in the performance measures that we derived. However, some of the key differences found to be significant in the performance data did not emerge as significant effects in the eye movement data. It is possible, however, that the eye movement measures were sensitive to more than one factor influencing a page's usability, and maybe two or more factors were cancelling out each other — so reducing the sensitivity of a measure. In this respect it is noteworthy that the eye movement measures of local search and processing in Goldberg & Kotval's (1999b) experiment were found to show quadratic relationships with the usability ratings. Goldberg & Kotval concluded that that the longer fixations and shorter saccades at both higher and lower levels of usability were not necessarily due to the same factor. It is likely that there is more than one type of search behaviour and more than one type of processing behaviour exhibited by users at an interface. Interpreting long fixations as being due to extended processing, and large spatial densities as being due to inefficient searching, is rather vague.

If different search strategies and processing types could be identified, and the eye movement patterns associated with them, then it might be possible to break down measures such as average fixation duration into separate measures according to search strategy or stage of processing. For example, the average fixation duration of all instances of stage 'a' processing could be calculated. All instances of stage 'b' eye movement patterns would be calculated separately, as would instances of stage 'c'. The interface could then be more precisely evaluated for which stages of processing it fails to support, rather than just saying it fails to support any type of processing. Assuming that several processing stages do exist and that the eye movement measure is capturing them all, then if one stage is supported by the interface but not the others, any effect is likely to be cancelled out. The eye movement measure used, therefore, would appear to be insensitive to all processing when, in fact, it might be trying to detect three different types of processing.

Although many differences were not significant in the data from the eye movement measures, qualitative differences can be seen in the graphs of the means (Figures 1–6). This implies that there is the potential that eye movement measures can be used to help further understand the usability problems indicated by performance measures. That is, eye movement measures appear to be sensitive to similar influences as the more conventional performance/usability measures.

An important issue that arises from both this study and those of Goldberg & Kotval is that the usability of the interfaces tested was only relative to the other interfaces. There is no absolute benchmark of what eye movement patterns a good or a bad interface produces. Also, individual differences in participants' performance make it difficult to say that a certain pattern of eye movements should occur for an interface to be of a particular standard. For example, doing Task 1 on Page A, one participant had a mean fixation duration of just 297ms, whilst another's was 738ms; one took only 17s to complete that task on that page, another took 42s.

Several issues have arisen from this exploratory study that would benefit from further research. First, it is necessary to establish a means of identifying benchmarks for eye movement patterns on a single interface design, rather than just for comparing a selection of interfaces. Second, it is important to investigate the types of processing and search strategies that are employed by users on interfaces and the eye movement patterns associated with them. It can then be considered how eye movement measures can be adapted to detect them more accurately. Third, it is probable that the number of possible correct targets on the interface affects the usability of the page. The Response Scores in the present experiment suggest that they may have some influence, but that the visibility of those possible targets is also important. Finally, it is possible that using a greater variety of tasks would reveal a greater sensitivity of the eye movements to various factors that affect the usability of an interface.

## References

Baccino, T. & Colombi, T. (2001), L'Analyse des Mouvements des Yeux sur le Web, *in* A. Vom Hofe (ed.), *Les Interactions Homme–Système: Perspectives et Recherches Psycho-ergonomiques*, Editions Hermès Science, pp.127–48.

Buckingham, B. R. (1931), New Data on the Typography of Textbooks, *in Yearbook of National Society for the Study of Education*, Vol. 30, Part II The Textook in American Education, National Society for the Study of Education, pp.93–125.

Crowe, E. C. & Narayanan, N. H. (2000), Comparing Interfaces Based on What Users Watch and Do, *in Proceedings of the Eye Tracking Research & Applications Symposium 2000*, ACM Press, pp.29–36.

Goldberg, J. H. & Kotval, X. P. (1998), Eye Movement-based Evaluation of the Computer Interface, *in* S. K. Kumar (ed.), *Advances in Occupational Ergonomics and Safety*, IOS Press, pp.529–32.

Goldberg, J. `H. & Kotval, X. P. (1999a), "Computer Interface Evaluation Using Eye Movements: Methods and Constructs", *International Journal of Industrial Ergonomics* **24**(6), 631–45.

Goldberg, J. H. & Kotval, X. P. (1999b), Eye Movement Derived Measures of Interface Usability, http://www.ie.psu.edu/people/faculty/goldberg.htm.

Gregory, R. L. (1990), *Eye and Brain: The Psychology of Seeing*, fourth edition, Weidenfield and Nicholson.

Henderson, J. M. & Hollingworth, A. (1999), "High-level Scene Perception", *Annual Review of Psychology* **50**, 243–71.

Jacob, R. J. K. (1995), Eye-Tracking in Advanced Interface Design, *in* W. Barfield & T. A. Furness (eds.), *Virtual Environments and Advanced Interface Design*, Oxford University Press, pp.258–88.

Kotval, X. P. & Goldberg, J. H. (1998), Eye Movements and Interface Component Groupings: An Evaluation Method, *in Proceedings of the Human Factors and Ergonomics Society 42nd Annual Meeting*, Human Factors and Ergonomics Society, pp.17–23.

Nielsen, J. (1994), Heuristic Evaluation, *in* J. Nielsen & R. L. Mack (eds.), *Usability Inspection Methods*, John Wiley & Sons, pp.25–62.

Palmer, S. E. (1999), *Vision Science: Photons to Phenomenology*, MIT Press.

Preece, J., Rogers, Y., Sharpe, H., Benyon, D., Holland, S. & Carey, T. (1994), *Human–Computer Interaction*, Addison–Wesley.

Rayner, K. (1995), Eye Movements and Cognitive Processes in Reading, Visual Search and Scene Perception, *in* J. M. Findlay, R. Walker & R. W. Kentridge (eds.), *Eye Movement Research: Mechanisms, Processes and Applications*, Elsevier Science, pp.3–22.

Rayner, K. & Pollatsek, A. (1994), *The Psychology of Reading*, Lawrence Erlbaum Associates.

SensoriMotoric Instruments (1999), *iView Version 3.01, Manual & Software Reference Document*.

Wharton, C., Rieman, J., Lewis, C. & Polson, P. (1994), The Cognitive Walkthrough Method: A Practitioners Guide, *in* J. Nielsen & R. L. Mack (eds.), *Usability Inspection Methods*, John Wiley & Sons, pp.105–40.

# Auditory Emotional Feedback Facilitates Human–Computer Interaction

## Anne Aula[†] & Veikko Surakka[†‡]

[†] *Tampere Unit for Computer–Human Interaction, Department of Computer and Information Sciences, Pinninkatu 53B, FIN-33014 University of Tampere, Finland.*

Tel: *+358 3 215 8871*

Fax: *+358 3 215 8557*

Email: *aula@cs.uta.fi*

[‡] *Department of Clinical Neurophysiology, Tampere University Hospital, PO Box 2000, FIN-33521 Tampere, Finland.*

Email: *veikko.surakka@uta.fi*

**The present study investigated psychophysiological responses to emotional feedback in a computerised problem-solving experiment. 40 subjects solved 27 series of mathematical tasks. After each series, a speech synthesiser gave emotionally negative, neutral, or positive feedback. Response times and error-rates to calculations following the different feedback categories were analysed. Pupil size was measured during and five seconds after each feedback category. Ratings of the feedback categories were also measured. The ratings showed that the different feedback categories were effective in eliciting congruent emotions in the subjects. The task times were significantly shorter after positive than negative feedback. Error rates were not affected by the feedback. The pupil size was significantly smaller after the feedback than during it. After positive feedback, there was a significantly faster decrease in the pupil diameter than after the other feedback categories. Thus, positive emotional feedback had beneficial effects on human behaviour and physiology in human–computer interaction.**

**Keywords:** emotion, feedback, cognition, pupil size, affective computing, synthesised speech.

# 1   Introduction

Affective computing is a new field of research that aims at integrating emotions in human–computer interaction (HCI). The reason for the growing interest in taking emotions into account in HCI is due to the fact that human emotions are beginning to be widely recognised as an integral part of human rational behaviour. It is known from both animal and human studies that emotions have a strong neural basis (Davidson & Irwin, 1999; Panksepp, 1998). In addition to the responses of the central nervous system, emotional responses can be observed and measured as changes in the neuromuscular system, for example, as changes in the activity of certain facial muscles and visually recognisable facial expressions (Ekman & Friesen, 1976; Surakka & Hietanen, 1998). Also vocal expressions are varied according to different emotional responses (Scherer et al., 1991). Emotion related changes in the activity of the autonomic nervous system have been found to include changes in, for example, heart rate, skin conductance, blood pressure (Ekman et al., 1983; Levenson et al., 1990), and pupil size (Goldwater, 1972; Hess, 1965; Hess & Polt, 1960; Janisse, 1974). Earlier studies on the association of pupil size and emotions have been somewhat contradictory (Hess, 1965; Hess & Polt, 1960; Janisse, 1974). Recent studies using carefully controlled auditory emotional stimuli have, however, consistently found significantly larger pupil dilation in response to both negative and positive emotional stimuli as compared to the dilation in response to emotionally neutral stimuli (Partala et al., 2000; Partala & Surakka, submitted). These findings are important because they suggest that the pupil size measurement could be utilised in the context of HCI, for example, as a computer input signal (Jacob, 1996).

There is also evidence of the significant effects of emotions on human behaviour. It has been shown that intact emotional processing is a necessity for rational decision-making (Damasio, 1994). Already relatively early auditory change detection processing in auditory cortex is significantly attenuated by positively valenced visual stimulation (Surakka et al., 1998). Zajonc (1980) showed convincing evidence that emotional processing can have primacy over cognition. For example, perceiving others' facial emotional expressions can significantly affect the interpretation of non-emotional information. Murphy & Zajonc (1993) showed that sub-optimally presented (4ms) happy and angry facial expressions modulated the ratings of subsequently presented neutral stimuli (i.e. Chinese ideographs) in a positive and negative direction, respectively. It has also been found that neutral faces are rated significantly more pleasant after seeing sequences of happy than sad facial expressions (Murphy & Zajonc, 1993; Surakka et al., 1999; Zajonc, 1980). The effects the emotions have on the cognitive processing differ generally according to the valence of the experienced emotion. The most common findings suggest that negative emotions or moods, for example, make people avoid the task that produces negative emotions, reduce working-memory capacity, distract the concentration from the task at hand, and impair the processing efficiency in a cognitive task (Bechara et al., 1997; Isen, 1993; MacLeod & Donnellan, 1993; Rickenberg & Reeves, 2000). Positive emotions are found, for example, to increase creativity, to result in a richer organisation of the material in mind, and to result in a more efficient and thorough decision-making (Isen, 1993; Zhou, 1998). However, when the task itself consists of emotional material, the effects of emotional state tend to be emotion-congruent. That is, the negative emotional state facilitates the processing of negative material and positive emotions facilitate the processing of positive material (Olafson & Ferraro, 2001).

In inter-individual behaviour, emotions and emotional expressions significantly affect the quality of the interaction. There is evidence that emotional expressions (facial and vocal) can evoke parallel emotional reactions in the observer in terms of electrical facial muscle activity and emotional experiences. In other words, emotions can be contagious (Hietanen et al., 1998; Surakka & Hietanen, 1998). Furthermore, several studies have shown that the tendency to act emotionally and socially exceeds the context of human-human interaction. The rules of emotional and social interaction used in human-human communication are frequently applied to human–computer interaction (Fogg & Nass, 1997; Picard, 1997; Reeves & Nass, 1996).

It seems to be possible to affect the emotional state of the user during HCI. Rickenberg & Reeves (2000) showed that an animated agent that monitored the user's work elicited anxiety in the user. In Riseberg et al.'s (1998) study, the subjects felt frustrated for being inhibited from attaining a good score in a computer game. It has also been shown that the users are highly susceptible to flattery from the computer. Although the users were told beforehand that the feedback they would receive from the computer would not be an accurate evaluation of their performance, the praise still had beneficial effects (Fogg & Nass, 1997).

Although the effects of informational feedback to different cognitive tasks have been studied widely — for a review, see Kluger & DeNisi (1996) — feedback with emotional content has received little attention. However, based already on the brief review of emotions above, it is conceivable, that emotional feedback could have profound effects in HCI. At present, it is not known whether the effects of emotional feedback would be advantageous or disadvantageous. Thus, more research is needed in order to find out the possibilities of emotional feedback in HCI.

As the current interfaces are frequently overloaded with visual information, the use of textual or other visual feedback could result in losing the feedback in the flood of the other visual information. The feedback could also distract the user from his or her current task. Synthesised speech offers a promising alternative for textual or other visual feedback. Emotions can be recognised from the contents of spoken messages, from the emotion-related prosodic cues, or by combining the two (Scherer et al., 1984). There is also evidence that perceiving other's vocal emotional expressions results in significant emotional reactions in terms of the electrical activity of emotion related facial muscles, pupil dilation, and emotional experiences (Hietanen et al., 1998; Partala et al., 2000). Prosodic cues that have been found to differ according to the emotional state are, for example, changes in the fundamental frequency, pitch range, intensity, articulation, and speech rate (Cahn, 1990; Murray & Arnott, 1993; Scherer et al., 1991). Some broad level prosodic manipulations related to different emotions have been applied to synthesised speech. Those manipulations have succeeded in producing recognisable emotional messages (Cahn, 1990). However, compared to the knowledge on the emotion related components of

| Negative | Neutral | Positive |
|----------|---------|----------|
| Your performance annoys me. | Average performance. | I am happy for your result. |
| I am disappointed with your result. | Your result was usual. | Your performance makes me glad. |
| Your performance was a disappointment. | Your result was average. | Now I am pleased for your result. |

**Table 1:** Feedback phrases used in the experiment (translated form Finnish).

---

facial expressions, the knowledge on the components of emotion related prosodic cues is still far away (Scherer et al., 1991). Fortunately, synthesised speech can be used to mediate emotional messages by varying the emotional content of the messages. Although emotions can be expressed as discrete expressions, such as happiness, sadness, etc.— see for example Ekman & Friesen (1976) — emotions can also be expressed and recognised on the basis of broad dimensional information, such as valence (from unpleasant to pleasant) and arousal (from calm to aroused) (Bradley & Lang, 1994). Although vocal expressions of discrete emotions can be recognised from the combinations of different prosodic cues, messages like "I am disappointed" or "I am happy" are easily recognised as being clear indications of the emotional valence of the feedback.

The present aim was to investigate the effects of emotional feedback during HCI. A fully computerised problem-solving task was created. Subjects were to perform 27 series of mathematical problems. After each series, the computer gave emotionally negative, positive, or neutral feedback to the subject (Table 1). We wanted to explore how computerised feedback with emotional content affects the subjects' emotional ratings, their pupil responses, and their cognitive performance.

## 2   Methods

### 2.1   Subjects

Forty subjects participated in the study (17 males and 23 females, the mean age of 23.2 years, range 15–47 years). The subjects were students from the University of Tampere and they got extra points for their classes from their participation. The subjects were right-handed, had normal or corrected to normal vision, and normal hearing by their own report. They were Finnish-speaking and ignorant about the purpose of the experiment. The data from one subject (female) was discarded from the analysis, because the performance in the experimental task was at chance level. For pupil size analyses, data from 12 subjects had to be discarded because of excessive eye-blinking or technical difficulties (the details are discussed later in the paper).

### 2.2   Equipment

The experimental tasks were run on an Apple Macintosh PowerPC computer running a PsyScope program, a graphic environment for designing psychology experiments

(Cohen et al., 1993). The display was 15.1″ Nokia 500Xa flat panel display with 1024×768 resolution. The PsyScope Button Box timing device was used to send timing information to the eye-tracker and as an input device for the responses of the subject. The speech synthesiser was a Finnish-speaking synthesiser, Mikropuhe version 4.20. Subjects wore Sennheiser, model HMD 410 earphones. The pupil size was recorded from the subject's left eye with the Applied Science Laboratories (ASL) series 4000 eye-tracker with a sampling rate of 50Hz.

## 2.3 Stimuli

The stimuli consisted of 80 different addition and subtraction tasks missing the operator (a plus or a minus) between the terms (e.g. 2 (–3) = –1). The subjects' task was to deduce the missing operator and answer + or –. The terms were either positive or negative and in half of the tasks, the correct operator was a plus and in the other half, a minus. There were only integer numbers between –9 and 9 in the tasks.

Nine different feedback phrases were produced using the male voice of the speech synthesiser (Table 1). The fundamental frequency of the voice was set to 100Hz and the speech rate was set at 95 words per minute. The pause between the words, the amount of changes in the intonation of the speech, and the random variation of the intonation were set to zero. The Mikropuhe speech synthesiser has a feature of automatically producing changes in the intonation according to the sentence structure (lowering the intonation towards the end of the sentence) even when the intonation is set to zero. Otherwise, the prosodic features of the voice were kept similar in all feedback phrases. The synthesised feedback phrases were stored and the same stored samples were then used for all subjects in the experiment. The feedback was delivered via headphones at a comfortable volume level.

## 2.4 Experimental Procedure

The laboratory was introduced and the subject was told a cover story that the purpose of the experiment was to study eye-movements during mathematical tasks. The subjects were also told that the experiment was not about measuring their mathematical skills *per se*. This was done to prevent the subjects from becoming anxious about their performance skills. The subject was seated in an adjustable chair that was in a separate, dimly lit experimental room. The distance between the subject's eyes and the computer screen was 75cm. A headrest was used to support the back of the subject's head so that the head remained still during the experiment.

Before the experiment, the experimenter told the subject that the computer would give feedback of his or her performance and that he or she should try to concentrate on the message of the feedback. After the subject was seated comfortably and the earphones were adjusted, a practice phase began. The speech synthesiser gave all the instructions about the experimental task to the subject. This way, the subject had time to get accustomed to the synthesised speech before the experimental tasks.

In the practice phase, the computer instructed the subject to solve mathematical tasks shown on the centre of the screen as quickly and accurately as possible. The subject was instructed to give his or her answer by pressing either the left button (i.e. the minus operator) or the right button (i.e. the plus operator) of the Button Box.

The tasks were presented in a random order and they stayed on the screen until the subject gave his or her answer. There were eight practice tasks that were similar to the tasks in the experimental phase. In the practice phase, the computer told that during the experiment, a cross would appear in the middle of the screen after each series of eight calculations (the cross was shown in the screen at that point). The subject was instructed to look at this fixation point for as long as it stayed on the screen. At the end of the practice phase, the computer told the subjects that they could ask for clarification from the experimenter if everything was not clear. If they did not have any questions, they proceeded to the experimental phase by pressing a button on the Button Box.

During the experimental phase each series of eight tasks was followed by a five second fixation. After the five-second fixation, the speech synthesiser gave randomly negative, neutral, or positive feedback. The fixation point disappeared five seconds after the end of the feedback. After each nine sets of calculations, there was a pause when the subject could improve her or his posture and take a rest before continuing the experiment. There were altogether 27 sets of eight calculations followed by nine times of each type of feedback.

After the experimental phase, the subjects rated their experiences evoked by the different feedback phrases in two dimensions, valence and arousal (Bradley & Lang, 1994). The ratings were given on two nine-point scales. On the valence-scale, the lower end of the scale represented a negative experience (unpleasantness), the centre of the scale represented a neutral emotion, and the upper end represented a positive experience (pleasantness). On the arousal-scale, the subjects rated the arousal they experienced from calm (the lower end) to aroused (the upper end). The rating scales were presented in the computer screen and the subject used a keyboard to give the ratings. The subjects heard each feedback phrase twice. On the first time, they rated the valence and on the second time the arousal. Finally, the subjects were interviewed about their awareness of the purpose of the study. None of the subjects realised the real aim of the experiment. Before leaving the laboratory, the subjects were fully debriefed.

## 2.5   Data Analysis

First, the eye blinks and artefacts were removed from the pupil size data. In addition to blinks, a sudden brief decrease or increase of 0.75mm within a 20ms interval was judged as an artefact (Partala et al., 2000). Four subjects were discarded from further analysis because of excessive eye blinking (i.e. more than half of the data had to be removed). Data from eight subjects had to be removed from the analysis due to technical difficulties (the eye-tracker lost the subject's pupil during the experiment so that it resulted in the loss of more than half of the data). After removing the blinks, the data was baseline corrected using a 500ms pre-stimulus baseline. Then the data was categorised according to the stimulus categories to two sets of data: data during the emotional feedback and data five seconds following the end of the feedback.

The statistical analyses were performed using repeated measures ANOVAs with Greenhouse–Geisser corrected degrees of freedoms. Post hoc comparisons were made with paired Bonferroni corrected pairwise t-tests.

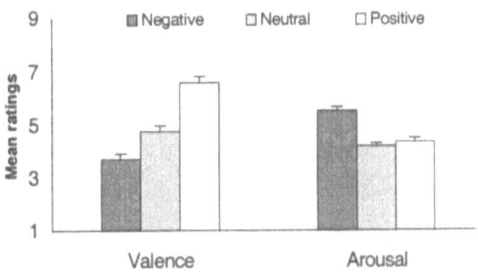

**Figure 1:** Ratings of valence and arousal (and SEM) of the different stimulus categories.

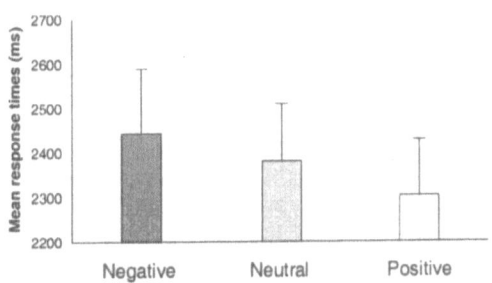

**Figure 2:** Response times (and SEM) following the different feedback categories.

## 3   Results

The ratings of different feedback categories were analysed with a one-way ANOVA that showed a significant effect of feedback category on the ratings of valence, $F(2,76) = 92.2$, $p < 0.001$. Pairwise comparisons showed that the ratings of valence were significantly smaller for negative feedback as compared to neutral, $t = 7.5$, $df = 38$, $p < 0.001$, and positive feedback, $t = 10.6$, $df = 38$, $p < 0.001$. The ratings of valence for neutral feedback were significantly smaller than for positive feedback $t = 8.8$, $df = 38$, $p < 0.001$ (Figure 1).

A one-way ANOVA showed also a significant effect of feedback category on the ratings of arousal, $F(2,76) = 11.8$, $p < 0.001$. Pairwise comparisons showed that negative feedback was experienced as significantly more arousing than neutral feedback, $t = 6.4$, $df = 38$, $p < 0.001$ and positive feedback, $t = 3.3$, $df = 38$, $p < 0.01$. The difference between neutral and positive feedback categories was not statistically significant (Figure 1).

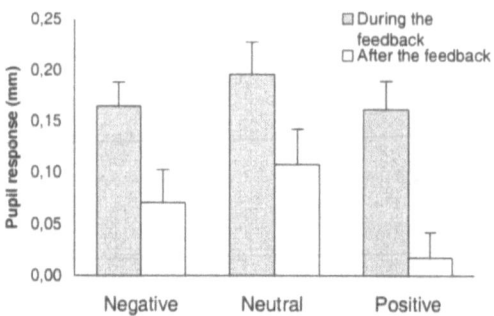

**Figure 3:** Mean pupil dilations from the baseline (and SEM) during and after the different feedback categories.

For response times following the different feedback categories ANOVA showed a significant effect of feedback category, $F(2,76) = 4.57$, $p < 0.05$. Pairwise comparisons showed that the response times were significantly shorter after positive feedback than after negative feedback $t = 3.1$, $df = 38$, $p < 0.05$. The other comparisons were not significant (Figure 2). For the error rates, a one-way ANOVA showed no significant effects of feedback category.

The pupil size data was subjected to a $3 \times 2$ ANOVA with feedback category and time (during and after the feedback) as within-subject factors. The analysis revealed significant main effects of feedback category, $F(2,52) = 3.7$, $p < 0.05$ and time, $F(1,26) = 48.7$, $p < 0.001$. The interaction of the main effects was also significant, $F(2,52) = 5.7$, $p < 0.01$. Pairwise comparisons showed that the pupil size was significantly larger during the feedback than five seconds after it in all feedback categories, $t = 4.7$, $df = 26$, $p < 0.001$ for negative, $t = 4.6$, $df = 26$, $p < 0.001$ for neutral, and $t = 7.4$, $df = 26$, $p < 0.001$ for positive feedback category (Figure 3).

Because of the significant interaction of the main effects two separate one-way ANOVAs were performed to analyse separately the effects of emotional feedback during and following the feedback. During the feedback, the ANOVA showed no significant effect of feedback category. After the feedback, the ANOVA showed a significant effect of feedback category, $F(2,56) = 4.7$, $p < 0.05$. Pairwise comparisons further showed that the pupil size was significantly smaller after positive feedback as compared with the pupil size after neutral feedback, $t = 2.8$, $df = 26$, $p < 0.01$, and negative feedback, $t = 3.2$, $df = 26$, $p < 0.01$. Other differences were not statistically significant (Figure 3).

## 4   Discussion

Our results showed that emotional feedback given by the speech synthesiser evoked significant differences in the users' ratings of different feedback categories.

Although the emotional stimuli were delivered by the content of the synthesised speech alone, the subjects rated the feedback categories as differing in their valences, that is, as negative, neutral and positive. The negative feedback category was rated as significantly more arousing than neutral and positive categories. The results also showed that the response times were significantly shorter after positive than negative feedback. The error rates were not affected by the emotional feedback. Pupil size data did not vary significantly by emotional category during the feedback. However, after the feedback, the different categories produced differences in the pupil responses. Specifically, following emotionally positive feedback, the pupil size was significantly smaller as compared to the pupil size following emotionally negative or neutral feedback.

The results showed only pupil dilations in response to emotional and neutral feedback. The current findings on pupil size variation by emotional stimulation are in line with those previous findings that showed pupil dilations, but not constrictions, to emotionally or psychologically meaningful stimulation (Janisse, 1974). The results are also in line with the very recent findings showing only pupil dilations to neutral, and emotionally positive and negative auditory stimulation (Partala et al., 2000; Partala & Surakka, submitted).

All in all, the feedback had marked effects on the physiological activity in terms of the pupil size variation. Both emotional and neutral feedback evoked autonomous nervous system activity as the pupil size clearly enlarged from the baseline during all feedback categories. The feedback produced an interesting difference between the pupil sizes during the five-second time-window following the end of the positive and negative feedback. The pupil size approached the baseline level significantly faster after the positive feedback as compared to the pupil size after negative feedback. The faster decrease in the pupillary dilation after the positive feedback suggests that recovery from autonomic arousal is easiest after positive than negative or neutral emotional feedback.

Although the ratings of arousal were relatively close to the middle of the scale (neither arousing nor calming) in all feedback categories, the negative feedback category was rated as significantly more arousing than the other feedback categories. It may be that this was the reason for a longer-lasting autonomic nervous system activity. On the other hand, the arousal ratings between the positive and neutral feedback categories did not differ significantly. Still, the pupil sizes following these feedback categories differed significantly, being smaller after positive than neutral feedback. These results suggest that the arousal dimension of the feedback operates in conjunction with the valence dimension in creating the emotion related pupil responses, see Partala et al. (2000), Partala & Surakka (submitted).

The behavioural results showed that feedback with negative emotional content resulted in a slower performance in the mathematical task as compared to the performance after positive feedback. Thus, positive emotional feedback facilitated emotional responding. This result is in line with the results by (Simpson et al., 2000), who showed that the subjects' decision-making performance was slower when negatively valenced pictorial material was used as compared to the use of neutral material. It may be argued that the decrease in the speed of the task performance after the negative feedback was due to the subjects trying to improve their performance by focusing on the task more intensely and being more careful. This, in turn, should probably have resulted in smaller error rates. However, this was not supported by the error rate data.

The pupil size was not analysed during the mathematical tasks, so this study cannot give a straightforward answer to the question whether the positive emotional feedback resulted in a decrease in the stress produced by the cognitive processing. As there is evidence that cognitive processing load is positively associated with autonomic arousal, for example Hyönä et al. (1995), it is conceivable that positive feedback could result in a facilitated recovery from it.

Importantly, in this study we used the content of the feedback, not the emotion related prosodic cues, in conveying the emotional feedback. Furthermore, the feedback was independent of the performance. Despite of these, the feedback produced significant effects in the subjects' cognitive performance and physiology. It is likely that performance-congruent emotional feedback with emotion-related prosodic cues would produce even stronger physiological and behavioural effects. It is known from the studies of facial expressions of emotion that genuine expressions of positive emotion elicit significantly stronger positive emotional responses in the receiver as compared to non-genuine emotional expressions (Surakka & Hietanen, 1998). By manipulating the synthesised speech with emotional-related prosody, it might be possible to make the sound of a synthesised speech even more efficient in the communication of emotions.

In sum, our results suggest that positive feedback might be a powerful method for facilitating HCI by providing one possible way of regulating the emotional state of the user. The present experiment offers a starting point for utilising emotion regulation to benefit people working with computers. An obvious application area for the emotion regulation is computer-supported learning. By providing an emotionally supportive learning environment, it might be possible to make the learning more fun and efficient. Another possibility for applying the emotion regulation comes from the finding that positive emotional feedback resulted in the improvement of the cognitive performance as compared to the performance after negative feedback. This finding implies that positive emotional feedback might be effective in increasing work efficiency. In addition to those, the results of this study suggest that positive emotional feedback might be used as a method for alleviating the stress caused by cognitive tasks. Because the computers are commonly used in cognitively demanding tasks, this stress-reducing capacity would provide significant facilitation of the HCI. As we have shown, it is fairly easy to make the computer act in an emotionally effective way. Further, this emotionally effective behaviour was shown to have significant effects in the user. Thus, integration of emotions seems to be a valuable method for improving the quality of the human–computer interaction.

## Acknowledgements

We would like to thank all the voluntary test subjects. This study was supported by the Academy of Finland (Projects no. 152,936 and 167,491).

# References

Bechara, A., Damasio, H., Tranel, D. & Damasio, A. R. (1997), "Deciding Advantageously before Knowing the Advantageous Strategy", *Science* **275**(5304), 1293–4.

Bradley, M. M. & Lang, P. J. (1994), "Measuring Emotion: The Self-assessment Manikin and the Semantic Differential", *Journal of Behavioral Therapy & Experimental Psychiatry* **25**(1), 49–59.

Cahn, J. (1990), "The Generation of Affect in Synthesized Speech", *Journal of the American Voice I/O Society* **8**, 1–19.

Cohen, J. D., MacWhinney, B., Flatt, M. & Provost, J. (1993), "PsyScope: A New Graphic Interactive Environment for Designing Psychology Experiments", *Behavior Research Methods, Instruments & Computers* **25**(2), 257–71.

Damasio, A. (1994), *Descartes' Error: Emotion, Reason, and the Human Brain*, Putnam.

Davidson, R. J. & Irwin, W. (1999), "The Functional Neuroanatomy of Emotion and Affective Style", *Trends in Cognitive Sciences* **3**(1), 11–21.

Ekman, P. & Friesen, W. V. (1976), *Pictures of Facial Affect*, Consulting Psychologists Press.

Ekman, P., Levenson, R. W. & Friesen, W. V. (1983), "Autonomic Nervous System Activity Distinguishes among Emotions", *Science* **221**(4616), 1208–10.

Fogg, B. J. & Nass, C. (1997), "Silicon Sycopaths: The Effects of Computers that Flatter", *International Journal of Human–Computer Studies* **46**(5), 551–61.

Goldwater, B. C. (1972), "Psychological Significance of Pupillary Movements", *Psychological Bulletin* **77**(5), 340–55.

Hess, E. H. (1965), "Attitude and Pupil Size", *Scientific American* **212**(4), 46–54.

Hess, E. H. & Polt, J. M. (1960), "Pupil Size as Related to Interest Value of Visual Stimuli", *Science* **132**, 349–50.

Hietanen, J. K., Surakka, V. & Linnankoski, I. (1998), "Facial Electromyographic Responses to Vocal Affect Expressions", *Psychophysiology* **35**(5), 530–36.

Hyönä, J., Tommola, J. & Alaja, A.-M. (1995), "Pupil Dilation as a Measure of Processing Load in Simultaneous Interpretation and Other Language Tasks", *The Quarterly Journal of Experimental Psychology* **48A**(3), 598–612.

Isen, A. M. (1993), Positive Affect and Decision Making, *in* M. Lewis & J. M. Haviland (eds.), *Handbook of Emotions*, The Guilford Press, pp.261–77.

Jacob, R. J. K. (1996), "The Future of Input Devices", *ACM Computing Surveys* **28A**(4es).

Janisse, M. P. (1974), "Pupil Size, Affect and Exposure Frequency", *Social Behavior and Personality* **2**(2), 125–46.

Kluger, A. N. & DeNisi, A. (1996), "The Effects of Feedback Interventions on Performance: An Historical Review, a Meta-analysis and a Preliminary Feedback Intervention Theory", *Psychological Bulletin* **119**(2), 254–84.

Levenson, R. W., Ekman, P. & Friesen, W. V. (1990), "Voluntary Facial Activity Creates Emotion-specific Autonomic Nervous System Activity", *Psychophysiology* **27**(4), 363–84.

MacLeod, C. & Donnellan, A. M. (1993), "Individual Differences in Anxiety and the Restriction of Working Memory Capacity", *Personality and Individual Differences* **15**(2), 163–73.

Murphy, S. T. & Zajonc, R. B. (1993), "Affect, Cognition and Awareness: Affective Priming with Suboptimal and Optimal Stimulus Exposures", *Journal of Personality and Social Psychology* **64**(5), 723–39.

Murray, I. R. & Arnott, J. L. (1993), "Toward the Simulation of Emotion in Synthetic Speech: A Review of the Literature on Human Vocal Emotion", *Journal of the Acoustical Society of America* **93**(2), 1097–108.

Olafson, K. M. & Ferraro, F. R. (2001), "Effects of Emotional State on Lexical Decision Performance", *Brain and Cognition* **45**(1), 15–20.

Panksepp, J. (1998), *Affective Neuroscience: The Foundations of Human and Animal Emotions*, Oxford University Press.

Partala, T. & Surakka, V. (submitted), Pupil Size Variation as an Indication of Affective Processing, Submitted for publication in International Journal of Human Computer Studies.

Partala, T., Jokiniemi, M. & Surakka, V. (2000), Pupillary Responses to Emotionally Provocative Stimuli, *in* S. N. Spencer (ed.), *Proceedings of ETRA 2000*, ACM Press, pp.123–9.

Picard, R. W. (1997), *Affective Computing*, MIT Press.

Reeves, B. & Nass, C. (1996), *The Media Equation: How People Treat Computers, Television and New Media Like Real People and Places*, Cambridge University Press.

Rickenberg, R. & Reeves, B. (2000), The Effects of Animated Characters on Anxiety, Task Performance and Evaluations of User Interfaces, *in* T. Turner, G. Szwillus, M. Czerwinski & F. Paternò (eds.), *Proceedings of the CHI2000 Conference on Human Factors in Computing Systems*, CHI Letters **2**(1), ACM Press, pp.49–56.

Riseberg, J., Klein, J., Fernendez, R. & Picard, R. W. (1998), Frustrating the User on Purpose: Using Biosignals to Detect the User's Emotional State, *in* C.-M. Karat, A. Lund, B. Bederson, E. Bergman, M. Beaudouin-Lafon, N. Bevan, D. Boehm-Davis, A. Boltman, G. Cockton, A. Druin, S. Dumais, N. Frischberg, J. Jacko, J. Koenemann, C. Lewis, S. Pemberton, A. Sears, K. T. Simsarian, C. Wolf & J. Ziegler (eds.), *Summary Proceedings of CHI'98: Human Factors in Computing Systems (CHI'98 Conference Summary)*, ACM Press, pp.227–8.

Scherer, K. R., Banse, R., Wallbott, H. G. & Goldbeck, T. (1991), "Vocal Cues in Emotion Encoding and Decoding", *Motivation and Emotion* **15**(2), 123–48.

Scherer, K. R., Ladd, D. R. & Silverman, K. E. A. (1984), "Vocal Cues to Speaker Affect: Testing Two Models", *Journal of the Acoustical Society of America* **76**(5), 1346–56.

Simpson, J. R., Öngür, D., Akbudak, E., Conturo, T. E., Ollinger, J. M., Snyder, A. Z., Gusnard, D. A. & Raichle, M. E. (2000), "The Emotional Modulation of Cognitive Processing: An fMRI study", *Journal of Cognitive Neuroscience* 12(Supplement 2), 157–70.

Surakka, V. & Hietanen, J. K. (1998), "Facial and Emotional Reactions to Duchenne and non-Duchenne smiles", *International Journal of Psychophysiology* 29(1), 23–33.

Surakka, V., Sams, M. & Hietanen, J. K. (1999), "Modulation of Neutral Face Evaluation by Laterally Presented Emotional Expressions", *Perceptual and Motor Skills* 88(2), 595–606.

Surakka, V., Tenhunen-Eskelinen, M., Hietanen, J. K. & Sams, M. (1998), "Modulation of Human Auditory Information Processing by Visual Emotional Stimuli", *Cognitive Brain Research* 7(2), 159–63.

Zajonc, R. B. (1980), "Feeling and Thinking: Preferences Need No Inferences", *American Psychologist* 35(2), 151–75.

Zhou, J. (1998), "Feedback Valence, Feedback Style, Task Autonomy and Achievement Orientation: Interactive Effects on Creative Performance", *Journal of Applied Psychology* 83(2), 261–76.

# Navigation in the Software Development Information Space

## Wayne Ho

*IBM Canada Limited, 8200 Warden Avenue, Markham, Ontario L6G 1C7, Canada.*
Tel: *+1 905 413 4461*
Fax: *+1 905 413 4974*
Email: *who@ca.ibm.com*

**This paper describes a usability study comparing two alternative interface designs used to navigate the software development information space. The results of this study were used to determine the default navigation design for a software development tool. The study provided insight into how programmers navigate the software development information space and the results are described in the context of navigational theories such as visual momentum.**

**Keywords:** usability, interface design, navigation.

## 1  Introduction

Software development tools have been designed to assist software programmers create, modify, and troubleshoot program code.  This software can range from simple to large, complex systems involving millions of lines of code. Development tools have been created to assist programmers in the task of navigating this large information space.  This paper focuses on how the programmer navigates this information space using a software development tool.

### 1.1  Navigating in the Software Domain

The software development domain is useful for studying navigational theory for several reasons.  Software systems are becoming larger and more complex.  In addition, software is often developed by a team, so programmers must navigate and understand code written by other individuals. Navigation within this complex information space is difficult and can place a large mental burden on software developers. The task is even more difficult when you consider this large information space can only be viewed through the narrow computer monitor display.  Woods (1984) refers to this as the *keyhole phenomenon*.

## 1.2   Keyhole Phenomenon

The *keyhole phenomenon* exists when an individual must view a large information space, in this case the software system code, through a relatively small viewport of the computer monitor display. The view through the narrow *keyhole* can degrade the user's ability to extract information and may require the user to integrate information across displays or views. In the case of software development, the primary task of designing and comprehending code requires the secondary task of navigating the code. The programmer must understand the purpose of the software system, the specific code in the system, and the programmer must understand the interdependencies of the code she is going to write. Her code may have impact on other parts of the system, and other code may have an impact on the code she is writing.

As a user navigates through an information space via the computer keyhole, the user often encounters various problems. Problems include:

- The getting lost phenomenon.

- Display thrashing.

- Cognitive tunnel vision.

The *getting lost phenomenon* occurs when users become disoriented as they move in the space of possible displays (Woods & Watts, 1997). *Display thrashing* occurs when users must integrate information from separate parts (e.g. different views) of the display. *Cognitive tunnel vision* occurs when the user's attention is focused solely on a subset of information and ignoring other, possibly important, information. If a user encounters these problems she will have to spend more time performing activities on the interface rather than performing the desired task itself. If the interface causes the user to perform activities on the interface that are not directly related to the user's task, mental workload is increased, and tasks will be completed more slowly.

This paper investigates the navigation of the software development information space using the IBM VisualAge for Java Integrated Development Environment (IDE). Specifically, two alternative designs that allow developers navigate software code are studied in a laboratory usability study. The results of the study were used to determine the default navigation method for the tool. The study also provided insight on how subjects navigate and retrieve information in the software development domain.

## 1.3   VisualAge for Java

The VisualAge for Java IDE is designed to assist the programmer navigate Java code and to provide her with a clear sense of where code is located in the environment (Chamberland et al., 1998). Java is an object-oriented programming language and code written in Java is structured into various objects including:

- Packages.

- Classes.

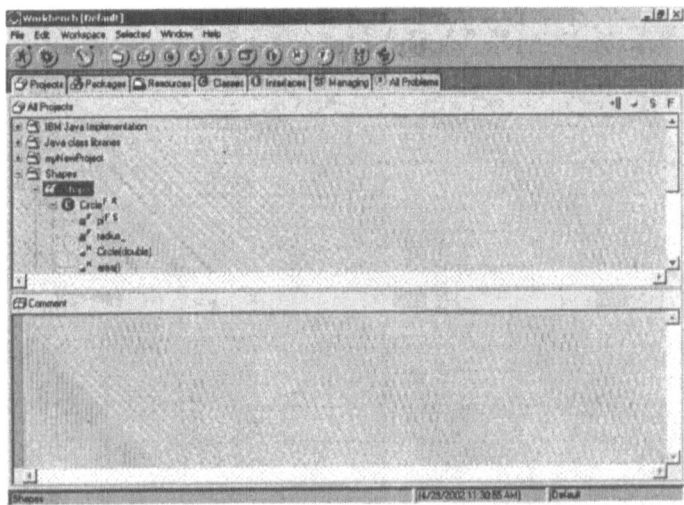

**Figure 1:** The Workbench: This view provides an overview of the entire information space.

- Methods.

These are hierarchical objects: a group of methods are contained in a class, and classes are contained in a package. VisualAge for Java provides a collection of browsers used to view and manipulate these objects. Each Java object has a dedicated browser. The main browser, the Workbench, provides a high-level view of all objects in the workspace (Figure 1). A new browser can be opened from the Workbench (i.e. by double-clicking on the object) to narrow the focus to one package, one class, or one method. Each browser provides a different scope and also provides different views of the information. The user can manually change views by selecting a tab within the browser. These tabs are much like tabs used in physical file folders, and when selected allow programmers to see different information while maintaining the same scope within the information space.

Each browser consists of a number of linked panes. The panes are similar to HTML frames, often used in Web pages, in that they can be individually resized. These panes are tightly coupled sub-windows that all sit in the same window and together make a coherent whole. These linked panes support hierarchical browsing. For instance, in a Package Browser (see Figure 2), the user is presented a list of the classes contained within the package being examined by the browser. The classes are displayed in the first pane, located at the top-left of the window. The next pane to the right contains the list of methods contained within the selected class. At the bottom of the window, there is pane that displays the source code of the selected method.

Using multiple browsers, programmers can browse multiple objects simultaneously on one computer display. In addition, VisualAge for Java provides a number of built-in search facilities allowing programmer to search for program elements in the information space.

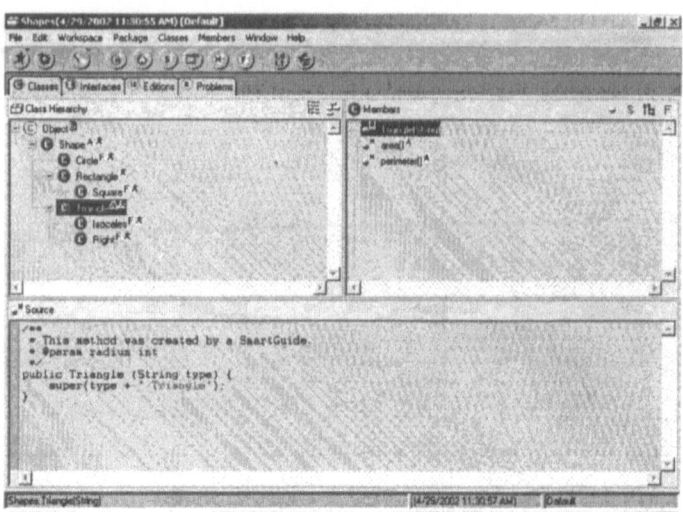

**Figure 2:** A Package Browser: This view provides a view of all classes, methods, and source code of a specified package.

---

### 1.3.1    Open Browser in a New Window Design ('Open in New Window')

In early versions of VisualAge for Java, when the programmer selects and opens an object within a browser (by double-clicking the object using the mouse) another browser is opened in a new window. This window is overlayed on top of the originating browser window (Figure 3). The programmer can continue to open new browsers that subsequently open up more and more windows. Providing multiple concurrently opened windows allows the programmer to view and reference other parts of the information space and manipulate or view one object and then move to the next.

Programmers may switch from one window to another by selecting the *Window* menu item at the top of the browser, or using the operating systems built-in windowing mechanisms. For example, in a Microsoft Windows environment, the programmer can click on the appropriate window that is visible on the desktop, use the Windows *Start menu*, or use the *Alt-Tab* keyboard combination to switch to the desired window.

However, in some cases programmers may open a large number of windows and become disoriented or spend a large amount of mental effort managing the windows rather than manipulating or viewing the actual code.

### 1.3.2    Open Browser in Place Design ('Open in Place')

An alternative design has been proposed to minimise the number of windows concurrently opened. Rather than opening a browser in a new window, the new design opens the browser in the same physical window replacing the originating browser. To move between browsers, *Back* and *Forward* buttons are provided. This allows users to move backward and forward through a *ring* of browsers, much like

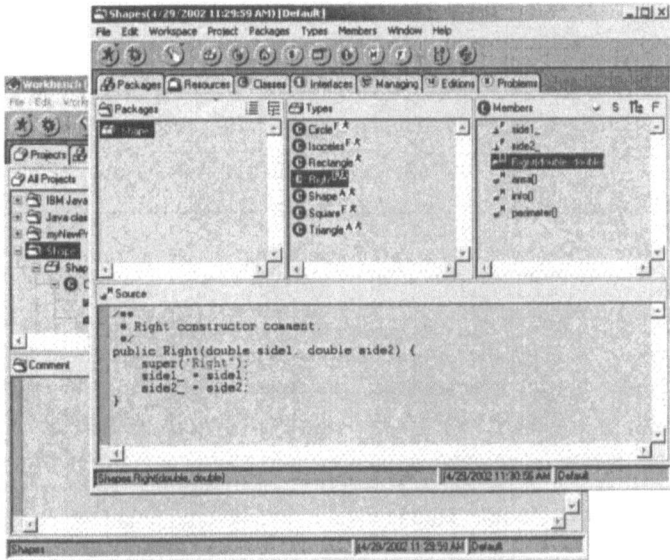

**Figure 3:** The 'Open in New Window' design overlays windows.

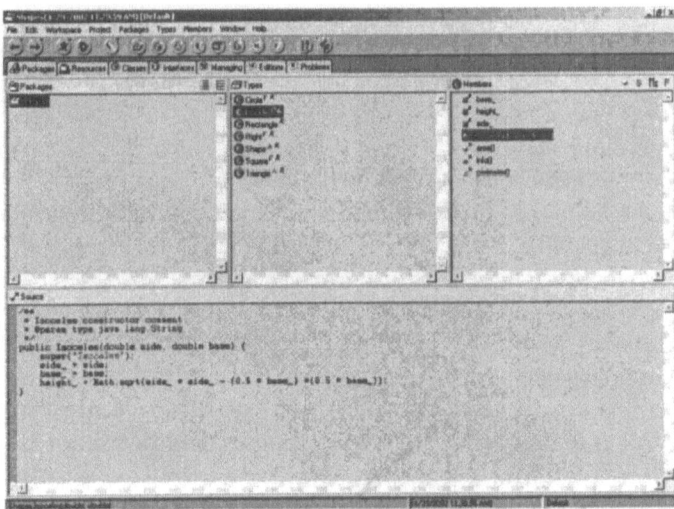

**Figure 4:** The 'Open in Place' design.

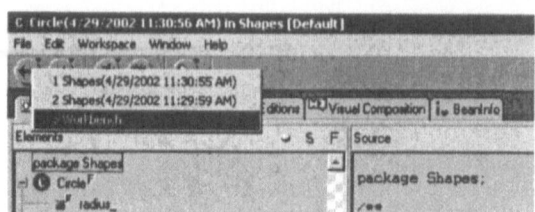

**Figure 5:** The history list in the 'Open in Place' design.

---

typical a Web browser (Figure 4). It is no longer possible to use the operating system's windowing-mechanisms to switch from one browser to another. Instead, the user navigates through the various browsers using the *Back* and *Forward* buttons. The programmer can jump several steps by right-clicking on the Back or Forward buttons to display a history-list of all browsers currently opened in the browser (Figure 5).

## 2 Methods and Procedures

### 2.1 Users

A usability study was conducted to explore how programmers navigate the programming information space using the two alternative designs for VisualAge for Java. Six users were recruited for this study. Users were experienced programmers with at least one year of Java experience. Both users with and without VisualAge for Java experience were recruited. Two users had little or no experience with VisualAge for Java, while the other four subjects had a minimum of six months practical experience with VisualAge for Java.

### 2.2 Tasks

Software developers typically perform two fundamental activities: composition and comprehension (Pennington & Grabowski, 1990). Composition is the activity of designing the software, and comprehension is the act of understanding how the program works in order to determine what goal it is trying to accomplish. Tasks were developed to represent these two fundamental activities. At the start of each session, users were given 10 minutes to explore the interface. Following this exploration period, the users were asked to browse an existing software application and to answer questions to confirm comprehension. The third task asked users to browse, understand, and then make modifications to an existing application. After this set of tasks was completed, users were asked to perform three equivalent tasks using the alternate interface design.

A within-subject study was performed with all users using both interfaces. Some users were asked to start with the 'Open in Place' design while others were asked to start with the 'Open in New Window' design. Users were not explicitly informed about the differences between the two interfaces. The users' navigation methods and problems were observed while they used both interface designs. This was not a highly controlled laboratory experiment, rather it was a usability study used to determine subjects' reactions to the different design alternatives, and to observe how subjects navigate the software code using a given interface. During the session, subjects were asked to speak out loud as they were performing the tasks. Following each task, interview questions were used to collect verbal responses from the subjects and to determine their satisfaction with the interface.

## 3 Results

The results of this study are presented in two sections. The first section describes the observations and navigational differences between the two alternative designs. The second section describes the factors that influenced navigation in this software-coding environment.

### 3.1 The Alternative Designs

The results of this study did not show whether one interface design was superior to another. Existing VisualAge for Java users preferred the original 'Open in New Window' design. This is not a surprising result since these four users already had experience with this design. These users also expressed dissatisfaction and experienced many navigation problems using the 'Open in Place' design. The other two users had little to no experience with VisualAge for Java and preferred the 'Open in Place' design.

#### 3.1.1 Observations from the 'Open in New Window' Design

The experienced VisualAge for Java users were able to easily manage opening multiple windows and used them to their advantage. They would use the Workbench to perform the majority of their work and open new windows to reference other areas of the information space or to narrow the focus. Some users would expand the Workbench to encompass the entire computer monitor. When they wished to examine an object at a more specific level of detail, they opened a new browser. Because this browser was located in another window, users were able to overlay the windows and move between one to the other relatively easily. The newly opened browser windows were often sized smaller than the Workbench and moved to a corner of the monitor. These experienced users moved easily from one window to another and closed windows they no longer required.

The inexperienced users expressed concerns about managing numerous windows. They were concerned that if too many windows were open, it would become difficult to navigate. These users simply avoided opening new windows when possible and worked almost exclusively within the Workbench.

#### 3.1.2 Observations from the 'Open in Place' Design

Inexperienced VisualAge for Java users in the study preferred the 'Open in Place' design. This design minimises the number of windows that are opened and reduces the effort required for managing windows. These users preferred this design as it reduced confusion caused by visual clutter on the computer monitor. When the users wanted to view another browser, the browser would open in place and replace the Workbench view. When they wanted to return to the Workbench, they were able to do so by using the Back button. It should be noted that these users did not open many additional views and worked almost exclusively with the Workbench. Therefore, they rarely had more than one additional view besides the Workbench. Navigation using the Back and Forward buttons was kept to a minimum and the depth of the various views in the 'ring' (the history of views) was kept to 2 or 3 views.

Other users experienced serious navigation difficulties using the 'Open in Place' design. A number of the users started in the Workbench and opened a new browser. The browser opened and replaced the Workbench. The users did not understand why the Workbench had disappeared from view and became confused. A number of users became disoriented when attempting to return to the Workbench after obtaining information from a new browser. To find the Workbench one user closed the visible window, this inadvertently exited the IDE. These users did not immediately discover the Back and Forward buttons nor the associated history lists.

Once these users discovered the Back and Forward button and the 'ring' of browsers in the window, they were able to navigate between the different views in the window.

A number of the users did not discover the history lists and found it difficult to remember what windows were open. One user commented:

> "...did not have a feel for what I had open and not open ... not necessarily sure where I'm going back to or forward to."

## 3.2  *Observations about Navigation*

The study provided insight on how programmers are navigating the software development information space using VisualAge for Java. A number of factors influenced the subjects' ability to navigate both the interface and the code. This included customising the interface, looking at the big picture, the use of landmarks, spatial dedication, and the use of searching and filtering. These factors allow users to cope with the problems associated with the *keyhole phenomenon*.

### 3.2.1  *Customising the Interface*

VisualAge for Java provides the users with a default organisation of information. Most users took the time to customise the interface to support their tasks. The users invested time to customise the interface and felt it was important to have the option to tailor the interface to better suit their working style and to facilitate completing their tasks and accomplishing their goals. By customising the interface, the users were able to minimise the amount of *display thrashing* and navigation of the interface.

### 3.2.2  *Looking at the Big Picture and Changing Scope and Focus*

Users applied various techniques to keep track of where they were in the information space. The users employed different browsers to widen and narrow the scope of the information space as they worked. *Cognitive tunnel vision* was minimised as users were able to easily change the scope and focus of their work. Most users used the Workbench, the main browser, for the majority of their work. The Workbench provided a high-level context and focus on the information space. When the users were interested in focusing on more specific information, such as an individual class or method in the Java code, they would open an additional browser that focused more narrowly on the relevant object. The users navigated back and forth from the Workbench and the more narrowly scoped browser to obtain information on a specific object and then make changes to the information space using the Workbench. In general, the users would always return to the Workbench and used it as a launching point for other browsers. The Workbench acted as a familiar and central location in the information space and appeared to be used as a point of reference and helped reduce the occurrence of the *getting lost phenomenon*. Once they had obtained the necessary information from an additional browser, the users would return to the Workbench to continue work or to move to another location.

### 3.2.3 Use of Landmarks

Both experienced and inexperienced users were able to easily navigate within one browser. Users were able to easily switch to different views of the same information within a single browser. They used the tabs (located towards the top of the browser) to change different views. The tabs act as landmarks that are easily visible and provide information about where the user is in the information space (Woods, 1984) thereby reducing the chances of *getting lost* in the information space. In this case, the landmarks provide information about the type of view users are currently using. Other landmarks include headings in the windows and panes, various icons that demonstrate the type of browser that is opened and the type of objects that will be located in a view.

Users also discovered and enjoyed a number of navigation aiding tools within VisualAge for Java. Within the Workbench, a bookmark facility is provided to allow users to keep track of a particular location in the Workbench. The users can associate a bookmark to a particular object, and the select the bookmark (located at the top-right of the window) and the interface will automatically return the user to that location.

### 3.2.4 Spatial Dedication

Users were able to navigate within a particular browser with relative ease. In a given browser, the user was able to navigate from one object to another with minimal effort. This was facilitated via the use of the structured panes in each browser. For instance, in a Workbench, the panes consist of the Projects pane, the Classes pane, the Methods pane, and finally the Source pane. The Project pane is always located in the top left corner of the browser and contains a list of all projects in the workspace in a tree structure. The Classes pane is located to the right on the Projects pane and displays all classes and interfaces in a tree view. To the right of the Classes pane, the Methods pane displays all methods. Below the last three panes is the Source pane that displays the actual code of the selected method. The Source pane is updated appropriately depending on what project, class, and method that is chosen. Each of these panes is always spatially located in the same position (although it is user configurable). This made it easy for users to locate desired information in a common location and, once again, minimise the possibility of experiencing the *getting lost phenomenon*.

## 3.2.5   Use of Searching and Filtering

Users were very positive about the searching and filtering capabilities of VisualAge for Java. They were impressed with the ability to search for objects in the information space. The simple search mechanisms assist users in locating required information quickly without having to *thrash* through the interface or manage windows. Users also enjoyed the filtering mechanisms that allowed them to simplify the views or to customise the views that were necessary.

# 4   Discussion

The 'Open in New Window' design provided multiple windows for users to perform their tasks. Bury et al. (1985) found windowed systems produced larger task-completion times than did the non-windowed (full-screen) environment. The interface with multiple smaller windows led to more time arranging the windows in the interface to bring the required information into view. Once the time arranging the display was completed, the task times were shorter and fewer errors were made for the windowed system. This may explain why experienced VisualAge for Java users preferred the 'Open in New Window' design. This design was a multi-windowed design. The experienced users had the expertise and knowledge to arrange and manipulate the interface to complete their desired tasks. The inexperienced users encountered the time-consuming task of initially arranging the windows and were concerned about the necessity to manage windows. To ensure programmers can take advantage of multiple windows, it is imperative that VisualAge for Java provide an effective design for window arrangement.

The 'Open in Place' design also had its advantages, and new user preferred this design. Tauscher & Greenberg (1997) found navigation using a Back button to be effective and simple to use in the Web environment. This type of navigation was particularly useful in the Web space since users tend to revisit Web pages. VisualAge for Java and most Web browsers base the Back and Forward navigation buttons on a stack model. Tauscher & Greenberg (1997) suggest this model may potentially be improved by basing it on a recency model. More investigation on how programmers navigate between windows is needed to determine the most appropriate Back button model for navigating the programming information space.

This study did not find one design alternative better for navigation than the other. However, the study found existing users of VisualAge for Java were quite negative towards the new 'Open in Place' design. A number of these users became lost and disoriented. Due to these reasons and some usability issues regarding the 'Open in Place' design, it was decided that the default design would be the 'Open in a New Window' design. However, the final design will allow users to select the 'Open in Place' design by changing it in the user customisable options.

Aside from specifically comparing the design alternatives, a number of observations from this study provide insight on similar studies and theories on navigating computer environments. Watts' (1994) study of navigation of computer spreadsheets found that users customised their interfaces to reduce time spent on navigation, that landmarks provided important cues for aiding navigation, and saw that information arranged in a spatially dedicated manner helped users better understand the structure of the information. Similarly, users in this study spent time customising their environments to minimise the amount of navigation necessary to complete the tasks. The users also found the tabs, icons, and other landmarks to be of great value when navigating the interface. Finally, the spatially dedicated panes in each browser allowed users to better understand and navigate the Java code.

The concept of visual momentum can also be used to understand and solve the navigation problems in computer interfaces. Woods (1984) defines visual momentum as:

> "A measure of the user's ability to extract and integrate information across displays, in other words, as a measure of the distribution of attention."

This concept was originally borrowed from film editing, as a technique used to make film cuts easy to comprehend (Hochberg & Brooks, 1978).

> "When visual momentum is high, there is continuity across successive views which supports the rapid comprehension of data following the transition to a new display. It is analogous to a good cut from one scene or view to another in film editing." (Woods, 1984)

High visual momentum will impact a user's ability to extract information via the computer display. If transitions to new displays are discontinuous, a high cognitive load is placed on users. Users are forced to integrate information from separate displays making it difficult for users to extract relevant information. Discontinuous transitions present information in a serial as opposed to parallel manner (Woods, 1984). In the computer medium, a lack of visual momentum can result in disorientation and the 'getting lost' phenomenon. This study supports the theory of visual momentum, as shown in the disorientation experienced by users working in the 'Open in Place' design.

Visual momentum provides a number of design guidelines for interface design (Woods & Watts, 1997; Wickens, 1992).

## 4.1 Use Graceful Transitions

Poor transitions from one display to another can disorient the user. In this study, users became disoriented when the 'Open in Place' design completely replaced one browser view with another. The design did not provide visible cues that other views were available. The Back and Forward buttons remained enabled at all times, instead of being enabled and disabled to indicate that navigation to other views was possible. In addition, the provided history list was not easily discovered and is not immediately apparent to the user. To improve the 'Open in Place' design, the transitions need to become more continuous and evidence for navigation to other views must be more salient.

## 4.2 Provide an Overview or Longshot Display

A longshot provides an overview of the display structure and can act as a viewable map of the world. This map can act to assist users navigate to important details in the display. As a result, the user does not have to maintain a model of the information space in memory, thereby easing the cognitive load. The longshot helps users relate a view to previous views and to integrate views. In this study, it was observed that users wanted to navigate via the Workbench browser. The Workbench provided an overview of the programming information space and assisted users in navigating to more detailed views. The Workbench acts much like a global map and helped users decide where to look next within the system. This may explain why some users had difficulties with the 'Open in Place' design. The Workbench was an important map of the world and they needed to return to it frequently. However, the 'Open in Place' design made it more difficult to return to this view. By replacing the Workbench with another browser view, users did not view both the overview display in parallel with the more detailed information. When using the 'Open in New Window' design, users often kept the Workbench open and another browser open in a separate window allowing the user to gather information in parallel.

### 4.3   Use and Highlight Landmarks

Landmarks are constant features in the interface that can be easily identified and located. Like their physical counterparts, landmarks in the computer medium can assist users navigate. A visible landmark can act as frame of reference from which to navigate. Landmarks in the computer medium assist users in locating relevant information. Landmarks in VisualAge for Java, such as the tabs and icons helped users locate appropriate views and information in the interface.

### 4.4   Use of Spatial Dedication

Information that is placed in a fixed location can act as a memory aid for users. If a particular type of information can always be located in a particular place in the interface, users can more easily learn where to find the information. As mentioned earlier, the pane design of VisualAge for Java places information in spatially fixed locations assisting users in locating specific information.

### 4.5   Provide Information in Parallel

Allow users to see related views in parallel. By displaying related information in parallel, the interface can assist the user integrate the individual pieces of information. In the computer medium, different views or windows may contain related information. Software programmers should be studied to determine what software development views need to be seen in parallel. One method of providing information in parallel is the use of overlayed windows, such as in the 'Open in New Window' design.

## References

Bury, K. F., Davies, S. E. & Darnell, M. J. (1985), Window Management: A Review of Issues and Some Results from User Testing, Technical Report HFC-53, IBM Human Factors Center, San Jose, CA, USA.

Chamberland, L. A., Lymer, S. F. & Ryman, A. G. (1998), "IBM VisualAge for Java", *IBM System Journal* **37**(3), 386–408.

Hochberg, J. & Brooks, V. (1978), Film Cutting and Visual Momentum, *in* J. W. Senders, D. F. Fisher & R. A. Monty (eds.), *Eye Movements and the Higher Psychological Functions*, Lawrence Erlbaum Associates, pp.293–313.

Pennington, N. & Grabowski, B. (1990), The Tasks of Programming, *in* J.-M. Hoc, T. R. G. Green, R. Samurçay & D. J. Gilmore (eds.), *The Psychology of Programming*, Academic Press, pp.45–62.

Tauscher, L. & Greenberg, S. (1997), Revisitation Patterns in World Wide Web navigation, *in* S. Pemberton (ed.), *Proceedings of CHI'97: Human Factors in Computing Systems*, ACM Press, pp.399–406.

Watts, J. (1994), Navigation in the Computer Medium: A Cognitive Analysis, *in Proceedings of the Human Factors and Ergonomics Society 38th Annual Meeting*, Human Factors and Ergonomics Society, pp.310–4.

Wickens, C. D. (1992), *Engineering Psychology and Human Performance*, Charles E. Merrill Publishing.

Woods, D. D. (1984), "Visual Momentum: A Concept to Improve the Cognitive Coupling of Person and Computer", *International Journal of Man–Machine Studies* **21**(3), 229–44.

Woods, D. D. & Watts, J. C. (1997), How Not To Have To Navigate Through Too Many Windows, *in* M. Helander, T. K. Landauer & P. V. Prabhu (eds.), *Handbook of Human–Computer Interaction*, second edition, North-Holland, pp.617–50.

# Selecting the 'Invisible' User Interface Development Tool

## Joanna Lumsden

*Department of Computing Science, University of Glasgow, Glasgow G12 8QQ, UK.*
Tel: *+44 141 330 6045*
Email: *jo@dcs.gla.ac.uk*
URL: *http://www.dcs.gla.ac.uk/~jo*

**Developers of interactive software are confronted by an increasing variety of software tools to help engineer the interactive aspects of software applications.   Typically resorting to ad hoc means of tool selection, developers are often dissatisfied with their chosen tool on account of the fact that the tool lacks required functionality or does not fit seamlessly within the context in which it is to be used. This paper describes a system for evaluating the suitability of user interface development tools for use in software development organisations and projects such that the selected tool appears 'invisible' within its anticipated context of use.  The paper also outlines and presents the results of an informal empirical study and a series of observational case studies of the system.**

**Keywords:** UIDT, evaluation, selection, context sensitive, project-specific.

## 1  Introduction

Developers of interactive software are confronted by an increasing variety of software tools to assist in engineering the interactive aspects of software applications. Not only do these tools fall into different categories in terms of functionality, but within each category there is a growing number of competing tools with similar, but not identical, features. Choice of user interface development tool (UIDT) is therefore becoming increasingly complex.

There is evidence to suggest that industrial software developers rely heavily upon right-brain (intuitive) decision making (Sauter, 1999) — based on little more than an ad hoc inspection of marketing material, journal reviews, and recommendations from colleagues — when selecting UIDTs (McKirdy, 1998). Although potentially adequate in some cases, this can result in poor choices, especially when the information from brochures, friends, and reviews is not relevant to the context in which the tool is to be used.

Acknowledging the place for intuition in the overall process of tool evaluation and selection, this research facilitates software engineers with a mechanism that allows them to approach UIDT selection from an analytical perspective without suppressing intuitive decision making so that, where necessary, it can be used to handle areas of uncertainty such as trade-offs.

This paper presents a framework, method, and data analysis tool for evaluating UIDT suitability for software development projects such that the selected tools appear 'invisible' within their anticipated context of use. Section 2 briefly outlines the background and motivation for this work. Section 3 provides a summary description of the framework and method, for greater detail see Lumsden (2001) and McKirdy (1999). This is followed, in Section 4, by an account of an evaluative study of their use. Section 5 introduces a data analysis tool that has been developed to support the UIDT selection process and describes its evaluation. This paper concludes by outlining some plans for future work.

## 2  Background

To systematically select a UIDT, one must identify assumptions that establish selection boundaries; with its decision space defined by high-level factors such as the budget allocation assigned to UIDT purchase and installation, the availability of staff training for the deployed UIDT, programming language restrictions, time constraints, development platform restrictions, availability of information, and cost/benefit ratio, UIDT selection takes place in a setting of variably negotiable, co-operating and/or competing goals and constraints.

Once delineated, the problem must be represented (modelled) in a manner that facilitates its solution. The delimited decision space that must be modelled includes criteria determined by the development requirements of a specific project — e.g. user interface specific components required for the end product user interface and necessary software engineering support — and by some of the delimiting constraints/assumptions. Once modelled, the selection problem is solved by deciding between different solutions — the principal aim should be to choose the UIDT that best fits with identified goals and values and is therefore 'invisible' within its context of use (Jacobs & Holten, 1995; Albers, 1996; Harris, 1998).

A UIDT selection decision is made within a decision space (delimited by factors such as budget allocation, programming language, and development platform) which determines the set of UIDTs that are considered during the selection process; UIDTs can be assessed against these criteria, and their suitability determined, without having to evaluate the low-level detail of the tools.

Decision makers tend to seek more information than is necessary to make a good decision (Harris, 1998). This often leads to delay in the decision, decline in decision making ability due to information overload, selective use of information to support preconceived solutions, mental fatigue which returns slower and poorer quality work, and decision fatigue which results in fast, careless decisions or even decision paralysis (Harris, 1998). UIDTs are assessed according to the degree to which they meet identified criteria and it is these criteria that determine the information that needs to be collected for each candidate UIDT.

Software development deadlines generally make optimised UIDT selection impracticable and therefore rarely performed (McKirdy, 1998); instead, although not ideal, satisficing is typically used (McKirdy, 1998). When satisficing, if no UIDTs are found to completely meet identified criteria, a complex process of goal, constraint, and criteria adjustment and trade-off is initiated to facilitate a selection. Where this is insufficient, the limiting boundaries of the decision space may also have to be adjusted.

UIDT selection decisions can be good or bad. A good decision is logical — based on available information — and reflects context-sensitive values set for the problem solution; a bad decision is based on inadequate information and does not reflect identified values (i.e. the context of use):

"It is better to expend a little more energy to solve a problem well the first time than have to redo the entire thing after a half energetic solution." (Harris, 1998)

## 2.1 The Importance of Context

The importance of context is recognised in software design. Clarke comments that:

"Designers often neglect to take account of contextual factors due to their focus on the artefact itself." (Clarke, 1997, p.10)

Disastrous consequences can arise when context is ignored during software development — e.g. with hindsight it was discovered that lack of consideration of the context in which the Patriot system (for Scud missile interception) would be used, contributed to loss of life in the Gulf War (Clarke, 1997). Making the relationships between context and design explicit allows accurate judgements to be made about the use of contextual information in design (Clarke, 1997).

Considering context of use during UIDT selection is similarly important; context of use determines the 'invisibility' of a selected UIDT. In this case, evaluators often fail to adequately consider contextual information when selecting a UIDT due to their focus on the tools themselves with the result that inappropriate UIDT selection is made (McKirdy, 1998; Kemerer, 1992). Often the choice that would perhaps be obvious to an evaluator may not function in the context in which it is used due to cost, time, and most importantly, lack of acceptance. Problem solving and decision making changes when an individual evaluator is asked to assume an organisational position to select a UIDT not for himself, but for members of a group. In these circumstances, evaluators are required to adapt their goals and values to their responsibility (Simon, 1986) — namely, the context of use of the selected UIDT. Without an adequate model of the UIDT's context of use, evaluators are prone to reverting to their individual set of preferences and goals. It is therefore important to identify and adequately model the context of use for the selected UIDT so that it can be considered when rating candidate UIDTs against selection criteria during the decision making process. Additionally, by identifying the context sensitive criteria to be considered during the decision making process it is possible to focus information-gathering for UIDT selection and thereby potentially prevent the hazards of excess information discussed previously.

A UIDT selection decision must always be made in light of the people who will be required to use the UIDT; those who must use the selected UIDT must accept it if it is to be used effectively and efficiently and 'invisibly'. Acceptance is critically important: even if technically 'brilliant', a UIDT that only reflects the preferences of the evaluator may be rejected by the anticipated users and therefore not represent a good decision. Acceptance of a selected UIDT is increased if the project team members who have to use the selected tool are considered when making the selection decision and the drawbacks of the selected UIDT are outlined in addition to the projected benefits — users are more likely to accept a decision if they understand the risks and believe that they have been given due consideration (Harris, 1998; Rumble, 1991). To achieve this, there needs to be a mechanism by which to record this context during the selection process, and to explicitly represent this influence over the suitability of any given UIDT.

## 2.2   *Previous Support Mechanisms For UIDT Selection*

The most substantial previous work on UIDT evaluation was conducted ten years ago by Hix et al. (Hix & Ryan, 1992; Hix & Schulman, 1991; Hix, 1991). Their approach is based on functionality- and usability-oriented checklists; tools are assessed against an extensive set of criteria and cumulative ratings generated which serve as the basis for tool comparisons. While their basic objective measure of functionality is appropriate, the mechanism as it stands suffers from several problems, namely: cumulative measures hide much useful evaluative information; their checklists are not adequately designed for extension in keeping with functionality increases and improvements in interaction techniques; and no account is taken of any factors other than functionality and usability.

Although other UIDT evaluation mechanisms have used different sets of attributes (Bass et al., 1994; Sundaram & Ramamurthy, 1996; Myers, 1996; Valaer & Babb, 1997), have made some effort to introduce tailorability (Valaer & Babb, 1997), and have introduced performance benchmarks for some attributes (Bass et al., 1994; Sundaram & Ramamurthy, 1996), they are all based on the common fundamental assumption that an evaluative UIDT judgement can be made largely independently of the context in which the evaluation takes place. Common to all of these techniques is an absence of the means to represent and therefore adequately consider the relationships between context of use and UIDT functionality. Despite its influence and importance none of these facilities either promote or support the consideration of context of use during UIDT evaluation and selection. They do not, therefore, facilitate good quality decisions as defined previously; while they all contribute to de-contextualised UIDT evaluation, they fail to fully consider the context in which a UIDT is to be used and thus do not adequately support the complexities of the decision making (evaluation) process described above.

To further investigate the precise nature of that context of use, a study of current industrial practice in UIDT selection was undertaken. Via questionnaires, software developers were asked about the tools they used, how they made their tool selections, and the context in which their selections were made (McKirdy, 1999). A correlation was observed between the type of application being developed and the type of tools used, and between tool type and other aspects of the project, including: team size; team member expertise; management structure; and the role of prototypes in the design process.

Additionally, it was found that amongst the respondents, there was little use of systematic evaluation methods but a general desire to introduce appropriate methods if they were available. Overall, the study supported the notion that UIDT evaluation methods need to be developed which reflect organisational and project context. That context is the core factor motivating and structuring the method, framework, and visualisation environment described in the remainder of this paper.

# 3   SUIT

SUIT, a framework and method for the selection of *u*ser *i*nterface development *t*ools, provides a context-sensitive, extensible, and systematic means by which developers can determine the UIDT that best fits their needs. Adopting a reference model-based approach to tool selection, SUIT can be used in three different ways:

- To select a UIDT based on a generic comparison of tools.

- To select the 'best-fit' UIDT for a project based on the specific context and requirements of that project where the project has no precedent within the organisation and hence no access to existing comparative data (see below).

- To identify an appropriate UIDT for a specific project based on comparisons with previous projects.

The applicability of each approach is based on the stage of design/development of the project, the precedence of the project within the context of the organisation, and the intended specificity of the outcome of the use of SUIT. Each approach dictates the appropriate route through the SUIT method (see Figure 1) and the manner in which the framework is manipulated.

Guided by the appropriate methodological setting, the SUIT framework is tailored (i.e. framework components are included or excluded from consideration) to provide a structure for data collection and thereafter a context for the interpretation of that data. The degree to which the framework *can be* tailored is determined by the amount of information available to the evaluator at the time of using SUIT. The degree to which the framework *is* tailored also depends on the intended use — e.g. generic comparison may require no tailoring.

In terms of what is possible and appropriate, the three different routes through the SUIT method reflect the natural progression of UIDT selection as an organisation matures — a pattern/process of maturation analogous with the Capability Maturity Model (CMM) of software development (Humphrey, 1989; Paulk et al., 1993). Just as the CMM was designed to guide software organisations when improving their software development strategies by identifying their current level of process maturity and those issues most critical to software quality and process improvement (Paulk

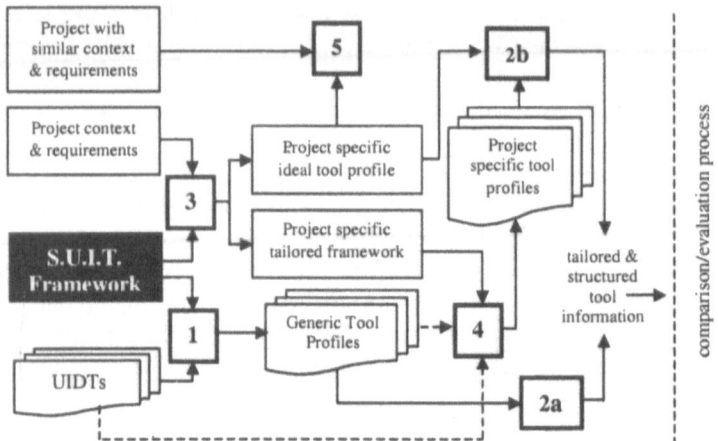

**Figure 1:** The route map of the SUIT method showing all possible paths.

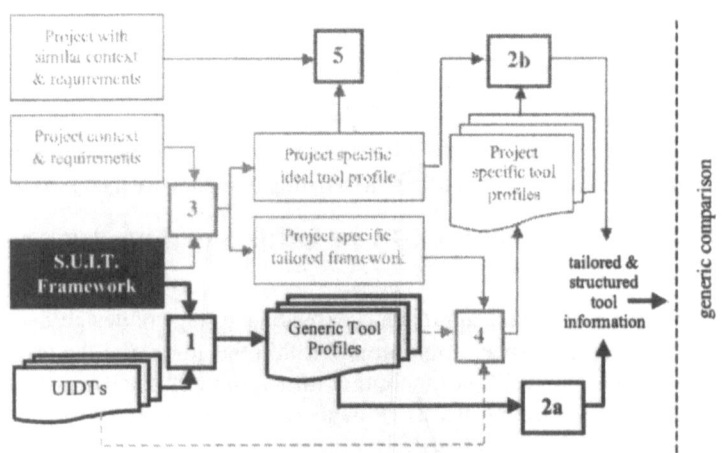

**Figure 2:** Performing a generic comparison of UIDTs using SUIT.

et al., 1993), SUIT is designed to guide evaluators when improving their process of UIDT evaluation and selection by identifying their evaluation capabilities and critical selection requirements and enabling them to perform increasingly sophisticated and/or efficient UIDT selection.

## 3.1  UIDT Selection Based on a Generic Comparison of Tools

When SUIT is used to perform generic — i.e. non project specific — tool comparisons, no knowledge of the project or its context is required.

Figure 2 highlights the path that would be taken through the SUIT method to perform a generic comparison of UIDTs. In this case the SUIT framework is used

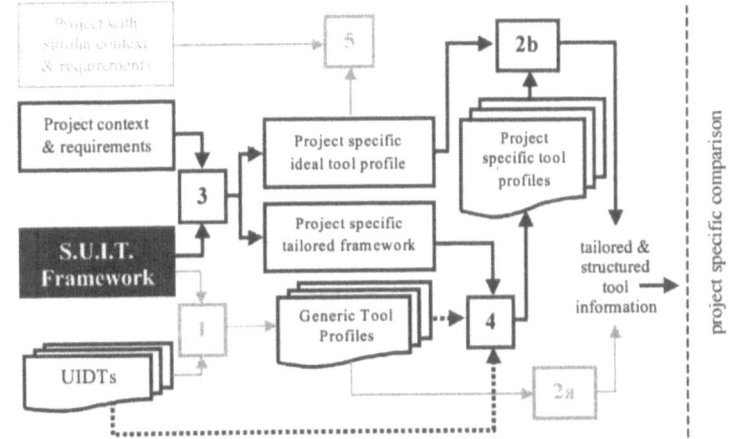

**Figure 3:** Performing a project-specific comparison of UIDTs using SUIT.

as a complete reference model, i.e. every component in the framework is an active criterion for the comparison of the tools.

At Step 1, each tool is examined to determine which of the components listed in the SUIT framework are/are not present. For each tool, the information recorded during this process forms a generic profile of the tool; these are collated (Step 2a) for use in the final stages of generic tool comparison or evaluation[1].

## 3.2   Project-specific UIDT Comparison

Generic comparisons highlight the differences between various tools, but it is in the context of a specific project that the significance of the differences becomes apparent. Hence, to select the tool which best fits (or is 'invisible' within) a specific project, the project's functional requirements and context of use have to be taken into consideration throughout the selection process. Figure 3 highlights the methodological path designed for determining the best-fit tool for an unprecedented project — i.e. a project for which there have been, within an organisation, no similar preceding projects which have themselves used the SUIT system to select a UIDT.

Given information about project requirements, the basic framework is modified to produce a project-specific tailored framework that only considers data relevant to that project. A copy of the tailored framework is augmented by adding contextual information to the functional requirements, creating a profile of the ideal tool for that project — see Step 3. It is against this profile that the data about real tools is compared to determine which tool best matches the ideal.

A project-specific tailored framework is used to pilot the collection of (only relevant) data for the real tools. This data can either be extracted/filtered from existing generic tool profiles or it can be collected via direct examination of the actual tools (Step 4); the result is a series of project-specific tool profiles (i.e. tool profiles

---

[1] SUIT does not stipulate how to perform the final comparison; this is the case for all uses of SUIT.

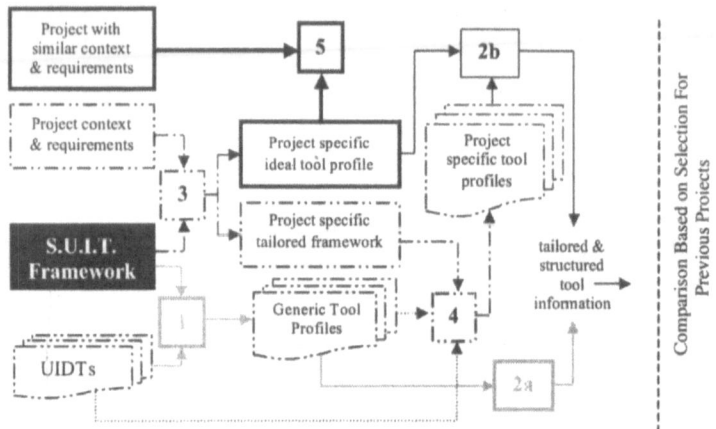

**Figure 4:** Performing a project-specific comparison of UIDTs using SUIT where selection information is available for similar preceding projects.

focusing only on those features relevant to the given project) which can be collated with the ideal tool profile (Step 2b) for use in the final stages of the comparison process.

## 3.3   Project-specific UIDT Selection Based on Comparison with Previous Projects

Project specific ideal tool profiles, tailored frameworks, and associated tool information form records of past UIDT selections using SUIT. Where software companies develop 'families' of projects, and where SUIT has been used to inform previous UIDT selections, new projects can exploit tool selection results of previous, closely matching projects. Figure 4 highlights the path through the SUIT method which would be followed under such circumstances.

When drawing on tool selection information from similar preceding projects, a new project's context and requirements are examined to determine whether they would generate a project-specific ideal tool profile matching an existing one (Step 5). In this case, the tool recommendation as made for the preceding project would also be the best fit for the new project. If there are only slight differences between the new and existing projects' ideal tool profiles, the project-specific tailored framework and ideal tool profile for the preceding project can be copied and tweaked (i.e. minor changes made) and the altered versions used to complete the selection process as described in Section 3.2, Steps 4 and 2b. Given either scenario, the time and effort expended on previous tool evaluations reduces the cost of tool selection for new projects.

## 3.4   The SUIT Framework

The SUIT framework — an extensible reference model of the functionality and support features that might be found in a typical UIDT — contains three main sections:

**Environmental Context of Use:** The human resources and institutional goals/constraints comprising the environment in which a project takes place.

**User Interface Specific Requirements:** Concrete requirements dictated by the design of the user interface to be developed using the selected UIDT.

**Developmental Context of Use:** Working practice and the ways in which the selected UIDT can enhance these practices, the design and development methodologies adopted by the organisation for project completion, and the technological support that must be provided by the selected UIDT for it to be successfully integrated into the developmental context of the organisation.

For the criteria in each of these sections (McKirdy, 1999), the following dimensions are recorded: the interaction mechanisms used to achieve the criteria; the interaction assistance provided by the tool; the cognitive demands placed on the user; the quality of feedback from the tool; and other miscellaneous factors relating to the tool and its use. Interaction mechanisms play a pivotal role in the selection of tools using SUIT; selecting a tool which lessens the disparities between the actual interaction mechanisms used and those appropriate for the anticipated tool users will in turn lessen the time taken for users to learn the tool and increase the levels of acceptance (and 'invisibility') of the new tool. Interaction assistance is similarly important in determining the suitability of a tool relative to its intended user-base. The remaining dimensions play a supporting role; they represent factors that may have to be taken into consideration when, after eliminating inappropriate tools on the basis of their mismatch with the ideal tool profile, the remaining evaluated tools are so similar as to make it impossible to make a rational decision on the basis of interaction style and assistance alone. Unfortunately, due to limitations of space, it is not possible to discuss these factors in greater detail; detail is, however, available from the author or alternatively from (McKirdy, 1999).

# 4 Evaluative Study of SUIT

The SUIT framework and method were the subject of an evaluative study to assess SUIT's viability as a paper-based mechanism for UIDT evaluation and to inform a set of requirements for a data visualisation environment to support the SUIT evaluation process. During this study, the use of SUIT was compared to that of the nearest alternative mechanism (Hix, 1991) but these findings are outwith the scope of this paper.

## 4.1 The Study

Twenty seven final year undergraduate computing science students were divided into pairs[2] and allocated an evaluation method (either SUIT or the Hix et al. method). They were taught how to use their allocated method and given a problem scenario outlining the requirements and context for a project. Each pair was given 30 man-hours to evaluate two web-authoring tools and, with respect to the scenario, make a recommendation for the selection of one. All subjects submitted an evaluation

---

[2]Twelve pairs and one group of three.

report, their evaluation forms, and a log sheet detailing their allocation of time to sub-task. They also completed a NASA TLX-based questionnaire (Hart & Staveland, 1988; Hart & Wickens, 1990).

## 4.2 The Results in Brief

Examination of the evaluation forms indicated that the subjects had correctly used the forms. They had been complete and thorough in their evaluation and there was noticeable intra-subject consistency in the use of the framework tables.

The evaluation reports were analysed to identify the use of terminology related to project requirements and context of use. The frequency, composition, and distribution of this term set indicated that SUIT directed evaluators' attention to the project-specific/contextual aspects of UIDT evaluation. In particular, the ideal tool profile was shown to play an essential role in the comparison process and as such would have to be readily accessible in any visualisation environment, for greater detail about this analysis, see Lumsden (2001).

The evaluation reports were also examined to gauge subjects' reactions to their evaluation method. Subjects' comments highlighted that the real difficulty in tool selection is deciding between two tools that are very close functionally and stylistically, confirming the need for visualisation tools which allow the evaluator to query the data during the final stages of the examination and decision making process.

The log sheets showed that subjects did not have to spend a large proportion of their time trying to understand and learn SUIT but that the greatest time was spent using the actual tools. Given the conditions under which the study took place, it was not possible to avoid experimenter influence in terms of the anonymity of the two evaluation methods. Thus, it is recognised that the Hawthorne Effect may have influenced both the motivation of the subjects using SUIT, and their subjective assessment of the method. However, the subjects had no knowledge of what was anticipated with respect to the relative importance of time vs. quality of evaluation, or the content of their completed evaluation checklists, and therefore this information is unlikely to be subject to method-oriented bias. Whilst recognising that the results were for a student-based subject group and that they might have been different had commercial software developers been included, the results of the study were nevertheless indicative of SUIT's viability as a paper-based evaluation method; there was evidence that SUIT is comprehensive and effective and that it directs the attention of the evaluator as it was designed to. Furthermore, the study identified the principal requirements for the SUIT data visualisation environment — both in terms of what needed to be visualised and how that visualisation might need to be manipulated/queried.

## 5 The SUIT Visualisation Environment

The SUIT visualisation environment extracts structure and data from external databases (reflecting the SUIT framework tables) and represents their contents using a combination of location and colour coding to allow data analysis. Figure 5 shows part of a visualisation that has been created for a generic comparison of two fictitious tools, annotated to highlight the main features.

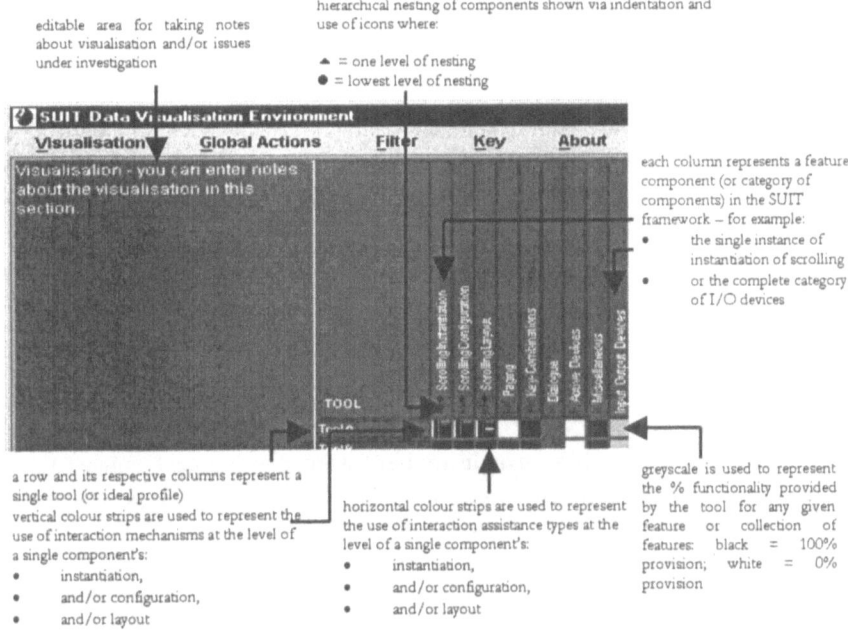

**Figure 5:** An example of a SUIT visualisation.

A SUIT data visualisation explicitly represents most of the data that is contained within the SUIT framework. The remaining data — that which is not visible above — is available on demand. To simplify a visualisation, the evaluator can chose to hide the information about interaction assistance. Each of SUIT's categories of criteria and the components therein (McKirdy, 1999) are represented by a column in the visualisation. On a category-by-category basis, evaluators can select the level of detail to view by expanding/contracting columns in the component/category hierarchy; this allows the evaluator greater control over, and flexibility of, analysis.

## 5.1  Interacting with a SUIT Visualisation

Components/columns can be selectively juxtapositioned and/or hidden to make visual comparison easier. If a feature is not provided by a given tool, these cells appear blank in the visualisation at this level.

An evaluator can query the data. SUIT queries are essentially predefined filters which can be applied to the active data set. Initially comprising all data, the active data set becomes progressively smaller as filters are applied; a textual record of the history of filter application is maintained so that the semantics of the active data set can be viewed at any stage. At any point in time an evaluator can chose to take a snapshot of the result of his/her data investigation so that the state of the visualisation can be maintained for reference during the comparison process. Once created, snapshots are independent of their source (i.e. the original visualisation or another snapshot of which they are a copy) and so can themselves be further manipulated allowing the evaluator maximum flexibility for data analysis.

## 5.2    Qualitative Evaluation Study

Qualitative studies were undertaken to investigate the manner in which evaluators use the environment to compare and analyse UIDT evaluation data[3], and thereby to establish an initial corpus of information regarding evaluators' strategies for analysis when using the SUIT visualisation environment in combination with the SUIT method to complete a project-specific tool selection. This information would help create a data comparison and analysis strategy model for (optional) use with the environment by future evaluators. The studies used a combination of direct (video-taped) observation, think aloud protocols, and question asking protocols plus an end-of-session interview to elicit the required data.

### 5.2.1    Performing the Study

After being piloted within an industrial software development organisation and amended prior to performance on account of feedback from the pilot, the studies were structured as follows. Five subjects were selected on the basis of their abilities, interests, and availability — all were software developers, one was a CASE tool expert, and one was an expert in the development and evaluation of a range of software tools. Prior to their evaluation sessions, each subject was given a short paper outlining the SUIT method and framework with which to familiarise themselves with the concepts underpinning the environment (Lumsden & Gray, 2000). Each subject was then given a short tutorial on the environment and, provided with a small data set, given as long as required to investigate and familiarise themselves with the environment before being asked to answer a series of questions designed to ensure they had all acquired the same basic understanding of the environment. Each subject was asked to return in 1.5 hours[4] and on their return were given 5 minutes to re-familiarise themselves with the environment before being asked to read an outline of an evaluation scenario and their task — given a project profile they were charged with the task of selecting one of two UIDTs for that project — whilst the researcher generated the required visualisation and started the video camera. Each subject was asked to outline their intended analysis strategy and then asked to begin, after being reminded to think aloud as they worked. At the end of their interactive session, each subject participated in a short interview/discussion session. Together the interactive session and interview lasted between 2 and 3 hours.

The videotape of each session was analysed to generate a content log describing the activities performed by the subjects and synopsising discussion that took place with the researcher and a transcript of the interview session (O'Neill, 1998). The accuracy of each content log was verified by an independent assessor.

## 5.3    A Model of SUIT Data Comparison and Analysis

The content logs were examined to determine subjects' actions and the sequence in which they performed these actions in order to derive an observational model of the

---

[3]No other similar environment having been available prior to the SUIT prototype, there was no specific previous research to indicate — at the detailed level — how evaluators might use such a tool.

[4]To avoid user fatigue which the pilot study identified as a likely hurdle in the evaluation.

manner in which evaluators analyse SUIT data using the visualisation environment. To facilitate the modelling of subjects' data analysis strategies, an appropriate notation was devised (Lumsden, 2001).

Subjects typically sub-divided their analysis into a period of global analysis and a period of category-by-category analysis. During their category-by-category analysis, subjects generally ranked their top-level categories according to the degree of difference across the different tools in terms of functionality provision. Thereafter, some started with the categories with least difference in the hope to be able to eliminate categories from their analysis (i.e. from their decision making process), and others focused primarily on the categories with the greatest degree of difference considering them to be categories in which the decision criteria would be found. The subjects selected each category in turn and (normally) expanded the category to the lowest level of detail. After examining the data at that level, they all returned the visualisation to the top-level category view.

Without exception, subjects focused their comparison on the differences between tools; given that the two tools were very similar in terms of functionality provided and interaction mechanisms used, this proved an effective strategy. In general, when analysing data at the lowest level of detail, subjects relied most heavily on 'manual' visual comparison of the data components — a process commonly referred to by subjects as 'eyeballing the data' — as opposed to using the provided query/filtering facilities.

When asked to prioritise the dimensions of measurement used in SUIT, without exception subjects rated the importance of tools' functional provision over that of the interaction mechanisms the tools promoted which in turn was rated more important than interaction assistance. During the course of each interactive session it was interesting to note that, had the ideal tool profile not been there, most subjects would have intuitively focused on the interaction mechanisms with which they were most familiar or favoured rather than the mechanisms identified as most appropriate for the project team as outlined in the scenario. Although most subjects compared tool data according to the prioritisation described here, some performed all comparisons at once (i.e. during a single full expansion of the top level category) whilst others repeated the category-by-category expansion for each of the dimensions in turn.

For those subjects who performed global analysis after category-by-category analysis, the former appeared to constitute a confirmation exercise; they had in general identified the points on which to base their recommendation but used the global analysis to 'double check' their observations. In some cases, it was at this point that subjects compared the data set on the basis of cognitive demands and quality of feedback to determine whether there was any other dimension, over and above functionality and interaction mechanisms, upon which to base their selection decision. Very rarely did subjects combine the effect of filters over their data set; instead they tended to work methodically through their desired filters, clearing the effects of one before applying the next.

A strategy map has been developed that, via flexibility of choice, captures the majority of approaches observed. Due to space restrictions, it is not possible to include the strategy map here but it can be viewed in detail in (Lumsden, 2001).

All bar one subject recommended the same UIDT; those who agreed on their recommendation adopted an often similar systematic strategy whereas the remaining one subject who differed on her recommendation was less obviously systematic in her approach. Although not taking into account the quality of their recommendations, this suggests that there may be a correlation between the strategy used and the result of evaluators' data analysis.

## 6  Conclusions and Further Work

The research described here provides a viable context-sensitive UIDT evaluation framework and method. Furthermore, to support their practical use, a novel visualisation environment for SUIT-specific data has also been developed and shown to be both useful and practicable. Evaluation of use of the visualisation environment has contributed an initial corpus of knowledge about, and thereby model of, realistic UIDT evaluation data analysis strategies.

It has been suggested that SUIT has the potential to be made sufficiently generic such that it could be used for any manner of evaluation activity (for example, CASE tools, data analysis tools etc., or even non-software products). It is hoped to investigate this possibility further.

SUIT offers the basis for addressing the issue of trustworthiness of UIDT evaluation data. Firstly, by virtue of being a repeatable documented method, it is possible to establish review procedures for SUIT evaluations. Secondly, the documents that can be generated using SUIT — completed evaluation frameworks, recorded visualisations, and structured and justified recommendations — have the potential to form the core components of evaluation audit trails. On these grounds, this research would aim to investigate and ultimately establish a 'community' of SUIT evaluators such that SUIT data can be shared and reused — an open (freely available) source of UIDT profiles and SUIT-related results.

Initial suggestions to tackle associated issues of trust are to allow a registered community of software engineers to update/alter/version UIDT profiles thereby establishing communally-agreed 'correctness' of profiles. On the basis of the accepted model of academic research publication review, it is anticipated that such peer-reviewed tool profiles would afford acceptable levels of trust from evaluators. Furthermore, using SUIT, evaluators could compare registered profiles for the same UIDT to determine the general consensus of opinion.

Were the 'open-source' idea to be extended to include not just tool profiles but also the results of SUIT-based evaluations and selections, issues of intellectual ownership and company confidentiality would have to be investigated. If these problems prove surmountable, the third use of SUIT (see Section 3) could be extended beyond the bounds of a single organisation to include a far wider community of software professionals.

## References

Albers, M. J. (1996), Decision Making: A Missing Facet of Effective Documentation, *in Proceedings of the Fourteenth Annual International Conference on Computer*

Documentation (SIGDOC'96) — Marshalling New Technological Forces: Building a Corporate, Academic and User-oriented Triangle, ACM Press, pp.57–65.

Bass, L., Abowd, G. & Kazman, R. (1994), Issues in the Evaluation of User Interface Tools, in R. Taylor & J. Coutaz (eds.), *Proceedings of the Workshop on Software Engineering & Computer–Human Interaction*, Vol. 896 of *Lecture Notes in Computer Science*, Springer-Verlag, pp.17–27.

Clarke, S. (1997), Encourage the Effective use of Contextual Information in Design, PhD thesis, Department of Computer Science, University of Glasgow.

Harris, R. (1998), Introduction to Decision Making, Technical Report, University of Southern California.

Hart, S. & Staveland, L. (1988), Development of NASA-TLX (Task Load Index): Results of Empirical and Theoretical Research, in P. Hancock & N. Meshkati (eds.), *Human Mental Workload*, North-Holland, pp.139–83.

Hart, S. G. & Wickens, C. (1990), Workload Assessment and Prediction, in H. R. Booher (ed.), *MANPRINT: An Approach to Systems Integration*, Van Nostrand Reinhold, pp.257–96.

Hix, D. (1991), An Evaluation Procedure for User Interface Development Tools Version 2.0, Technical Report, Virginia Polytechnic Institute & State University.

Hix, D. & Ryan, T. (1992), Evaluating User Interface Development Tools, in *Proceedings of the Human Factors and Ergonomics Society 36th Annual Meeting*, Human Factors and Ergonomics Society, pp.374–8.

Hix, D. & Schulman, R. S. (1991), "Human–Computer Interface Development Tools: A Methodology for Their Evaluation", *Communications of the ACM* **34**(3), 74–87.

Humphrey, W. S. (1989), *Managing the Software Process*, Addison–Wesley.

Jacobs, S. & Holten, R. (1995), Goal Driven Business Modelling — Supporting Decision Making within Information Systems Development, in *Proceedings of Conference on Organisational Computing Systems (COCS)*, ACM Press, pp.96–105.

Kemerer, C. F. (1992), "How the Learning Curve Affects CASE Tool Adoption", *IEEE Software* **9**(3), 23–8.

Lumsden, J. & Gray, P. (2000), SUIT — Context Sensitive Evaluation of User Interface Development Tools, in P. Palanque & F. Paternò (eds.), *Proceedings of Design, Specification and Verification of Interactive Systems*, Springer-Verlag, pp.91–108.

Lumsden, J. M. (2001), SUIT — A Methodology and Framework for Selection of User Interface Development Tools, PhD thesis, Department of Computing Science, University of Glasgow.

McKirdy, J. (1998), An Empirical Study of the Relationships Between User Interface Development Tools & User Interface Development, Technical Report TR-1998-06, University of Glasgow.

McKirdy, J. (1999), SUIT — A Framework & Methodology for the Selection of User Interface Development Tools Based on Fitness Criteria, Technical Report TR-1999-34, University of Glasgow.

Myers, B. A. (1996), UIMSs, Toolkits, Interface Builders, Technical Report, Human Computer Interaction Institute, Carnegie Mellon University. Was at http://www.cs.cmu.edu/afs/cs/user/bam/www/toolnames.html but now no longer available.

O'Neill, E. J. (1998), User-developer Cooperation in Software Development: Building Common Ground and Usable Systems, PhD thesis, Department of Computing Science, Queen Mary and Westfield College, University of London.

Paulk, M. C., Curtis, B., Chrissis, M. B. & Weber, C. V. (1993), "The Capability Maturity Model for Software", *IEEE Software* **10**(4), 18–27.

Rumble, C. D. (1991), The Human Element Approach to Decision Making… Let's Try Reorganisation, *in Proceedings of 19th ACM SIGUCCS Conference on User Services*, ACM Press, pp.345–50.

Sauter, V. L. (1999), "Intuitive Decision-making", *Communications of the ACM* **42**(6), 109–15.

Simon, H. (1986), Research Briefings 1986: Report of the Research Briefing Panel on Decision Making and Problem Solving, Technical Report, National Academy of Sciences.

Sundaram, S. & Ramamurthy, K. (1996), "A Measurement Methodology for Evaluating User Interface Management Systems", *Journal of Computer Information Systems* **37**(2), 54–61.

Valaer, L. A. & Babb, R. G. (1997), "Choosing a User Interface Development Tool", *IEEE Software* **14**(4), 29–39.

# VE and Games

# Non-Verbal Communication Forms in Multi-player Game Session

## Tony Manninen & Tomi Kujanpää

*Department of Information Processing Science, University of Oulu, PO Box 3000, 90014 Oulun yliopisto, Finland.*
Email: *tony.manninen@oulu.fi*

**The lack of intuitive and non-intrusive non-verbal cues is one of the distinctive features that separate computer-mediated communication settings from face-to-face encounters. The analysis of the non-verbal communication forms in a multi-player game session indicates that the participants of collaborative virtual environment can effectively use various forms of non-verbal communication to reduce the communication difficulties. A creative combination of various communication channels makes it possible to enhance the interaction. The limitations of computer mediation can be reduced by enabling more flexible and natural interaction. Although the naturalness and of face-to-face communication is hard to achieve, the virtual environments provide additional ways to enhance the weak areas of interaction.**

**Keywords:** collaborative virtual environments, interaction, behaviour, simulation.

## 1 Introduction

The communication difficulties in current 3D Collaborative Virtual Environments (CVEs) have not been overcome. The use of graphical representations of participants and environments does not always help the interpersonal interaction. The lack of intuitive and non-intrusive non-verbal cues is one of the distinctive features that separate computer-mediated communication settings from face-to-face encounters. Even multi-player games have fundamental problems in supporting social activity, although players constantly seek workarounds in order to fulfil their need to socialise.

The importance of non-verbal communication (hereinafter referred to as NVC) has been noted in the HCI and CSCW literature. For example Snowdon et al. (2001) raise 'backchannel' gestures (i.e. gestures and head nods, eye gaze and eyebrow raises) as crucial in determining the way in which utterances are interpreted. Moreover, cues from dress, posture and mannerisms provide much of the background context for verbal negotiations. However, in graphical CVEs such backchannel gestures are often hard to achieve with embodiments, in which subtle gesturing is not easily supported.

It can hardly be denied that NVC provides a substantial portion of the information that is shared between interacting participants. Thalmann (2001) points out that more than 65 per cent of the information exchanged during face-to-face interaction is expressed through non-verbal means. He argues that if the VR systems want to achieve the fullness of real-world social interactions, the systems must support NVC.

One solution that would enhance the communicative and collaborative activities in CVEs is to explicitly support NVC. If the participants are able to use multi-modal messaging and backchannel gesturing, they do not have to rely on verbal communication alone. They would, then, have more flexibility in representing themselves and their ideas by combining the various interaction forms.

Designing rich interaction that supports interpersonal activities, including NVC, is not a simple task. This paper analyses the usage of NVC forms in an experimental CVE setting, in order to support the creation of rich interaction design guidelines. The research problem addressed in this paper can be formalised as follows: How are the NVC forms used in an experimental multi-player game setting?

According to Fraser et al. (1999), there have been relatively few studies of the ways in which CVEs support and enable interaction between users. They argue that application of qualitative studies has been particularly successful in informing the design of collaborative virtual systems. The analysis presented in this paper follows qualitative research principles by providing rich descriptions of the phenomena.

The scope of this work covers the manifestations of NVC forms. The perceivable actions and behaviours have been described and analysed without tackling the social or cultural aspects of communication. The point of interest, thus, is to find more understanding about the possibilities and effects of NVC in the CVE context.

## 2   Non-Verbal Communication Forms

The following section illustrates the forms, or codes, of NVC. The categories have been put together based on the related aspects, and the corresponding authors of individual forms have been identified. Communication literature has variations in the form categories in terms of quantity and definitions, so this presentation aims at combining several existing models:

**Haptics** reflects the use of touch in communication situations (Burgoon & Ruffner, 1978). This category consists of *physical contact* such as handshakes and patting (Allbeck & Badler, 2001). *Bodily contact* stimulates several different kinds of receptors — responsive to touch, pressure, warmth or cold, and pain (Argyle, 1975). The physical aspect of NVC forms an effective part of interpersonal interaction both in positive and negative situations (Fiske, 1982).

**Physical appearance** defines the attributes of image and presentation of self (Burgoon & Ruffner, 1978; Fiske, 1982). *Appearance* contains the visual aspects of one's presentation. Argyle (1975) divides this into two: those aspects under voluntary control — clothes, bodily paint and adornment — and those less controllable — hair, skin, height, weight, etc. The aspects of appearance can, thus, be thought of as static or dynamic communicational messages depending on the attribute.

**Kinesics** includes all bodily movement except touching, commonly referred to as body language (Burgoon & Ruffner, 1978). *Head nods* are the up-down movements of one's head. These are involved mainly in interaction management, particularly in turn taking in speech, and can consist of one or several sequential (rapid) nods at various speeds (Fiske, 1982). *Posture* defines the way of sitting, standing and lying (Argyle, 1975). Interestingly, posture is less well controlled than facial expression. Gestures involve the hand and arm as the main transmitters, but gestures of the feet and head are also important. They are usually closely co-ordinated with speech and supplement verbal communication. In addition to gestures, Allbeck & Badler (2001) describe *body movements* as a form of NVC.

**Facial expressions** may be broken down into the sub-codes of eyebrow position, eye and mouth shape and nostril size. These, in various combinations, determine the expression of the face, and it is possible to write a 'grammar' of their combinations and meanings (Fiske, 1982). Furthermore, Argyle (1975) classifies blushing and perspiration as facial expression.

**Spatial behaviour** consists of proximity, orientation, territorial behaviour and movement in a physical setting (Argyle, 1975). Burgoon & Ruffner (1978) use the term *proxemics* to include actions relating to the use of personal space. Proximity consists of the various actions corresponding to the use of personal space, i.e. how closely we approach someone can give a message about our relationship. Different distances usually convey different meanings. *Orientation* defines the direction where a person is turned to. How we angle ourselves in relation to others is another way of sending messages about relationships. This code can also convey information about our point of interest, or, focus (Fiske, 1982).

**Paralanguage** is the non-verbal audio part of speech and it includes the use of the voice in communication (Burgoon & Ruffner, 1978). Masterson (1996) describes these as *Vocalics*, or non-verbal cues to be found in a speaker's voice. Furthermore, *non-verbal aspects of speech* contain prosodic and paradigmatic codes (Fiske, 1982). The former is linked to speech (e.g. timing, pitch, and loudness) and the latter are independent of the speech (e.g. personal voice quality and accent, emotion, disturbances). *Non-verbal vocalisations* (Argyle, 1975) are an essential part of communication as they can significantly change the meaning of the message.

**Occulesics** are movements in facial area and eyes, e.g. gaze (Masterson, 1996). *Eye movement and eye contact* depict the focus, direction and duration of gaze in relation to other participants (Fiske, 1982). Allbeck & Badler (2001) use the term *visual orientation* to differentiate this group from spatial behaviour. Argyle (1975) describes two groups of variables associated with the gaze: amount of gaze (e.g. how long people have eye-contact) and quality of gaze (e.g. pupil dilation, blink rate, opening of eyes, etc.).

**Environmental details** define the appearance of surroundings providing contextual cues (Masterson, 1996). These include *artefacts* that can be used and manipulated within the environment (Burgoon & Ruffner, 1978). Argyle (1975) states that moving objects and furniture, leaving markers, and architectural design can be used to communicate through space and place. Argyle originally describes *manipulating the physical setting* as part of spatial behaviour, but since the use of objects has been associated by others with environmental details, the category presented by Argyle is divided into two.

**Chronemics** involves the use and perception of time (Burgoon & Ruffner, 1978). Masterson (1996) describes the example of being punctual vs. being late as one illustration of this group. However, there are several other possibilities in using time as a communication tool. For example, pauses can be used to increase anticipation and to make others to pay closer attention to ones actions.

**Olfactics** reflect to the non-verbal communicative effect of one's scents and odours (Masterson, 1996). Perhaps the most common example of this category is the use of perfumes.

## 3   Previous Research on Non-Verbal Communication in CVEs

Masterson (1996) in his study of NVC in text-based virtual environments, has described the forms and functions of NVC categories. The work conducted by Masterson is highly relevant to this research as it provides a clear example of using a communication model as a framework for analysis. However, the focus being on textual environments limits the results in relation to this research.

Allbeck & Badler (2001) have summarised the channels of NVC in the context of embodied agents. Although their starting point originates from a communications background, the main focus of their work is to describe cognitive processes that can be used to co-ordinate the channels of communication and create consistent behaviour for autonomous agents. Their categorisation of the non-verbal channel differs from the ones provided by other authors referenced in Section 2.

Thalmann (2001) has studied NVC in the context of realistic avatars. He has argued for the need of NVC support in shared virtual environments. He emphasises postures and their indications on what people are feeling, claiming that NVC is essential in driving the interaction between people with or without contact.

Vilhjálmsson & Cassell (1998) have designed and developed a system that supports NVC by modelling and animating the subtle and involuntary cues that exist in face-to-face communication. However, their focus was on gaze and communicative facial expressions. The elaborate articulation required for human body animation forced them to exclude gestures and body posture from the scope, although they agree on the importance of these.

Cherny (1995) has categorised the main types of interaction forms available to MUD users. The commands, such as 'say', 'emote', and various programmed functions provide the textual counterparts of face-to-face communication. In particularly the 'emote' enables the simulation of most of the NVC forms by using textual descriptions. The 'emote' can also be used to portray feelings, states of mind, and other non-perceivable actions of the user.

Non-verbal communication control and behaviour have been studied, for example, in the context of autonomous agents (Badler & Allbeck, 2000) and communicative agents (Cassell & Vilhjálmsson, 1999; Vilhjálmsson & Cassell, 1998). Furthermore, the research conducted within user embodiment (Benford et al., 1995), NVC interface (Guye-Vuillème et al., 1999), embodied actions (Robertson, 1997), and acting in virtual environment (Slater et al., 2000) have partially considered the issues of NVC.

## 4 Experimental Distributed Game — Tuppi3D

The analysed game session was conducted with an experimental system that has been designed and constructed based on the rich interaction concepts (Manninen, 2001). The work is part of a research project involving the production of a computerised version of *Arctic Bridge* (or *Tuppi* in Finnish), a traditional team-based card game which has its origins in northern Finland. The aim of the project was to construct a team game that would follow the idea of the original real world version. The rich interaction experiment was constructed in the form of a 3D representation of the game, players and corresponding thematic environment.

The design follows the traditional lumberjack theme with various environmental and atmospheric effects that support and enrich the interaction and intensity of the experience. The main features of the experiment include various card manipulation possibilities and several forms of interpersonal interactions (e.g. non-verbal communication). The system is designed to provide a flexible and rich set of interaction, which can be freely combined by the players.

The main scene consists of a log cabin with a central table for card playing. The interior of the cabin is spacious enough to allow up to 16 people to be accommodated for an exciting card game. Usually four people take part in the actual game play, while others act as observers. Figure 1 illustrates the exterior of the log cabin which forms the arena for the card game and provides a view of the interior of the cabin with four players in the middle of a game of *Tuppi*.

The playing card simulator enables human-directed card play. This means that the players can define and agree on the rules, number of players, and corresponding parameters, without application-related restrictions. Rich interaction possibilities are increased by allowing the users to select the actions and activities they would like to do. The experiment is like a virtual 'sandbox', where users can freely play and fulfil their creative desires.

**Figure 1:** Log cabin with corresponding environment and four players in action inside the cabin.

| # | s | Actions, Expressions, Gestures and Sounds | Verbal Communication |
|---|---|---|---|
| 21 | 46 | | Tony: Two, may I have, thank you |
| 22 | 48 | Heikki observes the deck (beam indicating) | |
| 23 | 49 | Tony turns towards Heikki | Soili: One for me |
| 24 | 50 | Heikki puts three cards<br>Tomi focuses onto the table<br>Tony turns towards Tomi and glances at Heikki briefly. | |
| 25 | 52 | | Heikki: Three for me ... mmm ... no ... three ... yes ... sorry, mmm ... slight confusion ... |
| 26 | 53 | Soili turns to Tomi | |
| 27 | 56 | Tony pushes his two cards towards the table centre | |
| 28 | 59 | Tomi puts four cards onto the table<br>Tomi levels his view | |
| 29 | 00 | Tomi starts dealing new cards<br>Tony glances at Heikki (orientation) | |

**Table 1:** Excerpt from the interaction decomposition.

# 5   Research Method and Framework

This qualitative research uses the NVC model as a theoretical framework for the analysis of interaction in a multi-user computer game session. The analysis is presented with descriptions of the interaction phenomena observed in the filmed session. The video is filmed using a first-person view from one of the participants by capturing his monitor feed.

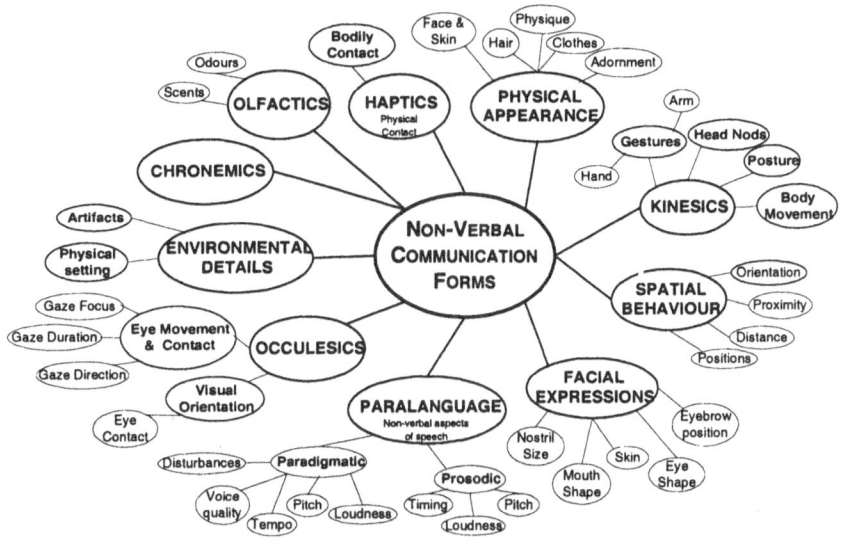

**Figure 2:** Concept model depicting the non-verbal communication forms.

The video material has been decomposed into small fractions using the interaction analysis techniques. The total number of fractions in the 2 minute and 33 second.video is 93. The fractions have been transcribed and analysed according to the corresponding utterances, actions, expressions, gestures and sounds. Table 1 gives an example of the decomposition. The transcription consists of sequential identification numbers of the fractions, the starting times and the actions associated with each fraction. Furthermore, verbal communication has been illustrated when available.

The main points implied by the fractions have been analysed and the results have been compared to the NVC model constructed from the theoretical background material. In addition to the categorisation of individual user interactions, the sequence and timing of the actions have been analysed. Issues, such as turn-taking, co-ordination and co-operation are of interest for this research. Although the emphasis is on the non-verbal aspects of communication, the transcribed verbal part provides more insight into the interaction.

Figure 2 depicts the satellite model of the NVC forms. The model is constructed from the communication literature by combining the individual classifications that have been presented by several authors. The aim in the synthesis of the combined model was to get as exhaustive a set of forms as possible. The communication forms have been categorised into 10 classes, each consisting of a number of sub-concepts. Some of the forms have to be considered differently when applied to the CVE setting. For example, various forms of *olfactics* are not directly applicable, unless the scents and odours are modelled within the CVE.

The conceptual model is merely a tool for analysis, and thus, is not meant for hard-coding the categories. The borders of individual concepts can be very vague, and some of the concepts can be categorised differently. For example, the placing of individual forms varies according to different authors, so the model is more or less a compromise of several previous models. The aim of this work is to explicitly illustrate the occurrences of these forms, and, therefore, the actual taxonomy is not the most important issue.

## 6  Video Analysis

This section describes the NVC forms that can be perceived from the video material. The use of these forms has been analysed in terms of what they mean and how and why they were used. The use of forms is analysed according to the proposed NVC form model and the descriptions are organised according to the categorisation.

### 6.1  *Perceivable Non-verbal Communication Forms*

The first part of the analysis describes and categorises the perceivable NVC forms according to the framework. The forms have been identified, their meaning has been interpreted, and a brief description of their use has been provided. The excerpts from the transcription have been presented when applicable.

#### 6.1.1  *Haptics or Physical Contact*

There are no direct examples of physical contact, even in its virtual form, in the experiment. The participants do not touch, pat or hug each other, although that might occur in a physical world. One of the reasons is the structured setting, in which the players stay more or less on their own sides of the table. Furthermore, the system implementation did not explicitly support actions such as handshakes or hugging. However, the need for physical contact became evident in the form of orientation and positioning. The participants imitated patting by making corresponding hand movements when close to the other person.

The non-violent use of physical contact seems to be hard to find in current games. Although there are plenty of examples in which participants hit, kick, throw and shoot each other in violent games, there are few features that support other type of contact. The lack of tactile and force feedback interfaces in desktop systems may be one of the reasons limiting the use of communicational physical contact. However, the text-based virtual environments such as MUDs and MOOs contain a relatively large amount of simulated physical contact between the participants.

If the category is slightly extended, there are several examples of physical contact between the participant and the virtual environment. For example, collision detection prevents the player from walking through walls, or through another participant. Moreover, card hitting can be used as a form of physical contact that provides indicative sound effects for other participants.

#### 6.1.2  *Physical Appearance*

The appearance of the avatars was not dynamically modifiable by the participants, so the main use of this form was to convey identity to others. Each of the players had a unique avatar, which, after a certain initial period, made the recognition easier. The experiment involved only four participants, and so the identification was not a major issue, even if the avatars had been more similar. However, the participants felt it was nice to have individual characteristics also in the virtual environment.

The photo-realistic approach to avatar implementation made it possible to use pictures of one's own face in the facial texture of the avatars. This seemed to highly increase the interpersonal immersion. The participants were not distracted by the unfamiliar features of their fellow players. This, of course, does not necessarily apply to a setting in which participants are not previously known to each other. In addition to the identification, it was observed that some faces were more interesting (appealing, funny) than others. It is possible that the proportions of the geometry in relation to the physical head created these side effects.

In the small group setting, the physical appearance could be most beneficially used to represent dynamic aspects of the participant. For example, variations in the height and width could be used, in the same manner as in animated cartoons, to illustrate some action or feeling. Furthermore, different sets of clothes could be used to convey meaning to others. Because any of the attributes could be controlled, by the participant or by the system, there is an enormous amount of possibilities for using them as communicative forms. The end result would not necessarily be realistic, but that is not a limitation in a virtual setting.

### 6.1.3 Kinesics

Gestures and body movement were implemented as explicit and implicit actions. Some of them were directly executed by the participants (e.g. waving, yawning, walking, jumping, and turning), while others were bound to certain actions in the form of additional representations (e.g. card hitting and picking). The former required explicit execution and concentration from the participants. The latter, however, being automatic, did not increase the participant's task complexity.

The explicit nature of gestures, in this experiment, is evident during the game phases in which participants concentrate on their tasks. There is hardly any movement when the players are managing their hand of cards. As this task is not indicated to others in any way, it stays more or less internal. On the other hand, there are a lot of slight changes in left-right and up-down orientations of the avatars. This effect is created by an almost involuntary movement of the mouse, which is directly mapped to the movement of the avatar.

One example of intuitive and transparent gesture is provided by Soili when she is sorting her hand of cards (i.e. there is no perceivable movement). After she has completed her task, she (involuntary) checks what is going on around her by executing a slight left-right turn. This clearly indicates that her focus is back onto the surrounding environment and she is about to proceed. In the previous round she did not signal her readiness in any way. This resulted in a sudden action in which she hit her card on the table without any early warning.

An illustration of the use of *kinesics* to support and enhance verbal communication is provided by Tony in his over-anxious request for more cards. Table 2 illustrates the request, which is enhanced by the avatar's rapid left and right turning movement that resembles shaking. When combined with the verbal message, the movement gives a feeling of rush and of high anticipation. The dealer

| # | s | Actions, Expressions, Gestures and Sounds | Verbal Communication |
|---|---|---|---|
| 32 | 03 | Tony starts shaking with rapid left-right movement | |
| 33 | 04 | | Soili: Mmhhmmh |
| 34 | 05 | | Tony: Cards ... cards ... (!?) |
| 35 | 06 | Tomi gives one card to Soili Tony stops shaking | Tomi: In a minute ... here's for Soili |
| 36 | 08 | . | Soili: Yes, thanks |

**Table 2:** Combination of kinesics, paralanguage and verbal communication.

---

also acknowledges the high-impact message by promising more cards soon. A similar example is the up-down jumping of Tomi when he believes he has won the game. In addition to verbal exclamation, he indicates his happiness by jumping.

The automatic movements can be combined with other forms of actions in order to provide additional communicational effects. For example, Heikki finishes his game by hitting his cards rapidly in succession onto the table in slightly different places. He then sweeps his hand back, almost as if showing off his invincible set of cards. As he had, only a five seconds earlier, announced that he had lost the game, this can be interpreted as a sort of demonstration. Moreover, the action ends with a yawning gesture, thus, indicating a resolution from Heikki's point of view.

### 6.1.4 Facial Expressions

The experiment has been implemented with a predefined set of facial expressions, which have to be executed explicitly by the users. Ten different expressions were available, with the possible add-on sound effects to support the message. In addition to these, some of the facial expressions were combined with the gestures of the avatars. The modelled expressions included, for example, different smiles, grinning, raising of eyebrow, blushing, yawning, and a serious expression.

The facial expressions were used in a similar way to the gestural movements; there were relatively few expressions during the actual game session. The explicit execution of expressions forced the players to concentrate on the enactment, which, on the other hand, was conflicting with the actual task (card game). However, there is one significant example of a facial expression that belongs to the actual game play. When Tomi signals verbally his (assumed) victory, Tony responds with a nasty grin accompanied by a sound effect. This seems to go unnoticed by the other participants, although it provides clear opposition to the declared winning condition (see Table 4 for an illustration of the example). The whole scene seems to get closer to the physical world situation, because the action of one user is not explicitly perceived by the others. This positive fuzziness in communication is not easily achieved, due to the computer's digital representations. Something is usually either visible or invisible.

During the game initialisation and aftermath, there was much more expressional by-play, either as a supporting act or as purposeful and playful interaction with other participants. Soili's welcoming greeting with a wave is one instant of pre-task action, while Heikki's yawn, after he has declared that he has lost the game, indicates a post-task action and perhaps a slight tiredness towards the situation (two of the participants are still actively engaged in the game). The expressional interplay between Tomi and Tony after the game has finished is a clear example of the playful possibilities of NVC. The participants exchange very little words, but still they interact with each other by representing expressions and by reacting to the ones presented by the other.

### 6.1.5   Spatial Behaviour

The card game does not provide too many positional changes of the players due to the relatively structured game environment. The proximity and position of the players stay more or less constant throughout the game with a few exceptions. The main spatial behaviour during the actual game play is the orientation according to the focus. Players constantly re-orient themselves, either when following the game, or when controlling the game by indicating to others of their turn.

The experimental implementation does not support individual head or eye movements, and, therefore glances, focus changes and other occulesics can cause changes in orientation if there do not fit within the limited field of view. This makes several actions to be categorised as spatial behaviour, although they would not necessarily be part of this group in the real world setting.

Most of the spatial behaviours originate from the participants' need to see what is going on around them, or from their need to see better. For example, as illustrated by Table 1, Tony, after putting his two cards onto the table, orients himself towards Heikki who is the next player in turn. Because there is no indication that Heikki has paid any attention to this re-orientation, the action is purely observational and does not necessarily control the flow of the game.

One of the most significant position changes occurs when Tomi realises that he is not winning the game after all. The truth is revealed when Tony asks "Do you want to see the winning hand?" and at the same time starts turning his cards one by one to show his hand. Tomi goes to take a closer look, as if he does not believe the outcome of the game. At this point, the two remaining players also orient themselves toward the winner, in order to see what is going on. The sudden action of position change, however, seems to disorient Tony as he spends some time trying to figure out where Tomi went. Table 3 illustrates the action.

### 6.1.6   Paralanguage

The use of the voice over IP verbal communication channel during the experiment allowed the participants also to convey a large amount of NVC. Both the speech contents related and non-related aspects of paralanguage were used by the participants — either via the voice channel, or by executing explicit sound expressions (e.g. laughter, whistle and yawn).

Although the sound is disturbingly muffled at times, it still enables the speech audio to convey a number of emotional and expressional messages. The limited number of other expressional features increases the importance of voice. Furthermore, the implementation made it possible to use a very natural form of voice

| #  | s  | Actions, Expressions, Gestures and Sounds | Verbal Communication |
|----|----|-------------------------------------------|----------------------|
| 75 | 15 | Tomi stands behind Tony and looks at Tony's cards | Heikki: Wow |
| 76 | 16 | Soili turns another card | |
| 77 | 18 | Soili turns to Tomi and Tony<br>Tomi focuses on Tony | Tomi: You're one heck of a guy!<br>...Dance for us! |
| 78 | 19 | Soili takes yet another card<br>Heikki arranges the cards<br>Tomi backs away from Tony slightly | |
| 79 | 20 | Tony starts turning left in order to find Tomi | |
| 80 | 22 | Tony turns back and further to the right (still in search of Tomi)<br>Tony waves | |
| 81 | 24 | | Tony: Why are you hiding behind my back? |

**Table 3:** Positional and orientation changes at the end of the game.

communication, which did not require any extra effort from the participants. This significantly enhanced the flexible use of different modalities in interaction.

An illustration of the use of paralanguage to support and enhance verbal communication is evident, for example, in the aforementioned over-anxious request for more cards by Tony. The prosodic aspects of voice enhance the messages provided by kinesics and verbal communication, resulting in quite believable and coherent action. Although the verbal content of Tony's line in Table 2 does convey any significant meaning, the combination of NVC forms makes it a clear request.

Table 4 illustrates additional uses of paralanguage. For example, Soili's line (59) does not have any verbal content, but it still is part of the communicational flow of the session. Furthermore, Tomi's happy and excited resolution (line 62) is a clear example of the paralinguistic aspects of speech. His joy over the situation is impossible to leave unnoticed. The third form of paralanguage perceivable from the material (e.g. line 64) consists of the explicit sound expressions that are usually combined with *kinesics* and facial expressions. Tony's smirk in response to Tomi's believed victory gives a clear indication of a different opinion.

One important area not described by the NVC theories is the meaning of sound effects in interaction. The paralanguage concept seems to cover only sounds that originate from the user. However, there are several examples of audio communication provided as the effect of actions and environment. For example, the type of card hitting is signalled through different sound effects. The open fire in the corner of the cabin provides a constant ambient sound, while the sound of birds and other creatures comes from outside the cabin.

| # | s | Actions, Expressions, Gestures and Sounds | Verbal Communication |
|---|---|---|---|
| 58 | 44 | | Tony: Yeah ... here are my cards |
| 59 | 49 | | Soili: Mmmm ... |
| 60 | 51 | | Heikki: I don't have like anything ... |
| 61 | 52 | | Soili: I don't have anything ... |
| 62 | 55 | Tomi hits five cards (two face-up, three face down) Tomi levels his view | Tomi: But I do ... hahhahaaaa ... Two Queens! |
| 63 | 56 | Tony finishes card arrangement Tony quickly turns to Tomi | Tony: ........... Do you want to see ... (conflict with Tomi's line) |
| 64 | 58 | Tony grins with nasty smirk (sound effect) | |
| 65 | 00 | Heikki starts putting cards on the table one by one, almost like showing off | Tony: Do you want to see the winning hand? |

**Table 4:** Examples of three types of paralanguage forms.

| # | s | Actions, Expressions, Gestures and Sounds | Verbal Communication |
|---|---|---|---|
| 1 | 10 | Tomi deals 5 cards for each player Soili glances around | |
| 2 | 11 | Tomi turns to Soili | Soili: So ... |
| 3 | 12 | Soili waves (hand & face) | |
| 4 | 13 | | Heikki: Ok |
| 5 | 16 | Tony looks around and glances at Heikki (orientation) Tomi focuses on his card pile Soili takes her cards | |
| 6 | 17 | Heikki takes his cards Tomi takes his cards Tony looks at the table | |
| 7 | 18 | | Tony: Right ... |
| 8 | 19 | Tony takes his cards | |

**Table 5:** Example of changes in gaze directions.

## 6.1.7 Occulesics

This group of NVC forms cannot be directly isolated from the video material because the implementation does not support individual head or eye movement. The direction of gaze, however, can be estimated by analysing the angle of the avatars. For example, the participants tend to be leaning slightly forward most of the time, thus indicating their direction of view towards the tabletop. This causes some problems for the analysis as well, because when the focus of the filming participant is most often towards the tabletop, the faces of the others are not visible all the time.

There are several occurrences of specific directional changes in the participants' gaze. Table 5 shows an excerpt of the game in which the participants take their cards from the table. Before taking his cards, Tony glances at the table, as if to make sure the cards are still there. This indicates that his gaze direction was targeted on a higher area (e.g. face level) before the action.

Most of the *occulesics* perceivable from the material are glances, while the mutual gaze is not strongly evident. The only significant mutual gaze example is in the post-game session in which Tomi and Tony start the interplay between their expressions. The lack of longer eye contact indicates that, in task-oriented interaction, the focus of the participants is mostly on the objects and actions. The faces of the others can be within the peripheral vision, or outside the field of view altogether. However, the frequent glances towards the other participants indicates the importance of gaze control. The mutual awareness and interaction seem to be enhanced by the possibility to glance at others.

An important aspect concerning the analysis of *occulesics* in this experiment is the measurement of accurate gaze direction. It is not visible to which direction the participant is directing his or her gaze if the target is within the field of view of the avatar. At some points the participants obviously wanted to have their target in the centre of the screen, thus re-orienting themselves accordingly. However, even the limited field of view made it possible to have every other participant within it, so it was possible to glance at others without making any visible signals.

### 6.1.8   Environmental Details

The main parts of the environmental details are the playing cards and their use in the game. The implementation allows the participants to manipulate the cards relatively freely, so the cards can be picked, dropped, hit, moved and turned in various ways. However, the rest of the setting is more or less constant, providing the players with a certain atmosphere and context within which to participate in the collaborative task.

The card manipulation can be executed by using an adequate level of abstraction. For example, at the beginning of the game the dealer selects a higher level action of 'deal 5 cards', instead of dealing them manually to each participant. However, the following card exchange is handled card by card by the dealer.

One example of purposeful modification of the environment is provided in Table 1, line 27, where Tony pushes his cards closer to the dealer so as to make an explicit note that he is ready to exchange. This, as many of the card arrangement tasks, can be seen as purely entertaining for the participant initiating the action. They do not seem to have any effect on the overall game. For example, the explicit note made by Tony did not speed up the game, which eventually led to the over-anxious request of more cards presented in Table 2. However, this kind of flexibility and self-fulfilment provide a feeling of control, even in situations where there is none.

The most significant example of environment manipulation is presented in Table 6 where Tony starts revealing his cards one by one after asking others whether they want to see his 'winning hand'. The act goes on for about 11 seconds before Tony states the value of his hand (two pairs). His action causes Tomi to move closer in order to see what are the actual values of the cards.

| # | s | Actions, Expressions, Gestures and Sounds | Verbal Communication |
|---|---|---|---|
| 66 | 02 | Tony starts turning his cards one by one | |
| 67 | 04 | Soili takes one card from the deck and puts it in the corner (!) <br> Heikki yawns <br> Tomi approaches the table and focuses on Tony | |
| 68 | 06 | Tomi jumps up and down | |
| 69 | 08 | Soili turns the card face-up | |
| 70 | 09 | Heikki moves back and forth | |
| 71 | 11 | Tomi starts moving towards Tony | |
| 72 | 12 | | Tony: There it goes … |
| 73 | 13 | | Tony: Two pairs |
| 74 | 14 | Tony finishes his card turning | |
| 75 | 15 | Tomi stands behind Tony and looks at Tony's cards | Heikki: Wow |

**Table 6:** Use of environmental details to increase anticipation.

### 6.1.9   Chronemics

The use of communication forms falling into this group is not very clear based on the material. However, there are a couple of examples that can be considered as use and perception of time. The first one is the difference in the perceived speed of the game events. Tony's request for more cards, while the dealer is still busy trying to manage all his task, indicates that Tony would like the events to flow at a faster pace. He cannot proceed before he gets more cards from the dealer, and thus, he is eagerly waiting for them. The second example is the anticipation build-up sequence, presented in Table 6, where Tony does not want to reveal his hand immediately, but instead causes purposeful delay in the game flow.

In the aforementioned examples the progress of time is both perceived as too slow and also purposefully slowed down. Similar examples can be found from card games in the physical world in which the pace of the game varies greatly depending on the situation. An additional example of controlling the time is the situation in which the dealer uses the combination of speech and action when handing out the exchanged cards. He reconfirms the number of cards while moving them one by one across the table.

## 6.2   Additional Findings

Although the task-oriented collaboration tends to direct the focus of the participants to the objects and actions related to the task, there are a lot of social interaction and 'show-off' movements before and after the game. This makes the pre- and post-activity sessions important from the design point of view as well. For example, the end of the observed game session results in a set of expressional actions, which resemble the relaxing and a sort of 'partying' kind of activity. Both the winner and the dealer start changing their facial expressions and gestures and they continue to have verbal commenting. The remaining two players, although not directly participating, still follow the course of action.

The sound effects seem to make a significant difference to the interaction. The participants were also trying the game without any other audio than their speech, and the resulting session provided much limited awareness of the actions. Furthermore, the audio environment (e.g. birds singing, dogs barking, fire crackling, etc.) creates a sense of warmth and increases the feeling of immersion. This can make the overall experience increasingly enjoyable.

Although characters remain frozen during the manipulations of the cards in hand, the spoken commentary is almost constant. This indicates that the intuitive skill of combined speaking and acting, provides good results, if it is supported by the environment. The dealer mainly uses voice to control the flow of the game and this activity is also conducted by individual players in their requests for more cards. Without the speech, the experience would have been much more limited.

## 7 Discussion

The NVC model was relatively well-supported by the findings. The communicational behaviour of the participants followed the face-to-face interaction conventions in most of the categories. However, the limitations in the user interface, animation and in the CVE system made some of the forms non-usable and reduced the possibilities for natural communication.

The focus of the NVC model is too limited when considering the overall rich interaction design. The model originates from the physical world where many of the things such as body, sense of touch and sensomotoric control are taken for granted. However, the CVEs do not follow the conventions of the physical world. The virtual environments and games require additional features and interaction forms which do not necessarily fit into the communicational model. The model has to be expanded to cover the most basic primitives of virtual environments. Still, the model provides a partial conceptual cover for the interaction phenomena. The familiar conventions and well-established categories help the designers to focus on the necessary interaction forms when designing new virtual environments.

The analysis indicates that even small-scale NVC support can greatly increase the natural and intuitive forms of interaction. Richer interaction possibilities provide the participants with flexible ways of communicating and acting within the virtual environment. First of all, the availability of various interaction mechanisms helps participants choose the ones fitting their purposes. Second, the combination of different communication channels makes it possible to enhance the messages, or to execute contradicting behaviours. Third, the tacit 'knowledge' can be conveyed by enabling sub-conscious and intuitive actions, which are perceivable by other participants.

The virtual environment provides novel ways of utilising the traditional NVC forms. Moreover, the virtuality makes it possible to introduce new conventions of communication that are not realistic or possible in the physical world. For example, various augmented information (e.g. gaze cues and sound effects) can be added to enhance the communication.

The design implications raised by the analysis include the following:

- The extended NVC model can be used as a basic set of requirements for communicational virtual environments. The communication forms should be implemented so that users have enough freedom to utilise the ones they see most fit for their needs.

- Automatic and autonomous gestures and expressions would greatly enhance the communication by providing a model for sub-conscious actions.

- Higher-quality speech audio would improve the utilisation of the paralanguage, which, in turn, would form a natural way of enhancing the communication.

- Gaze direction measurement and mapping it into the environment would enable more tacit and fine-grain communication.

## 8   Concluding Remarks

This research provides a detailed description of non-verbal communication forms in a multi-player game session that was run on top of an experimental virtual environment system. The system has been designed according to the preliminary rich interaction design guidelines.

The analysis of the non-verbal communication forms in a multi-player game session indicates that the participants can effectively use various forms of communication, if the system is designed to support them in a memorable, yet invisible, way. A creative combination of various communication channels makes it possible to enhance the overall interaction and further increases the usefulness of the collaborative virtual environments.

The results are significant for collaborative virtual environment designers as they illustrate the importance and possibilities of non-verbal communication in networked settings. Thus, it is possible to reduce the limitations and restrictions of computer mediation by enabling more flexible and natural interaction. Although the naturalness and intuitiveness of face-to-face communication is hard to achieve, the virtual environments provide additional and novel ways to enhance the weak areas of interaction.

The analysis provides several implications for design. The main task, however, is to use artistic selectivity and principles of game design in order to achieve engaging and compelling systems. The conceptual and theoretical models of communication and interaction should be utilised in order to make solutions natural and intuitive. The need to understand the whole concept of interaction in virtual environments is evident if the communicational needs of the users are to be supported.

## References

Allbeck, J. M. & Badler, N. I. (2001), Consistent Communication with Control, *in* C. Pelachaud & I. Poggi (eds.), *Proceedings of the Fifth International*

*Conference on Autonomous Agents (AA'01) Workshop No. 7: Non-verbal and Verbal Communicative Acts to Achieve Contextual Embodied Agents*, CEUR-WS. available at http://SunSITE.Informatik.RWTH-Aachen.DE/Publications/CEUR-WS/Vol-46/.

Argyle, M. (1975), *Bodily Communication*, International Universities Press.

Badler, N. I. & Allbeck, J. M. (2000), Towards Behavioral Consistency in Animated Agents, *in* N. Magnenat-Thalmann & D. Thalmann (eds.), *Proceedings of Deformable Avatars 2000*, Kluwer, pp.191–205.

Benford, S., Bowers, J., Fahlen, L. E., Greenhalgh, C. & Snowdown, D. (1995), User Embodiment in Collaborative Virtual Environments, *in* I. Katz, R. Mack, L. Marks, M. B. Rosson & J. Nielsen (eds.), *Proceedings of CHI'95: Human Factors in Computing Systems*, ACM Press, pp.242–9.

Burgoon, M. & Ruffner, M. (1978), *Human Communication*, Holt, Rinehart and Winston.

Cassell, J. & Vilhjálmsson, H. (1999), "Fully Embodied Conversational Avatars: Making Communicative Behaviours Autonomous", *Autonomous Agents and Multi-agent Systems* 2(1), 45–64.

Cherny, L. (1995), "The Modal Complexity of Speech Events in a Social Mud", *Electronic Journal of Communication* 5(4). Online journal paper available at http://www.cios.org/www/ejc/v5n495.htm.

Fiske, J. (1982), *Introduction to Communication Studies*, Routledge.

Fraser, M., Benford, S., Hindmarsh, J. & Heath, C. (1999), Supporting Awareness and Interaction through Collaborative Virtual Interfaces, *in* B. Schilit (ed.), *Proceedings of the 12th Annual ACM Symposium on User Interface Software and Technology, UIST'99, CHI Letters* 1(1), ACM Press, pp.27–36.

Guye-Vuillème, A., Capin, T. K., Pandzic, I. S., Magnenat Thalmann, N. & Thalmann, D. (1999), "Nonverbal Communication Interface for Collaborative Virtual Environments", *Virtual Reality* 4(1), 49–59.

Manninen, T. (2001), Rich Interaction in the Context of Networked Virtual Environments: Experiences Gained from the Multi-player Games Domain, *in* A. Blandford, J. Vanderdonckt & P. Gray (eds.), *People and Computers XV: Interaction without Frontiers (Proceedings of IHM-HCI'2001)*, Springer-Verlag, pp.383–98.

Masterson, J. (1996), Nonverbal Communication in Text Based Virtual Realities, Master of Arts Thesis, University of Montana.

Robertson, T. (1997), Cooperative Work and Lived Cognitions: A Taxonomy of Embodied Actions, *in* J. Hughes, W. Prinz, T. Rodden & K. Schmidt (eds.), *Proceedings of ECSCW'97, the 5th European Conference on Computer-Supported Cooperative Work*, Kluwer, pp.205–20.

Slater, M., Howell, J., Steed, A., Pertaub, D.-P., Garau, M. & Springel, S. (2000), Acting in Virtual Reality, *in* E. Churchill & M. Reddy (eds.), *Proceedings of the Third International Conference on Collaborative Virtual Environments (CVE 2000)*, ACM Press, pp.103–10.

Snowdon, D. N., Churchill, E. F. & Munro, A. J. (2001), Collaborative Virtual Environments — Digital Places and Spaces for CSCW: An Introduction, *in* E. F. Churchill, D. N. Snowdon & A. J. Munro (eds.), *Collaborative Virtual Environments — Digital Places and Spaces for Interaction*, Springer-Verlag, pp.3–17.

Thalmann, D. (2001), The Role of Virtual Humans in Virtual Environment Technology and Interfaces, *in* R. Earnshaw, R. Guejd, A. van Dam & J. Vince (eds.), *Frontiers of Human-centred Computing, Online Communities and Virtual Environments*, Springer-Verlag, pp.27–38.

Vilhjálmsson, H. H. & Cassell, J. (1998), BodyChat: Autonomous Communicative Behaviors in Avatars, *in* K. P. Sycara & M. Wooldridge (eds.), *Proceedings of the Second International Conference on Autonomous Agents*, ACM Press, pp.269–76.

# Support Robots for Playing Games: The Role of Player–Actor Relationship

## Loe Feijs & Mark de Graaf

*Department of Industrial Design, Technische Universiteit Eindhoven, PO Box 513, 5600 MB Eindhoven, The Netherlands.*

Tel: *+31 40 247 4522*

Fax: *+31 40 247 5376*

Email: *m.j.d.graaf@tue.nl*

**The impact of simple support robots on computer game play is studied. Two physical agents, outside the computer screen, provide additional feedback to the user. The study incorporates an analysis of the game play in terms of rewards and punishment. Concepts and a realisation of the agents (hardware and software) are developed and used as an extension of an existing game. Emphasis is on the role of player–actor relationships. Trials conducted using the game support robots are reported.**

**Keywords:** game support robots, affective computing, identification.

## 1  Game Support Robots

### 1.1  General

There is a general interest in exploring new types of human–computer interaction. Two trends can be observed. First, computers are used for other tasks than traditional computation and word processing; interesting worlds and interesting characters are created that 'live' in the computer and that present themselves through screens and a fast growing variety of interaction devices (virtual reality, avatars, simulation games, etc.). An advanced example of this is the ROCCO (ROboCup COmmentator) system. Based on analysis and interpretation of video images, this system generates TV-style live reports for matches of the RoboCup simulator league. Conversely, more and more traditional objects, devices, tools and toys get equipped with embedded processors and thus become more intelligent (next to the traditional embedded systems these include sensor-dolls (Yonezawa et al., 2001), teddy bear-like robot-phones (Sekiguchi et al., 2001), doll-packaged sensors (Clarkson et al., 2001), story-telling support toys as in the Rosebud system (Glos & Cassell, 1997), interactive toy characters such as Microsoft ActiMates Barney (Strommen, 2000), media-companion robots such as Tony (Jun, 2001), and of course well-known robots such as Furby, R100 and PaPeRo of NEC and Kismet at MIT). In the theme explored in this article computer games and physical toys meet: game support robots. These can be integrated into computer game design to provide richer game experiences. As conjectured by Strommen (2000), the size and presence of physical characters make them more appealing than screen characters, particularly for children. This conjecture is explored in the context of an enriched game while paying special attention to the design of the player-actor relationships involved. These relationships will be developed in a formal sense.

## 1.2   Plan of the Work

The first decision is to choose a game that is simple enough to study some assumptions and user reactions in a rather pure form. The game must be non-trivial and have the potential of providing real fun. The choice is for a Pac Man game, or one of its variants. Rather than programming the game from scratch, an existing public domain game is used. Thus only the game support robot software must be programmed, not an entire game. The actual research work is started with an overview of applicable concepts from literature. With these concepts in mind, the game is analysed. Subsequently the goals and assumptions under investigation are defined and the game support robots are designed. These are used in the game playing experiments. Results and conclusions from the experiments are described in e last paragraphs of this paper.

## 2   Introduction

One of the goals was to develop an extension that is fun and that enriches the game in a meaningful way. A variety of approaches can be found to improve games in a more or less systematic way. Carroll & Thomas (1988) were first to explicitly address the importance of fun as a human factor. Johnson (1997) stressed the importance of well-designed controls in a case study on an interactive movie game. Malone (1982) presented useful heuristics for designing enjoyable user interfaces, both for games and other applications.

In this work, an understanding of the player's psychology is chosen as a starting point. Therefore, once the game under investigation was chosen it was necessary find a model or theory that would improve the understanding of the player's motivation and his or her relation to the game characters. So the first question is: "why do people want to play this game", in other words, "what is the fun in the game?"

Two concepts considered highly relevant for developing an understanding of the question why people play computer games in general and for developing concepts to extend the existing class of games are *reward* and *identification*. This section contains a summary of articles addressing these concepts and providing some vocabulary and basic results.

The concept of reward, also called 'reinforcer' plays a central role in a publication of Hopson (2001) where he considers games from the viewpoint of behaviouristic psychology. He presents several examples of rewards in computer games, such as points to be earned; also the transition to a next phase in a predetermined game schedule is a reward in itself. He distinguishes two main types of rules (contingencies) that determine when the player gets another reward: *ratio schedules* meaning that the player gets a reward after a certain number of actions have been completed, and *interval schedules* meaning that the player gets a reward after a certain time. Hopson takes the position of a game designer who wants the player to go on playing as long as possible. For example, behaviouristic psychology tells that for a (fixed) ratio schedule there will be a period of low activity or even a pause, followed by a burst of activity when the reward is near. From the game designer's position this pause is a real issue because if the pause becomes infinite, it means that the player walks away. If the number of actions to be completed is not fixed but variable (variable ratio schedule) then the activity is steadier and the overall rate of activity is higher. Several special cases (extinction, avoidance, behaviouristic contrast) are discussed in detail and some of the results are translated into guidelines for game design.

The concept of identification is analysed by Schirra & Carl-McGrath (2001). They study it for various classes of computer games by comparing it to the identification that is possible in movies. Their main interest is in the possible negative effects of violence in computer games but although this is not the main focus of the present project, the analysis and the vocabulary introduced by Schirra & Carl-McGrath is nevertheless useful. They observe that computer games and movies can be classified into corresponding categories. Adventure games correspond to fantasy movies; shooting games (action games) correspond to action movies; strategic games correspond to movies about strategic themes. They also address the different physical viewpoint (the perspective) that the game player or the movie watcher (general term: media user) can have with respect to his or her game character or his or her hero ('Protagonist'). Two perspectives are discussed. Either the media user sees the world in the same way as his hero or game character, which is called the *first person* perspective, or the media user sees the world as an outsider and thus observes his or her hero or game character in the same way as the other figures, which is called the *third person* perspective. In movies the first person perspective occurs only rarely. In computer games the first person perspective seems to be no problem, mostly because of the motor actions and the direct feedback possible in interactive games. In movies, the relation between the media user and his or her hero builds on the concept of identification, defined in social psychology as the capability for a person to replace himself or herself into someone else, to understand the motivations of his or her actions, to make estimations of his or her perceptions and views and by doing so give a meaning to his or her acting. Essential for this type of identification is that the other person is supposed to have a rich mental life that, although not directly observable, is observed through the other person's acts and the responses upon his or her environment. It is an *empathic identification*, which is a very fundamental mechanism available to humans — essential for developing consciousness and a personality. Schirra & Carl-McGrath argue that in computer games there is not much need for a complex predefined inner life of the game character; it would only be in the way for the user who has to play it. In computer games there is a *role-playing identification* (Rollenausfüllende Indentifikationsform), which is very different from the empathic kind of identification. Several additional aspects of games and movies are discussed as well, such as suffering (not really possible in games) and experimenting (not really possible in movies). In the section 'design of the robots', *both* types of identification relations will be used in the design of the extended game, also the empathic identification.

Fritz & Fehr (1993) provide a classification of computer games into five classes: abstract thinking and skill games, fighting games, funny games, simulations and adventures. Of these, comic-like characters in a screen world characterise the funny games. They don't demand a high level of aggression. Many ingredients of a typical funny game are interpreted as traditional fairy tale themes by Fritz & Fehr: labyrinths, being eaten and ghosts. The large degree of acceptance of funny games is explained as follows: a very wide range of game users can recognise their wishes, expectations and backgrounds in themes such as chasing, being chased, eating, wealth acquisition and purification (cleaning the labyrinth from dots). If the game is not just about killing enemies it is potentially more attractive for female game players; gathering things, keeping them, and paying attention to threats are more likely to relate to their life background than actions for war and killing. It is also noted that both in computer gaming and in real life it is important to distinguish friend and enemy, positive and negative, and to behave such as to use one while avoiding the other.

## 3    Game Analysis

In order to design and extend a successful game, it is useful to start from an understanding of the original game because the new play options and the characters must be consistent with the unmodified parts of the game and since the original game was such a success there may be certain useful lessons hidden in it. Moreover, it is interesting to see whether the psychological concepts and theories of the previous section are consistent with the designer's presentation.

The original intentions of the game are expressed in a later interview with its designer Toru Iwatani (1986). Upon the question "What was the thinking behind the design of Pac Man?" Iwatani first explains that his design began with words, such as the kanji word 'taberu', to eat and the Japanese a slang word 'paku paku', describing the motion of the mouth opening and closing while eating. He notes that all the computer games available at the time were of the violent type — war games and space invader types. His goal was to come up with a 'comical' game also female players could enjoy. The Pac Man figure is kept simple: as Iwatani puts it: "once we added eyes, we would want to add glasses and maybe a moustache. There would just be no end to it." Food is a part of the basic concept; the maze provides a structure. The enemies are created to provide excitement and tension. The ghost-shaped monsters each have a different colour, also because Iwatani felt female players would like this. The monsters' invasions are designed to come in

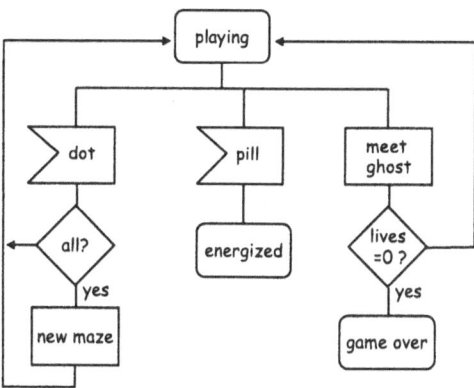

**Figure 1:** Snacky's behaviour (playing).

---

waves. Iwatani mentions the design of the spirit ('kokoro'), or the energy forces of Pac Man. If he eats an energiser (a pill) at one of the four corners of the screen, he can retaliate by eating the enemy. So Pac Man can be the hunter as well as the hunted.

Next, the behaviour of the screen character is described using an adapted type of SDL diagram (Saracco et al., 1989), see Figure 1.

SDL is the Specification and Description Language frequently used for telecommunication systems. Rounded boxes denote states, rectangular boxes denote actions and kites denote decisions (think of it as a mix of flow charts and state transition diagrams). Traditional SDL uses input boxes for receiving messages and output boxes for sending messages. Here only input boxes are used and they are given the special meaning of receiving reinforcers (no output boxes are needed, the response of the characters is implicit in the behaviour). The analysis given next is not about the original Pac Man of Iwatani but a version called Snack Attack, the source of which is available and which is described in some detail in Michael Packard's "crash course in game design". In this version, the screen character is called Snacky (not Pac Man). The description given here applies to Packard's character (Snacky).

In order to develop this theoretical description of the game two decisions were made. The first decision is that the main game states are playing / energised for Snacky and imprisoned / wandering / hunting / hunted for each of the ghosts. The second decision is not to use input boxes or other special symbols for punishments. This decision is justified by the observation that in this game the effect of punishments is sufficiently captured by the state transition behaviour (the bad thing about 'meet ghost' in the 'playing' state is that it leads to the 'game over' state). In Figure 1 the behaviour in the playing state is described.

In Figure 2 the behaviour in the energised state is described. In Figure 3 the behaviour in the imprisoned state and the wandering state is described. In Figure 4 the behaviour in the hunted state is described.

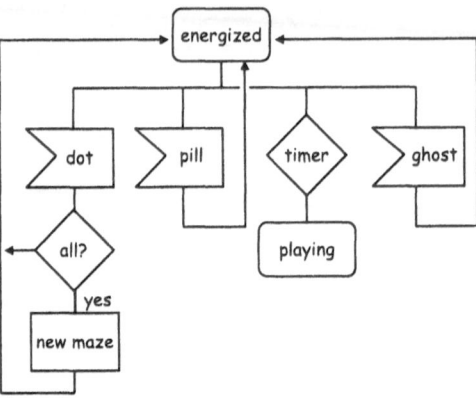

**Figure 2**: Snacky's behaviour (energised).

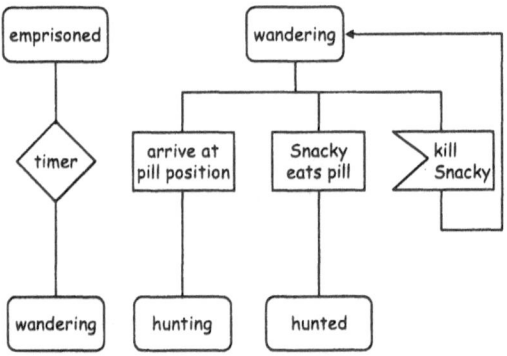

**Figure 3**: Ghost (imprisoned, wandering).

Combining the literature of section 'Introduction', the explanations of Iwatani and the diagrams of Figures 1–4, the following model is reconstructed:

**Classification:** In the terminology of Fritz & Fehr (1993) the game is a typical funny game.

**Relations:** There is a role-playing identification relation between the game player and Snacky since the game player controls Snacky. It is a third person game; in view of the role-playing identification, a first person perspective would have been possible too, but as it happens, this has not been chosen. There is a mutually aggressive relation between Snacky and the ghosts.

**Rewards:** The game player, in the role of Snacky, voluntarily engages into living in this maze and letting himself or herself be motivated by the rewards and

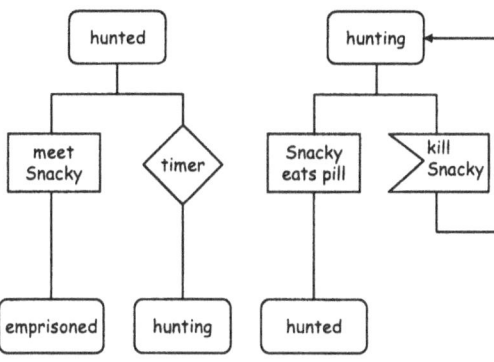

**Figure 4:** Ghost (hunted, hunting)

punishments that can be obtained in it. Positive reinforcers (rewards) appear at several levels: initially they are dots and pills and reaching new mazes (full of fresh dots) but once experienced, the game player may pay more attention to the points to be earned. Being killed by the ghost is easily perceived as a direct punishment, but it is also a kind of extinction because being killed three times means losing all the work done so far to get into the next higher maze.

**Randomness:** The old behaviouristic psychology predicts that a variable ratio schedule is even more stimulating than a fixed ratio schedule. This is not implemented in a direct way; indirectly however, there is certain randomness in the behaviour of the ghosts. Although on average they tend to move into the direction of Snacky (when they are in the hunting mode), they let a random generator influence their behaviour when choosing their path at a splitting point in the maze.

## 4 Design of the Robots

The main goal of designing two game support robots is to validate the hypothesis that the concepts of reward, empathic identification and role playing identification can be used fruitfully to design a game extension by adding support robots such that the resulting system delivers more fun and a richer game experience.

There are secondary goals such as to develop experience in constructing and programming game support robots, find solutions to the creative and technical problems to be solved, and provide an attractive demo, have fun with it, and use it as a source of further inspiration.

The theoretical concepts serve as guidelines, giving direction to the constructive work; using a conceptual framework is helpful to make a coherent and consistent design rather than perhaps bring together a loosely connected set of ideas. Conversely, once the experimental design robots are constructed, they can be

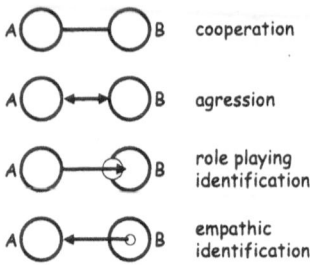

**Figure 5:** Four kinds of relations.

employed in user tests to gather feedback by real users and see whether the real user's behaviour and reactions confirm or contradict the hypotheses.

So precisely what are the theoretical hypotheses to be used in the design and to be put to the test in the experiment? They are based on the literature and the analysis results of the previous sections. There are two, more or less independent assumptions:

- For the nature of the identification relations in games it is assumed that the two types (empathic identification and role playing identification) are applicable, not only to the screen characters but also to the game play support robots. It is assumed that relations can be designed to be of either type and that the game player will recognise the roles.

- For the questions why it is that users have fun playing a game and how to design a game to let the user(s) have fun, it is assumed that the terminology of rewards and punishments is applicable. Thus it is avoided to give a direct definition of fun, but the question is shifted into another, more manageable, question because it is assumed that continued play signifies 'fun' and quitting the game signifies the fun to be less than the expected fun of alternatives outside the game.

For the next step some creative ingredients and specific choices have to be added: one of the initial ideas was that of an 'applause robot', a supporter of the player. Then an indirection was introduced: the robot applauses for Snacky and hence indirectly for the player. For creating form, colour and behaviour, the idea used is that if the robot is to be a supporter of Snacky, it must look like a Pac Man and behave like a Pac Man. For consistency reasons the original simplicity of the game character is reflected in the robot's design. Once it became clear that this could be worked out for the first robot, it was decided to develop the next robot along the same lines, but being a kind of supporter of the ghosts.

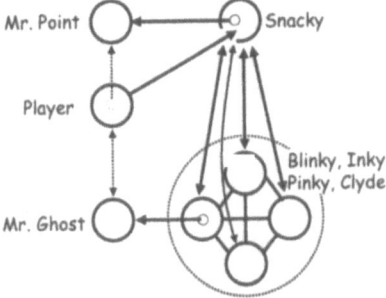

**Figure 6:** Relations in the extended game.

**Figure 7:** Game support robot Mr Point.

## 4.1 Relations

First the various relations are developed. Four types of relations are distinguished: cooperation, aggression, role-playing identification and empathic identification. They are listed in Figure 5. The symbol proposed for the last relation in Figure 5 needs an extra explanation: the idea is that A identifies with B, in other words, B is the hero of A. Following the terminology of Schirra & Carl-McGrath, B is supposed to have an inner life, depicted as the dot inside B's circle, which is understood by A. Therefore the arrow goes from B's dot to A.

Of these four types of relations, cooperation and aggression are easily recognised to exist amongst the screen characters. Both types of identification relations are used for the game support robots.

The specific relations in the case of Snack Attack, extended with two game support robots are indicated in Figure 6. The player has a role-playing identification with screen character Snacky. Snacky and the ghosts are in an aggressive relation with respect to each other. There are two game support robots, one designed to have an empathic identification relation with Snacky, and one, which is designed to have an empathic identification relation with a ghost (the dotted lines in Figure 6 will be explained later in this section). Note that, as in the original game, there are four ghosts, called Blinky, Inky, Pinky and Clyde. For example, Blinky is the red one and Inky is blue.

**Figure 8:** Game support robot Mr Ghost.

The game support robots were given Dutch names. The robot identifying with Snacky is called Mr Point (because it exhibits an interest in the game points earned by the player — through Snacky). Actually also an alternative for this robot (Snacky's supporter) was devised. The alternative version of Mr Point is called Mr Sweet (because it exhibits an interest in the eating going on). Mr Point is shown in Figure 7.

The robot identifying with one of the ghosts is called Mr Ghost. It is shown in Figure 8. The dotted lines in Figure 6 indicate induced relations: when the ghosts are in the hunting mode, the collection ghosts can be viewed as a single power; Mr Ghost is easily perceived as being the supporter of all ghosts, not just of Blinky. Also the relation between the game player and Mr Point is induced; it can be expected that the player perceives Mr Point to have an empathic identification with the player (who after all plays Snacky's role). The extra aggression relation is expected to be induced in a similar way.

## 4.2   Behaviour

The behaviour of the robots has been programmed. The program consist of three parts:

- Subroutines to control the robot's hardware through the COM port of the very same computer on which the game (Snack Attack for Windows 98) is running; examples of subroutines are hap(), haphap(), etc., to let Mr Point open and close his mouth fast one, two or more times, respectively.

- Subroutines called as 'hooks' by the main program of the game to recognise specific conditions; examples are eatghost, eatcandy and enternewmaze.

- E-rules (environment rules) that deliver certain actions (rewards to the game player) by a robot when specific conditions are met.

The program is written in Euphoria, a language with Pascal-like control and LISP-like data structures. The choice for this programming language is for convenience because the original Snack Attack is programmed in it too. An example of a simplified set of e-rules is given below (the variable c contains the condition). These e-rules describe the behaviour of Mr Sweet:

```
if c=eatpill then hap()
if c=eatghost then haphap()
if c=eatcandy then haphaphap()
if c=enternewmaze then haphaphaphap()
if c=die then haap()
```

Some e-rules of Mr Point are:

```
if c=hundred then hap()
if c=twohundred then haphap()
if c=threehundred then haphaphap()
if c=fourhundred then haphaphaphap()
if c=die then haap()
```

## 4.3   Physical Design of the Robots

The game support robots are kept very simple, not only for practical reasons, but also to be consistent with the simplicity and straightforwardness of the screen characters. Of these, Snacky is even simpler than the ghosts, both with respect to its form and behaviour; the ghosts are four in number and their behaviour is more difficult to be grasped.

Mr Point is a yellow polystyrene foam sphere of 10cm diameter from which a segment of 120° is removed. A 60° segment connected by a very simple hinge serves as the lower jaw, creating a mouth of about 0°–45°. It has two black feet, a white collar and two slightly protruding eyes. Driven by a small electromagnet the jaw lets the mouth close and open again (the state of rest is open). When closing a kind of snapping sound is produced ('hap' in Dutch). Although the width of the connection between the game computer and Mr Point is just 1 bit (a serial gate), there is a variety of behaviours: 'hap', 'haphap' etc., showing interest at reaching levels of 100 and 200 points, respectively. Also a slow mouth movement (closing the mouth during 1.5 seconds) is used to indicate that Mr Point is annoyed; typically this occurs when Snacky is killed.

Mr Sweet is very similar, but has another colour scheme (white body, pastel colours like green for the feet, and orange for the tongue). Two big gumdrops form the eyes and there is no collar.

Mr Ghost is connected through 3 bits (three serial gates operating in parallel): lighting eyes, an internal lamp to change the cloth from (default) red to blue, and a fan to make the cloth wave.

## 4.4   Game AI

A classical AI technique is used to provide Mr Ghost with the ability to recognise a state of affairs in which, in principle, Snacky is trapped. This occurs when it is enclosed in a certain part of the maze such that it cannot get out of it without passing either a wall or a ghost and moreover there is no pill (energiser) left inside this part. The method used is essentially Lee's algorithm (Lee, 1961; Moore, 1959) also known as *maze routing*, which has many applications in design automation. It maintains a set of reachable maze positions, which is initialised to the singleton containing Snacky's position. Now repeatedly, a set of reachable points is added (the wave front). At the same time, a check for the absence of pills is done. If the growth of the set stops within a fixed number of steps (here 30) then Mr Ghost 'knows' Snacky to be trapped and behaves actively (fast colour changes). During the game it still happens that Snacky survives, which is because of the fact that the four ghosts behave randomly (although on average they tend to move into the right direction). In other words: the ghosts do not have built-in AI, and although Mr Ghost does, he does not control the ghosts.

## 5 Trials

Three trials conducted. The first one was very informal. The subject group consisted of four children (girl 8, girl 11, girl 11, boy 13). The subjects were instructed by giving them a very short explanation of the Snack Attack game and mentioning the relationships and robot behaviour. This experiment was done in an early phase of the project when there was just one robot. The robot had no name yet. The spontaneous reactions and comments of the subjects were observed.

The second trial was done in a more systematic way. The subject group of the second experiment consisted of 18 children in the age of 10–11 year (girls and boys) from a primary school. The method was to let children play during 7 minutes with the system and after that elicit feedback through a structured form that included open questions. Also their scores, spontaneous reactions and comments were observed. The subjects were instructed by giving them a very short explanation of the Snack Attack game and by stating the name of the support robots (just "this is Mr. Point and this is Mr. Ghost", but not mentioning any relationships or behaviour). Each subject was allowed to play with a system configuration as follows:

game+(Mr Point or Mr Sweet)+Mr Ghost. Each child played with both Mr Point and Mr Sweet (the hardware supports hot plug and play for this robot) Also a systematic variation of the reward scheme was applied: next to the reward schedule already described, a variable ratio reward schedule was used. In the latter, each reward is only given when the condition is fulfilled and a Boolean random variable returns true (with a probability of 50%). Each subject played with only one schedule. The third trial was informal again. The subjects of the third experiment consisted of four children (boy 8, boy 11, girl 11, boy 14). Two of them were in the subject group of the first experiment too. The subjects were instructed by giving them the explanation of the Snack Attack game and the instruction to play at least 30 minutes with the system, both with the fixed and variable reward schedules (they could see that there were two different executables but the difference is not told). The children could ask questions and during conversation they were gradually told about the relationships of the robots and the game characters. From the trials, a number of interesting qualitative observations were made:

### 5.1 Observations on Identification

- It was found that if no separate name for the robot were available, there was a kind of identification where Snacky and the robot were considered to be just one character. Katinka (11) explaining the robot to her friend Lana said (when the robot did 'haphaphap' upon eating a candy): "you see, he really likes those very much."

- The role playing identification really worked as an identification; for example a boy (10) who had difficulties to grasp the fact that it is Snacky he controlled and not the ghosts or the candy asked "who am I?" meaning "which game character is it I control?"

- The relations were easily recognised and considered believable when told to the subjects ("you see, Mr Sweet is Snacky's friend", etc.). The children accepted the explanation and used similar terminology during subsequent conversation (it was harder for the subjects to explain the relations when nothing was explained to them first).

## 5.2   *Observations on Game Play*

- The differences in playing skills amongst the children varied largely; some children needed several minutes to before they controlled Snacky in an effective way; others were good players, reaching 600 points and the second maze within 7 minutes; also for a given player, the outcomes of subsequent games varied greatly: a player who got 600 points could get only 150 in the next game.

- The children considered the robots interesting and attractive; particularly the gumdrop eyes of Mr Sweet and the sound of both Mr Point's and Mr Sweet's feedback was considered fun; most children liked Mr Sweet more than Mr Point or Mr Ghost (probably because of its appearance).

- The non-visual feedback by the robots was most effective during play; the player had to keep his or her eyes on the screen; audio feedback could be dealt with at the same time, but the game just didn't allow for the player to turn his or her head. Changes of Mr Ghost's colours could still be seen, even in the outer parts of the visual fields, and the blower's sound could be heard and the wind could be felt (if Mr Ghost is positioned near the arrows keys, which usually was near the player's right hand).

## 5.3   *Observations on Understanding of the Robots*

- The behaviour of Mr Ghost was considered interesting, by some of the subjects, but only the more skilled players and only after several minutes; for example several subjects discovered viz. that the red/blue colour changes of Mr Ghost were useful (one of the ghosts was blue anyhow in Snack Attack, so without Mr Ghost it was easy to make the mistake of assuming it to be hunted when it was not); also the fact that Mr Ghost 'goes crazy' (fast colour changes see the paragraph 'game AI' in the section design-of-the-robots) when Snacky's death is immanent was considered interesting.

- The girls showed more interest in the robots than the boys; the boys tended to concentrate on the screen; the boys were better players, on average.

- No difference between the fixed and variable ratio schedules schemes could be detected: neither by a correlation with the scores nor in the explanations by the subjects.

- The explanations the children gave about the robot's behaviours are quite often just not true; an example, Mike (13) reported Mr Ghost 'going crazy' by fast red/blue flashing (true) and by making wind (not true).

## 6   Discussion

The approach of this work was to direct a very practical project (designing and building game support robots) from well-known theoretical insights proved to be very fruitful. The analysis of the computer game and the design of the robots were based on two hypotheses: reward and identification.

From the trials, role-playing identification and empathic identification are both clearly observed. This is consistent with the hypothesis on identification and in more detail with the model presented in Figure 6. Furthermore, judging the enthusiasm of the children, the robots clearly enriched the game experience. This enrichment was in general different for boys and girls. Boys tended to focus on the game play and the 'reward' of the snapping robots. Girls were often more interested in the robots, the way they were made and behaved, and fantasised more about the robot characters.

The concept of reward came out less strong. Though children sometimes did have a vague notion of the robots snapping when they collected points, in majority they didn't understand much of the behaviour of the robots in relation to their game play performance. The difference between fixed and random reward schedules wasn't observed at all. Still the actions of the robots were welcomed enthusiastically and greatly contributed to the fun of playing the game. Malone gives some clues why the why the reward schedules might be poorly understood:

> "An optimally complex environment will be one where the learner knows enough to have expectations about what will happen, but where these expectations are sometimes unmet."

In our experiments the 'learners' did not know enough to have expectations. In further work several ways are open to improve this. Longer trials or providing more information about the robots would help players to understand the relation between performance and robot behaviour. The relation could be reinforced, e.g. by letting the robot reflect the actual status of the player: the more advanced the player is, the more impressive the robot could look, sound and act. Also, the robot could get more than applause functionality. It could for example give vital information on the danger level, or give clues for favourable strategies.

The work can be related to the theme of affective computing (Picard, 1995); if affective computing may be considered as an ambitious research program to exploit a rich repertoire of sensing devices and complex modalities like face and voice recognition and generation, the present work is a domain-specific and bottom-up contribution. The contribution shows that by designing player-actor relationships in a systematic manner, even with moderate (game-specific) hardware facilities and moderate interfacing bandwidth, the game experience can be enriched significantly.

## References

Carroll, J. & Thomas, J. (1988), "Fun", *ACM SIGCHI Bulletin* **19**(3), 21–4.

Clarkson, B., Mase, K. & Pentland, A. (2001), The Familiar: A Living Diary and Companion, *in* J. A. Jacko & A. Sears (eds.), *Companion Proceedings of CHI2001: Human Factors in Computing Systems (CHI2001 Conference Companion)*, ACM Press, pp.271–2.

Fritz, J. & Fehr, W. (1993), Videospiele und ihre Typisierung, http://www.bpb.de/snp/referate/fritztyp.htm.

Glos, J. & Cassell, J. (1997), Rosebud: A Place for Interaction between Memory, Story and Self, *in* J. Marsh et al.(eds.), *Proceedings of Cognitive Technologies '97*, IEEE Publications, pp.88–97.

Hopson, J. (2001), Behavioral Game Design, http://www.gamasutra.com/features/20010427/hopson_01.htm.

Iwatani, T. (1986), TBS Interviews Book 1986, http://retrogamer.merseyworld.com/pacoz.htm.

Johnson, J. (1997), Symplifying the Controls of an Interactive Movie Game, *in* S. Pemberton (ed.), *Proceedings of CHI'97: Human Factors in Computing Systems*, ACM Press, pp.65–72.

Jun, H. (2001), Distributed Interfaces for a Time-based Media Application, MTD Thesis, Stan Ackermans Institute Center for Technological Design, The Netherlands.

Lee, C. (1961), "An Algorithm for Path Connections and its Applications", *IRE Transactions on Electronic Computers* **EC-10**, 346–65.

Malone, T. (1982), Heuristics for Designing Enjoyable User Interfaces: Lessons from Computer Games, *in* J. Thomas & M. Schneider (eds.), *Human Factors in Computing Systems*, Ablex, pp.62–8.

Moore, E. (1959), "The Shortest Path Through a Maze", *Annals of the Harvard Computation Laboratory* **30**(Pt.II).

Picard, R. W. (1995), Affective Computing, Technical Report 321, MIT Media Laboratory.

Saracco, R., Smith, J. & Reed, R. (1989), *Telecommunications Systems Engineering using SDL*, Elsevier Science.

Schirra, J. & Carl-McGrath, S. (2001), Identifikationsformen in Computerspiel und Spielfilm, *in* M. Strübel (ed.), *Film und Krieg — Die Inszenierung von Politik zwischen Apologetik und Apokalypse*, Leske and Budrich, pp.1–12.

Sekiguchi, D., Inami, M. & Tachi, S. (2001), RobotPHONE: RUI for Interpersonal Communication, *in* J. A. Jacko & A. Sears (eds.), *Companion Proceedings of CHI2001: Human Factors in Computing Systems (CHI2001 Conference Companion)*, ACM Press, pp.277–8.

Strommen, E. (2000), Interactive Toy Characters as Interfaces for Children, *in* E. Bergman (ed.), *Information Appliances and Beyond: Interaction Design for Consumer Products*, Morgan-Kaufmann, pp.257–98.

Yonezawa, T., Clarkson, B., Yasumura, M. & Mase, K. (2001), Context-aware Sensor-doll as a Music Expression Device, *in* J. A. Jacko & A. Sears (eds.), *Companion Proceedings of CHI2001: Human Factors in Computing Systems (CHI2001 Conference Companion)*, ACM Press, pp.307–8.

# Author Index

# Keyword Index